About the Author

Elizabeth Kelly is a historical fiction for *The Tudors Series*. She is a former teacher with a degree in Ancient History and Archaeology who is fascinated by historical research. She has a passion for investigating the Tudor period and exploring its dramatic potential. Her novels vividly bring to life the Tudor court, featuring a diverse cast of characters with unique perspectives. Her stories delve into the lives of kings and queens, noblemen and noblewomen, ambitious ladies-in-waiting and humble seamstresses, child actors and royal fools. Her imaginative writing offers readers an escape into the alternative reality of creative historical fiction.

The Tudors Series

(1) The Tudor Maid (the story of the seamstress Margery Hallows).

(2) The Tudor Lady in Waiting (the story of Lady Margaret de la Roche).

(3) The Tudor Fool: My Life with Henry VIII (the story of Will Somers).

(4) The Dark Lady: The Rise and Fall of Queen Anne Boleyn.

(5) The Shadow of the Tower (the story of Lady Margaret Pole).

This book is dedicated to my brother.

FIRST LADY OF THE REALM

Book 7 in The Tudors Series

Author: Elizabeth Kelly
Illustrator: Julia Bai

Copyright©2025 by Elizabeth Kelly

Illustrator: Julia Bai

All rights reserved. No part of this publication may be reproduced, distributed or transmitted in any form or by any means, including photocopying, recording, or other electronic or mechanical methods, without the prior written permission of the publisher, except in the case of brief quotations embodied in critical reviews and certain other noncommercial uses permitted by copyright law.

Historical Notes on the Text

(1) According to George Cavendish, Queen Catherine played card games with Anne Boleyn in order to deprive King Henry VIII of the pleasure of her company. On one occasion we are told that, *"the young lady's hap was much to stop at a king; which the queen noting, said to her playfellow, My Lady Anne, you have good hap to stop at a king, but you are not like others, you will have all or none."* (George Cavendish, *The Life and Death of Cardinal Wolsey*, 1558).

(2) Sir Richard Page was a gentleman of the Privy Chamber to King Henry VIII and the stepfather of Anne Stanhope. He was one of the seven men who were arrested for adultery with Queen Anne Boleyn in 1536. Five of the men were executed for treason including Lord Rochford (George Boleyn), Henry Norris, Sir Francis Weston, William Brereton and Mark Smeaton. Sir Thomas Wyatt and Sir Richard Page were both released from the Tower in June 1536 for reasons that are obscure. Sir Richard Page was offered his post back, but he preferred to leave court.

(3) Anne Stanhope was precontracted to marry another man before she married Edward Seymour in 1535, but his identity is unknown.

(4) Surrey's poem entitled *"To the lady who would not dance with me"* compared her to a she-wolf.

(5) In 1536 King Henry VIII wrote a letter to Mistress Jane Seymour to inform her about *"a ballad made*

lately of great derision against us." It circulated in London before the execution of Anne Boleyn. Sadly, the words of this satirical ballad remain unknown.

(6) According to the Spanish Chronicle, Lady Anne Seymour, duchess of Somerset saved her husband's life during the crisis of October 1549 by bribing the countess of Warwick with *"a very rich jewel of diamonds."*

(7) The rule of the Lord Protector Edward Seymour, the duke of Somerset, lasted for two years and nine months from January 1547 to October 1549. It includes some sensational stories that are so outlandish that they seem the stuff of fiction. Who would believe that the widowed Catherine Parr married Thomas Seymour only a few months after the death of King Henry VIII? Or that the duchess of Somerset made a night time expedition to raid the late King's silk house at Whitehall palace? Or that Thomas Seymour made a madcap attempt to kidnap King Edward VI from his bedchamber during which he shot his faithful spaniel and then ran off into the night. The excessive greed, pride and ambition of the Seymours discredited their rule and led to their downfall. How could such a story be left untold?

List of Principal Characters

The Seymour Family

- Edward Seymour; afterwards Viscount Beauchamp of Hache, Earl of Hertford, Duke of Somerset, Lord Protector of the realm.
- Catherine Fillol, his first wife.
- Sir John Seymour, his father.
- Lady Margery Wentworth, his mother.
- Thomas Seymour, his brother; afterwards Baron Sudeley, Lord High Admiral.
- Mistress Jane Seymour, his sister; afterwards Queen Jane Seymour.
- Elizabeth Seymour, his sister; married first to Sir Anthony Ughtred; second to Gregory Cromwell, Baron Cromwell.

The Stanhope Family

- Mistress Anne Stanhope; afterwards Lady Seymour, Lady Beauchamp, Countess Hertford, Duchess of Somerset.
- Sir Edward Stanhope, her father.
- Sir Richard Page, her stepfather, Gentleman of the Privy Chamber.
- Lady Elizabeth Bourchier, her mother.
- Sir Michael Stanhope, her half-brother, Groom of the Stool to Edward VI.
- Francis Newdigate, her second husband.
- Ned Seymour, earl of Hertford, her son.
- Anne Seymour, her daughter.
- Margaret Seymour, her daughter.

- Jane Seymour, her daughter, maid of honour to Elizabeth I.
- Master Richard Whalley, Chamberlain to Lord and Lady Somerset.

The court of King Henry VIII

- King Henry VIII (1509-1547).
- Queen Catherine of Aragon (1509-1533).
- Queen Anne Boleyn (1533-1536).
- Queen Jane Seymour (1536-1537).
- Queen Anne of Cleves (January 1540 – July 1540).
- Queen Catherine Howard (1540-1542).
- Queen Catherine Parr (1543-1547).

- King Edward VI (1547-1553).
- Queen Mary I (1553-1558).
- Prince Philip of Spain (1554 – 1558).
- Queen Elizabeth I (1558-1603).

- Lady Margaret Douglas, the King's niece.
- Lady Jane Grey, the King's great-niece (10th July 1553 – 19th July 1553).

- Pope Clement VII.
- Cardinal Lorenzo Campeggio.
- Cardinal Thomas Wolsey.
- Cardinal Reginal Pole.
- Archbishop Thomas Cranmer.
- Bishop Steven Gardiner.
- Bishop Edmund Bonner.
- Bishop Hugh Latimer.

- Bishop Nicholas Ridley.
- Richard Sampson, Dean of the Chapel Royal.
- Thomas Becon, chaplain to Lady Somerset.
- Mistress Anne Askew, Protestant martyr.

- Edward Stafford, Duke of Buckingham.
- Thomas Howard, Duke of Norfolk.
- Charles Brandon, Duke of Suffolk.
- Arthur Plantagenet, Viscount Lisle, Constable of Calais.
- John Dudley; afterwards Lord Lisle, Earl of Warwick, Duke of Northumberland.
- Henry Grey, Marquess of Dorset; afterwards Duke of Suffolk.
- William Parr; afterwards Earl of Essex, Marquess of Northampton.
- Henry Courtenay, Earl of Devon, Marquess of Exeter.
- Edward Courtenay, his son, Earl of Devon.
- Henry Percy, Earl of Northumberland.
- Thomas Boleyn; afterwards Viscount Rochford, Earl of Wiltshire and Ormond.
- George Boleyn, his son; afterwards Viscount Rochford.

- Seigneur Eustace Chapuys, Spanish Ambassador.

- Chancellor Thomas More.
- Chancellor Thomas Cromwell; afterwards Earl of Essex.
- Chancellor Thomas Wriothesley; afterwards Earl of

Southampton.
- Chancellor Richard Rich; afterwards Baron Rich of Leez.

- William Blount, Baron Mountjoy, Chamberlain to Queen Catherine of Aragon.
- Sir William Compton, Groom of the Stool (1509-1526).
- Master Henry Norris, Groom of the Stool (1526-1536).
- Master Thomas Heneage, Groom of the Stool (1536-1546).
- Sir Anthony Denny, Groom of the Stool (1536-1546).
- Master William Brereton, Groom of the Privy Chamber.
- Sir William Paget, the King's Secretary; afterwards Lord Paget de Beaudesert.
- Master Andrew Windsor, Keeper of the Wardrobe.
- Sir Henry Guildford, Comptroller of the Household 1522 – 1532.
- Sir William Paulet, Comptroller of the Household 1532-1537 and Lord Chamberlain of the Household 1543-1555.
- Sir Francis Weston, Gentleman of the Privy Chamber.
- Master Thomas Culpeper, Gentleman of the Privy Chamber.
- Sir Urian Brereton.
- Sir Thomas Wyatt.
- Sir Francis Bryan.

- Sir Nicholas Carew.
- Sir George Zouche of Codnor.
- Sir William Herbert.
- Sir William St Loe.

- Dr Thomas Wendy.
- Dr William Butts.
- Master Nicholas Kratzer, the court astronomer.
- Master William Cornish, the Master of the Revels.
- Master Hans Holbein, the King's painter.
- Master Robert Amadas, the King's goldsmith.
- Master Mark Smeaton, musician.
- Jane the Fool.

Ladies in Waiting
- Lady Margaret de la Pole, Countess of Salisbury.
- Lady Elizabeth Stafford, Duchess of Norfolk.
- Lady Agnes Howard, Dowager Duchess of Norfolk.
- Lady Margaret Howard.
- Lady Catherine Brandon, Duchess of Suffolk.
- Lady Jane Dudley; afterwards Lady Lisle, Countess of Warwick, Duchess of Northumberland
- Lady Gertrude Courtenay, Marchioness of Exeter.
- Lady Elizabeth Boleyn; afterwards Lady Wiltshire.
- Lady Maud Parr.
- Lady Anne Parr; afterwards Lady Herbert.
- Lady Maria de Eresby.

Maids of Honour

- Mrs Stoner, the Mother of the Maids.
- Mistress Jane Rochford; afterwards Lady Rochford.
- Mistress Mary Boleyn; afterwards Lady Carey.
- Mistress Margery Horsman.
- Mistress Elizabeth Darrell.
- Mistress Dorothy Badby.
- Mistress Anne Gainsford "Nan.".
- Mistress Mary Shelton.
- Mistress Anne Parr

Ladies in Waiting to Queen Mary

- Lady Frances Grey, Marchioness of Dorset; afterwards Duchess of Suffolk.
- Lady Catherine Grey
- Lady Mary Grey.

Contents

Chapter 1: The Maiden (1510 -1527) 13
Chapter 2: The Maid of Honour (1527) 29
Chapter 3: The Household of Mistress Anne Boleyn (1528) 93
Chapter 4: The Courtier (1531) 145
Chapter 5: Lady Seymour (1535) 193
Chapter 6: Lady Hertford (1537) 271
Chapter 7: Lady of the Court (1539 – 1547) 303
Chapter 8: Duchess of Somerset (1547) 393
Chapter 9: First Lady of the Realm (1547) 423
Chapter 10: The Tower of London (1551-1553) 477
Chapter 11: Restoration (1553) 495
Chapter 12: The Secret Marriage (1560) 519

Epilogue 537
Appendix 1 539
Appendix 2 541
Appendix 3 543
Book Group Discussion Guide 553
Bibliography 555

First Lady of the Realm

*"Who can find a virtuous woman? for her price is far above rubies.
The heart of her husband doth safely trust in her, so that he shall have no need of spoil.
She will do him good and not evil all the days of her life.
She seeketh wool, and flax, and worketh willingly with her hands.
She looketh well to the ways of her household, and eateth not the bread of idleness.
Her children arise up, and call her blessed; her husband also, and he praiseth her.
Many daughters have done virtuously, but thou excellest them all"*

(Proverbs 31 v10-13, 27-29)

CHAPTER 1

The Maiden (1510 -1527)

"There is nothing that doth so much commend a maid as silence"

(Thomas Becon, *Workes*, 1512-1567).

I always knew that I was destined for greatness. I was no ordinary woman, but a descendant of royal kings and queens. I was the daughter of Sir Edward Stanhope and Elizabeth Bourchier. I was my father's only child and a great heiress. He died when I was only an infant and my mother married Sir Richard Page. He had started his career as the chamberlain to Cardinal Wolsey. Now he was a gentleman of the Privy Chamber to King Henry VIII with good connections at court. My mother had a high regard for his abilities, but his background was undistinguished. But her family could boast of a noble pedigree. She was the daughter of Fulk Bourchier, the tenth Baron FitzWarin. They made a handsome couple for they were dignified, immaculate in their appearance and proficient in polite conversation.

I grew up at my stepfather's house at Beechwood Hall in Hertfordshire. I had a nurse until the age of seven and then I was put into the care of a capable governess. Learning came easily to me and I learned how to read, write and converse in French like a well-mannered lady. My mother did not leave my instruction solely to my governess. She believed that I could only learn how a lady conducted herself by the power of example. I learned all the skills that she had acquired from her own mother. She prided herself that she had a great deal to impart. I spent a great deal of time in the solar where my mother sewed with her maids and gentlewomen. There I mastered the embroidery patterns which she had learned from her mother as a girl. At the age of ten, I sewed a sampler to display them in an elaborate border. My stitches were neat, precise and exact, just like hers. The centrepiece was a moral verse entitled: *The Woman's Lesson.*

"Be thou modest, sober and wise.
And learn the points of housewifery.
And men shall have thee in such price,
That thou shalt not need a dowry."

The text so encapsulated the spirit of my mother's teaching that she had it framed and placed it upon the wall of my bedchamber. She believed that it would inspire my heart to follow in the path of virtue.

"When you go to court you will learn the latest patterns," she said. "Your courtly skills will form part of the dowry that you bring to your husband. You can teach them to your own maids one day and embellish your apartments. A serious man does not want to marry a pretty butterfly. He looks for a wife who will bring him credit as the mistress of his household. Remember the words of the King's mother in Proverbs 31: *A virtuous woman is far above rubies!"*

"Yes, mother," I replied dutifully. She regarded Proverbs 31 as the yardstick for a Christian woman and was fond of quoting its precepts. She had made me learn the entire chapter by heart when I was a child. Although, I noted that Queen Bathsheba was no paragon of virtue. She had seduced King David and conspired to put her son on the throne. And King Solomon had not heeded his mother's wise advice. He had gathered a harem of pretty pagan concubines around him which caused the downfall of Israel. He ought to have contented himself with finding a wife of outstanding qualities. One who would have assisted him to rule his kingdom.

But I knew better than to speak my thoughts aloud. A virtuous young girl was modest, industrious and silent. She did not parade her knowledge before her elders, but listened obediently to their instructions. My mother did not like pert girls and my stepfather spent most of his time at court. Whenever he had leave to come home, he would tell enthralling stories of his life in the royal circle. He was privileged to attend King Henry VIII daily in his apartments. The King was generous to his gentlemen and often gave them valuable presents and gifts from his wardrobe. Sir Richard dressed according to the latest fashions of the court and knew how to play the most popular card games. He knew everyone who was everyone and was privy to all their secrets. He held us enthralled by describing the court entertainments he witnessed at Easter and Christmas.

"King Henry VIII always celebrates the feast days with much nobleness and open court," he said. "The Great Hall of the palace is decorated with fine hangings and splendid banquets are prepared for his guests. Afterwards, pageants or plays are presented to the court. Sometimes there is a new form of entertainment from Italy known as a masque. I remember how one Epiphany the King and his companions dressed up in strange costumes with visors and caps of gold and requested the ladies of the court to dance with them. It was considered a scandalous novelty at the time but now it is regarded as quite commonplace."

"It sounds very wonderful," I said. I had never seen a pageant or a play. The revelry at Beechwood Hall was much more modest. A group of local mummers came to visit Beechwood Hall every Christmas. They told the story of St George slaying the dragon in rhymed speeches and in return we gave them cakes and ale.

"The King is very fond of disguisings," he said. "Once at Twelfth Night, he came to Westminster with a group of his friends wearing coats of Kentish Kendal and carrying bows and arrows like Robin Hood and his merry men. They burst into the chamber of Queen Catherine of Aragon and shocked her ladies with their roguish appearance. But the Queen kept her composure and complimented the King upon his artful surprise."

"What is Queen Catherine like?" I asked.

"She is the chief ornament of the court," he replied. "She enjoys taking part in the King's pastimes and understands how to play the game of courtly love better than any other lady. On May Day she presides over the tournaments and awards the prizes to the champions of the jousts."

"I wish that I could visit the court and see the King and Queen," I said.

"When you are older, I will take you there one day," he promised. "Then you will see them for yourself."

"Thank you, Sir Richard," I replied.

My mother smiled to see my eagerness. "Your stepfather once took me to court at New Year," she said. "It was the year after our marriage but I remember it as if it was yesterday. It is the custom that anyone may come to the palace that day to give their loyal greetings to the king and queen. Since Sir Richard is an important courtier, the royal steward admitted us to the Presence Chamber where they were receiving their visitors. In those days King Henry was a golden prince and Queen Catherine was a beautiful young wife. They were both much beloved by the people. We did not stay above an hour, for the press and the noise of the crowd was quite unsupportable."

"Did you ever visit the court again?" I asked.

She shook her head. "You were still an infant and it was not convenient for me to undertake such a long journey," she said. "It is useful for a young girl to gain some court polish, but a wife's proper place is in the home."

She did not appear to regret her curtailed opportunities at all. It seemed that one glimpse at the gilded life of the court had been enough to suffice her. I was certain that I would go further in life than my pious mother. She had sufficient skills to make a success of her marriage and her household. My stepfather's table was always well provided and he had no complaints when he dined. His house was comfortably furnished with embroidered hangings and cushions made by the hands of my mother and her maids. His gardens were planted with productive fruit trees and all manner of wholesome herbs. It was a testimony to her admirable competence as a wife. But I knew that I had a greater intellect and a stronger ambition. I was determined that I would go further in life. I would have a good marriage, a splendid house and a career at court. I had no doubt that one day my children would rise up and call me blessed for the many benefits that I had conferred upon them.

On the day of my fifteenth birthday, I stood before the great genealogical chart that hung in the entrance hall, its gilded edges gleaming faintly in the dim afternoon light. It was inscribed with the Bourchier coat of arms and a succession of names was penned in red ink as if written in blood. I knew them all by heart from Thomas Woodstock, Duke of Gloucester, at the summit, down through generations of nobility, to my mother, Elizabeth Bourchier, at the base.

Her voice broke the silence, sharp and commanding. "You are a descendant of King Edward III," she declared, her piercing gaze fixed upon me. The weight of her words hung heavy in the air, like the hewn stones of the hall itself. "You must make a marriage that is worthy of your noble ancestry. Such a glorious lineage is not to be diminished. It is your duty to uphold it."

Her tone left no room for argument. I swallowed hard, my throat tight with the enormity of her expectation. Duty—an inescapable chain, cold and unyielding. Though my heart rebelled, I knew better than to defy her. I was the daughter of Elizabeth Bourchier, a woman of iron will and unshakable resolve.

She stepped closer, her hand resting on my shoulder with a weight that felt far greater than its physical presence. "Sir Richard is going to arrange for you to serve at court," she informed me. "You will take your place in the household of Queen Catherine of Aragon. There is no greater honour for a young girl."

My pulse quickened at the mention of court. Images of gilded tapestries, knightly tournaments and the dazzling radiance of the queen herself flitted through my mind. A place at court—what young girl could resist the allure of such a life? As she gazed at me, her piercing eyes searching my soul for resolve, I straightened my back. It was not merely an honour; it was an opportunity. A chance to prove my worth, to secure alliances, to carve my place among the notables of the realm. My destiny was no longer in my hands alone. It belonged to the generations who had come before me and to the name I carried.

"I will make you proud, Mother," I said, my voice steadier than I felt. "I will fulfil my duty and honour our lineage."

She nodded, a flicker of approval in her stern expression. "See that you do, Anne. The court is no place for the faint-hearted. Be resolute, be vigilant, and always remember where you come from."

With those words, she left me standing before the chart. I turned back to it, the inked names seeming brighter now, their significance heavier. I traced the path upward with my eyes, from Elizabeth Bourchier to Thomas Woodstock, and onward to King Edward III. They were not just names—they were my inheritance and my calling. The road ahead would be fraught with challenges, I knew, but I would face them with the same unyielding spirit that my ancestors had possessed. The honour of our family demanded nothing less.

I expected to leave for the palace within the month. But two years went past and I was still not invited to court. One night I overheard my mother quarrelling with my stepfather. I put on my mantle and went to listen at the door of the privy chamber.

"When will you keep your promise and send Anne to court?" she demanded. "If you delay any longer, she will begin to lose her youthful bloom!"

"I am doing my best for her Elizabeth," he replied. "But I am not a great nobleman whose daughters have a right to such a privilege."

"But you serve in the King's chamber and he holds you in high regard," she said. "Surely that is enough?"

"He is besieged with requests every day," he explained. "He does not like his gentlemen to ask him for favours."

"I thought you were one of his favourites, Richard," she pouted. "Perhaps you have exaggerated your influence at court."

"There is a way, Elizabeth," he said. "But you might not like it."

What do you mean? she asked.

"The best time to make a request is when he is in a good humour," he said. "If I were to lose a considerable amount to him at cards then he would feel well disposed towards me. The King is very reckless at gambling and he is always complaining that his gentlemen make their fortunes from him."

"How great a sum would it require?" she asked.

"A few hundred pounds should suffice," he replied. "It is a fair price for such a favour. If I were to approach the Cardinal for his assistance he would expect to receive as much in return."

Sir Richard was absent at court for three months. But on his return, he summoned both my mother and I to come to his study. I had never been invited into his sanctuary before and I was filled with supressed excitement.

"I have good news and bad news to tell you," he said. "The bad news is that I lost three hundred pounds to the King in play. But I did not lose it in vain. The good news is that his Majesty has promised that the next opening among the maids of honour shall go to Anne." He looked at my mother triumphantly.

"That is wonderful news!" exclaimed my mother. "It was well worth the loss in order to gain such a chance. What do you say to your stepfather, Anne?"

I made a dutiful curtsey. "I am most grateful, Sir Richard," I said.

He basked in our praise. "That is not all," he said. "I have brought your court gowns with me. They have cost me a pretty penny for they are the finest fabrics and colours with matching Spanish hoods. I have told the steward to have the chest taken up to your chamber. You may go and try them on."

"I shall unpack them," interposed my mother. "Anne is not accustomed to handling such costly dresses. We must not risk any damage to them."

She rose and preceded me out of the study. Then she walked over to the porch. She supervised the transport of the precious chest upstairs. Then she proceeded to open it and examine the contents. She held up the gowns one at a time and then laid them reverently upon the bed. They were made of white satin, black velvet, dove grey silk, yellow satin, tawny velvet and deep green silk. The colours were rich and vibrant like a bowl of ripe fruit in the summertime. Her eyes gleamed with envy as she took in their quality.

"Sir Richard has never given me so fine a gown as any of these," she muttered to herself. "Why did he not consult me before undertaking so great an expense? Well, it is done now and we must make the most of this great chance."

Underneath, there was a long flat box containing a selection of sleeves made of silk and satin. Some were plain, but others were embroidered with gold and silver thread. The Spanish hoods had been carefully packed in square boxes in order to keep their shape. All this finery was the required wardrobe for a lady of the Queen's household.

"These fabrics were made in Italy," she remarked. "They are expensive imported goods."

I was transfixed by the sight of the splendid gowns. "May I try them on mother?" I asked.

"Yes, indeed," she said. "Sir Richard will expect to see how fine you look and his wishes must be gratified. I must check that they are a good fit for you. And I shall provide the linens for your wardrobe. They are just as necessary but he did not give any thought to it."

"Thank you, mother," I said. "Which one shall I wear?"

"The dove grey silk will suit your colouring best," she said.

I looked the mirror on the wall. I was a tall girl with fair hair and grey eyes. My reflection looked back at me with a cool and composed expression.

She sent for her maid to dress me in it. "It is not so bad a fit," she said judiciously. "Sir Richard has a good eye for such things. I shall put on the hood myself." She placed it upon my head carefully in order not to disarrange my hair.

I took another look in the mirror. Now I looked like a stranger to myself, and yet the image of that stranger compelled me to draw closer to the mirror. I raised my hand, touching the smooth silk that now hugged my frame with effortless elegance. The dove grey shimmered in the light like morning mist under the sun, and for the first time, I saw not just a girl—but the lady of the court that my mother and Sir Richard envisioned me to be.

Mary adjusted the gown once more, ensuring every detail was perfect. "There," she said. "You will turn heads in this, Mistress Stanhope."

I took a deep breath, my reflection still holding my gaze.

"Fine feathers make fine birds," my mother remarked approvingly. "But you cannot attend the court without jewels. Mary, fetch my casket."

"Yes, Lady Page," she said. She returned bearing a small wooden chest. It contained my mother's most treasured possessions.

"You will need a complete set of ornaments," she said, lifting the lid of the chest to reveal a dazzling array of jewels. Gleaming pearls nestled within a velvet pouch, sapphires shimmered under the warm glow of the firelight and golden chains coiled like sleeping serpents. Every piece was the finest quality.

My mother selected a necklace adorned with emeralds and diamonds. "These will bring out the colour of your eyes," she mused, fastening it around my neck. "And the earrings," she added, handing over a pair of matching emerald drops.

Mary stepped forward, holding a gold bracelet etched with intricate filigree. "Shall I, Lady Page?"

"Yes, it completes the ensemble," my mother agreed. She turned her attention to me, a satisfied smile gracing her lips. "Now you look like a lady from a noble house."

I gazed down at myself, marvelling at how the jewels transformed me—not just my appearance, but the very aura I projected. They seemed to imbue me with power, confidence, and the weight of expectation. I felt the pulse of the court already—its games, its intrigues, and my place within it.

"Be mindful," she said as she adjusted my bracelet one last time. "You are the daughter of an honourable line. You are also the heiress to a considerable fortune. The court is a splendid place but you must not let yourself get distracted. You are not going there for your own amusement but in order to serve the Queen. She has the reputation of being a good mistress to her ladies. So, you must serve her faithfully and loyally and in return she will find a worthy husband."

"Thank you, mother," I replied.

"Do not waste this opportunity," she warned me. "Your stepfather has been put to a great deal of expense to purchase your wardrobe."

I was determined that I would not. I was young, fair and I had every confidence in myself. I was going to be a success at court. I turned to my mother with resolution in my eyes. "I am ready."

She smiled. "Good. Sir Richard is waiting for you downstairs. Prepare yourself to meet him." And with that, she swept out of the chamber, leaving me and the stranger in the mirror alone to face what was to come. As the sound of her footsteps faded, I took one last look at my reflection. The finery gave me confidence, but my heart still raced at the thought of what awaited me. With a deep breath, I made my way downstairs, where my stepfather stood waiting to see me.

Sir Richard regarded me with a critical eye as I descended the staircase. "A fine sight indeed," he said, nodding approvingly. "Ladies are the flowers of the court. You must take good care of your wardrobe so that everything is immaculate. And whenever you stand or sit or curtsey you must do it with the grace and poise that characterise a lady of good birth. A maid of honour should reflect the majesty of the Queen. And you must be known for your virtue. You should wear a prayerbook at your girdle at all times. You will do well at court, Anne, if you remember the lessons we've taught you."

"Thank you for my beautiful gowns, Sir Richard," I said.

He smiled briefly to see my excitement. "I had them made for you by a dressmaker at court," he said. "They are in the latest fashion. One of the Queen's ladies advised me so they are all to her Majesty's taste."

"I shall be proud to wear them," I said.

"My dear Anne, the life of a maid of honour is an arduous calling," he said. "Let me offer you a few words of advice. Serve her Majesty with humility, diligence, and faithfulness. Be reverent to your superiors, courteous to your equals, and gentle with those below you. Avoid meddling in others' affairs and practice the silence which is fitting for a maiden. Let your words and actions aim for the good of all. Follow these rules, and you shall find great benefit in your service and bring joy to your friends."

"Yes, Sir Richard," I replied, keeping my eyes downcast. I was willing to be humble and devoted until I had achieved all my ambitions for myself. But did not intend to spend my life in silence. I was not going to become a nun, but a courtier. When I was a rich and titled lady, I intended to speak as I saw fit.

"It takes patience to mould oneself into a successful courtier," he said. "But the rewards are very great. I was a nobody when I entered the service of Cardinal Wolsey. There were dozens of other young men competing to gain his notice. But I succeeded in gaining his trust and preferment by the excellence of my service. Now I am an established courtier with a stipend and a fine residence. The King and the Queen have the power to bestow money, lands, houses and offices upon their favourites. So, close your ears to all unpleasantness and keep your eyes upon the prize."

His words made me eager to begin my service at court. I knew that I would make a perfect courtier. I was determined that I would be as successful as my stepfather had been. The path ahead was daunting, yet I felt ready to face it. I would not disappoint the expectations of my family.

CHAPTER 2

The Maid of Honour (1527)

"There is nothing that becometh a maid better than soberness, silence, shamefastness and chastity, both of body and mind"

(Thomas Bentley, *The Monument of Matrons*, 1582).

I received an invitation to join the court in time for Easter. So, it was springtime when I made the long journey to London. It was my favourite time of the year at Beechwood. The trees were beginning to show their new leaves, the green fields were dotted with yellow celandines and the young lambs gambolled in the bright sunshine. But I was not sorry to leave. My future lay ahead of me at the palace of Greenwich. The roads were sufficiently dry to support the weight of the cart which carried my wardrobe inside a locked chest. My box of jewels was hidden at the bottom of the chest. Their settings were rather old-fashioned, but there was nothing inferior about their quality. No woman of quality could attend the court without the dresses and jewels that signified her status. I wore my gown of tawny velvet with sleeves of yellow silk and a black woollen mantle for there was still a chill in the air.

Finally, we arrived at the palace of Greenwich. A great crowd thronged the entrance. I surveyed the jostling crowd with dismay. How would I ever gain entry to the palace? I wished that Sir Richard had accompanied me on my journey. He would have known exactly what to do. But he had returned to court a week ago to attend the King. A groom dressed in royal livery confronted the steward.

"Move that cart out of here," he ordered. "Get on your way."

"This is Mistress Stanhope," he replied. "She is here to enter the Queen's service."

"You have chosen a bad day," he retorted. "Today is Maundy Thursday. Queen Catherine is distributing alms to poor women in the Chapel Royal. And half of London has gathered here in the hope of receiving largesse. You will never make your way through the crowd and even if you did, there would be no-one to receive you. So, you had better return next week!"

The steward looked dumbfounded at this disastrous news. The groom folded his arms and smirked at his distress. Anger welled up inside me. I was a Bourchier and I would not be turned away by a mere groom. This was no time for maidenly modesty and silence. I resolved to take charge of the situation.

"I am here at the order of his Majesty the King," I snapped. "He will be most displeased to hear that I was received with such discourtesy. There must be another entrance into the palace. Where is it?"

He stared back at me coldly. "The Yeoman Guards won't allow you to pass," he said. "They have strict orders not to admit any strangers to the palace."

I stared back at him with equal coldness. I knew what he wanted. But I was not prepared to sit on a cart for the rest of the day. I would have to pay his price.

"My stepfather is Sir Richard Page," I said. "He is one the King's gentlemen. If you assist me then you will be well rewarded."

"So, they all say," he replied unimpressed.

I turned to the steward who was gaping like a fish out of water. "Give him what he wants," I said curtly.

He drew a purse out of his jerkin with a dubious expression. "A sixpence to admit the young lady into the palace and arrange for the carriage of her chest," he said.

He shook his head. "This is the King's palace," he said. "I can't do favours like that for just anyone."

"A shilling then," I agreed.

He grinned and held his hand out to the steward. He passed it over reluctantly. "I fear that you have been imposed upon, Mistress," he said.

The groom pocketed the coin and gave a piercing whistle. A young boy dressed in royal livery emerged from the crowd.

"Conduct this young lady to the Mother of the Maids," he said. "And send some servants to fetch her chest."

"Follow me Mistress," he said. "I am one of the royal pages. The guards will allow me to enter the door."

He escorted me round to a side entrance which was flanked by a pair of burly guardsmen bearing halberds.

"This lady is here to enter the Queen's service," he said. "I am going to fetch someone to take charge of her."

I waited while the page discharged his errands. Presently, a woman dressed in Spanish costume came to the door. She surveyed me with a look of deep suspicion.

Instantly I dropped a curtsey. "My name is Mistress Anne Stanhope," I said. "I am at your service Madam."

"I thought you were here to serve her Grace the Queen," she replied ironically.

"Yes, indeed, Madam," I answered politely.

"Who has sponsored you to serve her Majesty," she demanded.

"I am the stepdaughter of Sir Richard Page," I said. "He is one of the King's gentlemen."

She sniffed. "The Queen cannot even appoint her own choice of ladies," she said disdainfully. "His Majesty distributes her patronage to his friends just as he pleases."

I held my ground despite her extraordinary conduct. "I was told to report for duty before Easter," I said.

"And so, you arrive here during Holy Week," she snorted. "It shows that you are a girl without any reverence or common sense."

I would not allow the old harridan to intimidate me. "I am content to obey the King's orders," I replied.

Her eyes flashed at my insolence. "Are you related to the Boleyn family?" she demanded suspiciously.

I drew myself up to my full height. "I do not have the honour of their acquaintance," I said. "I am the daughter of Sir Edward Stanhope who was knighted by his Majesty for his valour in the French wars."

"The King has knighted many of his captains," she sneered. "I will conduct you to your mistress. Then you can explain yourself to her."

She nodded to the guards and they opened the door wide enough to admit me. I stepped inside and she turned her back and advanced rapidly along the corridor. I had no choice but to trail behind in her wake. Finally, she stopped before a door and knocked on it loudly. It was opened by a tall lady dressed in a black silk gown.

"Lady Maria de Salinas," she said. "What can I do for you?"

She shrugged dismissively. "I bring you a lost sheep for your flock, Mistress Stoner," she said. "She claims that she has come to enter the service of the Queen. Doubtless you can verify the truth of her story. But do not trouble her Grace today. She is quite exhausted from the ceremonies of Maundy Thursday. She has washed the feet of thirty-nine poor women, one for each year of her age."

"Of course, Lady Maria," she said. "You may leave this matter in my hands."

Lady Maria turned on her heel and left without vouchsafing me another glance. But I could not waste my attention on her. I needed to make a good impression upon Mistress Stoner.

I made a polite curtsey and lowered my eyes. "My name is Mistress Anne Stanhope," I said.

She surveyed me keenly as I stood before her. "You are young, fair and well presented, Mistress Stanhope," she said approvingly. "You must take care to dress well and keep your hair neatly under your hood."

"Yes, Mistress Stoner," I replied.

"Show me how you would make your curtsey to their Majesties," she said.

I swept into a deep court curtsey. I had been practising it for weeks.

"That is well enough," she said. "The Lord Chamberlain mentioned something about a new maid of honour coming. Normally, I shall would take you to see her Grace so that you could take your vow of service. But I did not expect you to arrive until after Easter. Tomorrow is Good Friday and the Queen cannot see you then. Nor on Holy Saturday either. And Easter Sunday will be quite impossible. You cannot possibly be presented to her Majesty until the court festivities are over. You will have to remain in the maid's dormitory until then."

I was filled with dismay at the thought of missing the celebrations.

"Perhaps her Majesty could see me this evening," I said.

"Didn't you hear what Lady Maria said?" she scolded. "Her Majesty cannot be disturbed. It seems you are a very impetuous young girl. You will have to learn patience in order to serve in the court."

I resigned myself to my fate. "Yes, Mistress Stoner," I replied.

"I will take you to the dormitory," she said. "Where is your chest?"

"It is outside in the courtyard," I replied. "My steward is guarding it."

"Very well, I will send some servants to fetch it," she said. "Come with me."

I followed her to the deserted dormitory. The other maids of honour are attending the Queen, she said. She has been ministering to the poor in the Chapel Royal all afternoon. I have no time to explain your duties to you now. I must return to my office.

She paused at the door. "When you hear the clock strike six o'clock, you should go to the Great Hall and take some repast," she said." Tomorrow is a fast day. You will see very little of the other girls during the next two days because they will be attending her Majesty in the chapel."

She left me to my thoughts. Half an hour later my chest arrived in the dormitory. I resigned myself to a dreary interlude. But I had not considered that the court was a hotbed of gossip. It did not take long before the Queen learned that a new maid of honour had arrived at the palace. She insisted that I should be presented to her at once. A page was sent to escort me to her privy chamber. I hastily opened my chest and put on my jewels. Then I placed my hood upon my head. The day had been filled with disappointments, but the moment had finally come for me to meet her Majesty.

Queen Catherine of Aragon was sitting upon her chair of estate with a canopy of cloth of gold above her head. It was hung with banners depicting the coats of arms of England and Spain. She was attended by several ladies dressed in the Spanish manner. All the ladies at court wore Spanish hoods and farthingales like the Queen. She was dressed in a gown of purple velvet with sleeves of cloth of gold. Around her neck she wore a gold cross inlaid with five rubies. On her bodice she wore a gold brooch with the letters IHS set with diamonds and three pendant pearls. A gold tablet of Our Lady hung from her girdle. Her face looked tired, but she smiled warmly as I was presented to her.

"It is most gracious of your Majesty to receive me," I said. I stood with my hands folded tightly before me, the embroidered hem of my bodice trembling ever so slightly. The air inside the Queen's privy chamber held the weight of ceremony, frankincense lingered faintly from morning prayers, mingling with beeswax and the fainter perfume of dried lavender tucked within the wall hangings. Outside, the rain ran down the mullioned windows.

"My dear, it would be unthinkable for you to miss the highlight of the Christian year," she replied. "The etiquette of the royal court is extremely strict, as indeed it should be. But we must all bear in mind that God's service takes priority of place."

"Thank you, your Grace," I said.

Her Majesty sat tall beneath her cloth of estate, the deep purple of her gown pooling regally about her. "I am pleased to welcome you into my service, Mistress Stanhope," she said, her Castilian accent brushing each syllable with dignity. "Please bring the Bible, Mistress Stoner."

Mistress Stoner stepped forward in silence, her face a hard cameo carved of duty. The great Bible she bore was bound in black leather, its spine stiff with age and reverence.

"Place your hand upon the Holy Bible, Mistress Stanhope," she said.

I stepped forward, heart hammering beneath my stays, and laid my right hand upon it. Lord Mountjoy, the Lord Chamberlain, stepped forward and stood beside me in his silk-fringed cloak. He looked down with a severity that might have melted iron.

"Repeat these words after me," he said. "I swear to be true and faithful to my sovereign lord, King Henry VIII and to my lady Queen Catherine of Aragon. I shall serve her with diligence and honesty, I shall keep her counsel and do nothing that shall be to her dishonour or displeasure. So, help me God and all the saints. Amen."

I drew a deep breath and recited the oath of service to her Majesty calmly and clearly. Then I took my hand off the Bible. I watched Mistress Stoner carry it away with an inward sense of relief. Finally, it was done and I was now a maid of honour in the service of Queen Catherine.

Her Majesty smiled with a genuine warmth that curled at the corners of her mouth and softened the lines around her eyes. "You shall join me in the chapel tomorrow morning," she said. "There we shall contemplate the glorious mystery of the passion and death of our Lord."

"Yes, your Majesty," I replied.

"I hear that you have lost your father, Mistress Stanhope," she said.

"Yes, your Grace," I replied. "He died when I was an infant. I never knew him."

"That is a grave misfortune for a young girl," she sighed. "But you are in my household now and you shall have nothing to fear while you are in my care."

"Your Majesty should rest now," insisted Lady Maria.

"I am not tired, Maria," she replied. "When I think of the faces of all those women on the chapel today, I can only be thankful. They were so grateful to receive my poor offerings that they wept for joy. It is a great comfort to me to think of their prayers. I am sure that I will reap great blessings from their intercession. Perhaps even the greatest blessing of all - the one that I have prayed for so earnestly and for so many years."

Lady Maria's stern expression suddenly became tender. "Perhaps, your Grace," she murmured.

"It is said that the ear of the Almighty is open to the cries of the poor," she said. "Perhaps He will be merciful to me for their sake and grant me the same miracle that He gave to the holy women Sarah and Elizabeth. A child in my old age. A son to inherit this kingdom."

"Nothing is impossible with God, your Grace," she agreed.

"This is the holiest time of the year," she said. "The heavens come close to the earth and the veil that stands between may be pierced by prayer and repentance. I shall spend this night at the altar in my closet meditating upon the last night of the Lord in Gethsemane."

"I beseech your Grace to take some rest," she urged her.

"It is true that the spirit is willing but the flesh is weak," she said. "When our Lord prayed in the garden of Gethsemane, his disciples Peter and John fell asleep. He reproached them for their weakness, saying, *Could you not watch with me for one hour?* What is one night out of a whole lifetime? It is little enough to spend in devotion to the Lord."

"If you cannot be moved to think of yourself, then think of his Majesty," said Lady Maria. "He will expect you to preside over the Easter festivities of the court. You cannot do justice to your duties unless you take some rest now."

"You are right to remind me, Maria," she sighed. "I cannot only be guided by my own desires. I must remember my responsibilities to the King and the court."

"There is a balance in all things, your Grace," she said. "Did not our Lord command us to render unto Caesar what is due to Caesar and unto God what is due to God?"

"You have an answer for everything Maria," she said. "You always have your way in the end."

"It is time for your Grace to dine," she replied. "It has been a long day."

"I shall only require a little, Maria," she said. "Remember that it is still a time of penance and fasting. Only when it is Easter Sunday will the court share in the great feast of celebration for the resurrection of our Lord."

I watched as the chamberlain directed the servants to bring in the dishes and place them on the side boards. The maids of honour stood behind the Queen as they were presented and served. I boldly took my place beside them. I was now a maid of honour too. The Queen waved away most of the dishes. Lady Maria watched her like a dragon as she took some manchet bread and drank a cup of wine. Then she pushed away her trencher.

"Your Grace should retire to her bedchamber and rest now," said Lady Maria.

The Queen nodded wearily and rose to her feet. Lady Maria shepherded her towards her bedchamber.

Mistress Stoner signalled to the maids of honour. "It is time to dine in the Presence Chamber," she said. "Afterwards you will return to the dormitory."

Some of the ladies in waiting joined the maids of honour at dinner. The rest withdrew to their own apartments to dine. Our repast consisted of a thin pottage and half a loaf of bread. I had expected to dine much better at the royal court. But I reminded myself that the Queen was a most pious lady and it was still Lent.

When we returned to the dormitory, Mistress Stoner introduced me to my companions.

"This is Mistress Stanhope, the new maid of honour," she said. "I trust that you will make her welcome among you."

Back at the dormitory, I had little time to take stock of my companions. They sat on their beds and whispered to each other while darting curious looks at me. There were six maids of honour altogether. I supposed that they were the daughters of noblemen and important courtiers. After an hour, Mistress Stoner returned to the dormitory to turn out the lights.

"You need an early night, young ladies," she said. "Tomorrow is Good Friday and I shall be here to take you to the chapel at six o'clock. Remember that the day will be spent in fasting and silence in memory of the sacrifice of our Lord. You should make good use of this time to pray earnestly on behalf of our gracious Majesty the Queen."

The maids of honour exchanged furtive glances with each other, but no-one ventured to enlighten me.

I lay down in silence and listened as the sounds of the palace—faint lute music from a distant hall and the rhythmic steps of the watch—faded into a breathless hush. The following morning, we dressed in the dark and waited in silence for Mistress Stoner. We followed her in pairs to the Chapel Royal and took our places on the benches behind the Queen and the ladies in waiting.

The chapel, stripped of its usual splendour, was a study in humility. It stood quiet and reverent, as if the very stones had taken a vow of silence. The tracery upon the fan-vaulted ceiling hung like frozen lace above us and the scent of cold stone and candle wax met us like a hush. The tapestries had been drawn back, revealing walls of pale ashlar that seemed to glow faintly in the early gloom. The altar stood bare, its usual gold and finery replaced by austerity. A lone cross, draped in rich purple silk, was the only focal point, reminding us of the sorrowful Passion of our Lord. The priest stood at the altar in purple vestments, his movements deliberate, his expression grave. A thurible hung motionless in his hand, unlit. There would be no music today, no incense to stir the senses, only stillness and the weight of reflection.

Queen Catherine sat with her hands folded tightly, her head slightly bowed beneath a hood of black damask. Even her jewels had been set aside for mourning. Mistress Stoner hovered discreetly at her side, watching for any sign of need, but the Queen neither moved nor spoke. One by one, the nobility entered and took their places with hushed solemnity. I recognised the Marquess of Exeter by his crimson cloak, now muted by the subdued light filtering through the leaded windows. Beside him walked Lord Mountjoy, his face grave, his steps deliberate. Their usual courtly finery seemed dimmed, the jewels and silks unable to compete with the weight of Good Friday's sorrow. Even the Duke of Norfolk had forgone his usual splendour, wearing a dark doublet that seemed to swallow light. No-one looked toward the Queen directly. No-one spoke. The silence of the day did not feel empty. It was ritualistic, devout, charged with undercurrents too dangerous to name aloud. I watched expressions flicker and fade, some tense, some mournful, some unreadable. But all knew where their gaze must rest eventually. On the veiled cross. And on the Queen.

It was then that the atmosphere in the chapel shifted. The distant sound of boots on stone announced the arrival of his Majesty King Henry VIII and his retinue. All eyes instinctively turned toward the grand entrance as the heavy oak doors creaked open, revealing the King in his full imposing presence. Despite the solemnity of the day, King Henry commanded attention with effortless authority. His figure was draped in muted yet rich fabrics, the deep crimson of his cloak lined with ermine a subtle nod to his royal stature. A simple gold chain adorned his neck, restrained compared to his usual finery, yet it gleamed in the dim candlelight, a reminder of his unmatched power. His face, though stern, bore a trace of piety, as befitted the occasion. On his head he wore a black velvet cap with seven pairs of triangular aglets.

Behind him, his courtiers followed in precise formation, a well-rehearsed display of regal order. The men wore dark doublets and cloaks, their swords carefully sheathed at their sides. The women of the court, with their modestly lowered eyes, moved gracefully in their subdued gowns of velvet and brocade. The faint rustle of fabric and the whisper of footsteps on the chapel floor were the only sounds as they took their places. As the King advanced, the Queen rose from her seat and curtsied deeply, her ladies and maids following suit in perfect unison. Henry acknowledged her with a solemn nod, his expression unreadable. Once he was seated, the chapel seemed to exhale, though the weight of his presence lingered like a shadow over all. The priest's voice resumed, leading the congregation in prayer, but my thoughts lingered on the magnetic force of the King's arrival. There was no denying that, even in the humblest of settings, Henry VIII was every inch a monarch.

The priest recited the opening words of the Latin liturgy: *"Deus in adjutorium meum intende."* The congregation responded with the words: *"Domine ad adiuvandum me festina."* Queen Catherine of Aragon sat in quiet reflection, her head slightly bowed, her rosary slipping through her fingers. The ladies in waiting mirrored her devout focus, their lips moving silently in prayer. My fellow maids clutched their own rosaries, murmuring the Hail Mary under their breath. I felt Mistress Stoner's unwavering gaze before I saw it, her stern eyes a constant reminder to maintain decorum. A moment's lapse, a single falter, and her reprimand would follow like a thunderclap.

I took my place and instinctively reached for the prayer book at my girdle. Its leather cover was cool beneath my fingers as I turned the pages, seeking solace in the well-worn prayers. As the hours passed, the day unfurled with solemn ritual. The offices came and went—sext, none, vespers, and finally compline. Each brought with it its own rhythm of psalms, readings, and reflection, yet the gravity of the day never wavered. By sunset, my knees ached from kneeling and my back felt stiff from the unyielding benches, but I dared not let my discomfort show. My thoughts strayed once to the gaiety I had left behind, the comforts I had forsaken in favour of this austere existence. But I clenched my jaw and steadied my gaze. This was my chance to serve the Queen, to prove my worth. I would not falter, not here, not today. When compline ended and we rose for the final time, the chapel seemed darker than before, the candles flickering against the encroaching night. My exhaustion was eclipsed only by the knowledge that I had endured. I followed Mistress Stoner out into the cold air, my breath visible in the twilight. Tomorrow would bring its own trials, but for now, I could at least be grateful for the silence.

Holy Saturday unfolded with the same air of solemnity as the previous day, a hushed reverence that permeated every moment. We rose before dawn, dressing in silence, the darkness outside a reflection of the penitential spirit within. Mistress Stoner guided us to the Chapel Royal once more, her stern demeanour ensuring no whisper or murmur broke the sanctity of the morning. The chapel, though unchanged in its stark appearance, seemed even more sombre today. The altar remained stripped, the cross still shrouded in purple silk, an ever-present reminder of the tomb where our Lord lay. The priest's purple vestments swayed gently as he moved about the altar, his voice steady and measured as he led us in prayer. I kept my focus firmly on my prayer book, unwilling to risk another reprimand from Mistress Stoner. The Queen, as always, was a model of devotion, her eyes closed in contemplation, her rosary a constant companion. Her ladies and the maids of honour mirrored her, each lost in their own prayers. Though my knees ached from kneeling and my back longed for relief, I dared not waver. Each word of the psalms, each line of the homilies, was a test of endurance and faith. Holy Saturday was another fast day. After the morning services in the Chapel Royal the maids of honour dined upon bread and pottage. But Queen Catherine ate nothing at all.

"Take a little, your Majesty," Lady Maria pleaded vainly.

She shook her head. "And did our gracious Lord eat upon this day?" she replied. "This is a time of penance and reflection. Let us share in His sufferings so that we may hope to share in His glory."

The afternoon stretched on, marked by the familiar rhythm of the daily offices. Sext brought a brief respite, though it was not for indulgence. None, vespers, and compline followed, each as solemn as the last. By sunset, the weight of the day pressed heavily upon us, yet none showed signs of faltering. As the evening fell and the last office concluded, I stepped out of the chapel into the cool night air, the stars faint against the darkened sky. Exhaustion threatened to overwhelm me, but I steadied myself, knowing that Easter Sunday would bring its own demands. For now, I was content to have endured another day, to have proven myself capable of the rigors of court life. The silence of the night was a welcome balm, a moment of peace amidst the trials of service. Tomorrow, I vowed, I would rise again, ready to face whatever challenges awaited.

Easter Sunday dawned with a sense of anticipation, a stark contrast to the sombre stillness of the preceding days. As I entered the Chapel Royal with the other maids of honour, the transformation was striking. The altar was resplendent with fresh blooms and glowing candles, their flames casting a warm light that seemed to dance upon the stone walls. The gold cross set with precious gems stood unveiled to our sight, its gleaming surface a beacon of hope and renewal.

We took our places on the benches behind the Queen and her ladies, and I found myself marvelling at the beauty of the scene before me. The priest, clad in white vestments that shimmered in the soft light, began the liturgy in a tone of exaltation. The joyful sound of hymns of praise filled the chapel, the voices of the choir soaring to the vaulted ceiling and enveloping us in their glory. I clutched my prayer book tightly, the familiar words of the Easter celebration resonating deeply within me.

King Henry VIII arrived shortly after the service began, his presence commanding as always. His attire, while muted compared to his usual grandeur, still bore the unmistakable marks of royalty: a doublet of rich red velvet, a golden chain, and a small jewelled brooch pinned at his chest. The Queen rose to greet him, her curtsy low and graceful, and he acknowledged her with a nod before taking his seat. The court followed his lead, a ripple of movement that brought the congregation to its knees in reverence.

After the service, the mood shifted from reverence to celebration. The palace halls bustled with activity as preparations for the Easter feast commenced. Long tables groaned under the weight of roasted meats, fragrant pies, and sweet confections, the scents mingling in the air and making my stomach rumble. I found my place among the other maids, savouring the flavours of the meal after the long fast of Lent. The hall was alive with conversation, laughter, and the soft strains of music played by minstrels in the corner.

"Christ the Lord is risen again,
Christ hath broken every chain.
Hark, angelic voices cry,
Singing evermore on high,
Alleluia!

He who gave for us His life,
Who for us endured the strife,
Is our Paschal Lamb today;
We too sing for joy and say
Alleluia!"

The afternoon was a blur of festivity. Dances were held in the Great Hall, and I watched as courtiers twirled in their finest attire, the vibrant colours of their gowns and doublets a celebration in themselves. Even I could not resist the lure of the music and joined a dance or two, though I was careful to maintain the decorum expected of a maid of honour. As the day faded into evening and the sun cast its golden light upon the palace, I felt a profound sense of renewal. Easter had brought with it not only the promise of salvation but also a reminder of the joy that could be found even within the confines of court life. I retired that night with a heart full of gratitude, ready to face whatever challenges my new role might bring.

Now that the austerities of Holy Week were concluded, an atmosphere of festivity pervaded the Tudor court. Music returned to the Great Hall, laughter arose among the courtiers, and the ladies of the Queen's household dressed in brighter silks. My companions were more disposed to be friendly and I learned their names. I sat upon a velvet-cushioned bench beneath a window glazed with armorial glass, the morning sun streaking the floor with mottled gold. Mistress Badby leaned toward me, fanning herself with a sprig of rosemary, her russet gown embroidered with a pattern of ivy and heartease.

"You are fortunate to gain a position in the Queen's service," she murmured, a tone of careful appraisal behind her words. "Most girls wait years for such an invitation."

I smoothed the folds of my kirtle, aware that half the chamber listened as they stitched, sipped wine, or plucked at their lutes.

"I have been waiting for two years for a chance to come to court," I replied. "I was told there were no openings."

Mistress Horsman glanced up from her embroidery hoop. "It is rare for a place to be open among the maids of honour," she said with meaning. "But one unexpectedly became vacant quite recently."

She spoke the last words with sly emphasis, and several heads turned.

"Did the young lady get married?" I asked innocently.

Mistress Horsman's mouth twitched with amusement. "She has not got married yet," she said, her voice lilting. "But she thinks that she will."

She and Mistress Badby exchanged glances, a silent ripple of mirth between them. Mistress Horsman gave a small titter behind her hand, and I felt the sudden tension coil in the air like a drawn thread.

"Margery, hush," said Mistress Darrell sharply, closing her prayer book with quiet force. She had been sitting in a sunless corner, watching with hawk-like stillness. "Mistress Stoner has told us not to gossip."

Mistress Horsman flushed and lowered her eyes. I said nothing, only folded my hands and looked out over the chamber. Somewhere in the distance I heard the bells toll to mark the passing of another hour. Mistress Darrell resumed her quiet vigil, her prayer book resting on her lap as if it were a shield. Around us, the mood shifted subtly. The maids bent closer over their embroidery hoops. The whispered laughter ebbed, replaced by the soft murmur of thread pulled through linen.

The door to the chamber opened and Mistress Stoner entered. At once the maids stood to attention beside their beds. She took her place beneath the tapestry of the Annunciation, her starched coif casting a shadow across her brow. The sunlight slanted through the tall windows and fell in fractured beams across the polished floor. She stood rooted like a sentinel and cast her gaze from one face to the next. No one dared to fidget. Her steel-grey eyes settled on Mistress Horsman first, who adjusted her girdle and glanced down, then on Mistress Darrell, who maintained her composure with effortless poise.

"Young ladies," she said, her voice clipped and flinty, "you are here to serve Their Majesties at court. You are not here to indulge your whims, gossip at leisure, or parade about like players on a May Day stage."

The words struck like rapier thrusts. Several girls shifted uncomfortably. I folded my hands with deliberate calm, willing myself not to be the subject of her next glance.

"His Majesty has ordered," she continued, "that all the ladies who attend the Queen must be fit for the room. In other words, you must be graceful, charming, and accomplished. Moreover, you must be attentive, dutiful and ready to entertain at all times. There shall be no slouching at meals, no idleness in your duties and no garish affectations. You are to be an ornament to her Majesty, not a burden."

"Yes, Mistress Stoner," we replied.

Mistress Stoner stepped forward, her shoes clicking crisply against the floor. "You shall master your court dances, your lute exercises, your embroidery. The hours are long, but you must never fail to smile and look pleasant. When the Queen plays cards, you will play cards. When she listens to her players, you are to attend with interest. And if any lady thinks her charms alone will secure her place, she will find herself excused from service before summer ends."

There was a silence so absolute it rang. One of the younger girls, pale-faced and trembling, dropped her fan.

"The Queen wishes to see all her ladies at chapel," she said. "So, you must rise early and prepare your appearance before attending mass in the Chapel Royal at six o'clock. You will stand behind the Queen's chair at all her meals and all her audiences. The rest of the time you will attend the Queen in her apartments and make yourselves useful. Remember that it is a great honour for a young girl to serve the Queen!"

The daily routine of a maid of honour included dressing the Queen, praying in the chapel and attending her at mealtimes. In the afternoons we listened to edifying readings in the privy chamber and diverted the Queen with music and cards. In the evenings we were entertained by the Queen's musicians. It was a busy life for a young girl. As I performed my duties, I weighed up my companions carefully in turn. Mistress Badby was a quiet little mouse with little of interest to say for herself. Mistress Darrell was as devout as a nun and dressed herself just as plainly. But Mistress Horsman had a witty tongue and lively sense of humour. I recognised her as a kindred spirit.

The Mother of the Maids was a vigilant guardian, but we could not be watched all the time. I made the most of the opportunities for conversation when she was called away. Everyone needed to have friend and allies at court, even a young girl like myself. The maids of honour frequently attended the Queen as she sewed in her Privy Chamber. One afternoon, Mistress Stoner summoned four of the maids of honour to accompany the Queen as she walked in the privy garden.

"Mistress Stanhope, you shall remain here with Mistress Horsman, she said. "She is an expert in blackwork embroidery and you need to master the skill. All of the maids of honour are renowned for their expertise in this art."

"Yes, Mistress Stoner," I replied.

We took up our workbags and sat in the window seats where there was good light. The walls were covered with rich tapestries depicting the legend of St George and the dragon. We spoke together in hushed tones as Mistress Horsman demonstrated the technique. I soon mastered the complex pattern and completed the border round the linen handkerchief.

She leaned closely to look at it. "That should satisfy our mistress, she said. How quickly you have learned the pattern. Most girls take much longer to acquire the technique."

"My mother taught me many embroidery patterns when I was a child," I replied. "She was even more particular than Mistress Stoner. I shall have to copy this new pattern and send it to her. She is anxious to learn about all the latest fashions at the court."

"You can send her another kerchief as a gift," she said. "It may prompt her to send you a present in return."

"She is not so indulgent," I said. "But it will please her to know that I am serving the Queen with diligence."

"Yes, we girls are the pawns of fortune, are we not?" she said. "We are obliged to please our families, our mistresses and our social superiors. But we are never free to please ourselves."

That afternoon I discovered that Mistress Horsman was a kindred spirit. Not only did she excel at needlework, but she had a great knowledge of court fashion. She had studied the ladies of the court with great care and she was the best dressed of all the maids of honour. She was a friend and ally who was well worth cultivating.

"You know, Margery," I said, "I want more than just a life of service. I want to be remembered, respected, sought after. There must be a way to rise here, even for girls like us."

She smiled faintly, understanding my hunger for advancement. "Of course, Anne," she replied, her gaze drifting to the gardens below where the Queen and her ladies strolled in silken gowns. "But the court is a place of games. Every step forward must be calculated and every word chosen with care."

I leaned closer, her intensity drawing me in. "Tell me, how do you manage it?" I asked. "You seem so composed, so admired. What's the secret?"

She hesitated, weighing her words. "A few secrets, perhaps," she admitted, leaning back slightly. "Firstly, align yourself with those who matter. The Queen herself, naturally, is the greatest ally one could hope for. Serve her loyally, and her shadow will protect you from the sharpest tongues."

I nodded, absorbing her advice like a sponge. "And the others? The ladies, the noblemen? How do you ensure they speak well of you?"

She smiled again, a little more knowingly this time. "Charm is a currency, Anne. Use it wisely. A kind word here, a compliment there—it costs nothing and often yields much. But never overdo it, lest you seem insincere. Let them think you are generous, but let them also wonder at your wisdom."

My lips curved into a small, thoughtful smile. "And the men?"

She held my gaze firmly, her tone sharpening. "Never underestimate the power of intrigue, but tread carefully. Men are easy to impress but quick to judge. A coy glance can win their favour; a misstep can lose it forever. Keep your ambitions close, Anne. Don't lay them bare for all to see."

I exhaled softly, my expression contemplative. "It's all a delicate dance, isn't it?"

"Indeed," she said, her voice tinged with a quiet resolve. "And we are the dancers. But remember, Anne—ambition can be our strength, or it can be our undoing. Walk the line wisely, and you might achieve all your desires. There is one who has already gone further than anyone might have imagined."

"Whom do your mean?" I asked.

She lowered her voice. "Your place formerly belonged to Mistress Anne Boleyn," she said. "But the King has just given her an apartment of her own in the palace. She is now his favourite lady at the court."

So that was the reason the maids of honour exchanged sidelong looks and spoke together in whispers when I entered the dormitory. It was not because I was new. It was because I had stepped into the raging of a silent storm. The Queen had a rival in the court and she was one of her own ladies. She had defied her oath of allegiance and stolen the affections of the King. Her unchecked ambition divided the court, forcing noble men and women to choose between their sovereign lord and sovereign lady. I had vowed to be equally faithful to the King and the Queen. But I realised that someday soon I might have to choose a side.

Queen Catherine was a pious lady and a devoted wife to the King. She endeavoured to teach her ladies how to be chaste, silent and obedient. These were the virtues most valued in a wife by men of good birth and breeding. Her maids of honour were forbidden to read romances. Seigneur Juan de Vives had drawn up the plan for the education of her daughter, the Princess Mary. He had ordained that virtuous young women should only read the lives of the saints. But the young men of the court could read whatever they liked. They would lend their tales of chivalry to the fair young maids to gain their favour and they passed from hand to hand around the dormitory. We took it in turns to read *The Castle of Love, The Four Sons of Amyon, The Knight of the Swan and William of Palerne*. They taught me to understand the code of chivalry that the King and his companions liked to embody. A gallant knight should choose a virtuous lady and pay his court to her. The lady might accept his homage but she must always remain a citadel of honour.

From time to time there were great festivities held at the court. It was then that I had the chance to see the glory and magnificence of King Henry on display. In April 1527 he agreed a Treaty of Perpetual Peace with France. The eleven-year-old Princess Mary was betrothed to Henri, duc d'Orléans, the second son of King Francis. Queen Catherine was pleased by the honour that was paid to her daughter.

"His Majesty intends to dazzle the French ambassadors with the glory of his court," she said. "A new banqueting house is being built in the tiltyard at Greenwich. It will be decorated by Master Holbein. A banquet of two hundred dishes will be served. And afterwards the guests will be entertained by a masque at which the princess and her ladies shall dance."

"It is a splendid project, your Majesty," said Lady Maria. "They will certainly report to the King of France that Princess Mary is a beautiful lady and a most graceful dancer."

On 4th May the court assembled in the Presence Chamber of Greenwich for the reception of the French ambassadors. The Bishop of Tarbes wore a gown of cloth of gold and a mantle of blue silk. He delivered an oration declaring the great love, league and amity between the kings of France and England. He was answered by Cardinal Wolsey who praised both rulers for their devotion to the peace and concord of their realms. He was an imposing figure dressed in the red robes of his office. I remembered what my stepfather had told me about him: *Take care to be very respectful of Cardinal Wolsey,* he said. *He is the most powerful man in the court. Not only is he a Prince of the Church but he is entrusted with the government of the realm. He is a very vain and self-important man. It would not do to offend him in any way. So, watch how you speak!*

After the signing of the treaty, the Cardinal made his way majestically to the Privy Chamber to dine with the King and the ambassadors. He held an orange in his hand against the pestilential airs of the crowd and disregarded the petitioners who clamoured for his attention. Queen Catherine and Princess Mary dined in the Queen's apartments while the rest of the court feasted in the Great Hall. Afterwards, the King brought his guests to visit his wife and daughter.

"We are most honoured to pay our respects to your Majesty and your Highness," said the Viscount of Turenne.

"Je suis enchante de faire votre connaissance," replied Princess Mary.

"You speak our language like a native French lady, your Highness," he said.

"She can speak Latin too," said King Henry. "Speak to our guests, Mary."

"Salvete, domini. Honor mihi est vos hic videre," she replied.

The King swelled with pride as the ambassadors applauded. "She is a most accomplished princess, your Majesty," said the Viscount of Turenne.

"She has inherited both my gift for languages and my love of music," boasted the King. "Sit at the harpsichord, Mary, and play something for our guests."

She made a polite curtsey. "It would be my pleasure, your Majesty," she said. She took her place at the harpsichord where she played and sang a lively French chanson:

"Ce moys de may, ma verte cotte je vestiray,
De bon matin me lèveray, ce joly moys de may.
Un sault, deux saults, trois saults, en rue je feray,
Pour voir si mon amy verray."

"This month of May, I shall wear my green coat,
Early in the morning I shall rise, this lovely month of May.
One leap, two leaps, three leaps, I shall dance in the streets,
To see if I shall find my love."

"Bravo, Madame," said the Viscount. "It seems that there is no end to your talents!"

"Now I shall play and the princess shall dance with you," said King Henry.

"I would be honoured, your Majesty," he replied with a deep bow. The King struck up the tune of a stately pavane and Princess Mary and the Viscount moved gracefully across the floor together. When the music ended, they made their obesiances to each other and the company applauded.

"I thank you for this great privilege, your Majesty," said the Viscount. "Her Highness is not only a great beauty but she is most admirable for her exceptional talents."

"She is the pearl of my world," replied King Henry. "But I am willing to bestow her upon France as the greatest treasure in my kingdom."

"His Majesty thanks you for the great honour of her hand in marriage for his son," he said. "Permit me to withdraw and write to him at once of the gracious reception that you have accorded me."

"Send my best wishes to my brother of France," he said with a beaming smile. He was satisfied that the signing of the treaty had been a great success.

The following day, the ambassadors were hosted at a grand banquet in the new banqueting hall. The entrance was designed in the form of a lofty triumphal arch. Above the archway was a spacious balcony for the musicians bearing the arms of the King and Queen and the King's motto, *"Dieu et mon droit."* The ceiling was painted to resemble ornamental coloured marble. The walls were hung with tapestries depicting scenes from the life of King David. The hall was illuminated by a row of torches arranged below the windows. I took my place behind the Queen as she dined beside the King and the French ambassadors at the high table. The representatives of Venice dined at a separate table and the Spanish envoys were not invited at all. A great banquet of thirty courses was served to the guests. The high table dined upon gold plate and the courtiers upon silver plate. I saw the ambassadors look admiringly at the fantastic display of gold plate that stood upon two cupboards, reaching from the floor to the ceiling. It was worth a king's ransom and not a single piece was used during the banquet. The King wanted the foreign ambassadors to appreciate the great wealth of his royal treasury. My feet began to throb in my new leather shoes long before the final course was brought out. But it was my role to represent the glory of the Queen.

So, I straightened my back and looked straight ahead as the conversation swirled around me.

"It is a great day," said the Queen. "This treaty with France will settle the future of my daughter."

"She will make a fine bride for the duc d'Orleans, your Grace," replied Lady Maria.

"It would have been better if she were to be married to King Francis or the dauphin," she sighed. "But Henri, duc d'Orleans is nearer to her age. So, the King thought that he would make a more suitable match."

"It is a pity that there is no Spanish prince for her," said Lady Maria.

"Yes, indeed," she agreed. "But Wolsey was determined upon a French alliance. Princess Mary is as accomplished as any lady in the French court. The ambassadors heard her play upon the virginals and tonight they will see how well she can dance in public. They are certain to send a good report to King Francis."

The banquet was followed by a splendid pageant in an adjoining hall. It had been designed to showcase the culture and learning of the English court and emphasise the rare qualities of Princess Mary. The floor was covered with cloth of silk embroidered with gold lilies. The ceiling was painted with a map of the world and the signs of the zodiac. At the far end of the hall a painted canvas depicted a verdant cave. Before it stood eight ladies dressed in the style of antique goddesses. Princess Mary wore a gown of crimson cloth of gold with her hair gathered into a net of pearls. She was adorned with so many brilliant jewels that her appearance was resplendent. Queen Catherine's eyes filled with tears as she watched her daughter being admired by the King and his distinguished guests. As her cheeks flushed with emotion, I could see how beautiful she had once been in her youth.

A blast of trumpets sounded and the ladies performed a sequence of stately dances that enchanted the audience. The trumpets blew again and eight noblemen appeared disguised in masks. They wore black satin gowns, gold doublets and caps of tawny velvet. They each chose a lady as their partner and enacted a series of courtly dances. When the dancing drew to a close, the men removed their masks. The guests applauded to see the King cast off his disguise and make himself known. He took great pride in his skill as a dancer. His partner was a young woman with black hair and dark eyes. She wore an elegant gown in the French fashion and from her girdle hung a tablet of gold with a device of Venus and Cupid. The King introduced her to the ambassadors and she spoke to them in fluent French. The joy on Queen Catherine's face faded into an expression of cold dignity. The King had just acknowledged his latest mistress in public. Margery nudged me, "That's her!" she whispered in my ear. I realised that this was the notorious Anne Boleyn. I overheard the Queen's Spanish ladies murmuring their disapproval.

"It is shameless," muttered Lady Maria. "How can he flaunt her before the eyes of the foreign ambassadors? Has he no regard for the honour of the queen or the reputation of his daughter? The French will not wish to select a bride from such a licentious court!"

Queen Catherine demonstrated her good judgement by ignoring the selfish conduct of the king. She rose to the occasion with admirable grace. She mastered her feelings and spoke with dignity.

"Mistress Anne Boleyn is the best dancer among my ladies," she remarked. "She learned her skills at the French court. Naturally his Majesty wishes to display her talent. It will make a good impression upon the foreign ambassadors."

It was a convincing performance but I wondered how much it cost the Queen to return loyalty in return for disloyalty. The King pulled off his daughter's coif to show off her abundant tresses which were a fine red-gold in colour. The ambassadors responded with a profusion of graceful compliments. But the attention of the court had shifted. Everyone was covertly watching Mistress Boleyn as she revelled in her moment of triumph. Her introduction to the distinguished guests emphasised her standing as the King's favourite. The Queen did not say another word until she had returned to her bedchamber. The evening had turned into a dreadful humiliation for her. She knew that the foreign ambassadors would report at length on the King's latest fancy. I marvelled at his selfishness in putting his own pleasure before his daughter's happiness.

"Do not grieve, your Grace," said Lady Maria. "The princess looked as splendid as an angel from heaven."

"But it cut me to the heart to see him parade his paramour before the court and the ambassadors," she sighed. "And all for the sake of gratifying her pride. What am I to tell my innocent daughter?"

"The King will grow tired of her by Christmas, your Grace," she replied. "Her sister caught his interest for a season, but after she had borne a child, he ceased to care for her."

The Queen took some comfort in the thought that her daughter had been honourably presented to the French ambassadors. But her consolation was not to last. The ambassadors reported that the Princess Mary was not ready for matrimony. Her figure was too small, thin and spare for the marriage bed. King Francis declined to ratify the match with his son. The failure of the embassy was a serious diplomatic embarrassment. King Henry was furious that all his efforts had been for nothing. He decided that Princess Mary was too frail a girl to be his only heir. He resolved to remarry as soon as possible in order to secure the succession to the throne. The following month, the King paid a visit to the Queen's apartments. His interview marked the beginning of her future trials.

"This is a pleasant surprise, Henry," she said. "It has been a long time since you last came to see me."

"My lady, I can keep silent no longer," he replied. "My conscience obliges me to speak."

"What is it that troubles you?" she asked.

"You know that you were married to my brother and lived for half a year with him," he said. "Therefore, we are not truly married and our union is an offence in God's eyes."

"How can you say so?" she said. "You know that Pope Julius II granted a dispensation for our marriage."

"Nevertheless, it is contrary to divine law and for many years we have lived in mortal sin," he insisted. "Leviticus states that if a man shall take his brother's wife, they shall be childless. This is the reason that I have no son."

"But we are not childless," Henry, she replied. "We have a fine daughter in the Princess Mary."

"But a daughter cannot rule and you cannot bear any more children," he said. "The matter is clear in my mind. We must separate and live apart from each other. You could enter a convent and dedicate yourself to prayer."

"I have no vocation for the religious life, Henry," she said. "I would never desire to go to a convent."

"Then you can choose any house in the realm and go to live there," he said. "You will be honoured as the Princess Dowager and maintain your household in the same state as you do now. Only you must agree to annul our marriage."

"I shall never agree to an annulment, Henry," she said. "I shall remain your wife and your queen until the day I die."

"If you will not consent, then the case will go to court for judgement," he said. "But I would spare from all that unpleasantness."

"I know that our marriage is good and true," she said. "I shall wait for an official verdict from the Church on our marriage."

"As you wish, Madam," he said. "I will leave you think on what I have said." He scowled and then turned and stalked out the door.

Queen Catherine began to weep. "I did not want to believe it, but it is true," she said. "He wants to put me aside and take another wife."

Lady Maria hurried to her side. "You are a daughter of Spain and your marriage was blessed by the Pope," she said. "He cannot possibly dissolve a marriage after eighteen years of wedlock. The Vatican will never agree to an annulment."

She took a handkerchief and dried her eyes. "Yes, you are quite right Maria," she said. "This conversation was intended to test my resolve. He has no just cause to end our marriage. I know that Cardinal Wolsey is behind this."

"Wolsey and that cursed Boleyn woman," she muttered. "She has bewitched the King's mind. May God damn her soul to hell for eternity!"

"Hold your peace, Maria," she replied. "Curse her not, but pray for her. One day the time will come when you shall have reason to pity her and lament her case."

Lady Maria pursed her lips but said no more. The Queen composed herself and tucked the handkerchief back in her sleeve. "I shall retire to my closet and pray for the welfare of the King," she said. "I know that he will come to his right mind and we shall be reconciled again." She rose and made her way to her closet and knelt before the altar. Her ladies joined her in prayer as she earnestly prayed for the welfare of the King. Afterwards, she rose and made her way to her bedchamber. Lady Maria unpinned her gown and sent me to fetch her nightgown. On my return, I found the Queen alone with Lady Maria. She had dismissed her other ladies. I lingered at the door as they spoke quietly together.

"I must send word to the emperor Charles V of Spain," the Queen whispered. "He needs to know the truth about my situation. But all my letters are monitored by Cardinal Wolsey."

"Can you send it through the Spanish ambassador, your Grace?" she asked.

"All his correspondence is being intercepted," she said. "And I cannot send any messengers to Spain either. I must find a way to get word through unofficial channels."

"Send for the duchess of Norfolk, your Grace," she said. "She is your devoted friend and she will move heaven and earth to assist you." She looked up and saw me standing at the door holding the garment in my hands.

"Bring that here at once!" she snapped. "Do not keep her Grace waiting."

I brought the nightgown and gave it to Lady Maria. Then I made my curtsey to the Queen.

"Leave us," ordered Lady Maria. "And close the door behind you. Her Majesty does not wish to be disturbed."

I withdrew from the bedchamber but I did not return to the dormitory. I sat on a stool covered in yellow velvet in a corner of the privy chamber and opened my prayer-book. Shortly afterwards, Lady Maria left the bedchamber and walked through the privy chamber into the palace. I suspected that she was on a secret mission for the Queen.

The following morning, Lady Elizabeth Howard, the duchess of Norfolk came to visit the Queen in her apartments. She wore a black velvet gown embroidered with silver with sleeves of carnation satin. She made a deep curtsey before the Queen. As soon as she arrived, Lady Maria ushered the ladies into the privy gardens to take a walk. We filed out the door leaving them alone to converse together. I dropped my handkerchief to give myself an excuse to return. It was a warm day and I saw that the window was open. I edged along the wall and stood beneath it to listen. I could hear the murmur of voices within and I strained to hear their conversation.

"How may I serve your Grace?" asked the duchess.

"Lady Maria has told you of my difficulty, Lady Howard?" she replied. "The matter is most urgent!"

"Your Grace may put your mind at rest," she said with a satisfied smile. "I have pondered this matter and thought of a solution. I will send a gift to Queen Mary of Hungary, the Regent of Flanders," she said. "A case of oranges and pomegranates. And I will hide your letter inside an orange. What do you want me to say?"

"Tell her that the emperor must speak to the King on my behalf," she said. "He must tell him that an annulment is unacceptable to Spain. And he must persuade the Pope to hear my case in Rome not in England. Otherwise, I will not get a fair hearing for all the clergy are too afraid to defy the King's wishes."

"Leave it to me, your Grace," she said. "I shall inform the Regent whenever you need to communicate with the emperor."

"You have relieved me of a great burden," she said. "I am most grateful for your assistance. Lady Maria will bring you my correspondence and money to pay for the cost of the carriage. It means everything to be able to communicate freely with Spain."

"I am very sorry for your Highness's troubles," she replied. "You can rely upon my discretion."

I looked around but there was no-one else in sight. I clutched my handkerchief tightly in my hand. Now I had learned a valuable secret. One day it might be of considerable importance to me. It seemed to me that Lady Howard was taking a great risk for the sake of the Queen. Her husband Norfolk was the uncle of Mistress Anne Boleyn. He would be furious if he discovered that the duchess was siding with the Queen and working against her. I put my handkerchief into my sleeve and returned to the privy gardens. The ladies were playing a game of pall-mall in an alley and the maids of honour were occupied in retrieving the ball. Margery smiled as I came over to join her.

"Where were you?" she said. "Meeting one of your admirers?"

"I left my handkerchief behind," I said lamely.

"You don't have to confide in me," she said. "But don't let Mistress Stoner catch you with a handsome young man or she'll have your guts for garters!"

Now Queen Catherine was fully aware of what was on the King's mind. She realised that Mistress Boleyn was not just a distraction. He fully intended to marry her. And Mistress Boleyn was equally determined to replace her as the Queen of England. She was the most stylish and admired lady at the court. She took delight in showing off her mastery of French, her skill at witty conversation, her knowledge of courtly verse. In the evenings she entranced the King by her grace in dancing and her expertise on the lute. She cast every other lady into the shade and she knew it. But her proficiency was marred by her vanity and pride. She took delight in her ascendancy over the Queen and did not trouble to restrain her spiteful tongue. There was nothing that she hated more than the reminder that she was the daughter of a simple knight and had once been a lowly maid of honour. She lost no opportunity of denigrating the Queen as a stubborn old woman.

Queen Catherine did her best to outshine her rival. She took to dressing herself with ever more splendid gowns with Spanish hoods and adorned herself with her most elaborate jewels. She presided over the Christmas court with great dignity and confidence. Mistress Boleyn retaliated by wearing a new gown every day with a round French hood. Her supporters adopted the new fashion as a sign of their allegiance. The court became divided between those who were faithful to the Queen and those who sought to gain favour with the King's new favourite. Their rivalry was unspoken but it was none the less bitter. Queen Catherine sent invitations to Mistress Boleyn to come and play cards with her in order to deprive the King of her company. On one occasion when they played a game of Noddy together, Mistress Boleyn turned over a king. The Queen eyed the card thoughtfully.

"Mistress Boleyn, I see you have the good fortune to take a king in your hand," she remarked. "But I see that you are not content like the others. You will have all or none."

Mistress Boleyn did not turn a hair at her gentle malice. "The King always plays to win and so do I," she replied.

The Queen set her own cards down with measured grace, folding her hands atop them as she studied the young woman before her. A slow smile curled at the corners of her lips.

"And yet, Mistress Boleyn," she murmured, "a wise player knows that a game is won not merely by seizing the strongest hand, but by knowing when to play it."

She lifted her chin slightly, refusing to flinch under her gaze. "Then I hope that the King sees me for the player I am, your Grace," she replied. "And not just another card to be discarded when the game is done."

For the briefest moment, a look of pity flickered across the Queen's face, but it vanished before it could take root. She picked up her cards once more and gestured for the game to continue.

"Then let us play, Mistress Boleyn," she said simply. "And may fortune favour the brave." The chamber was silent except for the quiet shuffle of cards upon the table. But everyone knew that they were no longer speaking of Noddy.

The Christmas season was approaching and I looked forward to seeing the celebrations at court. Christmas Eve was a fast-day and so the Queen and her ladies dined sparingly and spent their time in prayer and devotions. After attending Compline in the Chapel Royal of Greenwich, the maids of honour retired to their dormitory. It was lit by the flickering glow of candles, their golden light casting wavering shadows on the stone walls. Margery filled a bowl of water and placed it on the wooden table.

"Each of you must bring a candle," she said. "Drop the wax into the water and it will reveal the identity of your future husbands. It is the custom on Christmas Eve."

"The Queen does not approve of fortune telling," objected Mistress Darrell.

"Well, you don't have to play," she retorted. "You can sit on your bed and read your prayer book if you like!"

The other maids of honour gathered around the table, their hushed giggles and murmured excitement filling the air. The scent of beeswax mingled with the faint chill of the winter's evening. Margery steadied the bowl of water as each girl stepped forward, holding her candle aloft. The wax dripped in delicate streams, cooling instantly upon the surface, forming strange, curling shapes which sank to the bottom. The girls vied with each other to interpret their meanings. "A sword for a soldier! An anchor for a sailor! A key for a merchant!"

I watched them in amused scepticism, but when my turn came, I hesitated before stepping forward. What if the ritual did reveal my future? It tipped the candle so that great drops fell into the bowl. The moment the wax met the water, the liquid rippled, swirling around the solidifying form. As the shape took hold, one of the maids gasped.

"It's a pair of wings!" whispered Mistress Badby.

I leaned closer, studying the wax pattern, my brows knitting slightly. It did resemble a pair of pointed wings. Margery grinned knowingly. "Perhaps you're going to marry an angel!"

"A falconer, you mean," laughed Mistress Zouche.

"It could represent a man of great piety," said Mistress Darrell thoughtfully.

"It's all nonsense," I said. But I could not dismiss the thought that this strange symbol might be a sign of my future.

On Christmas Day the King and Queen attended Mass in the Chapel Royal. King Henry wore a doublet and hose of cloth of gold and a black velvet cap adorned with gold brooches set with diamonds and rubies. Queen Catherine wore a gown of cloth of silver with a Spanish hood bordered with sapphires and pearls and from her girdle hung a tablet of gold with a device of Adam and Eve. Their splendid attire signified that they presided as the sun and the moon of the court.

After the celebration of Christ's Mass, they attended a banquet in the Great Hall where a great Yule log burned in the fireplace. The door was wreathed with branches of holly and ivy. It was guarded by two Yeomen of the Guard dressed in scarlet liveries embroidered with roses and crowns. They held long halberds in their hands to show that they were the king's personal bodyguards. The walls were hung with purple cloth embroidered with Tudor roses and Spanish pomegranates in gold and silver thread. At the far end of the hall stood two tall cupboards which displayed rows of gleaming gold and silver vessels.

The King and Queen sat at the high table and I took my place behind my mistress. The board was laid with a salt cellar of gold in the form of a ship. Next to it stood a golden flagon of wine, a pair of trenchers and manchet loaves wrapped in fine napkins. The long tables were filled with the noblemen and ladies of the court in order of precedence. However, there was no sign of Mistress Boleyn. She remained in her own apartments throughout the festivities because she did not like to meet the Queen.

At the commencement of the feast, the choristers of the King's Chapel dressed in their scarlet gowns and white surplices entered the hall. They assembled before the King and Queen and sang the words of a traditional Christmas carol:

"Gaudete! Gaudete!
Christus est natus ex Maria virgine.
Gaudete!

Tempus adest gratiæ, hoc quod optabamus;
Carmina letitiæ devotè reddamus.

Deus homo factus est, Natura mirante,
Mundus renovatus est à Christo regnante.

Ezechielis porta clausa pertransitur;
Unde lux est orta, salus inuenitur.

Ergo nostra concio psallat iam in lustro;
Benedicat Domino; salus Regi nostro.

Rejoice! Rejoice! Christ is born of the Virgin Mary. Rejoice!

The time of grace has come, as we had hoped;
Let us render songs of joy with devotion.

God has become man, to the wonder of nature;
The world is renewed under Christ's reign.

The closed gate of Ezekiel is passed through;
From where the light has arisen, salvation is found.

Therefore, let our gathering now sing in brightness;
Let it bless the Lord; salvation to our King."

The flickering candlelight cast golden halos around the gathered singers as their voices soared through the great hall. The melody of *Gaudete!* still lingered in the air, a bright echo of celebration. Queen Catherine smiled with pleasure to hear their recital. As the final note faded, she lifted her hands in applause.

"Such beauty and such devotion," she murmured. Turning to her husband, she remarked. "Surely such talent should not go unrewarded?"

King Henry, seated with his customary regal command, observed her for a moment and then nodded. "Indeed," he declared, his voice carrying easily throughout the hall. "You have pleased the Queen and therefore, you have pleased me too. Come forward!"

The young choristers stepped forward hesitantly, their eyes wide with astonishment. The King gestured toward his steward. "See to it that each of these singers receives a shilling," he ordered.

A murmur of thanks arose from the choir and they made deep bows before they departed. Queen Catherine, watching them, allowed herself one last smile. The atmosphere was filled with warmth and merriment, the hearts of the court uplifted by the glad sound of the hymn of praise. Then a fanfare of trumpets sounded and a procession of servants led by the Lord Chamberlain entered the hall. A roasted boar's head on a silver platter was presented to the King and Queen and placed upon the buffet. Then a variety of exotic dishes passed before my astonished eyes. Two ushers brought in a roast peacock served in its feathers followed by a suckling pig gilded with gold leaf and a great venison pie in the shape of a castle. The second course consisted of stewed lampreys, sturgeon in galatine, a leg of mutton stuffed with garlic, hare in black sauce, roast woodcocks, capons stewed with oranges, and venison pasties. Finally, the subtleties of coloured jellies, gingerbread angels, gilded marchpane, mince pies and sugared almonds were served. Throughout the great feast, pleasure and good cheer flowed as freely as the wine itself.

Afterwards, the company withdrew to the Presence Chamber for the festivities. It shimmered with candle-light, flickering against the priceless series of tapestries of King Solomon that adorned the walls. The King and Queen took their places upon their chairs of estate. The courtiers gathered in clusters, their silken sleeves brushing as they whispered among themselves, eager for the entertainment to begin. At the head of the chamber stood The Master of the Revels, William Cornish, his robe heavy with embroidery, his expression sharp with anticipation.

"Your Majesties, I have the honour to present a disputation upon whether riches are greater than love," he announced. With a flourish of his hand, he signalled the start of the debate. Two figures stepped forward—a young scholar with a parchment tucked under his arm, arguing for the power of riches, and a poet with a book of verses, insisting love was the greater force. The scholar stepped forward with measured confidence, adjusting the parchment under his arm before speaking.

"Riches, my lords and ladies, are the foundation upon which kingdoms rise. They build fortresses, fund armies, and feed the hungry. A ruler with wealth commands power beyond sentiment, for gold does not waver in the face of misfortune. Love is fickle, as fleeting as the breath of spring, but riches endure. When kingdoms fall, it is not love that rebuilds them—it is the coin pressed into the hands of craftsmen, the jewels that secure alliances, the grain purchased to nourish the starving. Would a prince rule by love alone? What use is devotion if his coffers are empty and his subjects rebel from hunger?"

He paused, surveying the room, his argument glinting as sharply as a blade. *"Love may inspire loyalty, but wealth sustains it. A ruler who lavishes gold upon his faithful retains their service longer than one who relies upon sentiment alone. Let riches be the master of love, and not the other way around."*

He bowed and stepped aside. The poet advanced with unhurried grace, his expression almost wistful.

"What are riches without love? A hollow crown upon a ruler's brow, a kingdom filled with obedience but devoid of joy. Gold may buy bread for the hungry, but it cannot nourish the soul. Wealth may purchase loyalty, but never devotion. A prince revered in love is truly served, for his subjects do not follow him for mere coin, but for belief, for admiration, for the assurance that he rules not only their land but their hearts."

His voice rose like a tide, gentle yet irresistible. *"A kingdom built upon riches alone is a kingdom bound in chains. It is love that unites, love that heals, love that compels men to fight not just for survival, but for honour. It is love that makes a ruler's command just, love that ensures his reign endures long after the gold in his vaults has faded to dust. To rule without love is to rule without life. To love without riches is to struggle, yes—but I say a struggling heart is richer than an empty one filled with gold!"*

The crowd murmured, stirred by the fervour in his words. Then, from the edge of the dais, an old man with a silver beard rose. He did not hurry, nor did he speak until the room fell silent in deference to his presence. He smiled, a slow, knowing curve of his lips.

"Riches may feed the body, and love may nourish the soul," he said, in a hushed voice. *"But neither alone can sustain a kingdom. A prince should rule with love so that his subjects serve him willingly. And with his riches, he should reward his loyal friends and servants."* He spread his arms as if embracing the room itself. *"Only in harmony do these forces create true strength. Love without means is fragile. Wealth without devotion is cold."*

A moment of silence followed, then a murmur of approval swelled into applause. Master Cornish, watching with amusement, inclined his head. "A verdict most fitting," he declared. "And now, my lords and ladies, I pray you give ear to the players of the King's Music!"

From the gallery, the minstrels struck up the tune of a pavane, the strings and woodwinds weaving together in a melody that rippled throughout the hall. The courtiers, flushed with excitement, assembled in pairs, the silken gowns of the ladies swirling like petals caught in a gentle wind. After the first dance, the Queen signalled her permission for her ladies to join in the festivities. I stood at the edge of the revelry, my gown of tawny satin glowing in the candlelight. I watched the courtiers gliding in practiced steps, until a voice pulled my attention.

"Sir Urian Brereton, at your service, Mistress."

I turned to meet the keen gaze of a courtier with brown eyes and brown hair. His doublet of russet silk, embroidered in silver thread, caught the light as he extended a hand. There was confidence in his stance, a quiet assurance that intrigued me. "Do you merely admire the dance, or might you be tempted to join it?" he asked.

"And if I decline?" I replied, amusement flickering at the edges of my tone.

His smile broadened. "Then I would count myself most unfortunate this Christmas."

I paused for a moment and then placed my hand into his. I knew myself to be an accomplished dancer and I was eager to demonstrate my talents to the court. We moved onto the floor, the dance unfolding between us in smooth, measured steps. The music swelled, guiding them in silent accord, each turn a quiet exchange, each glance a word unspoken. The world beyond the dance faded, leaving only the rhythm between us, the pulse of motion and anticipation. As the final notes settled into silence, he released my hand with a slight bow. "A pleasure, mistress."

I inclined my head and curved my lips in the faintest suggestion of a smile. "Perhaps you shall have another," I murmured. The dancing continued late into the night and I partnered with a number of young gallants in turn. The feast of Christmas was celebrated that year to the great honour of the King and Queen and the pleasure of their court.

The climax of the festivities was the presentation of the New Year's gifts in the Presence Chamber. King Henry and Queen Catherine of Aragon took their places upon a raised dais beneath a huge crimson canopy of state. I stood behind my mistress and gazed in wonder at the magnificent scene. The chamber was set with a line of trestle tables which were covered with costly gifts. There were numerous purses filled with gold coins, quantities of gold and silver plate engraved with strange birds and beasts, splendid jewels of every kind, books bound in velvet covers and ingenious clocks and astronomical devices. These were the tokens of respect which were given by the courtiers to the King. Each one testified to the wealth and goodwill of the donor.

The King reciprocated the devotion of his loyal subjects with gifts of silver plate which they collected from the Master of the Jewel House. He gave Queen Catherine a gold pomander and a pet marmoset. She gave him a silver inkwell and stand in the form of a dragon and a cambric shirt with a collar of blackwork. But there were rumours that he had sent a great many extravagant presents to Mistress Boleyn in compensation for missing the public festivities that year. The revelries continued until the Feast of Epiphany on 6th January. After the celebration of mass in the Chapel Royal, my stepfather came to seek me out.

"My dear Anne," he said. "How did you enjoy your first Christmas season at court?"

"It was most agreeable, Sir Richard," I replied. "I have never seen such splendid entertainments nor known such good cheer as their Majesties keep in their households."

"His Majesty would be pleased to hear you say so," he remarked. "He prides himself upon the magnificence of his court and the hospitality of his house."

"We are most fortunate we are to serve their Majesties and share in their pleasures," I agreed.

"I am the bearer of good news," he said with a broad smile. "I have received an offer for your hand in marriage. It is Sir Urian Brereton. He says that you are everything that he is looking for in a wife."

"He is not noble, is he?" I replied doubtfully. I had thought little of my encounter with Sir Urian, but it seemed that I had made a much deeper impression upon him.

"He is the son of Sir Randle Brereton which makes him your social equal," he said. "Moreover, he is a groom of the Privy Chamber and that is an important post. He is rich and well propertied. He knows everyone at court. He could not be a better match for you, my dear!"

"I fear that my mother will be disappointed in this match," I said. "She had hoped that I would marry a nobleman rather than a courtier. Perhaps we should wait for a better offer."

"There is no question of refusing him, Anne," he said. "He is a most eligible suitor. He could marry any lady at court."

"I would like to meet Sir Urian," I replied.

"That is a sensible answer, Anne," he said. "I will arrange the meeting. But let him do the talking. Men do not want forward wives."

Sir Richard Page, arranged the meeting without delay and three days later he came to call at his apartments. The spring sunshine bathed the room as I entered, but the warmth in the air did little to soften my apprehension. I wore my gown of deep green silk and a gold brooch set with a green agate. I kept my composure carefully measured, as Sir Richard had advised. Sir Urian was a tall man with an air of confidence, though his manner seemed kind rather than imposing. His dark eyes sparkled as though they betrayed a smitten heart, but his expression remained composed.

"Mistress Anne," he said, bowing deeply, "it is an honour to meet you once more."

"And you, Sir Urian," I replied, curtsying with quiet grace.

Sir Richard, standing beside me, gestured warmly for him to sit. "Well, Urian," he said, his tone jovial, "you requested this meeting and you are at liberty to speak."

For a moment, Sir Urian looked slightly hesitant, as though choosing his words carefully. Then he turned to me, his voice steady but earnest. "Mistress Anne, from the moment we danced together, I was struck by your beauty and elegance," he said. "In truth, I could not stop thinking of you thereafter. I have come here today with the intention of asking for your hand in marriage. I believe I can offer you a good match, both in means and in standing."

His sincerity took me by surprise, but I masked it well. "That is high praise, Sir Urian," I said, my voice calm, "and I thank you for it. But I am bound to ask you this question. What is it that you seek in a wife?"

He smiled at the question, a flicker of admiration passing across his face. "I seek a partner who is poised and intelligent, one who would stand by my side at court with grace and good counsel," he said. "You, Mistress Anne, possess all these qualities and more."

Sir Richard beamed approvingly from his chair. "A fine answer, indeed!" he said. "What do you think, Anne?"

"I would be honoured to accept Sir Urian's proposal," I replied.

"You have made me a happy man, Mistress Anne," he said. "I shall inform their Majesties of my intention to take a wife. I am sure that they will be pleased to give their consent."

"Let us drink a toast to celebrate this happy occasion," said Sir Richard. He poured out three cups of wine from a flagon on the sideboard. "To my stepdaughter and my friend," he said, raising his cup. "I drink to your health and your happiness!"

I sipped the good wine appreciatively, feeling a warm glow spread throughout my body. Sir Richard filled up Sir Urian's cup again. Then the two men turned to each other to discuss the terms.

"Let us get married in June next year when Mistress Anne is eighteen," said Sir Urian.

"An excellent idea!" Sir Richard concurred. "That will give us plenty of time to plan the ceremony. I shall write to tell my wife the good news at once."

"And I shall make arrangements for a clerk to draw up the precontract," he replied. "With your permission I shall go to inform his Majesty at once."

Sir Urian bowed and took his leave, leaving me alone with my stepfather.

"You have done well to accept this offer, Anne," said Sir Richard. "Sir Urian is one of my closest friends and companions. I can assure you that he is a good man. Moreover, the King has shown him great favour by granting him lucrative posts. He is the Ranger of Delamere Forest and the Keeper of Shotwick Park."

The following day Sir Urian sent me a gold girdle set with opals as a betrothal gift. I was pleased. It showed that his intentions were serious. I took it to show my stepfather.

"It is jewel fit for a noblewoman," he said. "He must have commissioned it from the royal goldsmiths. I am sure he will prove himself to be a devoted husband."

I nodded at my stepfather's words, feeling a sense of quiet satisfaction as I traced the delicate opals embedded in the gilded surface. The girdle was exquisite, and its craftsmanship spoke of the thoughtfulness and wealth of the giver. Nonetheless, I was no foolish girl to be dazzled by the sight of a pretty bauble. I would judge him not by his gifts but by his deeds. Sir Urian had pledged himself, but it remained to be seen whether his heart and his actions aligned with the promise of his opals. For now, I held my hopes carefully in balance, neither rejecting them nor embracing them fully. Time would tell, as it always did.

"Soon you will be a married woman," he said. "How do you like the name Lady Anne Brereton?"

"I like it well," I replied.

"The King is always considerate to his servants," said Sir Richard. "He might attend the wedding and give you a present of money."

"I do hope so," I said. I returned to the maid's dormitory and showed my gift to Margery.

"How fortunate you are," she sighed. "Your first season at court and you are snapped up like a ripe plum. The other maids of honour have already served here for several years, but they are still unmatched."

I felt a sense of quiet satisfaction at her words. Sir Urian was not a great nobleman, but it was still an accolade to have received an eligible offer so soon. The next week the precontract was drawn up and signed. Now we were betrothed. Queen Catherine congratulated me on receiving such an eligible offer. I ordered a splendid wedding dress to be made by a palace seamstress. I looked forward to moving out of the maid's dormitory into an apartment of my own as Lady Anne Brereton. I hoped that the queen would honour me by inviting me to serve as a lady in waiting.

But my hopes and plans for my future married life proved to be in vain. In May 1528 an outbreak of the sweating sickness struck the court. The King took the Queen and a small number of attendants and fled to Waltham Abbey to escape the infection. The courtiers were ordered to go back to their homes until the danger had subsided. I returned to Beechwood to stay with my family. It proved to be a wise precaution for soon we heard terrible news. By the end of June 1528 forty thousand people in London had contracted the sickness.

"It will mean postponing the wedding until later in the year," said my mother. "You cannot possibly get married until everything has returned to normal again at court. It is a trial for you to have to wait, but there is no alternative."

During that dreadful time, Mistress Anne Boleyn fell ill at Hever Castle in Kent. The King sent one of his own doctors to treat her and she recovered. But several members of the King's privy chamber were not so fortunate. William Carey, Francis Poyntz and William Compton all died of the malady. My stepfather was deeply grieved to hear the news. I wondered how Sir Urian was faring, but I received no word of him. Then a messenger arrived at our house from Sir William Brereton. He informed us that his brother Urian had taken the sickness and died within the hour. He regretted that it had not been possible to invite us to attend the burial service. I had been widowed before I was even a wife.

"It is most unfortunate that he should have died before the wedding," sighed Sir Richard. "If only you had married him, you would have got your widow's jointure. Then you would have had no difficulty in finding a second husband. Now it is all to do again. But you must not let yourself get discouraged by this setback."

The sickness raged all summer long and then it disappeared. The court reconvened at Westminster in the autumn. I wore mourning for Sir Urian as a sign of my respect. Now I was neither a widow nor a fresh young maiden. I was slightly tarnished goods in the eyes of the court. Any mention of the dreaded sweat made people shudder and turn away. There were no more offers of marriage. But I had no time to dwell upon my sorrows. The contention between the Queen and her rival had reached a new level of intensity.

Mistress Anne Boleyn had returned to court. She looked thinner and paler after her illness, but her eyes glittered with a new determination. The King had written countless letters to her during their separation. He said that she had captured his heart and promised his eternal devotion. Finally, she accepted his proposal, but upon her own terms. She would not be his mistress, but only his wife. He swore that he would set aside Catherine and make her his queen. She sent him a jewel in the form of a lady upon a storm-tossed ship. It was her token and her pledge to him.

Cardinal Wolsey had persuaded the Pope to send a legate to England to rule upon the King's Great Matter. On 22nd October 1528, Cardinal Campeggio arrived at Westminster for an official audience. The King received him in his Presence Chamber where all the bishops and nobles were assembled to meet him. The tension among the Queen's household was palpable. As one of her maids of honour, I moved quietly, attending to her needs while the storm brewed around us. When word came that Cardinal Campeggio requested an audience with the Queen in her privy chamber, I could feel the air tighten—like the world itself was holding its breath.

Queen Catherine rose to meet him with a grace that belied the turmoil of the moment. Her face bore the calm dignity of a woman who had weathered many storms. "I am honoured by your visit, your Eminence, she said. "Please take a chair for I can see that the journey to England has wearied you."

"I thank your Majesty," he replied as he settled into his chair. "My visit here is of the utmost importance. I beg you to consider not only your own position, but the welfare of the realm. If you were to retire gracefully, you would spare yourself and the King further anguish. A convent is a noble and pious path, deserving of the deepest respect."

Queen Catherine did not flinch. Her hands folded neatly in her lap, she regarded him with unwavering eyes. "Your Eminence, I am certain that you speak from concern for my well-being," she replied. "Yet, you ask me to deny the truth upon which my very life rests. My conscience will not allow it."

Campeggio leaned forward, his brow furrowed with what seemed to be genuine concern. "Your Majesty, conscience is a guide—but it must not become a chain," he said. "There is wisdom in compromise, and strength in humility. The Church does not seek to dishonour you, but to find peace for all."

The Queen straightened her back, her voice cool and commanding. "And I shall show peace by upholding my vows—vows made before God, vows that cannot be undone by the whims of men. My first marriage was unconsummated, and I stand as the lawful wife of King Henry. To abandon my station would be to betray the truth, and I shall not betray the truth."

I dared to glance at Campeggio as he absorbed her words. He looked fatigued, like a man carrying the weight of many burdens, yet he pressed on. "Do you not fear, Your Majesty, that this path may lead to greater strife? The King has shown his will. Resistance may bring further hardship upon yourself and those loyal to you."

Her voice softened, though her resolve remained. "Fear is not my companion, Your Eminence," she declared. "I draw strength from my faith and my duty. If hardship comes, I shall meet it with the same grace I meet your words now. The truth is steadfast, and I am bound to it."

The Cardinal exhaled, seeming to acknowledge the futility of his endeavour. He offered a murmured blessing before departing, his robes sweeping behind him as he bowed and left the chamber. I watching as the Queen rested her fingers upon the crucifix she wore around her neck.

"My loyalty is to the truth," she whispered to herself. "And I shall endure."

"Now we know for certain what is upon the mind of the King, your Grace," said Lady Maria.

"Yes, indeed," she sighed. "I see how this matter has been framed against me. I had hoped that the King would tire of his inamourata. But now I see that he has no desire for a reconciliation. He seeks to make an end of his lawful marriage. But I shall never agree to enter a convent! And I shall never agree to an annulment. I shall live and die as the rightful Queen of England!"

"Your Majesty is tired," said Lady Maria. "You should retire to your bedchamber and rest now."

"This is no time to rest," she replied. "I must write a letter to the Pope at once to protest against this tribunal. My case cannot be fairly judged within this realm, but only in the courts of Rome. Send for Bishop Fisher to come here at once. I must have proper legal counsel in this matter."

I had to admire her resolute courage. The Queen had spoken with dignity and conviction, and in that moment, I knew there would be no force or persuasion that was strong enough to break her spirit.

The King lavished presents upon Mistress Anne but sent no gifts to the Queen. He considered that she had no right to receive any signs of his favour. She had failed in her duty as the Queen. She had denied him a son. His neglect of the Queen sent a message to the courtiers. She received less visitors and fewer tokens of goodwill. She had the name of the Queen but no influence at court. She could not make recommendations for patronage. It was all in the hands of Wolsey and the King. Those seeking favour now turned to Mistress Anne and her father, the earl of Wiltshire. They were the new power in the court.

In December 1528 the court moved to Greenwich for the Christmas festivities. Mistress Anne did not attend the official revels in the Great Hall because she had no wish to defer to the Queen in the manner that etiquette required. Queen Catherine presided over the court festivities as usual. But she found it hard to look cheerful since her mind was so troubled. My stepfather came to see me to urge me to dress in my best gowns.

"You should take off your mourning clothes and take part in the Christmas festivities," he said.

"But it has only been six months," I protested.

"You are not a widow," he reminded me. "You were only betrothed. It is time for you to put your sadness behind you and move forward with your life."

"As you wish," I said indifferently.

"So, what is like in the Queen's household these days?" he asked.

"Everyone is fearful," I said. "Everyone except the Queen. She is as fearless as a lion."

"The Queen's intransigence is not courage, it is folly," he said, waving his hand dismissively. "She will never bear the King another child. Her position is hopeless. She ought to have settled for the best possible terms at the beginning. The King would have treated her generously then. But now he is bitter and angry. She will lose everything and so will all her supporters. You must leave her service before it is too late. Why should you suffer with her?"

"You think that I should leave the setting sun for the rising sun?" I remarked.

"Of course, you should," he said. "Every courtier comes here in the hope of making their fortune. We spend our lives in the service of the King and Queen. But the Queen is no longer the true Queen. She is only an encumbrance. Do you want to be sent back home empty-handed?"

"No," I replied. "I came to court to make a good match. I cannot leave until I have succeeded."

"Look around you," he said. "It is Christmas and yet the King is spending it with Mistress Anne and not the Queen. Her day is over whether or not she is willing to accept it. It is time for every courtier to show their allegiance."

"I am a member of the Queen's household," I insisted.

"The Queen will not need any attendants in a convent," he replied. "When the legate gives his ruling, she will have to accede to the King's wishes. You would do better to join the household of Mistress Boleyn instead. And do it sooner rather than later."

"Why are you backing Mistress Boleyn?" I asked. "She has nothing particular to recommend her. The King may grow tired of her in a few months."

"I am taking the side of the King in this matter," he said. "It is what every loyal courtier should do. The Queen has fallen from grace. She will not survive the King's displeasure. Soon she will be forced to submit to his will and retire to a nunnery. Her supporters will be dismissed from court."

"What do you propose that I do?" I asked.

"Someone is passing secret messages between the Queen and the emperor of Spain," he said. "It is imperative that this should be stopped."

I shook my head. "That is the Queen's business," I replied. "It does not concern you or me."

"The King has entrusted me with this task," he said. "It will help both of us if you can find out who it is and how they are doing it. What do you say?"

I did not hesitate any longer. I could see the signs of decline every day. The King sent gifts to Mistress Boleyn every day. But fewer and fewer courtiers came to pay their respects to the Queen. She did her best to pretend that nothing was amiss. But everyone in the household was despondent.

"The courier is the duchess of Norfolk," I said. "Her letters are hidden inside oranges. Then they are smuggled out of England and taken to the court of Flanders."

"It is most ingenious," he remarked. "No-one would have suspected her. She is the aunt of Mistress Boleyn. Her husband will be furious with her. I will inform the King of your loyal services."

The following week, the duchess of Norfolk was banished from court for her disloyalty. But Sir Richard was appointed as the Captain of the King's Bodyguard as a reward. And I was transferred to the household of Mistress Anne Boleyn as one of her attendants.

CHAPTER 3

The Household of Mistress Anne Boleyn (1528)

"Women should have a sweetness in language and a good utterance to entertain all kind of men with communication worth the hearing"

(Castiglione, *The Courtier*, 1561).

The King had given Mistress Boleyn her own set of apartments in the palace. It meant that he could see her in private whenever he liked. Her lodgings testified to his devotion for they were as richly furnished as those of the Queen. The walls of the privy chamber were hung with Flemish tapestries depicting the story of Venus and Cupid. On the mantelpiece a portrait of the King was prominently displayed. On either side of it stood a gold clock and a mirror of Venetian glass. At the back of the chamber was a tall cupboard of silver plate. Costly gifts arrived for her daily which she pretended to disdain: a set of gold brooches in the shape of love-knots, a lute made of ivory tied with purple ribbons and a pair of white greyhounds wearing gold collars.

Mistress Boleyn presided over her luxurious household with the confidence of born noblewoman. She was not conventionally beautiful but she was very alluring. She had black hair, dark eyes and an oval face. Her time at the French court had given her a degree of sophistication above other English ladies. She was adept at witty conversation, she danced with grace and she played the lute skilfully. The proofs of the King's favour had made her very proud. She dressed herself in the richest clothes and the finest jewels. She had set herself to be the model of fashion at the court and every day she made a change in the style of her clothing. But still, she was only the daughter of a knight. I was curious to learn how she had grown so high in the King's regard. She sat in her privy chamber dressed in green velvet the colour of springtime orchard leaves. Her French hood was edged with pearls as big as chickpeas and from her girdle hung a sapphire the size of a robin's egg. Her face bore that inscrutable half-smile, as though she knew the end of a jest the rest of us had yet to hear.

King Henry arrived to bid her good morning. He was a striking figure, his frame broad and thick-chested, the power of youth now softened by indulgence but no less imposing. His eyes—bright blue, intelligent, and volatile—burned with the fire of command. He wore a doublet of cloth-of-gold, its fabric stiff with embroidery in red silk thread, edged with ermine and sewn with pearls the size of teardrops. Over it he sported a surcoat of rich burgundy velvet lined with lynx fur, the sleeves slashed to show glimpses of white satin beneath. His broad shoulders bore a heavy gold chain of livery from which hung the royal badge of the Tudor rose entwined with a H and A. At his hip swung a sword with a jewelled pommel and on his hands were many rings—one a signet bearing the crowned Tudor arms, another set with a deep red ruby that caught the light like a drop of blood. His cap, set at a jaunty tilt, was black velvet adorned with a single ostrich feather and a gold medallion of St. George. Beneath it, his auburn hair curled neatly, carefully groomed to frame a face that could turn from mirth to menace in a heartbeat. And yet it was not only his clothing that marked him. It was the aura—the expectation that the room would bend to his will, that no voice dared rise too brightly in his presence. He was every inch a king—and every inch aware of it. As he reached her, Anne did not rise to curtsy, nor even incline her head. She remained upright in her chair, her chin high.

"My lady," he said, softly, almost with a tremor. "Are you displeased with me?"

She tilted her head, one brow arching the barest degree. "Majesty, you dined last night with the Queen," she replied, her voice as cold as ice. I felt everyone freeze around me as we waited for the storm to break.

King Henry's jaw tightened. "It was a matter of state."

Mistress Boleyn stood up, her skirts framing her slim figure. "And so, I am someone of no importance. I thought I had your entire heart. But I see that I was mistaken."

His face flushed a deep red with the wounded pride of a king unused to rebuke. He took a step forward, his jewels catching the light, his breath heavy in the chamber's tense silence.

"No," he said, his voice low and rough with restraint. "You are not mistaken, Anne. You are the very pulse of my heart. But must you wound me so?"

She did not flinch. "I am the one who is wounded," she insisted. "You injure me every time you lavish your attention upon her."

Henry's hands twitched at his sides, then slowly curled into fists. "You know not what burdens I bear—parliament, councillors, the Emperor's spies and the Pope's prevarications."

"And yet," she cut in sharply, "you find time for Catherine still, for her letters, her petitions, her company at your bed and your board."

He recoiled slightly, eyes narrowed. "You would dare name her to me?"

"I dare everything for the truth," she said, her eyes flashing. "That is what you claimed to love in me. Or has your courage failed you, my lord?"

And in that moment, I saw it—not just his anger, but his awe. She stood before him like a tempest, unafraid, unbowed, every inch the queen she meant to become. He stared at her, jaw tight, eyes burning—and then, with a sound like a growl, he seized her hand and pressed it hard to his lips.

"None shall stand between us," he swore, voice hoarse. "Not Catherine. Not the Pope. Not even God Himself."

Mistress Boleyn looked down at him, her smile slow and dark with triumph. "Then prove it."

He said nothing. His hand, heavy with rings, twitched at his side. "I will prove my love before the whole world before I am done," he declared.

She reached for him—not with longing, but with deliberation—laying a hand upon his chest where the medallion glittered in enamel and gold. "You gave me your promise," she said, low. "You would not make me a byword, Henry. I will not be cast aside like those who came before."

"We shall never be parted, Anne," he said. "I swear it by all that is sacred!"

Mistress Boleyn did not soften. She withdrew her hand and turned to the window, the light framing her like a figure from a stained-glass panel. Only then did she reply, "I will believe you when you set a ring upon my finger and a crown upon my head." And in that moment, I understood: Anne Boleyn did not simply enchant the King. She commanded him.

Mistress Boleyn was attended by a circle of ladies from the Boleyn and Howard families. She was suspicious of me for I had no connection to her family. She could sense the ambition and the intellect that lay behind my polished exterior. I had a driving confidence that matched hers. And I was equally young, fair and well-born. She preferred her associates to be inferior to herself in their looks, accomplishments and wit. And she was not prepared to harbour any rivals in her circle. So, I knew that I would have to tread carefully. I sought the advice of my stepfather, Sir Richard Page.

"How do you find Mistress Anne?" he asked.

"She is a difficult mistress to serve," I said. "She is insufferably arrogant. She does not have the kind and gracious manner of Queen Catherine."

"It is easy to serve a kind mistress," he replied. "The challenge is to please a demanding one. I got where I am today by impressing both the Lord Cardinal and the King with my talents. It is the task of a courtier to serve the office not the personality. You don't want to leave court, do you?"

"No, I don't want to throw away everything that I have accomplished," I said. I knew that I was an exemplary maid of honour. I intended to make my career at the court.

"Then see this as a golden opportunity," he said. "Study the tastes of your mistress. Set yourself to anticipate her wishes. Always have a smiling countenance and an agreeable manner. Use flattery to gain her trust. In time your efforts will pay off and she will see you as the perfect attendant."

"I know that I have the aptitude for service," I said. "But nothing seems to please Mistress Anne."

"Then you must redouble your efforts," he said. "Be the first to attend her in the morning and the last to retire at night. Take care to be perfect in your manners and attire so that you add to her renown. Always be ready to entertain her with a conversation or a game. And never fail to compliment her upon her appearance and accomplishments. Then she will value your company and your opinions. Keep yourself lowly and never show resentment. Only then will you truly deserve the name of a courtier."

"Thank you, Sir Richard," I said.

"Good fortune comes to those who cultivate their opportunities," he admonished me. "You are an intelligent girl. You will soon find ways to recommend yourself to your mistress."

I took his words to heart and returned to the apartments with a renewed sense of determination. I would persevere until I had won over Mistress Boleyn. I would be the most faithful lady in her service. In the end, I would gain her confidence and her favour. The following morning, I arrived at her bedchamber before the rest of the ladies were awake. I greeted her with a curtsey and a pleasant smile.

"You again," she remarked dismissively. "Why are you so eager to put yourself forward?"

It seemed that the Cardinal had been easier to please than Mistress Boleyn. However, I remembered the advice of my stepfather and kept a pleasant smile on my face. She ignored me and turned to her mother.

"Today I shall wear my new gown of rose-pink silk," she announced proudly. "It is still in my privy chamber for it only arrived yesterday."

In my eagerness to serve, I brought it from the privy chamber and held it up before her. She glared at me in fury.

"Leave my gown alone!" she snapped. "It is a present from his Majesty. Only the Mistress of the Robes may handle it. I don't want it spoiled by clumsy hands!"

"I beg your pardon, Mistress Boleyn," I replied. "I will return it at once."

"And why would you do that?" she demanded. "Didn't I say that I intended to wear it?"

"Yes, Mistress Boleyn," I said. "Pray accept my humble apologies for displeasing you."

"Don't distress yourself, my dear," said Lady Boleyn. "Why not let the girl go and do some sewing for you?"

"I doubt that she can even edge a handkerchief fit to be seen," she retorted. "Put that down on the bed and get out of my sight!"

"Yes, Mistress Boleyn," I replied. My cheeks were scarlet with humiliation as I withdrew from the bedchamber and took sanctuary in a quiet corner of the privy chamber. I realised with a pang of regret that I had been far more contented serving Queen Catherine. But Mistress Boleyn was the King's favourite. I would have to bide my time and try to find some way to secure her goodwill. But I feared that she would rebuff my overtures out of spite.

I drew a deep breath and blinked back my foolish tears. I was not going to cry like a child. If Mistress Boleyn did not require my services, then I would employ my time to good advantage. I drew a linen cap out of my work bag and occupied myself by embroidering it with an intricate border of whitework. I had mastered the current court fashions in needlework and had set myself to embellish my plain linen garments. I intended to provide myself with a complete set of embroidered linen like a great lady.

Lady Boleyn took note of my efforts. "You are most adept with your needle, Mistress Stanhope," she remarked. "When this is finished, you may embroider my caps in the same style as this one."

Her daughter bristled at once. "Mistress Stanhope is my attendant, mother," she said. "As soon as she is finished, she shall embroider my linen caps."

"It is my pleasure to serve you, Mistress Boleyn," I replied.

It took me a fortnight to embroider a dozen linen caps with delicate patterns of whitework. But when the work was completed, she did not praise me for my efforts. I realised that I needed to take a different approach in order to win her favour. I set out to cultivate Mistress Anne Gainsford. She was a silly little thing but she was Mistress Anne Boleyn's favourite attendant. She called her Nan and treated her like her little sister. Most of the other ladies disdained her for her childish ways. But I did not. I saw that she could be useful. And it would not require a bribe or a favour. She could be bought for friendship. Soon I had gained her confidence and she shared her secrets with me. I learned that she was being courted by Sir George Zouche of Codnor.

"We must find you a sweetheart," she said carelessly. "Someone handsome and charming."

"Someone of birth and intelligence," I replied. "I want my children to be well-bred and well provided for."

"Don't you want them to be handsome too?" she teased me. "You have been at court for over a year now. Surely you have seen someone who is worthy of your favour?"

"The best ones are already taken," I said evasively. I did not want to relate the sad story of Sir Urian Brereton. I had resolved to put that episode behind me.

"Then it will have to be an Irish lord," she said. "Mistress Boleyn was nearly married to her cousin in Ireland. Fortunately, the plan came to nothing. Otherwise, she would never have become the favourite of the King."

"I don't believe half the things you say, Nan," I said.

"It's true," she retorted. "But it was her father's plan. She had no wish to go to Ireland. Afterwards, she thought that she would marry young Henry Percy. Oh, I am not supposed to talk about it."

"Then you shouldn't tell me," I replied.

"It's common knowledge," she said. "They were sweethearts once. But the Cardinal broke off their romance because she was only the daughter of a knight. Young Percy tried to defy him but the Cardinal forbade the match and sent him back to his father in Northumberland."

"How do you know all this?" I asked.

"Sir George told me," she said. "He has friends in the Cardinal's household. They heard him storming and raging at the poor young man for his deceit and ingratitude. It caused quite a scandal at the time."

"Then what happened?" I asked.

"He was forced to marry Lady Anne Talbot," she said. "Mistress Boleyn was heartbroken. She swore that one day she would take her revenge on the Cardinal for frustrating her plans. She left court for a time and returned to live at Hever. But when she returned to court, the King began to pay his court to her. So, everything worked out for the best. Instead of becoming the countess of Northumberland she will become the Queen of England!"

If it all works out for her, I thought.

"It's quite the romance, isn't it?" she sighed. "The King is completely devoted to her. He cannot do enough to show his love. He sends her splendid presents nearly every day."

"A remarkable story," I agreed.

"I have asked Mistress Boleyn to let me serve her when she is crowned queen," she said. "She has promised that she will find a place for both me and George. And you must be one of her ladies too."

"Yes, of course," I said. "We shall be the three Anne's. Nothing should ever separate us!"

"How witty you are, Anne!" she said. "I shall tell Mistress Boleyn what you said. It is bound to amuse her."

"It is our duty to please the King's favourite lady," I replied.

But not everyone was successful in pleasing Mistress Boleyn. I noticed a fair-haired lady who sat quietly sewing next to Lady Boleyn. She rarely spoke and I wondered who she was. Mistress Anne shot her a look of irritation.

"Isn't that glove finished yet?" she demanded. "You know I need to wear it this evening!"

She bit her lip and bowed her head at the rebuke.

"You are quite useless here," she snapped. "You might as well leave the court and go home."

Her lovely face flushed scarlet and her eyes filled with tears. But she remained silent. Lady Boleyn did not say a word.

"Who is she?" I whispered to Nan.

"That is Lady Mary Carey," replied Nan. She is the sister of Mistress Anne. Her older sister. She was once the King's mistress, you know."

I looked at her again. She was far more beautiful than her sister. "Why did she fall out of favour?" I enquired.

"She lacks spirit," said Nan. "She is sweet-tempered, but she is much too dull to keep the interest of the King for long. Beauty and charm only take a woman so far at the court. Even accomplishments count for little if a woman lacks vivacity. Mistress Boleyn served at the French court and learned the arts of attraction there. She may not be a beauty, but she knows how to allure. The men are drawn to her like moths to a flame."

"How is it that Lady Carey is treated so poorly by her mother and her sister?" I asked.

"She was too eager to please," said Nan. "She asked for nothing in return. They say that the King loved her passionately, but he never gave her a set of apartments nor such splendid presents. You see, she consented to become his mistress, but Mistress Boleyn refused him. She scorns her sister for giving herself too freely. She has nothing to show for her time in the sunshine. No titles, lands or house. No riches at all. So, she threw away her chance of becoming someone at the court."

She did not prize herself enough, I thought. *She had no pride or ambition. Now she is a nobody at court and everyone despises her.*

I stole another look at Lady Carey. She was beautiful, but she lacked drive and ambition. She had already used up her chances and now she was doomed to remain in the shadow of her younger sister. It was not enough to gain favour at court. One had to have the skills to keep it.

I glanced over to where Mistress Anne sat gazing out of the window at the garden. She was fiery and tempestuous where her sister was calm and placid. Her mercurial moods were fascinating. They drew the King in further in spite of his frustration. It was a matter of pride. He would stop at nothing to make her his own. Just as he tamed his spirited horses and hawks, so he longed to control her. But she was too elusive to be captured. She was a challenge that could not be resisted. Lady Carey did not have the temperament that distinguished a great lady. She was too yielding and complaisant. She did not know how to guard herself or command the respect of others. However, Mistress Boleyn had the force of personality to challenge the Queen in her own palace. She was fearless, resolute and determined. I wondered how a mere knight's daughter had the audacity to oppose a reigning Queen and a daughter of Spain. I resolved to study Mistress Boleyn and learn her secrets.

Mistress Boleyn was no great beauty but she had the power to captivate her admirers. Her mysterious charm had persuaded the King to grant her whatever she desired. Furthermore, she had the personality and dominating will of an empress. She was single-minded in her determination to become the next Queen of England. She was a demanding mistress to her servants and eagle-eyed to notice any failure on their part. She wanted to create the illusion that she was a great noblewoman and make that illusion into a reality.

Her greatest fear was that she would lose her hold upon the King before she had got the crown upon her head. Her sister had barely lasted two summers before the King had lost interest in her. She was determined not to repeat her mistake. But withholding her favours was a dangerous strategy. It left her vulnerable to rivals who would willingly grant their virtue to the King. She could hardly fail to notice the parade of noble daughters and noble wives who sought to entice the King. The strain of her precarious situation told upon her temper and she lashed out at everyone around her. She even rebuked the King for his failure to keep his word.

"I wish you would not quarrel with the King," said her mother, her voice heavy with concern. "If you drive him away, he may not come back to you again. You should welcome him with smiles and offer him a pleasant diversion from his cares whenever he honours you with a visit."

"That is good counsel for a wife," she replied coldly. "But he has not made me his wife. Sometimes I wish he would leave me altogether so that I could make an honourable marriage with a worthy man before it is too late."

Lady Boleyn inhaled sharply, her brows knitting in dismay. "That is no way to speak of the King," she chided. "Your father and your uncle would be most displeased by such wanton talk."

She laughed bitterly. "They have profited enough from my endeavours. What efforts do they make to secure a divorce?"

"How can you say that?" she countered. "Your father works constantly to promote your future. Has he not made an embassy to Rome in order to persuade the Pope to grant an annulment?"

"Rome is a lost cause," she snapped. "The Pope will never grant the King his desire. He ought to make use of his own authority as a King instead of supplicating the Bishop of Rome like a beggar."

"These are high matters, my dear," her mother said in a reproving tone. "You should not seek to meddle with affairs of state."

"I am surrounded by enemies, Mother," she murmured, lowering her voice as though the very walls might betray her. "Most of the courtiers sympathize with the Queen and try to undermine me. Unless the King takes action, he will be tied to that old woman for the rest of his life. And then what will become of me?"

Mistress Boleyn was not mistaken in her judgment. The duke of Suffolk warned the King that his favourite was a light woman who had already granted her favours to the poet, Sir Thomas Wyatt. But the King was too enamoured of her to heed any criticism. He hurried over to her apartments at once to seek reassurance.

"Suffolk told me that Wyatt was once your sweetheart," he complained. "Is it true?"

"How dare he accuse me?" she said passionately. "He has always been my enemy. Wyatt is just an old neighbour from Kent. He means nothing to me."

"But he writes poems about you," he said. "He boasts of your love for each other."

"Wyatt is a married man," she said. "Why would I grant my favours to such a one? I have more respect for what is due to myself and my family. But I see that you are determined to think the worst of me."

He reached out, taking her hand in his own. "Nay, sweetheart," he murmured. "It is not your fault if a poet writes verse in praise of your beauty. It is no reflection upon your virtue."

"So, you will send Suffolk away from court," she demanded. "It will stop these evil tongues from wagging."

"Yes, of course," he agreed. "He has no right to spread gossip around the court to blacken the name of an honest woman."

And so, Suffolk was banished from court. His departure served as a warning that anyone who dared to whisper against the King's favourite would find themselves cast into the shadows. His downfall emboldened Mistress Boleyn and the next day she celebrated her victory. She organised a picnic in the privy garden and invited all her friends to attend. She sat upon a chair of estate in the rose garden surrounded by her ladies. The sweet scent of lavender and honeysuckle filled the air and she laughed at the antics of her fool who imitated all the chief courtiers in turn. Meg the Fool was a simple soul dressed in blue and yellow livery who had a natural gift of mimicry. She had no idea that her foolery was a dangerous pastime at the court.

"Show me the duke of Norfolk paying his suit to the King," said Mistress Boleyn.

"Your Majesty, I pray you will grant me a divorce from my wife," she said. "If you can have a fair young bride, then surely, I deserve no less!"

"You are a naughty wench," she chided her. "You deserve a box on the ear for mocking his Grace. But we all know that a divorce is the chief desire of his heart. If he were free, he would gladly make his mistress into his duchess!"

"Really my dear, you give the girl too much license," said Lady Boleyn uneasily. "Suppose your uncle were to hear of her unseemly jests!"

"He is a pompous old fool," said Mistress Boleyn. "I care nothing for his opinion." Her cheeks were flushed with excitement and her dark eyes glinted with malice.

"For my sake, leave off these foolish japes," she said. They are unbecoming to your dignity.

"I find her banter amusing," said Mistress Boleyn defiantly. "Tell us where the Spanish Queen and her ladies belong, girl!"

"At the bottom of the sea with the Pope and the emperor," she replied.

Lady Boleyn frowned and shook her head but the other ladies giggled at her temerity. I laughed as loudly the rest of the company. But inwardly I wondered how many spies were listening to her careless words. They would undoubtedly report her insolence to the Queen, the Spanish ambassador and the duke of Norfolk. It was folly to make such powerful enemies at court. But Mistress Boleyn was bolder than a lion.

"Well said," she replied with a broad smile. "You shall have a sweetmeat for that and another one if you say it again in the presence of the King!"

"I beg you to have a care," urged Lady Boleyn. "Remember how the King said that you were greatly beholden to him since he had made many enemies for your sake."

"I do not give a straw for any of them and neither should he," she retorted. "He is too moderate in his dealings but I am not. Let them beware of provoking my vengeance. If I had my way, I would send all the Spaniards and the Papists to the Tower where they belong!"

Lady Boleyn compressed her lips but Mistress Bolen looked around herself in triumph. She seemed to have unshakable confidence in her ability to do anything. But her recklessness only emphasised her lack of decorum. It would have served her better to have practised the graciousness of a born noblewoman. She had served at both the French and English courts and ought to have known how circumspectly a queen behaved. I vowed that one day I would be a great lady with a train of servants to wait upon me. I would have a noble husband, a fine residence and a host of children to inherit my fortune. And I would conduct myself with the pride and dignity of my royal ancestors. No-one would have any cause to question my virtue or my prudence.

Mistress Boleyn prided herself upon her splendid wardrobe, her extensive jewel collection and her impressive library of books. She was interested in the religious reformers and commissioned her brother George to obtain banned books from the Continent. He brought her a copy of *The Obedience of a Christian Man* by William Tyndale.

"But take care not to let anyone see it," he cautioned. "It has been proscribed by Cardinal Wolsey."

"You need not concern yourself," she replied. "He never comes to my apartments."

She read the book avidly for the next few days and then laid it down with a sigh. "What is it about?" asked Nan.

"How Christian rulers ought to govern and the false power of the Pope," she said, handing it over. "You may read it for yourself."

But a few days later, Nan came to her in tears. "Mistress Boleyn, a terrible thing has happened," she sobbed. "It will bring disaster upon us all!"

"You are not making any sense," she complained. "What is all this to-do?"

"It is about the book you lent me," she said. "I was sitting by the window reading it when Sir George Zouche came to see me. I told him that it was difficult to understand so he took it and said that he would read it and explain it to me. But on his way home he encountered Richard Sampson, Dean of the Chapel Royal. He demanded to see what book he had in his hand and asked him how he came to have such a heretical book in his possession. Sir George begged him to let him have it back, but he said that he would take it to his master Cardinal Wolsey and he would have to answer to him. So now he is in dreadful trouble and so am I!"

"Dry your eyes, Nan," she said. "I swear that this shall be the dearest book that ever a dean or a cardinal took away. The King shall hear of this matter. I will go to see him at once."

She returned looking like the cat that had got the cream. "The King sent his ring to the Cardinal and ordered him to return the book at once," she said. "I persuaded him to read it himself and showed him the pages that I had marked. He read how the Pope's doctrine seeks nothing but the possessions of the world and the authority in the world, and to bear rule in the world. He declared that it was a book for him and all kings to read. So, you see, all is well again."

"I am so thankful," said Nan. "I was afraid of what might happen to my poor George."

"The Cardinal will think twice before he confiscates any of my books again!" she said smugly. "He thought that he would cause me displeasure but this time he has burned his own fingers!"

Mistress Boleyn soon took her revenge upon Cardinal Wolsey. The next time she encountered him she had prepared a deadly stroke.

"I have met with Cardinal Campeggio, your Majesty," he said. "I warned him that if your Grace's desire was not granted it would mean the total ruin of the kingdom and the Church's influence."

"Do you hear that sweetheart?" said King Henry. "The Cardinal has served us well and we shall soon have an annulment."

"The Cardinal has served himself well," she replied. "You have given him everything that a man could desire – titles and posts, houses and riches. Yet what has he done to deserve such honours?"

Cardinal Wolsey was stung by the accusation. "I would give your Majesty anything to show my loyalty," he declared. "You have only to name it!"

The King's eyes narrowed with thought. "Would you give me your palace of Hampton Court?" he asked.

"Gladly, your Majesty," he replied unflinchingly.

"Then I will receive it in the same spirit of friendship with which it was offered," he said, beaming with pleasure. "Do you hear that, my dear? It will be a palace for you and I alone, with no sign of the Queen anywhere."

Her eyes glinted with satisfaction. "His Grace the Cardinal is most generous," she replied.

But his generosity was not enough to win her friendship. She chafed at the continual delays in annulling the King's marriage. She blamed the Queen and the Cardinal for contriving to postpone the matter and turned her frustration upon the King.

"You are much too kind-hearted," she complained. "The Queen takes advantage of you. She will never willingly relinquish her position as the Queen. She will hold onto you until her dying day even if it deprives the realm of the chance of having a lawful son and heir."

"I have tried every means to persuade her," he replied. "But the Cardinal assures that he can convince the Pope to grant me an annulment. The case could not be a clearer one. I sinned in the sight of God by marrying my brother's wife. Consequently, I have no son. But it is essential for the peace and prosperity of the realm that I take a lawful wife and ensure a legitimate son and heir to succeed me. It is a matter of the greatest importance both for England and the whole of Christendom."

"I do not share your confidence in the Cardinal," she replied. "He will always put his loyalty to the Pope above his loyalty to the King."

"Peace, sweetheart," he said. "The Cardinal has never failed me. As soon as I have obtained an annulment, we shall be married."

"We would not have to wait if the Queen was not acting so selfishly," she said. "She ought to agree to enter a convent and allow you to remarry."

"I have already reasoned with her, but to no avail," he said. "I have offered her own choice of house, a generous pension and no diminution of her royal status. But she will not hear of it. I have sent bishops and noblemen to plead with her. None of them could persuade her to consent."

"Why should you plead?" she said. "You are the King and she is your subject. Why don't you just order her to go?"

"I do not wish to compel her against her will," he said. "After all, she is a daughter of Spain. But she will have to accept the decision of the Pope. His ruling will resolve all the difficulties that are standing in our way."

So, the King and his lady waited impatiently to receive the judgement of the Pope. But Cardinal Campeggio was in no hurry to convene a court. He insisted that his first duty was to seek a reconciliation between the King and the Queen.

Mistress Boleyn was furious to hear the news. "I have been deceived," she protested. "Wolsey promised that he would grant the King an annulment. But it is no such thing. He has come here to uphold the Queen and send me packing!"

"I am sure the King will not hear of a reconciliation," said Lady Boleyn.

"He is being led by the nose and he cannot see it," she said. "He thinks that Wolsey is his steadfast friend, but both these Cardinals are in league with Pope. I have no faith in any of them!"

It was not until 31st May 1529 that the Legatine court finally assembled. The Great Hall of Blackfriars was transformed into a theatre of judgment, its vaulted ceiling echoing with the quiet rustle of silk and the measured tread of high office. Sunlight slanted through tall, mullioned windows and fell in angled light across a raised dais, where the two papal legates sat beneath canopies of state—Cardinal

Campeggio, grim-faced and stoic, and Cardinal Wolsey, his expression carefully composed into neutrality. Their chairs were resplendent, covered in cloth of gold, the cushions embroidered with ecclesiastical emblems that caught the flicker of torchlight like hidden messages. A dormant table stretched before them, railed and swathed in heavy tapestries and Turkey carpets, the surface empty but for parchments, inkwells, and the silent weight of Rome's authority. Courtiers clustered along the sides, their velvet sleeves brushing as they leaned inward, eyes flicking between the central figures of this living tableau.

On 21st June 1529, King and the Queen were both called to give evidence. To the right of the hall, a cloth of estate shimmered above the chair of King Henry VIII, its red and gold heraldry glowing like a flame. He sat imperiously, hands resting on the lion-headed arms of his seat, the jewels of his doublet glinting with each impatient shift. His crown rested on a cushion nearby, untouched, yet omnipresent—a reminder that even in this court of foreign legates, his will was not absent. Opposite, beneath a mirrored cloth of estate, sat Queen Catherine of Aragon, her gown of black damask setting her apart like a shadow in daylight. Her chair matched the King's in form, but not in posture. She sat erect, hands folded calmly in her lap, her eyes fixed not on her husband but ahead, where judgment and dignity would collide. A hush followed her every movement, as if gravity bent itself gently in her direction. Behind the monarchs stood their respective households—ladies in waiting with veiled brows, gentlemen of the chamber, and a sea of curious faces drawn from every corner of the court. Whispers eddied like wind through rushes. The matter before them was no simple plea—it was the unravelling of a marriage, a Queen's fate, and the very shape of England's soul. Mistress Boleyn awaited the outcome of the trial in her apartments in the company of her mother. As the afternoon passed, she became increasingly impatient for news.

"How can the proceedings take so long?" she muttered. "It is a straightforward case and the Cardinals know what judgement the King expects to hear."

"Peace, Anne," Lady Boleyn replied. "His Majesty promised you should be the first to hear the outcome."

Late that afternoon the King arrived at her apartments. His face was black with suppressed rage. "The Queen humiliated me in public," he stormed. "She did not give her evidence to the court in a dignified manner. Instead, she knelt at my feet and pleaded with me to grant her justice. She swore that when we were married, she was a true maid without touch of man. Then she turned to the legates and said that she did not recognise the authority of their court and asked for the case to be referred to Rome."

"What did the judges say to her plea?" asked Mistress Boleyn.

"They refused her request and she defied them," he said. "She left the trial. She just walked out."

"She can't do that," she snapped.

"I tell you she did," he replied. "But it matters not. The trial will proceed without her."

"As long as it reaches the right conclusion," she muttered.

"It will, my love, I assure you," he said. "Wolsey has given me his word."

On 23rd July 1529 the Legatine court reassembled at Blackfriars to conclude the cause. King Henry sat in a gallery near the door to hear the judgement. Cardinal Campeggio stood up and announced that he would give no sentence until he had consulted with the Pope. Consequently, the court would now be adjourned until October. The duke of Suffolk slapped the table with his hand and shouted, "By the mass! There never was never a cardinal that did good in England!" The King walked out of the court in a rage.

The collapse of the trial infuriated Mistress Boleyn. She did not hesitate to denounce her enemy. "I said all along that the Pope and his Cardinals were deceiving you," she said. "They never had any intention of granting an annulment. They have made a fool of you in your own kingdom!"

The King sent for Cardinal Wolsey at once. He had to bear the brunt of the King's anger and disappointment.

"Where is my justice?" he demanded. "What of the sons that are due to me and to the realm?"

The Cardinal fell to his knees. "Pray hold back your hand, most pious King," he pleaded. "I swear to your gracious Majesty that next unto God, I desire nor covet anything in this world but the attaining of your gracious favour and the forgiveness of my trespass."

He ordered the Queen to move out of Greenwich and go to live at Richmond. Then he set out on his summer progress in the company of Mistress Boleyn and his closest companions. They travelled to the palace of Woodstock in Oxfordshire where King Henry II had entertained the fair Rosamond Clifford. There Mistress Boleyn kept state more like a queen than a simple maid. They remained there the whole summer so that the King could alleviate his grief by hunting the stag and hosting parties of pleasure in the forest. He wanted Mistress Boleyn to share his favourite pleasures.

"The best of all pastimes is to hunt in the forest during the summer months," he said. "It lifts the mind and strengthens the body. And when the hart runs true, and you match it stride for stride there is no excitement to match it."

She tilted her head and smiled, her eyes flashing beneath her arched velvet hood. "Your Majesty makes poetry of the chase," she said. "Though I wonder whether the beasts of the forest partake quite so willingly."

He chuckled, low and warm. "Not willingly, no—but the whole pleasure of the chase lies in the pursuit and the capture. No woman of spirit would care to hunt tame beasts."

A ripple of laughter stirred his companions and behind them, a steward galloped up with news: a great stag had been sighted nearby, its antlers wide and proud. King Henry leaned forward, his mood sharpened by anticipation.

"Let us ride," he said, his voice suddenly fierce and boyish. "And show the forest what true sport looks like." He spurred his horse forward with an eager flick of his reins, the animal snorting as it bounded into motion, hooves flinging earth beneath its stride. The courtly procession surged after him, velvet and ermine trailing in his wake like a royal banner unfurling through the trees. Mistress Boleyn's eyes followed him with a mixture of admiration and ambition. She was no longer a mere court lady enjoying the pleasures of the summer. She had become the King's established favourite. And now she had taken the place of the Queen on the royal progress. The cry of the master huntsman rang out through the dappled woods: *"Soho! Soho! The hart is up!"*

King Henry liked to set out at dawn, so every morning I had to rise in darkness and dress Mistress Boleyn by candlelight. He had provided her with riding habits of the finest velvet embroidered with gold and silver thread. I fitted her bodice of dark blue velvet bordered with intertwining vines. I looped her girdle around her waist and fastened the last of the long pearl pins in her hair. Then I placed the velvet hood adorned with jewelled spangles upon her head. She picked up her looking glass and smiled to see her reflection. She would ride like a queen, even if crowned only in desire.

Outside, the courtyard crackled with tension and cold. A banner flapped overhead—the Tudor dragon snarling against a pale morning sky. The horsemen adjusted stirrups and tightened reins. The hounds barked in their traces, nostrils steaming, paws stamping in rhythm with impatience. The King sat astride his great stallion Governatore looking around with impatience. Mistress Boleyn moved toward him with all the grace of ceremony. He reached down and pulled her onto the pillion seat behind him. A groom led her own horse Joyeuse which was trapped with a velvet saddle. The trumpets blew and the hunters rode out of the gate followed by the hounds and their keepers. The King spurred ahead and she clutched his waist, laughing into the wind. Her veil whipped behind her like a pennant and he turned slightly to catch her smile.

"The hunt is up, the hunt is up,
And it is well-nigh day;
And Harry our king is gone hunting,
To bring his deer to bay.

The east is bright with morning light,
And darkness it is fled;
And the merry horn wakes up the morn
To leave his idle bed.

Behold the skies with golden dyes
Are glowing all around;
The grass is green, and so are the treen,
All laughing with the sound.

The horses snort to be at the sport,
The dogs are running free;
The woods rejoice at the merry noise
Of hey taranta tee ree!"

The ladies rode out at midday to meet the royal party. We were accompanied by the musicians and the pages. Deep in the heart of Wychwood Forest, beneath a purple canopy that shimmered in the summer light, the King's court emerged into view. Tents of damask and cloth-of-gold billowed in the breeze, hung with garlands of honeysuckle and threaded with ribbons in the Tudor colours. The soft grass beneath it was strewn with Turkey carpets and coloured silk cushions upon which the King and his company were reclining. The cooks had already roasted a deer upon a spit and served a feast to the hunters. Now they were ready to enjoy an afternoon of entertainment. The King was dressed in russet and gold, his face flushed from wine. He wore a crown of woven oak leaves and resembled some wild god of the chase. Beside him sat Mistress Boleyn in her riding habit of emerald green looking like the goddess Diana in her secret woodland glade.

"Here are ladies and the minstrels at last!" the King cried, his voice rich with anticipation. "You are welcome to our rustic bower in the forest. Let us sit upon the ground and take our ease. We shall listen to lively tunes and merry songs! Master Smeaton, is your lute awake?"

I glanced at the boy, barely more than sixteen, with brown eyes and dark hair. "It is at your Grace's command," he replied with a bow. He took his lute in his hands and at once the forest fell quiet, even the breeze waiting to hear the first verse. As the music began, I watched the King lean into its rhythm, his great frame softened by pleasure. Mistress Boleyn kept her eyes fixed on him—not adoring, but calculating. She smiled as though the song were written for her alone:

"My lute awake! perform the last
Labour that thou and I shall waste,
And end that I have now begun;
For when this song is sung and past,
My lute be still, for I have done.

As to be heard where ear is none,
As lead to grave in marble stone,
My song may pierce her heart as soon;
Should we then sigh or sing or moan?
No, no, my lute, for I have done."

Chapter 3: The Household of Mistress Anne Boleyn (1528) | 123

The company applauded. "Play us another one, boy," said the King. Master Smeaton bowed low, his fingers already dancing across the strings before the King's voice had finished echoing. The air in the glade shimmered with expectation—courtiers leaned forward, ladies tilted their heads, and even the hounds quieted, ears twitching as if attuned to the mood of their sovereign.

"Pastime with good company
I love and shall until I die;
Grudge who will, but none deny
So God be pleased thus live will I
For my pastance
Hunt, sing, and dance
My heart is set:
All goodly sport
For my comfort
Who shall me let?

Youth must have some dalliance
Of good or ill some pastance;
Company methinks then best
All thoughts and fancies to digest:
For idleness
Is chief mistress
Of vices all;
Then who can say
But mirth and play
Is best of all?"

It was the King's own anthem, his philosophy of kingship wrapped in melody. His voice bellowed out the words of the second verse, louder than anyone else dared. "A good song, indeed!" he remarked contentedly. "Honest pastimes are good for the soul since idleness only leads to evil. Now sing us a hunting song!"

"Were Love to go hunting,
He'd bring a poet along for fun,
And follow the ladies' tracks.
For the latter are as fair and playful,
As the former is graceful and handsome."

"A bold song, boy!" he declared. "But it needs another verse to it. I would like to know which lady's track this lovestruck poet would follow?"

I held my breath. The company did too.

"I would not presume to take any names into my mouth, Your Majesty," Smeaton said, his eyes lowered. "I can only say that in this company there is a lady so fair that she exceeds the rest just as the dazzling moon outshines the light of the stars."

"Well said, boy," the King replied, tossing him a purse that landed on the moss. "Here is a reward for your gallant words and discretion!"

"Master Smeaton is a fine player, Your Majesty," said Mistress Boleyn. "And he sings just like an angel."

"If the boy pleases you, then he shall be yours," replied the King magnanimously. "I would not deny your slightest wish."

She smiled graciously at him and from that day forward Master Smeaton became the most devoted servant of Mistress Anne.

On his return to London, the King sent the dukes of Norfolk and Suffolk to take the Great Seal from Cardinal Wolsey. He was ordered to surrender York Place and all his lands, offices, goods and possessions. The loss of the King's favour left him a broken man. He departed to live at Cawood Castle in his archbishopric of York.

"I grieve for the fall of the Cardinal," said Sir Richard. "He was a great man and a good master. It is a great pity to see him fall so far."

"It is fortunate that you had already left his service to join the household of the King," I remarked. "There is nothing you can do for him. Mistress Boleyn was determined to destroy him."

"Indeed, she is the one who now has the ear of the King," he said. "You must take care not to offend her."

But the downfall of the Cardinal was not enough to satisfy Mistress Boleyn. The strain of her position made her irritable. She had secured the affections of the King, but she had not obtained the crown. Every day, King Henry promised her that soon he would gain his annulment and make her his queen. She seethed with frustration and vented her temper on those around her. Her household officials and servants wore sullen expressions on their faces. Their silent campaign of hostility provoked Mistress Boleyn to distraction. She retaliated by adopting a new motto and had it embroidered upon her servant's liveries: *This is how it will be, grumble who may.* But her defiant gesture backfired. The whole court sniggered when they read the new motto. They saw it as an admission of defeat. Mistress Boleyn did not want to become a laughing stock. She ordered it to be removed.

The rivalry between Queen Catherine and Mistress Anne Boleyn finally reached its climax. One day she saw one of the grooms of the privy chamber carrying a bundle of fine linen down the corridor. The fine weave and impeccable whiteness showed that it was from the royal stores. Her suspicions were aroused at once. She stepped forward and intercepted him with a raised hand.

"That is the finest linen in the palace," she said. "Where are you taking it?"

The groom hesitated, his eyes darting like a cornered hare. "To the Queen's apartments, Mistress Anne," he stammered. "The King wishes her to make him some new shirts."

She flew into a rage." You are a fool," she hissed. "His Majesty said no such thing. Take it back to the stores at once!"

The unfortunate groom turned around and hurried out of sight. Lady Boleyn tried vainly to calm her daughter who was pacing up and down in a fury.

"It is no great matter if the King asks the Queen to make him a few shirts," she murmured soothingly. "It means nothing."

Mistress Anne whirled on her, her eyes blazing with outrage. "It means everything!" she retorted. "It is always the wife that makes her husband's shirts. It shows that he has no regard for me. He still thinks of her as his true wife!"

I suspected that it had been convenient for the King to disregard the matter. He was a vain man and took pride in his regal attire. Queen Catherine of Aragon was a notable needlewoman and considered it her duty to sew her husband's shirts. His collar and cuffs were always splendidly embroidered with the delicate blackwork that she had learned in Spain. The King had been married to the Queen for twenty years. I wondered if he would really cast her aside for another, when he still relied upon her to see to his comfort.

"The Queen has always made his shirts for him," she insisted. "Do not excite yourself over a mere trifle."

Mistress Anne snorted, crossing her arms. "No doubt he scorns my skills in needlework," she said bitterly. "He does not trust me to make a shirt that is fit to be seen."

"I am sure it is no such thing," she said gently. "I expect that the King did not wish to trouble you with such tiresome duties."

Her face darkened. "He is making me the laughing-stock of the court," she snapped. "His prevarication will encourage her to cherish false hopes of a reconciliation. But I shall put a stop to it at once. In future, his linen will be sent to me!"

She turned and stormed away, her skirts swirling in a silken cascade behind her. The door slammed shut behind her leaving Lady Boleyn looking stricken. The murmur of the ladies faded into silence as they exchanged covert glances with each other. Mistress Anne Boleyn had always been formidable, but now, in the throes of courtly warfare, she was relentless. An hour later the door burst open, and there she was again—breathless but triumphant. Around her neck gleamed a string of matched pearls, bound by a green velvet ribbon. She lifted them with delicate fingers, letting the sunlight dance upon their surface.

"A token from the King?" murmured Lady Boleyn, taking in the gift with measured patience.

Mistress Anne lifted her chin. "A peace offering," she announced, her voice rich with satisfaction. "He seeks to mend what he nearly shattered."

"You will do well to be careful," sighed Lady Boleyn, shaking her head.

Mistress Anne smiled exultantly. "He is the one who must prove himself worthy. Not I."

A ripple of laughter spread among her ladies. I joined in the merriment but I could see the careful calculation that underlay her veneer of confidence. The following morning, the groom returned with his arms full of fine linen. He laid it upon the table and bowed, retreating as swiftly as he had arrived. Mistress Anne Boleyn sat amongst her ladies, a triumphant queen in waiting, and embroidered the collar and cuffs with purposeful hands. I watched her stitching her claim with every thrust of the needle. *She will rule*, I thought to myself. *And woe betide anyone who stands in her way.*

On St Andrew's Day in November 1529 Mistress Boleyn sat beside the fireplace in her apartments. She was reading verses aloud to Lady Rochford and polishing the tones of her French. On that cold winter's evening, the fire roared in the hearth and the tapestries depicting mythic hunts rippled gently in the draught. Her apartments glowed with warmth and taste and the heady scent of ambergris and rose oil hung in the air.

King Henry arrived unannounced at the door. He was wearing a fox-lined cloak thrown hastily over his doublet of black velvet, embroidered with gold thread in the pattern of Tudor roses. His collar sat askew, the rubies at his throat dulled by the pallor of his skin. Beneath the heavy fur, his posture was collapsed and weary, as though the weight of court and conscience pressed into his bones.

Mistress Boleyn rose swiftly from her cushioned chair. Her gown of deep russet silk glimmered in the firelight, tight-laced and daring, the sleeves slashed to reveal pale gauze beneath. Pearls danced in her hair, braided into dark coils that crowned her like a diadem.

"Whatever is the matter, Henry?" she asked. "Are you ill?"

He dropped into the nearest seat with a breath that sounded more curse than sigh. "It is no wonder if I am ill," he replied, sullen and sharp. "I went to dine with Queen Catherine this evening. It was a gracious gesture on my part—for I am not obliged to visit her at all."

I exchanged a glance with Lady Rochford. We had heard whispers of the Queen's defiance, but few of us expected the King to admit such a blow so plainly.

"But she was not in the least grateful to me for my consideration," he said, his voice rising like a storm gathering its wind. "She offered me no warmth nor thanks for my kindness."

"What happened?" she asked, her eyes narrowing, the flicker of firelight sharpening the amber in her gaze.

"She complained that I had treated her very badly by neglecting to visit her and dine with her and she was suffering the pains of Purgatory on earth," he said. "I explained that I was much occupied with affairs of state since the downfall of the Cardinal, but she paid me no heed. So, I told her that she ought to know by now that I was not her legitimate husband as many theologians, including my own almoner Doctor Lee, were ready to maintain."

"Very true," remarked Mistress Boleyn.

"But she declared that did not care a straw for Doctor Lee's opinion since it was a matter for the Pope to decide," he said. "She insisted that for every theologian who decided in my favour, she would find a thousand to declare that our marriage is good and indissoluble. She is an impossible woman!"

"I have told you so for the past two years," she said.

"Anyway, I said that if the Pope failed to declare our marriage null and void, I would denounce him as a heretic and marry whom I pleased," he said. "I was so upset by her obstinacy that I could not eat a single morsel and so I took my leave of her."

Mistress Boleyn looked at him scornfully. "Didn't I tell you not to dispute with the Queen for she was sure to gain the upper hand?" she retorted. "I see that one fine day you will succumb to her reasoning and cast me off!"

"Nay, sweetheart," he protested. "I would never do such a thing!"

"I have waited long for you to keep your promise," she said. "By now I might have made a good marriage and borne children for my consolation. But I have wasted my time and youth to no purpose at all!"

"How can you say such a thing?" he replied. "I am your truelove and you are mine. There will never be anyone else for either of us."

"So, you keep saying, but what are you doing about it?" she said. "The Queen will never let you go and I am despised by everyone. When will we be married, Henry? Why can't you find a way?"

"I swear I shall make you my wife and my Queen," he declared. "You must trust me, my love. I promise that will not let you down!"

I marvelled to hear the tempestuous way in which Lady Boleyn spoke to the King. But her imperious manner did not lessen his desire. It only stoked the fires of his love for her.

The King made it up to his beloved by granting her a title. "I will have no-one hold you in disdain, my love," he declared. "I am creating your father the earl of Wiltshire. So, you will become Lady Anne Boleyn. It will show the world my regard for you!"

"Lady Anne Boleyn," she said. "It sounds very well!"

"Moreover, I have decided to turn York Place into a royal residence," he said. "I will name it Whitehall and it shall be our very own palace."

"It is a splendid idea, Henry," she said. "How I have longed to live with you in our own house away from the Queen and her gloomy Spanish ladies."

"I intend to grant all the desires of your heart," he said. "You shall see what it means to be loved by a King!"

The King celebrated the ennoblement of Lord Wiltshire with a splendid banquet in the Great Hall. Naturally, Queen Catherine of Aragon refused to attend an occasion which honoured the family of her rival. However, all the other great noblewomen of the court were present including the King's sister Mary, the duchess of Suffolk, the dowager duchess of Norfolk and the marchioness of Exeter. All of them eyed the empty chair of estate next to the King. Each of them was ready to claim their right of precedence.

"Come, my love," said the King to Lady Anne Boleyn. "You shall sit beside me!"

I had stood behind her chair before, but never when it was the Queen's chair. I could hardly breathe as I watched Lady Boleyn settle herself into the seat that belonged to a crowned queen. A hush swept through the hall, a brief moment where the conversation faltered and the heavy silver goblets clattered upon the table. It was the duchess of Suffolk who stiffened first, her hand tightening over the stem of her cup as though she might crush it. This was no small slight. The duchess of Suffolk was a royal Tudor lady who outranked everyone here—but tonight, the King had made his meaning clear. Lady Boleyn was to be honoured above all.

"I give you a toast," he said to the company. "To my good friends, Lord and Lady Wiltshire. I wish them both good health and prosperity!"

The dowager duchess of Norfolk muttered something beneath her breath, too low for me to catch, but I saw the way her eyes burned as she watched Lady Boleyn lift her goblet to the King's toast. I had served long enough to recognize the quiet daggers hidden behind polite smiles—the way noble women wielded their offense like weapons, disguised behind murmured courtesies. Throughout the banquet the duchess of Suffolk sat sullenly in her place and refused to eat a thing. Even without words, the air was charged with quiet resentment. Finally, the dishes were cleared away and the musicians entered. It was the sign for the dancing to begin. But the King's sister was in no mood for merriment. She made her way to the King's side to express her seething resentment.

"I never thought you would treat me with such disrespect!" she spat. "I am your own sister and the former Queen of France. And yet you set me at naught while you raise the daughter of a knight above me!"

"I am the King and I will give honour where it is due," he replied.

"Your Majesty must excuse me if I do not attend the court in future," she declared. "I have no wish to see the unworthy set on high above their betters."

"You have my good leave to go, Mary," he replied.

"You shall never see me again, Henry," she retorted. "Your

wife, Queen Catherine, has my sympathy. She is a much abused lady!"

The King's eyes burned with anger as his sister flounced out of the hall. "Strike up a measure," he called to the players. "Lady Boleyn wishes to dance." I knew that this night would be spoken of for years to come.

The King showed his regard for Lady Anne Boleyn by enlarging her household. Several ladies were transferred from the service of Queen Catherine to serve her. Among them was my old friend, Margery Horsman. I was pleased to see her again and she was glad to enter the service of the King's favourite. Her stylish dress made her stand out among the maids of honour. She soon contrived to gain the notice of her new mistress.

"Let me see those embroidered sleeves of yours, Mistress Horsman," said Lady Boleyn. "Is this one of the new patterns from France?"

"The stitch is mine, but the motif is French, my lady," she said. "The knotted cords speak of constancy in love. I hear that the ladies of the French court favour the use of allegory. Flaming hearts, crowned serpents and intertwining vines express the language of courtly love."

"Yes, I have seen such devices when I served in the household of Queen Claude," she said. "It is time that they were popularised here at the English court."

"The courtiers of France wear such symbols boldly, my lady," she said. "Both men and women flaunt them upon their sleeves. It's the fashion to be seen as both virtuous and mysterious."

"Virtue laced with mystery," she mused. "What a delightful conceit. I have plans for a new wardrobe for Christmas. What symbols would you propose for my gowns?"

"There is the rose for love and beauty, my lady," she replied promptly. "Oak leaves and acorns for strength and endurance. And ivy leaves for fidelity and eternal love as it clings and endures."

"Such emblems are far too commonplace," she said. "I shall require a much bolder theme for my dress."

"Then I would suggest suns, moons and stars, my lady," she said. "They represent destiny and good fortune."

"A design of silver moons and stars embroidered upon a gown of white satin would suit me well," she said. "It shall signify that just as the King is the bright sun, I am the radiant moon."

"Yes indeed, my lady," she agreed. "You shall appear as the glorious Queen of the Night."

"And I shall require a pair of new sleeves," she said. "I have heard that in France, they now wear them slashed to reveal a coloured under-lining."

"It is the latest style among the most fashionable members of the court, my lady," she said. "It creates the illusion of petals blooming. I suggest a combination of night-blue damask and silver tissue. It draws the eyes without seeming gaudy."

"I see that you have a good understanding of matters of dress, Mistress Horsman," she remarked. "I shall send for the tailor and commission this design at once. It will make a splendid impression. The King shall see the court move where I move."

"The Queen of France herself could not parade herself with more splendour, my lady," she replied.

"Then I shall be France to his England," she said. "My wardrobe shall demonstrate my purpose to the world. I shall be adorned with stars and moons, flaming hearts and a crown."

At Christmas that year, the King and Queen held court together beneath a golden canopy. The nobles and courtiers mingled in their presence like chessmen in a gilded game. But all heads turned as Lady Anne Boleyn entered the Great Hall of Greenwich. She wore a gown of white satin that shimmered like moonlight on still water. Silver thread wove a cascade of crescent moons and six-pointed stars across her skirts and bodice. Tiny seed pearls trace their edges, catching the torchlight with every movement. A silver girdle wound like a constellation at her waist. Her veil trailed behind her like a wisp of cloud, her French hood set daringly low. A gasp of admiration arose from the assembled company and a host of whispers erupted:

She makes herself the moon and implies that His Majesty is the sun. She means for us to see it!

King Henry wore a doublet and hose of tawny velvet striped with threads of Venice gold. Around his neck was a gold collar set with rich jewels. He gazed at his beloved Anne like a man possessed. Queen Catherine of Aragon wore a Spanish hood and a gown of heavy crimson velvet with a high square neckline, adorned only by a plain cross at her throat. Her hands were still and folded in her lap. Only her eyes betrayed the storm within. The court held its breath. Lady Boleyn approached their Majesties to make her curtsy. The fabric of her gown rustled like the wings of a swan. Her eyes met the Queen's for the briefest instant—cool, composed and unreadable.

"Lady Boleyn, how brightly you shine this evening," she remarked. "You must take care not to outshine the heavens themselves."

"Your Majesty is ever gracious," she replied. "I seek only to reflect His Majesty's splendour."

"But the moon may forget that it has no light of its own," she said. "Its lustre is merely borrowed and its glory soon passes away."

A murmur stirred through the court like the wind through the reeds. The ladies eyed each other with equal intensity. Finally, the King broke through the tension in the hall.

"Since Lady Moon is fair but transient, we should make the most of the opportunity to bask in her beauty," he declared. "She is the finest ornament of our court!"

The courtiers applauded his wit. The King beamed with pleasure and Lady Boleyn gazed at Queen Catherine in triumph. Her bold ploy had succeeded just as she had intended. She had announced to the court her intention to take the Queen's place.

Now Lady Boleyn reigned supreme at court. But her arrogance had made her many enemies at court. They resented her presumption in taking the place of the rightful Queen. One afternoon she found a strange drawing lying upon her pillow. It showed three figures labelled with the letters H, K and A. She showed it to Nan.

"Someone has sent me a warning," she said. "Here is the King, this the Queen, weeping and wringing her hands, and this is myself with my head off. It foretells my certain destruction if I marry the King."

She recoiled from the dreadful image. "If I thought it were true, then I would not marry him though he were an emperor, my lady," she replied.

"I think the book a bauble," she said. "Yet for the sake of the children that I will bear, I am resolved to have him whatsoever may become of me."

"Who would do such a thing, my lady?" she asked.

"Some agent of the Spanish ambassador or the Queen, no doubt," she said. "They think they can frighten me away but I am no so easily daunted."

I had my doubts that the prophecy was the work of the Spanish ambassador or a member of the Queen's household. How would they gain access to her bedchamber? Her chamberers were questioned and they vehemently protested their innocence. I cast my mind back to the events of that morning. The only unexpected visitor had been Lady Mary Carey who had brought a book of poetry as a gift. That had surprised me because I knew that there was no love lost between the sisters.

"Nan, what happened to that book of poetry?" I asked.

"Lady Carey took it into the bedchamber," she said. "She said that she wanted it to be a surprise for her sister."

It would have been easy to conceal the paper inside a book and then leave it on the counterpane. But no-one would have believed that she would try to warn her sister against marrying the King. I shared my suspicions with no-one.

In November 1530 the King discovered that Cardinal Wolsey had been intriguing with the Pope and the emperor. He signed a warrant for his arrest on the charge of treason. He sent it to Henry Percy, earl of Northumberland, who was instructed to conduct him to the Tower of London. Everyone wondered if the King intended to execute him. On the last day of December, a messenger brought the news of the death of the Cardinal to the King. He had died at Leicester Abbey on his way to London. The King was grieved by the death of his once beloved friend and confidante. If he had intended to grant him a pardon, he had left it too late to make the gesture. But Lady Boleyn rejoiced in the downfall of her enemy. She sent for the Master of the Revels to attend her at once. At New Year she celebrated his demise with a masque entitled: *Sending the Cardinal to Hell.*

The Cardinal's effigy was brought out, clothed in the deep scarlet of his office, his gilded cross swinging against his chest. A mockery of Wolsey himself, his expression drawn in exaggerated arrogance with heavy theatrical paint. Then, with a sudden rush, the demons descended upon him - four shadowy figures clad in jet-black, their faces obscured by devilish masks with gaping mouths and glaring eyes. The crowd gasped, then shrieked with delight as the demons set upon him with ruthless abandon. One seized his silken sleeves and twisted them tight, forcing him to bow as if in supplication. Another cuffed his ears, making his powdered wig tilt absurdly atop his head. The third dragged him backward, clawing at his robes and tearing them to tatters. And the fourth, with a triumphant howl, snatched the cross from his neck and flung it into the flames.

Lady Boleyn laughed, her eyes flashing with unrestrained pleasure, clapping her hands in time to the torment. She delighted in the spectacle, watching as Wolsey—her great enemy—was dragged, flailing and tossing, toward the gaping maw of Hell painted upon the stage. The demons tossed him bodily through the fiery threshold, disappearing behind the red velvet curtain as the audience erupted into cheers. Lady Boleyn applauded the masque gleefully. But the King remained stony-faced and did not join in the merriment of the court. He considered it unseemly to deride the memory of such a great man. It reminded me that no-one at court was too high to fall. And once fallen, there would be no mercy.

In Jan 1531 King Henry came storming into Lady Anne's privy chamber waving a document in his fist. His cheeks were flushed and his eyes burned with anger. "Look at this letter!" he bellowed. "The Pope has ordered me to put you aside. He says that if I remarry, I will be excommunicated. I know that Catherine has put him up to this!"

"Of course she has," she replied scornfully. "Didn't I say that one day she would persuade you to abandon me?"

"I shall marry you regardless of his decisions," he insisted. "I have lost patience with his underhanded dealings. And I will not be threatened or coerced by a Pope who is in the pocket of Spain!"

"The Pope is only the Bishop of Rome," she said. "He has no right to interfere in your realm. You are the King and you alone should be recognised as the head of the church in England."

"That is right," he replied. "I am the Lord's anointed sovereign and my authority should not be restrained by any popish laws or decrees. I shall order Convocation to grant me the title of Supreme Head of the Church in England. That will put the high and mighty Bishop of Rome in his place!"

"Let us take a cup of wine," she said. "We shall drink to your exaltation and to his disgrace!"

"Down with the Pope!" he declared. "I swear that he shall never frustrate me again!"

"Glory to King Henry VIII, Defender of the Faith and Supreme Head of the Church," she replied.

Bishop Fisher and several other clergymen protested that only Christ could be head of the church. So Master Cromwell, the former lawyer to the Cardinal, suggested a compromise by adding the phrase *"so far as the law of Christ allows."* Convocation agreed to grant the King the title of Supreme Head of the Church in England. King Henry proclaimed that the Pope should now be referred to as the Bishop of Rome.

King Henry had settled his score with the Pope, but he did not have his annulment. He was still bound to Queen Catherine as his wife. In July 1531 he finally took matters into his own hands. He set out on his summer progress in the company of Lady Boleyn and left the Queen behind at Windsor. He left orders that she was to move her household to The More before he returned. The Queen sent a rider after the king to bring him a message.

King Henry read the message and then tore it up in a rage. "The audacity of that woman!" he declared.

"What does she want?" asked Lady Boleyn coldly.

"She says that she regrets that she was not able to bid me farewell," he said. "As if I have any wish to speak to her after her obstinate refusals. She has caused me annoyance and sorrow in a thousand ways. I shall make no more pretence at amity but treat her with the harshness she deserves!"

"You, Master Messenger," he snapped. "Ride back to your mistress. Say that I care not for her adieux. And tell her that I forbid her to send me any further messages or visitors!"

"Yes, your Grace," he replied. He turned his horse around and galloped away as fast as he could.

The King watched him depart in a seething temper. "She is determined to defy me to the uttermost!" he muttered. "But I shall brook her defiance no longer. I shall never live with her again!"

"You should have broken with her long ago," said Lady Boleyn. "You see how she delights to trouble us and spoil our pleasure. Let her abide in her own household from now on."

"Indeed, she shall disturb us no more," he said. "I am the King and she is my subject. She shall dwell apart in her own residence. She is not my wife and I have no desire to see her ever again!"

In August 1531 Queen Catherine moved to The More and her household was reduced. Several of her ladies were transferred to the service of Mistress Anne Boleyn including Mistress Jane Seymour. She was the eldest daughter of Sir John Seymour. She had gained a place at court as a favour to her father. But she was unremarkable for her beauty or accomplishments and her timidity greatly irritated Mistress Anne. She complained loudly that some of her ladies were unfit for service in the house of a city merchant let alone the royal household. In fact, they ought to seek employment as a gentlewoman spinster in a sewing room of a convent. Mistress Jane made no complaint but bowed her head and accepted it all. She knew that she could not compete for notice in a circle dominated by such accomplished ladies. She focused upon the needlework at which she excelled and made herself indispensable to the mother of the maids.

CHAPTER 4

The Courtier (1531)

"The most noble and pleasing treasure in this world is a woman of noble rank who is beautiful, young, chaste and well-mannered"

(Anne de Beaujeu, *Lessons for my Daughter,* 1497).

I remember the first time I saw Sir Edward Seymour. It was at one of Lady Boleyn's soirées. She liked the handsome young men to come and pay their court to her as if we were still living in the age of chivalry. For some reason she to a dislike to him. Perhaps it was because he was Jane's brother. Or perhaps because he was not captivated by her charms.

"A paltry knight's son," she said dismissively despite the fact that she herself was the daughter of a knight.

But there was something about him that impressed me. He did not fawn upon Lady Boleyn like the other young gallants. He had a dispassionate air and a calculating look in his eyes. He studied the court just as closely as I did and yet he did not wear that scrutiny like a mask. There was no artifice in his posture, no borrowed charm in his smile. He held himself with quiet confidence despite his lack of high rank. He spoke little, which was rare in a court that prized wit above substance. But when he did speak, it was with economy and intent. His restraint was a rare and admirable quality. The most powerful men were not those who boasted, but those who watched and waited. I remember thinking: *This is a man who will rise in the court.*

That Christmas it was the turn of Lady Boleyn to preside over the court festivities. She remembered the grand reception at which the Princess Mary had been presented to the French envoys. She wanted to be the focus of an equally memorable display. She sent for the Master of the Revels.

"Master Cornish, His Majesty wishes to celebrate the occasion with good cheer," she said. "There shall be no more of these tiresome moral dialogues. Instead, there shall be masques and revels on the theme of courtly love. My ladies and I will take part and dance for his pleasure. I would like to hear your proposals."

"His Majesty is most partial to the gallant tales of King Arthur and his knights, my lady," he suggested.

"And would you have me play the role of the faithless Guinevere?" she retorted. "Suggest something else!"

"Yes, my lady," he replied. "There are many heroic stories in the Greek myths. What about the famous romance between Paris of Troy and Helen of Sparta?"

"That ended in disaster," she snapped. "I am talking about a romance, not a tragedy!"

"Of course, my lady," he said, looking flustered. "Perhaps you would prefer the myth of Perseus and Ariadne."

She narrowed her eyes. "What are you trying to insinuate, you fool?" she demanded. "That one day I shall be deceived and abandoned?"

"No, no, my lady," he stammered. "Perhaps a Biblical story would better suit your purpose. The romance of Boaz and Ruth is a most edifying tale."

She frowned at the idea. I could see that she did not relish the reminder of her own humble origins. He might as well have suggested King Cophetua and the Beggar Maid.

"It is too simple a tale for a masque," she replied. "We shall present the arrival of the Queen of Sheba at the court of King Solomon. It is a most devout theme and suitable for the Christmas season."

"Yes, my lady," he replied.

"I shall play the Queen of Sheba dressed in a magnificent robe," she announced, her eyes glittering. "My ladies shall follow me in a great train. The court musicians will be garbed like the Magi of the East. I shall give a speech in praise of the King's wisdom and then we shall dance before him for his pleasure."

"I am sure that His Majesty will be most astonished," he replied.

"That is my intention," she said. "It will provide a great spectacle to impress the foreign ambassadors and the King's distinguished guests."

Lady Boleyn commissioned a splendid gown of crimson cloth of gold and her ladies wore gowns of white satin. We practiced our dances for hours before she was satisfied.

The Great Hall blazed with torches, the polished floor gleaming beneath our slippered feet. We stood in perfect formation, our gowns of white satin whispering as we shifted in anticipation. The scent of evergreen and frankincense clung to the air, mingling with the subtle, heady perfume Lady Boleyn had chosen for the evening.

I dared not move as the trumpets sounded, announcing our entrance. At the head of our train, Lady Boleyn stood resplendent, her crimson robe glimmering with gold embroidery that caught the light like flames. She had styled herself magnificently, her jewels rivalled the offerings of the Magi, and when she stepped forward, it was with the slow, measured grace of a queen who expected the world to bow.

The court musicians, dressed as Eastern sages, struck up a melody of lilting, foreign tones, and we followed her in solemn procession, advancing towards the dais where His Majesty sat in regal splendour. The foreign ambassadors sat upon chairs beside him, their eyes fixed upon our spectacle. Lady Boleyn halted her procession before the throne. Her gaze swept across the assembled court before settling on the King. She stepped forward with regal poise and swept into her prepared speech.

"Most wise and noble King, sovereign over hearts and minds alike, I stand before you as the Queen of Sheba stood before Solomon, drawn by the brilliance of your wisdom, the magnificence of your reign. In distant lands, men speak in hushed awe of your judgment, your prowess, your unparalleled grace—for truly, none among rulers rival your majesty. I bring no gold nor spices, no ivory nor gemstones, for England is already rich beyond measure

under your guiding hand. Instead, I offer devotion, loyalty, and the tribute of those who serve you with unwavering faith. May this evening's spectacle be but a mirror of the glory that flourishes in your court, the radiance of your power reflected in every step we take, in every note of music that graces your ears."

She inclined her head, her jewelled gown glimmering like firelight as she completed her declaration. The court held its breath awaiting the King's response. He leaned forward on his chair of estate with a look of great satisfaction on his face. He allowed a measured pause, letting the weight of her words settle upon the gathered court before replying.

"You speak with great eloquence, my lady," he said, his voice carrying through the hall, rich and commanding. "If Solomon was honoured by the visit of the Queen of Sheba, then I am no less honoured by yours. You bring a spectacle most pleasing to mine eyes, and a tribute well suited to the season."

A murmur of approval rippled through the courtiers. Lady Boleyn dipped into a graceful curtsy, satisfaction glinting in her gaze.

"Your Majesty is most gracious," she replied smoothly. "It is but a small reflection of the magnificence of your reign."

The King nodded, a faint smile touching his lips. "Then let the revels continue."

With that pronouncement, the musicians struck up an exotic Eastern rhythm and the masque unfolded in full. Lady Boleyn commanded the space as though she were the Queen of Sheba in truth and not merely in play. The dance wove a story of the admiration and honour of a great Queen for an even greater

King. She glided along as though borne on the air itself, her rich robe trailing behind her like a tide of molten gold and crimson. Her movements were deliberate, each step a display of regal control. With a slow turn, she raised her arms, The torchlight flickered upon the embroidery of her opulent gown and the rings that flashed like captured stars upon her outstretched fingers. Then the tempo shifted. She twirled, her skirts flaring in perfect symmetry, her ladies mirroring her steps in disciplined unison. She swept forward, lowering herself briefly in reverence to the King before rising again, her form poised and commanding. The music soared, and she led her ladies in a cascading sequence of spins and flourishes, our white satin gowns fanning out like petals in a winter breeze. As the last note hung in the air we sank into our final pose of obeisance before the King.

There was a moment of silence and then the court erupted in applause rolling like thunder across the hall. The King smiled in appreciation of her tribute. Lady Boleyn had achieved her triumph. She had transformed the dance into something more than mere entertainment. It was a testament to her power, her place, and her mastery over the art of illusion. And we, her ladies, were part of the spectacle that ensured her glory.

The King arose and came forward to greet her. "Now it is the turn of King Solomon to dance with the Queen of Sheba," he declared. "Come forward my lords and claim a dance with the lady of your choice. Show these fair ladies of Sheba the nobility and gallantry of our court!"

The musicians struck up the melody of a familiar pavane and the gentlemen hurried over to take themselves a partner. In the midst of the chaos, I found a familiar figure standing at my side.

"Sir Edward Seymour, at your service," he said with a faint smile, extending his hand. "Pray allow me the honour of this dance."

I took his hand, feeling the strength and steadiness in his grip. There was something reassuring about him, something solid and dependable. He had the confidence and skill of a courtier and performed the dance with easy grace. At the end of the measure, he showed no desire to surrender me to another partner. We danced three pavanes in succession.

"You dance superbly, Mistress Stanhope," he said. "It was a pleasure to see you performing in the festivities tonight."

"Thank you, Sir Edward," I replied, surprised by how easily the words came. "It was an honour to take part in the court masque. I had seen you before, but I haven't had the pleasure of meeting you until now."

"Then let me remedy that," he said. "This is the perfect opportunity for us to get to know each other better.

When he offered me his arm, I accepted without hesitation, and we moved toward the hearth where others had gathered. As the evening unfolded, I found myself surprised by how Edward Seymour could hold both gravity and warmth in his demeanour. He seemed a man of purpose, yet not without a sense of humour—a rarity among the ambitious men of court. The festivities continued late into the night, the spirit of Christmas warm and encompassing. I returned to my chamber that night with thoughts of him lingering in my mind. Time would reveal the truth of the connection, but for now, the night had been ours.

The following morning, I sought out Jane Seymour. "Tell me about your brother," I said.

"Which one?" she asked owlishly.

"Your eldest brother," I said impatiently.

"Sir Edward is an Esquire of the Body to the King," she said proudly. "He is married to Catherine Fillol, but she never comes to court. She lives with my parents at Wulf Hall and takes care of her two sons."

So, he was a married man. I put him out of my mind. The following year he disappeared from court for a time. I assumed he had to attend to some family business. But I did not know how scandalous it was. It was Lady Boleyn who enlightened me. She knew the gossip before anyone else.

"Sir Edward Seymour has gone home to Wulf Hall," she smirked. "He has sent his wife to a nunnery for her lewd conduct. She took a lover while he was away fighting in France. And not just anyone. It is said that it was his own father. I swear there will be thunderstorms at Wulf Hall over this! I doubt that we shall see his face at court again!"

I was certain that she was right. There was nothing that the court relished more than lurid scandals. It was a terrible humiliation for such a proud man. But Sir Edward was not the sort to be undone by the conduct of an unworthy wife. He resumed his duties as Esquire of the Body and seemed indifferent to his disgrace. He petitioned the King for permission to disown his two sons since he could not be certain of their paternity. The King readily granted his suit.

"You have our sympathy, Sir Edward," he said. "You deserve to have a worthier wife than the one you have now."

But although they were separated, there was no possibility of annulling the marriage. *It is a shame that such a fine man should be tied to an unfaithful wife,* I thought.

In September 1532, a rumour spread like fire through the palace corridors: the King had decided to seek the support of the French King for his divorce. He planned to make a grand state visit to France and he would not go alone. Lady Boleyn was going to accompany him, not as a mere mistress, but as his consort-in-waiting. The court buzzed with gossip and speculation. It was no ordinary journey. It was a declaration of intent.

"I shall present you to the King of France and the occasion will outshine the glory of the Field of the Cloth of Gold," he said. "Once he has recognised you, then the rest of Europe will follow."

"But will he agree to meet with me?" she asked.

"Yes, for I have decided to ennoble you," he said. "You shall have the title of Marquess of Pembroke and the income and estates to support you in that honour."

"Marquess of Pembroke," she repeated. "It sounds very well. I shall require a wardrobe and jewels that are worthy of the court of France."

"You shall have everything that you desire, my love," he said.

"If I am to meet the King of France as your consort then I ought to wear the jewels of the Queen of England," she said.

"You shall have them," he said. "Catherine has no further need of them. I shall send for them at once."

But the messenger returned empty handed. "She has refused," he said. "She says she will not give them to someone who is the scandal of Christendom."

"How dare she abuse me?" she cried. "You see how poisonous she is and how she denounces me at every opportunity!"

"I will send her my express command," said the King. "She will not dare to defy my wishes!"

Queen Catherine submitted to the King's order and surrendered her jewels. However, Lady Boleyn's victory was soured by the news from France. King Francis regretted that neither his wife nor his sister was prepared to receive Lady Boleyn, even if she did have the rank of a marquess. He proposed that his *maitresse-en-titre* should welcome her to court instead. Lady Boleyn was enraged by the suggestion.

"How dare he suggest that I meet his mistress," she stormed. "The duchess of Vendome is a notorious woman. He means it as an insult to me!"

"It is the fault of the Queen of France," said King Henry. You know that she is a Spaniard. I have no wish to set eyes on her either."

"You had better go to France on your own," she pouted. "I can see that they intend to humiliate me."

"You shall accompany me and I shall see that you are treated with great honour," he insisted. "King Francis knows better than to let his women dictate his foreign policy."

But the French ladies stood firm in their refusal to condone such a breach of etiquette. It was impossible for Lady Boleyn to make an official state visit. In the circumstances, King Henry decided not to go to the French court. It was agreed that he would go to meet the French King at Boulogne and then King Francis would make a return visit to Calais. Lady Boleyn would be presented to him there.

King Henry hosted a grand banquet in honour of King Francis at the Staple Inn. The Great Hall was adorned with tapestries depicting the Trojan War. The torchlight illuminated the rows of gold and silver vessels displayed upon the cupboards. The banners of England and France flanked the chairs of estate. The air was thick with the scent of rosemary, sweet wine, and anticipation. I stood among the ladies-in-waiting, our silk sleeves rustling as we watched the French King laugh at one of Suffolk's witticisms. King Henry, flushed with triumph, played host to his brother monarch with the exuberance of a man who believed God smiled upon his cause. His laughter rang through the candlelit hall, bold and unguarded, his gestures wide as he toasted Francis across a table set with jewelled goblets and imported delicacies—spiced pheasants, sweetmeats shaped like roses, wine so dark it looked like spilled blood. The two kings embraced as brothers, but the truth shimmered between them like heat above flame: this was politics dressed as friendship. Henry wore red and gold, his doublet heavy with heraldic lions and crowned Tudor roses. Francis was more refined in blue velvet embroidered with silver *fleur de lis*. But it was not Henry or Francis that the courtiers watched—it was Anne.

She made her entrance with the confidence of an empress. Her gown was scandalous and glorious: cloth of gold slashed with crimson tinsel, the bodice scalloped with pearls, her kirtle stiff with gold lace, her sleeves trailing like banners. Her hair was coiled high and adorned with spangles set with opals. Her face was concealed behind a gold mask inlaid with diamonds and rubies. She did not pause at the threshold; she advanced, slow and deliberate. All conversation thinned to whispers. Even the French courtiers, so accustomed to elegance, leaned forward in their seats. Francis smiled, polite and appraising. Henry's gaze was fixed, almost possessive, as if willing her presence to declare the legitimacy Rome had denied. It was not merely her beauty they admired. It was her audacity in presenting herself before the monarchs as their equal.

She stepped before the kings, curtsied with measured grace, and turned as the masquers entered behind her. Eight ladies dressed in flowing raiment, their costumes echoing ancient goddesses, followed her lead. I was robed as Athena in a helmet-shaped headdress pinned with a diamond star. We performed a stately routine to the strains of viol and recorder, moving between the tables in steps rehearsed for weeks. The scent of clove oranges and wine filled the air as we weaved through the candlelight like myths reborn. When the dance ended, the monarchs applauded. Lady Boleyn curtsied low, her gaze never leaving the French King's face, and then gestured for the goddesses to take partners from among the gentlemen. She bowed—neither too low, nor too proudly—and offered Francis her hand. He hesitated, just briefly, before taking it. I felt the weight of the moment in which the royal mistress was acknowledged by the French King. His visit to Calais had become her triumph.

As the music began, they stepped into the dance together, a slow pavane that turned the banquet hall into a theatre of diplomacy. I watched Lady Boleyn draw King Francis into conversation and the way she leaned in—head tilted, voice soft but deliberate—was not the gesture of a lady entertaining a monarch, but of a woman weighing her chances against centuries of precedent. She spoke in French, of course, her words smooth as the silk of her gown, and her smile just wide enough to charm, not provoke. Francis responded with courtly grace, his eyes flickering towards Henry, as if to measure how far he could indulge her audacity. When the music ended, Francis bowed with faultless grace. Lady Boleyn curtsied again, this time just a shade deeper. Her eyes held his for one heartbeat longer than protocol allowed.

"Let the ladies take off their masks," said King Henry. "Allow these worthy gentlemen to see the beauty of their partners."

Lady Boleyn removed her visor and smiled. King Francis took her hand and kissed it. "So, this is the beautiful Lady Pembroke," he said. "You dance most delightfully."

"I learned my skills at the French court, your Majesty," she replied. "Let us take a cup of wine together."

King Francis was captivated by her charms and threw protocol to the wind. "It would be my pleasure, my lady," he replied.

Lady Boleyn sat beside the French King and smiled serenely at the company. The French ladies may have scorned her, but she had outwitted them. They would be furious when they heard that King Francis had treated her with such honour. As they conversed, I studied Francis's retinue. Some looked amused. Some looked sceptical. One or two looked scandalised. But none of them were blind. They saw what this was: a bid to legitimise her, cloaked in revelry.

On 12th November 1532 King Henry and Lady Boleyn sailed back to Dover in triumph. He was convinced that the visit had been a success and King Francis would support his cause to the Pope. They were certain that their heart's desire was now close at hand. The sea was iron-grey, restless beneath the slate-coloured sky, but the royal flagship cut through it like a blade through silk. Pennants snapped in the wind—crimson and gold, the colours of triumph—and from the prow fluttered Henry's standard, a lion rampant glinting wet in the morning light. Dover's cliffs loomed ahead, chalk-white and resolute, as if England herself had been waiting for her sovereign's return.

King Henry stood at the helm, his cloak billowing around him, the salt wind reddening his cheeks and catching the edge of his feathered cap. He laughed as he recounted the grandeur of Calais, the obeisance of Francis, and the masque that had set tongues wagging across courts. In his eyes, it had been a coronation in all but name. The Pope's resistance was a paper fortress now, ready to be swept away by the tide of his royal will.

Lady Boleyn remained at his side, her face veiled, though the shape of her smile was unmistakable. She wore a gown of sapphire velvet, its sleeves embroidered with Tudor roses, and her hair was bound with gold ribbon that gleamed like conquest. She did not speak often, but when she did, Henry leaned closer, as if her words carried the weight of divine approval. Some said her hand brushed his when no-one watched. Others said she no longer cared if they did.

"Are you happy, my dear?" he asked.

"I am the happiest of women," she replied. "I am sure that King Francis will stand as our friend and acknowledge me as your true wife and your lawful Queen."

As the barge neared the port, trumpets sounded from the cliffs, and men-at-arms lined the dock in perfect formation. The crowd gathered despite the cold, craning for a glimpse of the woman who would wear roses not as decoration, but as claim. King Henry turned to Lady Boleyn then, clasping her hand with theatrical solemnity, and she—never one to squander a moment—inclined her head like majesty answering its call.

The Christmas season of 1532 was celebrated with great joy at the court. The galleries of Greenwich Palace were strung with evergreen and holly, the courtiers feasted on platters of roasted swan and gilded marchpane and the musicians played from morning to midnight. On New Year's Day, I watched King Henry stride into the Presence Chamber. He was dressed in crimson velvet trimmed with ermine and his mood was buoyant. He had sent Lady Boleyn a set of costly hangings made of cloth of gold and crimson satin for her apartments.

When she entered, the hush that followed her was almost reverent. She wore a gown of crimson cloth of gold to match the hangings, the bodice stiff with pearls, the train trailing behind her like a queen. She presented him with a set of boar spears—

richly decorated, their shafts carved with hunting scenes, the blades etched with Tudor roses and French fleur-de-lis. A bold gift. A martial one. He laughed as he received them, loud and delighted, and bent to kiss her hand with fervour.

The courtiers drank toasts and exchanged merry greetings. It was then that Queen Catherine's messenger arrived. He stepped forward, bowed deeply and offered the King a gold cup of exquisite craftsmanship. Lady Boleyn looked at Catherine's cup as if it were a ghost. King Henry stared at it as though it had offended him personally. His smile vanished.

"We are not husband and wife," he said, loud enough to halt the conversation among the courtiers. "And it is not seemly that we should exchange gifts."

The messenger paled. He began to speak, but Henry turned sharply. "Take it back," he snapped, then gestured for a page to clear the space. I felt the weight of the moment settle around us. A sovereign had rejected his Queen not in parchment or decree, but in public ritual.

Twelfth Night was celebrated with a splendid banquet in the Great Hall at Greenwich. The final course of subtleties was served in the Presence Chamber so that the tables and benches could be cleared away. After the cups of sweet wine and the dishes of sugared fruit and wafers had been consumed, Master Cornish made an announcement to the court:

"Ladies, gentlemen and honourable guests," he said. "His Majesty bids you to return to the Great Hall and take your places for a masque entitled: *'An Allegory of the Romance of the Rose.'*"

At the back of the hall a dark castle bearing the image of a red and white rose had appeared. It was surrounded by a walled garden made of painted screens, but the gate was barred by a thick barrier of thorns. The courtiers murmured in anticipation as they assembled themselves to view the performance. I stood among the onlookers eagerly watching as the masque unfolded before us. I had never lost my taste for courtly entertainments. A group of trumpeters blew a fanfare and the King strode forward as the embodiment of Ardent Desire. He was resplendent in a doublet of scarlet velvet, embroidered with golden flames, as though his passion could scorch the very air. His purple cloak billowed as he moved, and his hat bore a jewelled plume—bold, imperious, a statement of conquest. I could not help but marvel at how well the role suited him.

His Majesty, sword drawn, laid waste to the barrier of thorns that blocked the entrance to the castle garden. The gate opened and the Guardian of the Castle Perilous strode forward to confront him. He was tall and broad-shouldered, his armour blackened with soot, as if he had stepped from the very forge of Mars. His dark helm bore a crest of twisted briars, and his voice rang out like a tolling bell as he stood before Ardent Desire. He raised his sword, the point levelled at his opponent, and declared:

"Halt, bold heart, and speak thy name!
Who dares approach the Castle Perilous,
Where Love is chained by ancient vow,
And thorns guard Beauty's sacred bower?
Turn back, lest steel and sorrow be thy prize!"

The hall held its breath, as His Majesty stepped into the challenge with the bearing of one born to triumph. He lifted his sword in salute, the torchlight glinting along its edge like fire caught in metal. His eyes, set with purpose, never left the dark figure of the Guardian. Then in a voice that filled the hall, he spoke the words of a true knight-errant:

"I am he whose heart knows no retreat,
Whose spirit scorns the bramble's barbs.
Ardent Desire, sworn to Love's command,
I come not to plead, but to prove.
Though shadows rise and steel be drawn,
I claim the right, by noble cause,
To cross thy gate and win the Rose."

He lowered his blade slightly, his gaze steady. Somewhere behind me a lady gasped with fear. The Guardian gave no reply, but advanced upon his challenger and the contest began. The clash of wood against steel rang through the hall as Ardent Desire vanquished his foe. The audience murmured their approval.

Through the gate stepped Anne Boleyn in the guise of Lady Virtue. Her gown was white, the fabric thick with pearls that caught the candlelight, turning her into some celestial vision. The damask train spilled over the stage, and at her throat gleamed the familiar pendant—the letter 'B' suspended on a delicate gold chain. She held her chin high, her gaze unflinching, as if she dared him to meet the trials of his quest.

Ardent Desire bowed and made a speech: "Lady Virtue, thou art the fairest rose that blooms beneath God's heaven," he declared, his voice rich and commanding. "I have overcome peril and doubt to defeat the barriers that kept me from thee. Boldness and courage are the banners beneath which I ride, and with them I claim thee as my own."

But Lady Virtue did not bow her head in submission. Her expression was unreadable, the flicker of a smile playing at her lips. When she spoke, her voice was cool and measured.

"Boldness and courage, my lord, are worthy virtues indeed," she said, "but they alone do not win a woman's heart. A rose may be plucked with force, yet without tenderness, it wilts."

A murmur rippled through the watching courtiers. His Majesty stepped forward, a glimmer of amusement flashing in his eyes.

"Lady Virtue, thou dost test me still," he said, the flourish of his earlier proclamation tempered with sincerity. "I am no mere combatant, but a knight who seeks the honour of love. I have come not to compel, but to offer you marriage, devotion, and loyalty."

Her gaze lingered upon him. Then, slowly, she extended her hand. "My heart is won, gentle knight," she said. "Thou hast conquered it as surely as thou hast overcome the thorns."

The audience erupted in applause as he took her hand and pressed it to his lips. He took a ring from his hand and set it upon her finger. Lady Boleyn beamed in triumph. The mysterious figure of the Guardian got up from the floor. Then he removed his helm to reveal the grinning face of Charles Brandon. Everyone at court wondered whether the masque was just a performance. Or was it intended to reveal a hidden truth about the relationship between the King and his lady? It was a question not easily answered.

For the next two months the court buzzed with excitement and a succession of wild rumours circulated through the palace corridors. I heard a number of whispered stories claiming that the King had secretly married Lady Boleyn in Calais, in Dover or in the gatehouse of Whitehall Palace. Others insisted that they were not married but only betrothed. The foreign ambassadors promised substantial rewards in return for a genuine eyewitness account of the nuptials. But nobody dared to ask how the King could possibly marry again when he still had a wife and the Pope had refused to grant him an annulment.

I paid a discreet visit to my stepfather. "Several people have assured me that Lady Boleyn has married the King, but she isn't wearing a wedding ring," I said. "I don't know what to believe. Can you confirm if a wedding has taken place?"

"I have heard the same stories, but I don't know if any of them are true," he said. "Mind you, Henry Norris has been looking very smug lately. I think he knows something but he won't say a word."

I returned to Lady Boleyn's apartments and sought out Margery. "Did the Queen order a special wedding dress for herself?" I asked.

She shrugged her shoulders. "She took a whole wardrobe of finery over to Calais," she said. "She might have worn any of her gowns as a wedding dress. If there really was a wedding at all."

She pursed her lips and I realised that she would not tell me even if she knew. She was too astute to risk her position by betraying any confidences.

Finally, I took Nan aside and put the question to her. I knew that she was incapable of keeping a secret.

"Is it true?" I demanded. "Has she married the King?"

She blushed scarlet and bit her lip. "They were married last November at Dover," she admitted. "The wedding was conducted by his chaplain Dr Lee and I was one of their witnesses. But it is a most profound secret. You must swear not divulge it to anyone!"

"How did the King persuade his chaplain to perform the marriage?" I asked.

"He swore that he had a licence from the Pope in his chambers at Whitehall," she said. "He commanded him to perform his office without any further delay. I saw the King put a ring upon Lady Boleyn's finger and kiss her. Afterwards Lord and Lady Wiltshire congratulated him. So, it must have been a proper wedding."

"If they are married, then why haven't they announced it to the court?" I asked. "It doesn't make any sense. Perhaps you were mistaken and it was only a betrothal."

"Lady Boleyn said that it was a true marriage," she said. "But she warned me not to tell anyone or else the King would be angry and banish me from court."

"What does Sir George Zouche think?" I asked.

She looked down at the floor in embarrassment. "He says that the meeting with the French King emboldened King Henry to take matters into his own hands," she muttered. "He thinks that I shall soon be in the service of the Queen."

I was left none the wiser. Nan would believe whatever she was told, but Sir George was nobody's fool. I could not puzzle it out. Perhaps she had watched a rehearsal. Or maybe the whole thing was intended as a hoax to mislead the Spanish ambassador.

At the end of February 1533, Lady Boleyn entertained the King to a banquet in her apartments at Whitehall Palace. The Privy Chamber, reserved for her closest attendants and most intimate guests, was a marvel of opulence. Costly tapestries depicting scenes from Roman legend hung from the walls, their silken threads catching the candlelight in hues of crimson and gold. Turkey carpets muffled the sound of footsteps, and an entire cupboard stood open, its shelves gleaming with gold plate—goblets, chargers, and ewers etched with heraldic emblems and Latin mottos.

The King, resplendent in a doublet of cloth-of-gold and a collar heavy with diamonds, surveyed the chamber with a look of great satisfaction. His eyes lingered on the carved oak panelling, the perfumed air, the discreet musicians playing a pavane in the adjoining room.

"Has she not made a good marriage?" he asked, turning to the dowager duchess of Norfolk, who had paused mid-step, her expression unreadable. "Does she not have a great dowry?"

"Yes, indeed, your Majesty," the duchess replied in a measured voice. She glanced toward Lady Boleyn, who stood near the hearth, her hands folded, her gown of deep garnet velvet trimmed with sable. The duchess wondered if the King had consumed too much wine—or if he was merely indulging in one of his sudden whims, those unpredictable flashes of sentiment that could turn courtly favour into ruin.

Lady Boleyn met the duchess's gaze with an inscrutable smile, her eyes unreadable beneath delicately arched brows. She said nothing, but her silence was not empty. It was the silence of calculation, of a woman who knew the weight of her position and the power of her triumph.

The King, oblivious or pretending to be, took a goblet from the cupboard and raised it. "To fortune," he said, "and to the women who know how to seize it."

Lady Boleyn inclined her head, the firelight catching the jewels at her throat. "To fortune," she echoed softly, though whether it was a toast or a warning, none could say.

That same month, Queen Catherine was sent to live at Ampthill Castle and her household was reduced to just ten ladies. At the end of March 1533, Thomas Cranmer was consecrated as the new Archbishop of Canterbury. He lost no time in pronouncing the King's marriage to Catherine of Aragon to be null and void. Shortly afterwards, he declared his marriage to Anne Boleyn to be valid.

The secret of the King's marriage was finally revealed at Easter 1533. Queen Anne attended mass in the Chapel Royal wearing a gorgeous dress of gold tissue adorned with diamonds. She was attended by sixty ladies in accordance with her new rank. Afterwards, King Henry invited his nobles to make their court to his new queen. The duke of Norfolk was dispatched to inform Queen Catherine that she need not trouble any more about the king, for he had taken another wife. She was no longer the queen and her new title was the Princess Dowager of Wales. Furthermore, the King would no longer pay the wages of her servants. Queen Catherine replied that as long as she lived, she would call herself Queen of England. And if there was nothing for herself and her servants to live upon, she would willingly go about the world begging alms for the love of God.

After his marriage to Queen Anne, the King made arrangements for her coronation celebration. He sent a letter to the Mayor of London commanding him to see the city furnished with pageants in her honour. The festivities began on 29th May 1533 with a great water pageant on the river Thames. At three o'clock in the afternoon Queen Anne and her ladies travelled in her royal barge from Greenwich to the Tower of London. She wore a magnificent gown of cloth of gold adorned with gold spangles set with diamonds. A flotilla of fifty barges decked with banners and streamers had assembled in her honour displaying the emblems of the mayor, aldermen and city guilds of London. They escorted her on the journey accompanied by the sound of musicians playing and minstrels singing. At the head of the procession was a barge with a great dragon casting wild fire. It was followed by another barge with a white falcon upon a hill of red and white roses which was the Queen's device. It was surrounded by young maidens who were singing and playing sweetly. As the Queen's barge arrived at the Tower of London a thousand guns were fired in her honour. King Henry was waiting to receive her and he escorted her to the royal apartments which had been splendidly furnished.

On the day of the formal entry into London, I arose early and dressed in my new gown of crimson velvet with a border of red cloth of gold. Queen Anne wore a gown of white cloth of gold adorned with rubies and a mantle trimmed with ermine. Her black hair hung loose about her shoulders and she wore a circlet of gold set with gemstones on her head. She took her place in a rich chariot of white cloth of gold and a canopy of cloth of silver was held over her head by the four Lords of the Ports. I rode in a chariot with Nan, Margery and Jane Seymour. We drove through the streets of London which were newly laid with gravel and decked with rich hangings of scarlet and gold in celebration. We saw the city guilds in their bright liveries lining the streets. We were welcomed by a series of pageants in which speeches were made in honour of the queen. At Fenchurch a party of children dressed like English and French merchants welcomed the Queen to the city. At Gracechurch Corner a living tableau of the gods of Mount Parnassus was presented. At the top of the mountain sat Apollo with his lyre. He was surrounded by the Nine Muses who recited verses in praise of the Queen. At Leadenhall a castle was constructed in honour of Queen Anne. It was surmounted by the effigy of a white falcon in a bower of red and white roses. An angel in armour then appeared and crowned the falcon:

"Honour and grace be to our Queen Anne.
For whose cause an Angel Celestial
Descendeth, the falcon as white as a swan
To crown with a Diadem Imperial!

In her honour rejoice we all,
For it cometh from God, and not of man.
Honour and grace be to our Queen Anne!"

The great Conduit in Cheapside was brightly painted in white, red and gold and a fountain ran continually with white wine and claret. The Standard was adorned with images of Kings and Queens, and hung with banners of arms and the intertwined initials H and A. It was a splendid spectacle but the watching crowds remained as silent and solemn as if was a funeral. Few of them cried out, *"God save the Queen!"* as she passed by. The Mayor of London and his aldermen stood assembled at the Cross which was newly gilded. He gave her a thousand marks in a purse of gold in the name of the city.

"Why don't you tell the citizens to cheer and doff their caps?" she demanded.

"I cannot command the people's hearts, your Grace," he replied. "Not even his Majesty the King can make them rejoice."

A hush fell over the square. The purse of gold gleamed in her hand, but its weight was suddenly less than the silence that followed the Mayor's reply.

Queen Anne's eyes narrowed—not in fury, but in something colder. Calculation. She turned her gaze upon the assembled aldermen, their faces stiff with civic duty, their eyes avoiding hers. The citizens beyond the Cross stood in uneasy clusters, some curious, some sullen, a few whispering behind gloved hands.

"So," she said, her voice low but clear, "the city gives gold, but not loyalty."

The Mayor bowed his head, neither confirming nor denying.

She placed the tribute inside her fur-trimmed mantle. "Let them keep their silence," she said to no-one in particular. "It will not last."

At the Little Conduit we were greeted by a pageant of the Judgement of Paris. The three goddesses Pallas, Juno, and Venus hailed the Queen and made their obeisances. Then Paris of Troy presented her with the prize of a golden apple in honour of her beauty and grace:

> *"Here is the fourth lady now in our presence,*
> *Most worthy to have it of due congruence,*
> *As peerless in riches, wit, and beauty,*
> *Which are but sundry qualities in you three.*
> *But for her worthiness, this apple of gold*
> *Is too simple a reward a thousand-fold."*

At the gate of St Paul's Cathedral, the Queen was greeted by three ladies wearing costly dresses who held out crowns to her. Above them was a banner inscribed with the words: *"Queen Anne! Advance with success, go forward, and reign!"* The procession moved on to Ludgate where the Queen was entertained by a choir of men and children who sang ballads in her honour. Finally, we arrived at the palace of Westminster where King Henry was awaiting her arrival. He took her in his arms and embraced her.

"How did you like the look of the city?" he asked.

"Sir, I liked it well enough, but I saw a great many caps on heads and heard few tongues," she replied.

"The people shall grow to love you as much as I do," he promised.

The following day, Queen Anne was crowned at Westminster Abbey. She wore a robe of purple velvet edged with ermine and a gold coronet with a cap of pearls. The clergy and lords of the realm preceded her dressed in their robes of state. The crown was carried by the duke of Suffolk and the dowager duchess of Norfolk bore her train. She was followed by the chief noblewomen in scarlet robes trimmed with ermine and coronets on their heads. Then came the Queen's ladies dressed in gowns of scarlet edged with white Baltic fur.

The Queen took her place on the throne before the high altar and a canopy of cloth of gold was held over her head. And there she was anointed Queen of England by the archbishop of Canterbury and the crown was set upon her head. The choir sang a *Te Deum* in thanksgiving and a solemn mass was celebrated. Afterwards she proceeded to Westminster Hall for the coronation banquet. The Great Hall was hung with tapestries of the Nine Worthy Women. A table was set upon a high dias at the upper end of the hall where Queen Anne dined under a rich cloth of estate. The guests sat at four tables along the hall in order of precedence and a feast of three courses was served. King Henry looked on from a private balcony for he wanted the glory of the occasion to be hers alone. He now had a lawful wife and Queen and he awaited the arrival of his legitimate son and heir.

Due to Queen Anne's pregnancy, it was not possible for the King and Queen to embark upon a triumphal summer progress around the kingdom. King Henry went hunting in

Epping forest and the great park of Richmond while Queen Anne travelled by barge from Westminster to Greenwich. In the golden hush of late summer, Greenwich Palace seemed to breathe with expectancy. The gardens were riotous with colour, bees humming lazily amid the lavender, as Queen Anne was borne through the arched gatehouse in a litter draped with green silk. Inside the Great Hall, shadows danced upon tapestries depicting the Twelve Labours of Hercules. Courtiers kept their tones hushed and deferent; all knew this was no ordinary season of confinement—this was the waiting of a realm for its heir.

The Queen was conducted to the bedchamber which had been prepared for her lying-in. The walls were covered in blue arras which was supposed to have a calming effect. In the midst of the chamber stood a magnificent bed of estate which had once belonged to the Duke of Alencon. It was draped with rich hangings of cloth of gold, cloth of silver and richly embroidered crimson satin. The canopy was fashioned of crimson cloth of gold embroidered with the joint crowned arms of the King and Queen surrounded by a garland. The tester for the bed-head was made of white cloth of silver with a border of purple velvet. It displayed the initials H and A embroidered in gold thread. The counterpane was made of crimson and white damask with the badges of the King and Queen in the four corners and a wide border of cloth of gold. The valance that surrounded the base of the bed was made of white satin embroidered with acorns and honeysuckles. Queen Anne's eyes widened with pleasure when she saw this testimony of the King's great favour. It signified that nothing was too good for her or the child that she carried. Nevertheless, she refrained from making any remark about it. Her mother was not so reticent.

"It is the finest bed I have ever seen," Lady Wiltshire exclaimed. "You must be sure to thank His Majesty for his generosity."

"I am the Queen of England," she replied haughtily. "It befits my royal rank and status."

"You must change out of your clothes and lie down now," she said. "Your child needs rest."

Soon Queen Anne lay propped up on her bolsters dressed in a black satin nightgown lined with black taffeta and edged with velvet. A smile edged her lips, as if even weariness could not dim the triumph that cloaked her. I stood near the foot of the bed, having just smoothed the damask counterpane. Around the bedchamber, the embroidered cushions, chair-backs and carpets mirrored the pattern emblazoned around the valance. The acorn for strength and the honeysuckle for love. They were the private motifs of the King and Queen. The ceiling was carved with the intertwined initials H and A. The furnishings announced the fidelity and devotion of King Henry for his wife to everyone. As I watched her lying there so composed and splendid beneath her embroidered canopy, I felt a sense of admiration for her. She bore the future in her womb, and all of England tilted on its axis in response.

She turned her gaze on me. "Bring me water to wash my hands, Mistress Stanhope," she said imperiously.

"Yes, your Grace," I replied. "Would you prefer lavender or rosewater?"

"I will have rosewater," she replied. "The lavender is far too pungent."

I stepped forward with a bowl and a fine lawn cloth. I poured the scented water into the bowl, dipped the cloth and gently bathed her hands. We would remain here in this chamber for the next three months until the child was born. It was my duty to care for the Queen, to entertain her and distract her from the slow burn of time and the weight of expectation that burdened us all.

The following week, King Henry summoned the best doctors, astrologers and soothsayers in the kingdom to the Queen's bedchamber. He was eager to confirm his hopes for the birth of his child. He stood before a celestial globe, one hand resting on its carved surface, the other drumming impatiently on the pommel of his sword.

"Your Majesty," said Doctor Butts, bowing low, "her Grace's humours are in harmony. The child thrives. The Queen will be delivered safely, God willing."

"The heavens concur," added Master Kratzer. "Mars rises favourably in the house of the Lion. A son is foretold—one who shall be great in dominion and fierce in purpose."

The King's eyes gleamed. "A son – a fine son!" he said. "He shall be named Henry after his father and grandfather. He shall be King Henry the Ninth! Mark it well!"

With a flourish, he waved to his steward. "See that these wise men are rewarded with fifty marks apiece. Let their tongues tell everyone of this auspicious day."

"Your Majesty, her Grace the Queen, needs to rest," said her mother. "Too much excitement is not good for her health. She needs peace and quiet to await the birth of her child."

"You are quite right, Lady Wiltshire," he replied. "We shall withdraw and leave you to rule the bedchamber as you see fit."

He departed, satisfied with the assurance that he would have a fine son. The Queen missed the company of the King and the amusements of the court. She was confined to her chamber with her ladies. She chafed against the inaction and the oppressive heat. She would have loved to have spent these glorious sunny days following the chase, shooting at targets or enjoying a picnic in the garden. Since she could indulge in none of these pleasures, she consoled herself with dreams of her son's future.

"Little Henry shall have the most splendid christening service that ever was seen," she said. "I am determined that it shall far outshine the christening of Lady Mary. We shall invite the foreign ambassadors to attend and send announcements to every monarch in Europe. Then we will celebrate the occasion with a pageant and a tournament. The people will rejoice to hear the good news of the birth of a son and heir!"

"I remember the christening of Lady Mary," said her mother. "It was held in the Church of the Observant Friars at Greenwich and it was a very grand occasion. The church was hung with fine tapestries and coloured banners with the coats of arms of England and Spain. The infant was wrapped in a rich gold cloth from Spain and carried to the font by the Countess of Surrey."

"Then my son shall also be christened at this church," she replied. "He shall be carried by a duchess and wrapped in the same christening cloth. Where is it?"

Lady Wiltshire gave an apologetic cough. "I believe that it was the property of the Dowager Princess," she said. "But you can have another made that is just as fine or even finer!"

"I will not have another," Anne retorted, her voice sharp with entitlement and the brittle edge of insecurity. "My son shall have the royal christening cloth. The King must send for it at once—for I wish to see it."

Her ladies exchanged glances but said nothing. The Queen's mood had grown mercurial in recent days, her triumph shadowed by whispers and the weight of expectation. The christening cloth, embroidered with Tudor roses and Spanish pomegranates, was more than ceremonial—it was symbolic.

King Henry dispatched a messenger to the Dowager Princess with instructions to surrender the cloth. However, she indignantly refused to give it up. "It is my own property which I brought with me from Spain," she told the messenger. "Tell him I will not yield it. Not now. Not ever."

The cloth remained locked in a cedar chest, guarded by her loyal chamberlain. King Henry showed his displeasure by ordering her to move her household to Buckden Towers. Queen Anne was displeased that her wish had not been gratified.

"The King ought to have insisted," she complained. "She has no more need of it."

"But only consider, my dear," said her mother. "Her christening cloth was unlucky. It is much better to have a new one made."

"Very well," she conceded. "I shall have a mantle of the finest purple velvet with a long train furred with ermine. That is more fitting for the son and heir of the King!"

But the wise men were mistaken in their predictions. On 7th September 1533, Queen Anne gave birth to a daughter. She was named Elizabeth after the King's mother. The King was disappointed and cancelled the planned entertainments. Three days later Princess Elizabeth was christened in a silver font in the church of the Observant Friars at Greenwich. The Dowager Duchess of Norfolk carried the child in her purple mantle and her grandfather, the earl of Wiltshire, held the train. Afterwards, the heralds blew their trumpets and the Garter King of Arms cried aloud, "God of His infinite goodness, send a long and prosperous life to the high and mighty Princess Elizabeth of England!"

The King and Queen did not attend the ceremony, but afterwards the christening gifts were carried out of the church in procession for everyone to see and brought to the Queen's chamber. She watched with satisfaction as they were presented before her by the Lord Chamberlain:

"From his Grace, the Archbishop of Canterbury, a standing cup of gold," he announced. "From her ladyship, the dowager duchess of Norfolk, a standing cup of gold, set with pearls. From her ladyship, the Marchioness of Dorset, three gilt bowls with covers and from her ladyship, the Marchioness of Exeter, three standing bowls with covers."

Queen Anne turned to her mother in triumph. "I am certain that Lady Mary had no such gifts nor honours paid to her!"

The following day, Lady Mary was informed that she would no longer be referred to as Princess. Her household badges were replaced by the King's insignia. It signalled to the world that Queen Anne Boleyn's ascendancy—and Princess Elizabeth's claim—was now the sanctioned future of England.

On 9th December 1533, Princess Elizabeth—barely six months old—was taken from the royal nursery to reside at Hatfield House, her new household established with all the trappings of princely dignity. The procession that bore her through the city was a deliberate spectacle, orchestrated to affirm her legitimacy and future. The dukes of Norfolk and Suffolk rode at the head of the entourage, their cloaks lined with sable, their banners fluttering with heraldic pride. Behind them came a train of great lords, privy councillors, and household officers, each chosen for their loyalty to the Queen and their willingness to endorse the new order. Gentlemen ushers, nurses, and servants followed, their livery emblazoned with the falcon badge of Anne Boleyn, now gilded and crowned.

The streets of London were lined with citizens who watched the majestic display in silence. The city had not yet warmed to Queen Anne, and the memory of Queen Catherine still lingered in the hearts of the common folk. But the grandeur of the procession was undeniable. Trumpeters sounded at each major crossing, and banners of scarlet and cloth-of-gold were hung from windows where loyal merchants had been instructed to display their allegiance. Elizabeth's cradle, carved from walnut and inlaid with mother-of-pearl, was carried in a covered litter, its silken curtains drawn back just enough to reveal the infant swaddled in crimson damask. A herald walked beside the litter, announcing her titles: "Princess Elizabeth of England, daughter of His Majesty King Henry and Her Grace Queen Anne." This was not merely a child's relocation—it was a declaration of dynastic intent, a public assertion that Elizabeth was not simply the daughter of the King, but his chosen heir. The royal pageantry that surrounded her asserted an intentional challenge to those who still whispered of Mary's rights and Catherine's dignity.

"It is much healthier in the countryside than in London," said the King. "Lady Margaret Bryan will become her Lady Governess and take charge of her household."

"I shall miss her," sighed the Queen. "She is so dear to me."

"It is fitting that she should live in the state of a Princess of England," he replied. "We can go to visit her from time to time."

"And what of your other daughter?" she asked. "It is entirely unfitting that Lady Mary should live in the same princely state as the heir to the throne."

"Indeed, she should not," he agreed.

"She is not only a bastard but an ingrate," said the Queen. "She is unworthy of the privileges you have given her. You should take away her household, her costly wardrobe and her jewels. Send her to wait upon the Princess Elizabeth. It will humble her stiff-necked Spanish pride."

"I have treated her with great kindness, but she continues to defy me," he complained. "My patience is at an end. I will send Norfolk to inform her that she will no longer enjoy these honours. She is an obstinate girl and needs to learn the obedience that is due to her sovereign."

So, Lady Mary's household was dismissed and she was sent to live at Hatfield House. Her splendid residence at Hunsdon was given to George Boleyn and his wife Jane.

At Easter 1534 the Queen announced that she was expecting another child. She boasted that this time it was sure to be a son. The triumphant King ordered a silver cradle adorned with jewels and Tudor roses from his goldsmith. The court celebrated Easter that year with extravagant banquets and masques. On May Day a tournament was held at Greenwich on the theme of Love Triumphant. Queen Anne presided over the jousts in a gown of cloth-of-gold embroidered with intertwining vines. Her wide sleeves were patterned with Tudor roses. Her pregnancy gave her a new sense of assurance. The spring air was scented with may blossoms from the thick hedges of hawthorn that surrounded the tiltyard.

A blast of trumpets sounded and the tiltyard below the pavilion burst into action: plumes of crimson and azure, banners with hearts pierced by arrows, and the herald's cry of *L'amour triomphe*. I watched King Henry enter the lists with an exaggerated flourish, his silvered armour catching the sun. His stallion pawed the earth with impatience. He carried

Queen Anne's favour—a scarf of rose-pink silk—tied proudly to his lance. It fluttered like a flame. He turned towards her and bowed from the saddle, his visor raised. She smiled, just enough to be seen. Around us, the nobility murmured their admiration like a chorus of players in a masque.

The Queen's hand drifted to her belly, unconsciously, as if to remind the court what all this splendour celebrated. I caught the look that flickered across the face of Lady Mary Shelton beside me—admiration mingled with calculation. Even in celebration, the court was a battlefield.

Sir Nicholas Carew was the first to ride, his banner a sun rising over storm-tossed waves. His lance struck true, shattering against his opponent's breastplate in a glorious explosion of splinters. The crowd roared. Queen Anne clapped politely, but her eyes flicked to the King, gauging whether Henry relished the contest more than her approval. I had seen her wield her glances like daggers or garlands, depending on the moment.

My own heart beat a little faster when young Henry Norris rode out—noble, handsome and with the air of a man who knew the Queen watched. He tilted his lance with elegance, striking with precision, and bowed deeply toward the dais as he passed. His gaze lingered—but then, she looked away.

By midday the tiltyard was a sea of mud strewn with hoofprints, love tokens and broken wood. The Queen leaned back in her chair, triumphant and glowing beneath her cloth-of-estate. I knew then that this whole courtly display was not just a celebration but a demonstration of power. It underlined her status as the mother of the future sovereign. I remembered that May Day for many years. It was a moment of shining glory and splendour before the wind changed and the roses wilted.

In the autumn of 1534, Lady Carey made a startling confession. She stood before the Queen's chair of estate with her head bowed and her hands clenched tightly at her sides. She wore no jewels or rich embroidery, only a modest gown of murrey cloth, faded at the seams.

"Your Majesty, I appeal to your compassion and generosity," she murmured. "I am in great need of assistance."

Queen Anne's eyes narrowed with suspicion. "Why don't you ask our father for help?" she replied.

"He has no concern for what happens to me," she said. "In fact, he has cast me off entirely."

"Cast you off?" echoed the Queen. "What have you done?"

"I have married William Stafford," she said. "He is a soldier of the garrison of Calais and the second son of Sir Humphrey Stafford. He is a gentleman but he is poor. And I am expecting a child."

Queen Anne closed her eyes and shuddered. "Have you no shame, Mary?" she demanded. "Does the blood of Boleyn mean so little to you that you would squander it on a nobody?"

Mary raised her eyes defiantly. "I married for love, Anne. Not for a title nor for money."

The Queen glared at her sister, her dark eyes aflame. "Love?" she echoed, the word laced with scorn. "You dare speak to me of love while I bear the weight of a kingdom and carry a child who will be the next King of England? It was your duty to make an honourable match approved by myself and the King. But you have thrown yourself away upon a second son of no consequence, as though your family were worth nothing!"

"I have no wish to shame you," Mary said quietly, "but I am desperate. My children are hungry and Stafford is too proud to beg. I thought you might ask the King to grant me a pension."

The Queen shook her head. "You are no longer my sister but Mistress Stafford," she said. "You have chosen to marry a poor man with nothing to his name. Go from here and do not return."

Mary looked her straight in the eye. "The King has a fickle heart," she said. "One day he will tire of you and then you will have nothing too."

She curtsied with the quiet grace of a court lady and departed. I felt a shiver run through me. Lady Carey had cursed her unforgiving sister to suffer the same fate as herself. Shortly afterwards, the Queen lost her child. The King was deeply disappointed and distanced himself from her. She was left to console herself among the company of her ladies. He did not speak to her again until a bright day in September. He happened to be walking in the privy garden when he came across the Queen and her ladies. She was making merry with a game of pall mall. We were laughing and racing along the alley in pursuit of the ball. But at the sight of him we stopped and made our obeisances.

"What a pleasant surprise to see you here," she said. "Why don't you join our game, your Majesty?"

Once, he would not have hesitated to take part in the Queen's pastimes. He paused for a moment and then frowned as he remembered his grievances. He was not prepared to forego them for the brief diversion of a game.

He shook his head. "I will not interrupt your pleasure, your Grace," he replied. He turned to walk away. It was then that he caught sight of Jane Seymour. She was sitting apart on a bench. She had taken out her prayer book and was reading it intently. A shaft of sunlight shone upon her fair hair. She looked like an angel from heaven.

The King was intrigued and drew nearer. She became aware of him and looked up. Their eyes met in a moment of mutual recognition. Then she blushed and closed the book. She jumped to her feet and sank into a deep curtsey.

"I beg your pardon, your Majesty," she said. "I did not know that you were in the garden."

"There is no need to apologise," he replied. "It pleases me to know that there are ladies of such piety in the court. I shall not disturb you, my dear. Sit down and go on with your prayers. Say one for the King who is burdened with the care of this realm."

"Yes, your Majesty," she replied. "I shall always pray for you."

She sat down and opened her book. He stood there looking at her as she read it devoutly. His eyes lingered upon her as she sat below the bower of trees. The King was a sentimental man and the meeting made a great impression upon him. Henceforth he always thought of Jane as a very pious lady.

In November 1534 Parliament passed a law declaring the King to be Supreme Head of the Church of England. Everyone at court was required to swear an oath recognising his new title and acknowledging his marriage to Queen Anne Boleyn. Princess Elizabeth was named as the heir to the throne and Lady Mary was declared a bastard. Those who refused to take the oath would be charged with treason. The Lord Chamberlain, Baron Sandys, summoned the Queen's household to a meeting in the Presence Chamber.

"Everyone at court is required to swear the oath of supremacy," he said. "But since we are the servants of the Queen, we shall set a good example to the rest. Tomorrow we shall be the first to take the oath. We shall assemble here after breakfast."

"Is it a sin to swear this oath?" I whispered to Margery.

"It is our duty to obey the King," she replied. "We are his loyal subjects."

"But the King's title denies the authority of the Pope," I said. "And he is the descendant of St Peter."

"Parliament has made the King's Supremacy the law of the land," she said. "So, it is our bounden duty to accept it. My conscience is clear on the matter."

"Are you quite sure, Margery?" I said uneasily.

"It is no sin to obey the law", she said firmly. "Or if it is a sin, then it falls upon the head of the King."

But regardless of the grim penalty, the Carthusian monks of the Charterhouse, Bishop Fisher and Sir Thomas More all refused to take the oath. They were sent to the Tower as a sign of the King's displeasure. The Pope appointed Bishop Fisher a Cardinal as a sign of his support. But King Henry had lost all respect for the authority of the Pope. Queen Catherine and her daughter likewise refused to swear. Queen Anne Boleyn denounced them as traitors to the King.

"Now you see their true minds," she said. "Their loyalty is to the Pope and not their lawful sovereign."

"I expected that Catherine would defy me," he replied. "But it grieves me that my daughter Mary should choose to take her mother's side. It is unnatural of her to disobey her father and her King."

"They should both be executed for defying the law of the land," she urged. "The realm would be well rid of them."

King Henry sighed deeply. "I am gravely afflicted by their defiance," he said. "It is a great distress to me."

Queen Anne tried another tactic. "I will not be able to bear you a son while Catherine and Mary still live," she insisted.

The King said no more on the matter. He was not prepared to put his former wife and his daughter to death. Neither did he send them to the Tower. His councillors warned him that such a provocation could lead to a war with Spain. And it would inflame the feelings of his subjects against him. The execution of Lady Mary would weaken the realm. She was eighteen years old whereas Princess Elizabeth was just an infant.

"She is my death and I am hers," she muttered. "I will never rest until I have her put out of the way."

The Spanish ambassador, Seigneur Eustace Chapuys, tried to intercede on behalf of Catherine and Mary. He stood before the King with the measured dignity of a man who knew he was treading dangerous ground. His voice, though respectful, carried the weight of a foreign crown and the might of the Spanish empire.

"It is a matter of their conscience, Sire," he said. "They act not out of defiance, but from devotion—to Your Majesty, to the Church, and to the truth as they understand it."

King Henry's eyes narrowed. He had heard this argument before, and it no longer evoked his patience. "My conscience is quite clear on the matter," he retorted, his tone clipped, his jaw set. "I am the head of the Church in England. It is not for my daughter to instruct me in matters of conscience. She has no right to plead it. She ought to be guided by me."

There was a pause—tense, brittle. Seigneur Chapuys did not flinch, but he felt the chill in the air. King Henry's words were not merely paternal; they were sovereign. To question them was to question the very structure of the realm.

"She is but a child, Sire," Seigneur Chapuys ventured, "and yet she suffers as though she were a traitor. Her household diminished, her titles stripped, her mother cast aside. Might Your Majesty not show her some mercy?"

King Henry rose from his chair of estate, the movement sudden, deliberate. "Mercy?" he echoed. "I have shown mercy enough. I have offered them comfort, position, even reconciliation—if they would but yield. But they choose obstinacy. They choose Rome. They choose to defy me!"

He turned away, pacing toward the window where the winter light slanted across the floor. "Mary is my daughter, yes. But she is also my subject. And subjects do not govern kings."

Seigneur Chapuys bowed, sensing the futility of any further appeal. I watched him as he withdrew, his shoulders heavy with failure. I had seen the King's wrath fall swiftly before, and I knew that it would not be softened by any ties of blood or memory. Lady Mary was in deadly danger and I feared for her future.

In December 1534 Sir Edward Seymour returned to court. He was dressed in black mourning for he had received the news that his estranged wife had died in her convent.

"He will need a new wife now," said Nan. "He has no heirs any more. But it won't be easy for him. Not many fathers will be willing to give their daughters to such a scandalous family!"

Sir Edward visited the Queen's apartments to pay his respects to her. He took his place among the gentlemen and surveyed the company. His eyes lingered upon mine. The following week he brought me a copy of *The Romance of the Rose* as a New Year's gift.

"Permit me to read you a passage from this poem, Mistress Stanhope," he said.

If you wish, Sir Edward, I agreed. It was clever of him to read me a text since he had no skill as a poet.

"From here to Jerusalem no woman has a more beautiful neck; it was smooth and soft to the touch.
She had a bosom as white has the snow upon a branch when it has just fallen.
Her body as well-made and svelte; you would not have had to seek anywhere on earth to find a woman with a more beautiful body.
She had a pretty chaplet of gold embroidery. There was never a girl more elegant or better arrayed;
nor would I have described her right. Above the chaplet of gold embroidery was one of fresh roses, and in her hand, she held a mirror, and she had arranged her hair with a rich head-band."

"What are you trying to say, Sir Edward?" I asked.

"This is just how I think about you, Mistress Stanhope," he said. "You are fair and elegant beyond compare. And what is more, I know you to be an honourable lady."

"My virtue has never been called into question," I replied.

"My wife has died and I have been left a widower," he said. "I would like to offer you my hand in marriage, if you will graciously condescend to take me."

"But I hardly know you," I said.

"I am the eldest son of Sir John Seymour," he said. "I fought in the King's wars and was knighted in France. Now I am an esquire to the King. I can assure you that my intentions are most honourable and my prospects are favourable."

"That is not all, is it?" I said coldly. "Your wife was estranged from you and died in a convent."

"It is true that we were separated," he said. "But the circumstances were such that no blame can be imputed to me."

"My family would never let me marry you, Sir Edward," I said. "My mother is a very proud woman. And my stepfather sponsored my arrival at court in order that I would make a good match. He would never permit me to marry a man with a scandalous history."

But Sir Edward was a resourceful man. He sought out Sir Richard Page and persuaded him to agree to a betrothal.

"Sir Edward Seymour is a very capable young man," he said. "He has a promising career at court. And he is a widower with no legitimate children. So, there is no impediment to your marriage, my dear."

I considered the matter dispassionately. Sir Edward was cold, calculating and politic, not the sort of man to be led by his emotions. He was young and ambitious, the eldest son of a knight, a polished courtier and a determination to better himself. He would go far with the right wife at his side. I was twenty-five years old and it was time that I was married. I resolved to accept his proposal.

In February 1535 Queen Anne discovered that she was pregnant again. But her joy was short-lived because the King began an affair with her maid of honour, Madge Shelton. She had never imagined that he would become indifferent to her charms or careless of her feelings. She was left to console herself with the empty honours of her queenship. Her own family gave her little support. Her parents had retired from court, her sister was banished and she detested her uncle Norfolk. Only her brother George was a comfort to her. Now she understood the selfishness of her royal husband. His passionate love for her had burned out within a year of their marriage. Now he had no compunction about treating her just as badly as her predecessor. She clung to the hope that she could revive his affections by bearing him a son.

CHAPTER 5

Lady Seymour (1535)

"Therefore, love your husband here and if they reward it not, it shall be rewarded in heaven; be humble and lowly here and ye shall be exalted in heaven; be clothed in modesty here and ye shall be clothed with honour in heaven; be patient here and ye shall be crowned with glory in heaven"

(Francis Mere, *God's Arithmetic*, 1597).

Edward and I were married in the Chapel Royal on 9th March 1535. On the day of my wedding, it was my stepfather Sir Richard who walked me down the aisle and gave me away. Mistress Jane Seymour served as my bridesmaid and carried my train. On each side of the nave hung banners which proudly displayed the Seymour coat of arms: a pair of golden wings upon a scarlet background. Below the device was emblazoned the family motto: *Faith for Duty*. For a moment I almost stumbled when I recalled that Christmas Eve fortune telling of long ago. Here was the proof of it. Sir Richard held me up and I regained my poise. No doubt he thought that I was a nervous bride. Edward smiled at me as I approached him. He looked handsome in his new doublet and hose of dark brown silk. *Our union was meant to be,* I thought to myself. *We were destined for each other.*

Queen Anne graciously sent her favourite lute player, Master Smeaton, to play at our wedding feast. Edward's younger brother Thomas fulfilled his duties as the groomsman by urging the guests to drink heartily. He was the opposite of his prudent brother. Compared to Edward he was just a callow youth. But he was his mother's favourite on account of his good looks and easy charm. I saw at once that he was a vain peacock of a man. He would never amount to much. His best chance in life was to marry a wealthy heiress.

"Second time lucky eh, Edward?" he smirked. "Let's hope this one has more sense than your first wife."

"Anne is the ideal match for me," he replied coldly. "I chose her for her good sense and intelligence. She will make me an admirable wife."

"Not for her good looks or charm then?" he taunted him. "Still, she is an heiress so she is not a bad bargain."

"I must apologise for Thomas," said Edward in a level voice. "He has clearly drunk too much wine."

"I was not paying any attention, dear Edward," I replied. "Your brother is always talking nonsense."

But I never forgive him for disparaging me on my wedding day. From that day onwards, I was his deadly enemy.

After the banquet, my mother brought me upstairs to the bridal chamber. "You have a nobler lineage than your husband, Anne," she reminded me. "Your children will inherit royal blood through your ancestors."

"Edward did not inherit a title, but he will gain one through his loyal service," I replied loyally. "He will raise up his children to a higher state than his own."

"This is what all courtiers hope to gain from the King," she sighed. "But very few succeed in their ambitions."

"He made Charles Brandon the duke of Suffolk," I said. "Edward is just as loyal and far more capable. I know that he will prove his worth in time."

She pursed her lips and rose to her feet. "The King rewards his good friends much better than his good servants," she sighed. "But it is too late for you to repent now. I shall send in the maid to make you ready for your husband."

It wounded me to know that my mother was disappointed in my choice of husband. But I had every faith in Edward. He would be a good husband to me and I would be a loyal wife to him. I heard the sound of footsteps and laughter outside the door. Then I heard a raised voice taking command of the situation.

"Take yourself off, Thomas," he ordered. "My wife and I would be private together."

"You were always a spoil-sport, Edward," his brother replied. "It is customary to tease the bride a little."

"She has no taste for your foolish pranks," Edward snapped. "Leave now or I will kick you downstairs."

"You are well suited to your sourpuss of a wife," he retorted.

He stamped away and then I heard a quiet knock on the door. I was pleased that Edward had shown the respect that was due to his wife.

"Come in," I called out. I was sitting upon the bridal bed in my best linen nightgown. My long fair hair was loose around my shoulders.

He pushed the door open and gazed at me in admiration. He shut the door behind him and smiled. "This lovely vision is for no-one's eyes but my own."

"I am glad that you find my attire pleasing," I said. "Do you like it better than my wedding gown?"

"Much better," he replied. "I have dreamed of this moment ever since I first saw you."

"Fie upon you," I teased him. "You were still a married man!"

"I know that you would never betray me, Anne," he said. But the expression on his face showed no such certainty.

"I swear that I will be a faithful wife to you, Edward," I replied. "I will bear you many children and together we will give them a golden future."

His doubt turned into relief at my reassuring words. "You have always understood me, Anne," he said, taking my hand.

"Your first wife had no pride or dignity," I replied. "But I am a Bourchier and a descendant of King Edward III. I would never do anything to demean my noble lineage. We shall share our future and our fortunes whether the times be good or bad."

"You are the finest lady in the court," Anne, he said. "No-one else would have given me such a resolute answer."

"I have every confidence in your abilities, Edward," I said. "You should forget the shadows of the past and focus upon your career at court. I shall do everything in my power to help you succeed."

"You are a gift from heaven, Anne," he replied. "The boldest and most beautiful lady in the court. I consider myself fortunate to have such a fine lady as my wife."

He leaned over and blew out the candle. Then he pulled me down next to him on the bed. I smiled as I felt his passionate kisses falling upon my face and lips. I congratulated myself that I had made a good choice of husband in Edward. He would always be grateful to me and appreciate me because I had all the qualities that were lacking in Catherine Fillol.

I returned to the court as Lady Anne Seymour. Now I was no longer a humble maid of honour. I could dress as befitted the wife of a courtier of good birth. I was entitled to wear the Seymour family jewels. My new status brought me to the attention of the young noblemen of the court. Among them was Henry Howard, the earl of Surrey and heir to the duke of Norfolk.

"The beauteous Lady Seymour," he remarked with a curl of satisfaction tugging at his mouth. "The whole court speaks of your fine endowments." His eyes lingered upon my snow-white bosom with appreciation.

I knew what he was thinking. Now that I was a married lady of the court, it would be safe to take me as his mistress.

He assumed that I would be honoured to receive his attentions. In my view, Surrey was a young popinjay and the worst kind of courtier. He prided himself upon his noble birth and regarded his poetry as the highest form of service to the crown.

During the evening dances at court, he advanced towards me and casually held out his hand in invitation. I was vexed by his lack of courtesy and declined to take it.

"My lord, you do me too much honour," I said. "But I have no wish to dance this evening."

His cheeks flushed scarlet with mortification. "So fair and yet so proud," he replied in a tone of reproach. "Yet it is an honour for a knight's lady to partner with a duke's son."

Queen Anne Boleyn laughed to see his predicament. "Never mind, Surrey," she said mockingly. "You may now compose a verse dedicated to the lady who refused to dance with you."

"Your wish is my command, your Grace," he replied. "I shall indeed write a sonnet to this proud lady."

"I shall look forward to listening to your woeful laments," she said.

The Queen now turned her malice upon me. "You are fortunate to receive so gentle a rebuke, Lady Seymour," she remarked. "Perhaps you are unfamiliar with the temper of the Howards? If you had refused the duke of Norfolk so scornfully, he would have knocked your teeth out and then planted a dagger in your husband's breast to avenge his honour."

"Then it is fortunate that he is not present tonight, your Majesty," I replied. "Although it is unlikely that his Grace would have condescended to ask me in the first place."

"But what objection do you have to Surrey that makes you spurn his company?" she mused. "Do you fear that his great clumsy feet will tread upon your dainty shoes?"

"A married lady is not obliged to give a reason for declining an invitation to dance," I said.

"True enough," she conceded. "Young maidens are obliged to dance every dance for fear of being regarded as cold and haughty. Whereas a married lady may be as capricious as she pleases since she has already snared her marital prey."

Edward was dismayed that I had made such a scandalous scene. "My dear Anne, you must be more circumspect in future," he said. "We do not want to make an enemy of the Howard family."

"They need not boast of their noble lineage to me," I said. "I am descended from King Edward III. My bloodline is just as distinguished as theirs."

"Take heed, Anne," said Edward. "The duke of Buckingham liked to boast of his Plantagenet heritage. But it did him no good in the Tudor court. I pray that you will be more circumspect in your speech!"

"Surrey is the most foolish proud man at the court," I said. "Someone had to bring him down a notch."

The following day, Surrey returned with his verse. He bowed to the Queen. Your Majesty, I have the honour to present these lines on a lady that refused to dance with me.

Then let us hear them at once, she said, darting a malicious glance in my direction.

He unfurled the scroll and began to read aloud:

To her whose eyes do pierce the night's dark veil,
A lady proud, untamed by courtly grace,
Thy gentle hand unyielded, love's avail
Denied with words as sharp as silken lace.

Oh, how thy countenance doth shame the morn,
Thy beauty brighter than the sun's embrace,
Yet in thy pride my tender hopes are torn,
And honour bends beneath thy haughty face.

Shall I in verse thy fleeting spirit bind,
Immortalising all that I've withstood?
Fair lady, though cruel, thy will doth charm my mind,
For even scorn can fashion something good.

So here I write, both vexed and yet inspired,
By thee, whose proud disdain my muse has fired.

Queen Anne smiled to hear his biting words. "You are a poet who can draw blood with his words, she said. This will make my ladies show more discretion in the future. Is that not so, Lady Seymour?"

"It might daunt some ladies, your Grace," I said. "But others will not be affected in the least."

"Do you wish to enter the lists, Lady Seymour?" she asked. "It is only fair to grant you the right to reply to his rebuke. But only if you wish to accept the challenge."

"I am glad to accept it, your Grace," I replied.

"Then I shall hear your verse tomorrow," she said.

The following evening, I presented myself before the Queen. Surrey had assembled all his friends to witness my reply. They stared at me with scornful derision in their eyes. I knew that they had no opinion of women poets.

"I have the honour to present my verse, your Majesty," I said. I recited the lines from memory:

My lord, thy tender verse hath reached mine ear,
Yet duty binds my heart, not fleeting chance.
A lady's honour stands both proud and clear,
Not swayed by beckoning to courtly dance.

What merit lies in steps that quickly fade,
When steadfast virtue must not be delayed?
A knight's lady values deeds long made,
And places worth in vows securely laid.

Though beauty may inflame a moment's art,
True love is tempered by its patient fire.
To gain my hand requires far more a heart,
Than fleeting words or passing lord's desire.

Thus, 'tis not pride that bars thy fair request,
But thought that guards what cannot be possessed.

"So, you protest you are blameless?" she remarked. "As I recall, it was only an invitation to dance a measure, not a design to steal your virtue."

"Words can defame a lady just as surely as deeds," I replied.

"Well said, Lady Seymour," she said, inclining her head. "Every lady has the right to guard her reputation, just as every gentleman has the right to defend his honour. But I could not say which one of you has the greater degree of self-love. I think you are as well-matched for pride as you are for writing verses. So, you may divide the honours of the contest between you."

"Your Majesty is most gracious," I said, with a curtsey. A sense of triumph filled me. Surrey looked sullen and his friends gave me black looks. They had hoped to see me confounded and humiliated. But that day would never come. Thereafter, I gained the reputation of being the proudest lady at the court. Surrey muttered that I was the greatest she-wolf in the realm. But he took care never to cross swords with me again. Queen Anne was impressed and treated me as a lady who was worthy of respect.

"No-one has ever contested Surrey before," she said. "Henceforth no court gallant will dare to affront you, Lady Seymour!"

My triumph increased my standing and my confidence. By contrast, my sister-in-law, Jane Seymour, was a signal failure at court. Queen Anne tolerated her presence as long as she sat in a back corner of the privy chamber and attended to her sewing. She set her to embroider her pillowcases and bedsheets with intricate borders of blackwork. She did not dare to complain and spent her days diligently plying her needle. Queen Anne frequently made her the target of her mockery and renamed her jester Jane the Fool out of spite.

"I don't know which one of you is the greater fool," she said, her lips curling with disdain.

Jane flushed and bit her lip. She had no idea that making a clever retort would have redeemed her standing. She might have said, "Better a fool with wit than a Queen without grace." She might have said anything. But she said nothing. She had no sense of humour and I had never heard her tell a joke. Queen Anne's taunts invariably made her retreat into silence and confusion. She should have maintained her dignity and remembered that her royal mistress was no better born than herself. Her meekness made her small. She should have claimed her space among us, she should have learned the rhythms of laughter and card play, the flirtations, the dancing. We ladies knew how to please the Queen—not simply by our looks, but by our spirit.

I turned towards the fireplace where Master Smeaton strummed a merry galliard on the lute, and Nan spun in a slow circle, her skirts sweeping in time. The rest of us were gathered around the Queen's card table, playing a round of Primeroe. I had just laid down my card with a flourish and drawn a smile from Her Majesty when I saw Jane still seated at her embroidery frame like a ghost. No one called her to join us. No one offered her a place. In truth, I had no sympathy for her. The court was no place for dull wits and fragile hearts. It demanded cleverness dressed as charm, ambition veiled as devotion, and the strength to smile when your pride was bruised. The court was a stage, and if she would not play her part, she deserved the shadows she'd chosen.

Her ineptitude was an embarrassment to Edward. "I fear that my sister lacks your confidence and poise," he said. "I wish that she would make more of an effort to transform herself into a successful courtier. Perhaps you could help her to become more outgoing."

"Your sister is not suited to the life of the court," I said. "She would be much happier taking care of her own home. If you want to help her then you should arrange a match for her with one of your friends."

"I will do my best," he said. "But it would be easier if she was not so ridiculously shy and retiring. No courtier wants to have a goose for a wife."

I smiled politely, but said nothing. To my mind it had been a great mistake to send a girl like Jane to court. Her father should have given one of his other daughters the chance to make something of themselves. Her younger sister Elizabeth Seymour was already married to Sir Anthony Ughtred. She was undoubtedly the beauty of the family. In my opinion, Jane was a born spinster.

Edward did his best to find a match for his sister among his circle of friends. He introduced her to William Dormer, a gentleman of good family. He arranged a series of meetings to promote their acquaintance. Master Dormer was a reserved young man who took a liking to the quiet and submissive Jane. Edward congratulated himself that he had succeeded in settling the future of his sister. But her betrothal to William Dormer was broken by his mother. She had greater ambitions for her son than marriage to a mere knight's daughter.

Edward was furious. "Lady Dormer does not think that a Seymour girl is good enough for her precious son," he muttered. "It is an insult to our family."

"It is high time that Jane retired from court," I said. "She is on her way to becoming an old maid. There won't be any more offers now. And she is too old to serve a maid of honour any longer."

"Perhaps she should go to live at Elvetham," he proposed. "She could help to care for our children."

I pursed my lips. "She must return to Wulf Hall and take care of her parents, as is her duty." I could not abide his fool of a sister and I was determined not have her cluttering up my household.

"Of course, my dear," he agreed. "I will speak to my father at the first opportunity."

At the beginning of June 1535 Queen Anne sent for Master Cromwell. The King had appointed him as Visitor General of Religious Houses, and commissioned him to organise visitations of all the monasteries in the realm. He was now a prosperous man. He dressed in the finest velvet and wore an emerald ring on his hand.

"What do your commissioners say of the condition of these religious houses?" she asked.

"My commissioners have reported many cases of corrupt living at these houses, your Grace," he replied. "Some of the communities have dwindled to below a dozen. It is my opinion that the smaller houses should be closed. Their goods and property will revert to the crown."

The Queen countered swiftly. "Not so, Master Cromwell," she objected. "It would be a better plan to turn these houses into schools and poorhouses."

He shrugged indifferently. "The Church is very rich, your Grace," he remarked. "Its reform is likely to be a very profitable enterprise for his Majesty."

Her eyes flashed with temper. "You go too far, Master Cromwell," she said. "These reforms are not intended for profit but for the benefit of the people."

He pursed his lips. "It is for his Majesty to decide how he will make use of this revenue, your Grace," he replied.

"You are a baseborn varlet who is unfit for the King's councils," she said. "I would like to see your head taken off your shoulders!"

"I am his Majesty's faithful servant, your Grace," he replied. He bowed stiffly and took his leave. His eyes were dark with anger.

Queen Anne was furious that he refused to accommodate her wishes. "He thinks he is another Wolsey," she muttered. "But I shall see that he regrets defying me."

Later that month Cardinal Fisher was beheaded on Tower Hill for denying the King's title as Head of the Church. The people were greatly shocked by his death. Soon afterwards, Queen Anne suffered a miscarriage. King Henry ordered it to be kept secret for fear that the people would say that it was God's revenge for the execution of such a saintly man.

The following month, Sir Thomas More followed Bishop Fisher to the block. The axe fell, and with it, one of the last voices of measured defiance was silenced. His refusal to endorse the King's marriage to Anne Boleyn and the Act of Supremacy had echoed across Europe. But the news of his death brought no satisfaction to the King. In the days that followed, King Henry spoke little of More. But his courtiers knew better than to mention his name. His death had cast a dark shadow over the King's conscience. The King had won, but his victory tasted of ashes.

He snapped at the Queen: "You are the cause of his death!"

"He was a self-confessed traitor," she protested. "He brought his fate upon himself."

"But you persuaded me to it!" he muttered.

That summer the King and Queen set out on a progress through the West Country. She was glad to leave the burdens of the court behind her. They stayed at Sudeley Castle, Berkeley Castle and Thornbury Castle. Afterwards they made a visit to Wulf Hall in Wiltshire. The King was in a good humour because it was a fine summer and there were plenty of opportunities for hunting. He greeted Sir John Seymour at the entrance to his house like an old friend.

"My dear Sir John," he said. "You have been too long absent from the court. So, I am forced to come to see you instead."

"I am greatly honoured by your visit, your Majesty," he replied. "Let me present my wife, Lady Margery. A good wife she has been to me. Ten children she has borne me and six of them are sons!"

"Six sons," remarked the King. "A good wife indeed. Would that I had been so fortunate!"

Queen Anne glowered at his words. She raised her hand to her forehead. "I have endured such terrible heat upon the road," she said. "And the horses kicked up so much dust that I thought that I would faint along the way."

"Please come inside, your Grace," said Sir John. "Pray take this chair and take your ease. We have wine ready prepared for your refreshment."

The Queen sank down upon a chair in the entrance hall and unfurled a silken fan. The steward hurried to serve the King and Queen. He poured wine from a fluted silver ewer into a set of silver chalices.

"A toast to his Majesty and his gracious Queen," said Sir John. "Your chambers await you upstairs as soon as you are ready."

"Upstairs?" replied the Queen imperiously. "I am far too weary to ascend the stairs. I shall require a set of apartments on the ground floor. I wish to retire there immediately!"

"You shall have my own chambers, your Grace," said Sir John. "Whatever you desire for your comfort and good cheer shall be provided at once. Lady Margery shall escort you there and attend to your every need."

The King's brows knotted but he said nothing. He swallowed his wine in silence and watched his wife depart in triumph. He could not abide a fuss and she knew it. Yet at every opportunity she insisted upon making herself the centre of attention. Once again, she had spoiled his pleasure by her petulant demands.

"I will take a turn about your gardens, Sir John," he said. "Send someone to fetch me when it is time to dress for dinner."

"I myself shall escort your Majesty," he replied. "Our rose garden is very fine this year. Please allow me to conduct you there."

The King's face brightened. "It will be pleasant to take a stroll in the sunshine. I rode past many fine fields of wheat and barley on my journey. No doubt our farmers will enjoy a bumper harvest this year."

"Yes indeed, your Majesty," he replied. "We have brewed plenty of fine ale for your reception. It would please me to hear your opinion of it this evening."

"It would be my pleasure, Sir John," he replied. He had already recovered his good humour.

"Tomorrow morning, I have invited the gentlemen of the county to join us for a hunt," he said. "In the evening, we shall feast together upon roast venison and fat partridges."

"There is nothing that I enjoy more than the simple pleasures of life in the country," he replied. "You are a fortunate man to take your ease among such comfort. What more does any man require than a library, a garden and a fine horse to ride?"

"I consider myself blessed," he replied. "But my greatest blessings are my wife and children. I take great pride in the reports I receive from my son Edward at court. He is a most dutiful boy and a worthy heir to my name."

The King's mood darkened at once. "Indeed, there is no greater blessing than a son," he muttered. "Pray God that I shall soon be granted an heir for my kingdom."

Sir John was stricken into silence by his blunder. At that moment, his daughter Jane entered the hall. Her blonde hair had come loose from her cap and she held a great basket of cut roses in her arms. She placed the basket upon the floor and made a deep curtsey.

"Pardon, your Grace," she said. "I brought some roses from the gardens to set upon the dining table." Her cheeks were flushed from the exertion and she looked almost pretty for once.

"This is my eldest daughter Jane," said Sir John. "She is a maid of honour to the Queen."

"To be sure, I know her well," replied the King courteously. He looked at her with renewed interest.

"We are deeply honoured by your visit, Sire," she said.

"So, you have a rose garden, Sir John," remarked the King. "It is one of my greatest pleasures to take a walk in a pleasant garden. Perhaps Mistress Seymour would do me the kindness of showing me the way to your bower."

"It would be my honour, your Grace," she replied. "Please step this way and I will lead you through the herb garden into the rose arbour. There is a bench in the shade where you can rest and take your ease."

"Nothing would please me more," he replied. "You shall tell me all about yourself and your delightful home."

That evening Mistress Seymour appeared at dinner wearing a heavy gold ring upon her finger. Queen Anne

Boleyn eyed it thoughtfully. It was a ring from the King's own hand and an unmistakeable sign of his regard. The unexpected meeting with Mistress Seymour had aroused the King's romantic sentiments. For the rest of his visit, he sought her out at every opportunity. Edward changed his mind about persuading his father to bring her home from court. Since she had succeeded in gaining the King's favour, there might be a hope of finding her a good match.

In October 1535, Queen Anne found that she was pregnant again. She knew that it was her last chance to win back the favour of the King. She tried to cast her rivals in the shade by dressing with great magnificence. Every day she shimmered in the finest silks and velvets, each gem carefully placed to enhance her beauty. Yet for all her splendour, she could not recapture the King's wandering desire. He had grown weary of the charms that once enraptured him. I saw it in his hollow smiles, his perfunctory conversation and his inattention. Once he had been inseparable from her and had only found pleasure in her presence. He had courted her favour and overwhelmed her with costly presents. Now he had no interest in pleasing her and rarely visited her apartments. She bore his neglect with forced indifference, but I knew that it burned within her. She sought solace in the attentions of the young gentlemen of the court. Master Weston was among them, a gallant figure in his bottle-green doublet. She smiled as he stepped into her chamber again.

"Master Weston," she said, her voice honeyed but edged with amusement, "that is the third time you have visited my apartments clad in that same doublet and hose."

He bowed low, feigning humility. "Alas, Your Majesty, I am but a poor man. I cannot afford a new outfit until I have won a prize at a tournament."

She laughed, though the light in her eyes was knowing. "Until you have won a hand at cards, you mean."

Then, with a careless wave, she added, "Fortunately for you, I am a gracious Queen, and I shall bestow a purse upon you to remedy your deficiencies."

I felt Margery stiffen beside me. Such generosity—a purse gifted from the Queen's own hand—could be dangerous. It would have been more prudent of her to have asked the King to grant him a purse.

Weston straightened, one hand to his chest. "I am indebted to Your Majesty for such kindness."

"In return," she said, "you shall write me a verse in praise of my benevolence."

There was no hesitation, only the easy confidence of a courtier well-versed in flattery. "I would gladly write a book of verses in honour of your bountiful goodness," he said.

"Just one verse will do," she said, eyes glinting. "But it must be your own composition."

He inclined his head with practiced ease. "I shall praise Your Majesty as the most beloved lady of this age. Indeed, Your Majesty exceeds the heroines of all other ages. You are fairer than Helen of Troy, wiser than the Queen of Sheba, and more virtuous than the noble Lucretia."

She tilted her head, appraising him with narrowed eyes. "Well enough, Master Weston. But these are well-worn comparisons. You must present a more original theme in order to win my praise."

He bowed again. "I shall not fail Your Majesty."

Three days later, he returned, now adorned in tawny velvet trimmed with silver lace. The costly outfit was a conscious effort to prove himself worthy of the Queen's notice.

"That is more fitting for your prestige, Master Weston," she observed.

He produced a parchment with a flourish. "By Your Majesty's leave, I would like to read a few lines dedicated to your gracious presence."

"A rose grew on a silver branch,
The fairest of the fair.
Its petals were crimson and white,
Of all flowers the most rare.

The rose grew in a garden,
The paradise of a King.
It was the envy of all eyes,
The glory of the Spring.

I gazed upon that lovely rose,
For many a long day.
I wished that I might pluck that branch
And steal the bloom away.

But since I am a humble man,
I dare not act so bold.

*I hide my thoughts within my heart,
Never to be told."*

The Queen smiled, a slow, satisfied curve of her lips. "Bravo, Master Weston. You have the courtly speech of a true poet. I think you tell your heart very plain for all your modest words."

She basked in the tribute, reassured that she remained desired. But such extravagant flattery was reckless. It overstepped the mark of respectful devotion. I saw Margery's eyes widen at such familiarity. I wondered if she was in the pay of France or Spain. We were both married now and our first loyalties were to our husbands. The Queen saw herself as the focus of courtly love for the young gentlemen. She refused to see the danger she courted. But one of these days her intemperate language would reach the ears of the King and these gallant young men would find themselves banished.

The third year of the reign of Queen Anne began with joyous news for her. The dowager princess Catherine of Aragon died at Kimbolton Castle at the age of fifty. The woman who had once worn the crown, who had defied both annulment and exile, was finally gone.

"Thank God that we are free from the fear of war!" said the King.

"Now we can live together in peace," replied Queen Anne. At last, her rival was gone and she was the undisputed Queen of England. Her child would be born without any stigma over his legitimacy or her marriage to King Henry.

They celebrated by dressing themselves in yellow. Their daughter Elizabeth was taken to mass to the sound of trumpets and with great display. In the evening, the King brought her to the Great Hall where the ladies were dancing and showed her off to his courtiers.

"Is she not a fine child?" he said with a beaming smile.

Everyone agreed that she was a most worthy Princess of England. Queen Anne watched the scene with great satisfaction. She had never felt more secure than she did at that moment. But only two weeks later disaster struck. King Henry had grown restless with the inactivity of the court during the long winter months. He wanted some excitement to break the monotony.

"You are turning into slothful beasts," he chided his companions. "Tomorrow we shall have a joust to stir up your blood and renew your vigour!"

The winter sun hung pale over Greenwich, glinting against the burnished helms and gilded spears of the king's retinue. Trumpets blared as the tiltyard filled with mounted riders. Their banners flickered in the brisk wind—crimson dragons, white greyhounds and the Seymour phoenix rising bright beside the Tudor rose. King Henry VIII, clad in a shimmering suit of gilt-embossed armour, sat astride his towering destrier. At forty-four, he was still flushed with vigour and felt himself equal to any challenge.

"We shall ride against each other Suffolk," he declared. "And may the best man win!"

Atop the gallery, courtiers leaned forward in anticipation. Queen Anne, her eyes narrowed beneath her hood, clutched the edge of the canopy with white-knuckled fingers.

"It is folly," she whispered. "Why could he not content himself with a game of archery? But no, he must prove his manhood by jousting in the full view of the court!"

Henry wheeled his steed into position with his visor down and his lance angled. The signal was given. The great horse surged forward like a thunderclap. But just as it reached full gallop and the King lowered his lance to strike, the beast stumbled and collapsed. A collective groan rippled across the gallery as the horse and rider crashed to the ground. King Henry's body disappeared under the bulk of the stallion, the dust rising like smoke from a battlefield. For one breathless moment, all was still. Then came a flurry as grooms and guards dashed forward to heave the great carcass out of the way. The King lay motionless on the ground. I thought he must surely be dead.

Queen Anne was frozen in shock. "Dear God, somebody help him!" she said.

The duke of Suffolk dismounted and hurried across the tiltyard to take charge. "Send for the King's doctors!" he said. "Bring a door and place the King upon it. He must be taken to his bedchamber at once!"

The Yeomen of the Guard carried the King into the palace. He lay speechless for two hours and everyone feared the worst. Then he rallied and regained his senses. The courtiers were filled with relief. The Queen was so shaken that she took to her bed.

"Thank God that he was spared," she said. "If he had died then Elizabeth is nothing. A bastard. And I am discarded, or worse. How could he do this to me?"

The day after the King's fall, she was prostrate with exhaustion. She lay half-upright among silken pillows, her dark hair unbound, spilling across the embroidered counterpane like spilled ink. Her face was pale, her lips bitten red. Tremors still coursed through her, though she clutched at the edge of her counterpane as though it might anchor her.

Lady Wiltshire, composed in her jewelled hood and heavy sleeves, sat beside her daughter, the embroidery in her lap forgotten. She dipped a cloth into a bowl of lavender water and gently pressed it to the Queen's forehead.

"You must not go to visit his Majesty," she said. "You should rest here in your bedchamber. You must think of your own condition."

"I ought to check on what his doctors are doing," she replied. "If he were to die, then what would become of us?"

"Your uncle Norfolk would protect you," she said. "He is the Earl Marshall of England. He would become the regent for the Princess Elizabeth."

"He would marry her to one of his family and rule the kingdom," she said. "I will not allow him to usurp the throne. I shall become the regent for my daughter."

Lady Wiltshire smoothed her daughter's brow with trembling fingers. "You must not worry yourself," she said. "The King is a strong man and he is sure to recover. His surgeons say that nothing is broken."

The Queen's eyes flicked to the door. "Send a messenger

to bring me news of the King," she ordered. "One of the pages can go to his chamber."

"None of these boys have the wits to find out what is going on," said Lady Wiltshire. "Send one of your ladies to speak to the doctors."

Her eye fell on Mistress Jane Seymour and she signalled to her to leave. She departed at once on her errand. But an hour later, she had still not returned.

"Something is wrong," said Queen Anne. "Perhaps the King has grown worse. Or maybe he has died and she does not dare to tell me the news. I shall have to go there myself. Bring me my mantle!"

"Let me go in your place," said Lady Wiltshire. "You can depend upon me to find out what has happened."

"I must see the King with my own eyes," she insisted. She got up and put her feet into her velvet slippers and made her way to the door. I rushed after her with her mantle of powdered ermine as she strode determinedly along the corridors.

"He is a fool to try to joust at his age," she muttered to herself. "It is a pastime for brash young men, not for kings. He must never do so again."

The Yeomen Guards stepped back as she approached the King's Privy Chamber. The door swung open and I followed her inside the chamber. King Henry was sitting on his chair of estate in front of a blazing fire.

Queen Anne's voice rang out, sharp and edged with fury, stopping me in my tracks. "How dare you?" she spat, her skirts rustling violently as she strode forward. The rich crimson velvet of her gown, embroidered with golden thread, caught the fire's light, turning her into a figure of blazing wrath. The Queen's hand trembled upon her swelling belly, her dark eyes locked upon the scene before her— on his lap sat Mistress Jane Seymour, her fair hair tumbling softly over her forehead and a meek smile playing upon her lips. The King shifted, his expression tightening though he did not rise.

"You disgrace me, my Lord," she snapped. "Am I not your wife? Have you no regard for my honour or my unborn child?"

Henry's lips pressed together into a firm line. I saw the flicker of irritation, the impatience that had begun to mark his demeanour towards her these past months.

"Madam, you will not speak to me thus," he rumbled, his voice carrying the weight of warning. "I am your sovereign as well as your husband."

Anne's chin lifted, defiance sparking in her gaze. "I am your Queen," she countered, her voice trembling with the force of suppressed rage. "I am the mother of your heir, and yet you humiliate me." Her glare cut to Jane, who lowered her eyes in feigned humility.

Henry sighed, shifting Jane from his lap with slow deliberation, then stood up. "You fret too much, Anne. Mistress Seymour is nothing but a gentle lady of my court. Unlike some, she knows how to be pleasing."

Mistress Seymour remained silent, her downcast eyes masking whatever satisfaction she might have felt at having captured the King's favour. I saw the subtle tremor in her fingers as she smoothed the folds of her gown—a soft dove-grey damask, modest yet deliberate in its understated elegance.

The Queen's shoulders slumped in defeat. "I came to see how you fared, Henry," she replied. "Since I see that you are so well recovered, I shall retire to my apartments and rest."

I followed her out of the door, my heart hammering with the knowledge that I had just witnessed the beginning of the end. And I feared—more than I dared admit—that Queen Anne knew it too. By the time she returned to her bedchamber she was as pale as a ghost. Her mother was alarmed by her distraught appearance.

"Is it bad news, your Grace?" she asked.

The Queen sat down on her bed and clutched the bedspread in her hands. "I found that slut Jane Seymour sitting on the King's knee!" she said.

"You must not upset yourself," said Lady Boleyn. "She will not matter a jot to his Majesty once you have borne him a son."

"I will have her banished from the court," she said. "She is a devious little hussy. She has taken advantage of the King's illness to worm her way into his affections. I will make her rue the day that she presumed to take liberties with my husband."

"Try not to think about it," urged Lady Boleyn. "Lie down and take some rest. You cannot afford to become ill."

Tears began to slide down the Queen's face. "He has no affection for me anymore, mother," she said. "I could see it in his face. He is a cold and heartless man."

"Take off your dress and put on your nightgown," she said. "I will bring you a cup of wine to drink."

I unpinned the sleeves and unlaced the dress. Then I brought the Queen's satin nightgown and put it on her. She lay down on her bed and began to weep into her pillow. Lady Boleyn put down the cup of wine on the sideboard and frowned.

"Let everyone withdraw," she said. "The Queen needs to rest quietly in her bedchamber."

I took the opportunity to return to my apartments at once. I found Edward seated at his desk writing a letter. I did not pause for pleasantries.

"The Queen visited the King today," I said. "And she found your sister Jane sitting on his knee!"

His head snapped up and his sharp gaze fixed upon me. For a moment, there was silence and then exultation.

"This is it," he said, rising to his feet. "The Queen's days are numbered. The King has grown tired of her tantrums. And now he has seen how quiet and obedient Jane is." He turned to me, his expression alight with triumph. "Jane must remain resolute. She must not yield to his advances, not yet. If she does, she will be just another mistress. She must uphold her virtue and make him wait."

I swallowed, shifting uneasily. "You must speak to her, Edward," I said. "You must tell her what is expected of her."

He smiled—an expression of calculation rather than joy. "If she plays her part well, then the Queen will fall."

I shivered, the weight of his words settling heavily upon me. "But what if she bears a son?" I asked, forcing myself to meet his gaze. "You know how vengeful she is. If she gives the King an heir, we will all suffer the consequences."

For the first time, Edward hesitated. His jaw tightened, his fingers flexing as he considered the possibility.

"She will not," he said at last, though his voice carried none of its usual certainty.

I stepped closer, lowering my voice. "And if she does?"

"Then we must ensure that Jane does not falter," he said. "The King must become besotted with her. His love for her is our best protection. We have come too far to hesitate now."

The words settled in the air like a prophecy. The Queen's triumph would mean our ruin. And the game had never felt more perilous than at that moment. But Edward was proven right. At the end of January 1536, Queen Anne miscarried her child. As she lay weeping in her bedchamber, King Henry came to visit her. But he offered her no words of comfort.

"I see that God does not intend to give me sons," he said coldly.

Queen Anne turned on him in a rage. "You did this!" she snapped. "Your lechery with that little slut caused me such grief that I lost my child. It is all your fault!"

King Henry frowned. He could never bear to be told that he was at fault. "I shall speak to you later when you are up," he replied. "I bid you good day, Madam." He turned and left the bedchamber.

The Queen was distressed by his lack of sympathy. "He has broken my heart," she said. "How can I bear a healthy child when he treats me like this?"

She was now thirty-five years old. It was unlikely that she would bear any more children. The courtiers whispered that she had miscarried of her saviour. A son would have secured her position as the Queen. But now she was just another barren wife. And now that Catherine of Aragon was dead, it would possible for the King to set her aside and marry again.

The following month, I gave birth to my first child. It was a daughter. Edward was disappointed. He had hoped for a son.

"We shall have a son next time," I said.

"Yes, of course," he replied.

"What shall we name her?" I asked.

"She will be Anne after her mother," he said.

I was touched. "We will say that we named her after the Queen," I replied.

I found a wet nurse for my daughter and sent them to live at Elvetham. It was healthier for children to be raised in the countryside. And a court lady could not play the nursemaid.

The King did not trouble himself to speak to his wife. He had nothing more to say to her. Instead, he continued to seek Jane out. He was charmed by her beauty and innocence. He began to send her costly presents as a sign of his favour: a rosary of coral beads, a gold tablet engraved with the Passion of Christ and an illuminated Book of Hours in a cover of dark blue velvet.

He sent her messages saying that these gifts were intended as tributes to her piety and virtue. Suddenly, Jane became the focus of attention in the court. Edward was as astonished as I was that his dull sister had managed to gain the King's notice. He was determined to make the most of the opportunity. He sent for her to come to our apartments immediately.

"You have had the good fortune to catch the King's eye, Jane," said Edward.

"I haven't encouraged him," she replied defensively.

"Soon he will begin to court you," he said. "But you must not give in to his advances. You must be like Anne Boleyn and not like her foolish sister Mary."

"What do you mean?" she asked.

"I mean that he will try to persuade you to become his mistress," he said bluntly. "But you must refuse him. Then he will respect you as a virtuous woman."

"I am a virtuous woman," she protested indignantly.

"At the same time, you must make yourself agreeable to his Majesty," he lectured her. "We don't want him to go elsewhere. You must kindle his affections until he is willing to make you his lawful wife and Queen of England."

"But he is already married," she protested.

"The King has grown tired of Anne Boleyn," he said. "She is too petulant and demanding. And she has failed to give him a son. He wants to take another wife. And you shall be that wife if you follow my instructions to the letter."

"But the Queen will be furious with me," she said doubtfully.

He snapped his fingers. "A fig for the Queen! Let her scold and storm. It won't make any difference. The King has fallen in love with you. He will refuse to send you from court."

"I don't think I can do it, Edward," she said.

"Of course you can," he replied impatiently. "The more you refuse him, the more determined he will be to have you. You must hold out for marriage and settle for nothing less!"

"Yes, Edward," she agreed.

Under normal circumstances, the King wouldn't have looked twice at a commonplace girl like Jane. She was plain, quiet and dull. She had spent years at court without attracting his attention. But now he looked at her in a new light. Everything that had once dazzled him about Anne now repulsed him. He did not want a wife who was fascinating, temperamental and demanding. He wanted a virtuous and obedient lady who would bear his children and never contradict him. Someone who resembled his first wife but without any powerful family connections. Jane fitted those requirements to perfection. In his eyes she was the ideal chaste and demure maiden. Now Jane had the opportunity of a lifetime in front of her. She was fortunate that the Queen's powers were waning. The King would not be deterred by her tantrums any more. He would pursue any woman who took his fancy. He started visiting the Queen's apartments again. She was delighted until she realised that he was not coming to see her, but to see Jane.

"What do you see in that little fool?" she demanded. "She is the least accomplished of my ladies. She is unworthy of your interest."

"She has qualities which you do not value because you do not possess them, Madam," he retorted. "She is not a frivolous woman but a virtuous lady. It is surprising to find such a one in your circle."

"She is no pure maiden but a snake in the grass," she muttered.

As a special sign of his favour the King sent Jane a large gold locket on a chain. Inside was his portrait surrounded by diamonds. It was the kind of lavish present that was sent to kings and princes rather than members of the court. Jane was delighted by this proof of his regard. She wore it the following morning to chapel. She held it up in her hand and clicked it open and shut several times. She spent the entire time opening it and closing it again. Then she looked across the chapel and smiled at the king. He smiled back at her and the Queen's face turned as black as thunder. By the end of the service everyone at court was aware that Jane had received a token from the King. I was surprised by her temerity in parading her good fortune. She was not the meek little mouse that she seemed to be. She relished the opportunity to show off her favour and make herself the centre of attention. Now she could settle her score with the Queen after having endured so many years of humiliation at her hands.

Queen Anne confronted her as soon as they returned to the privy chamber.

"What is this bauble that you are parading in front of everyone?" she demanded. "Is it a pledge from your lover?"

"I could not say, your Grace," she replied.

"Show it to me," she insisted.

"As you wish, your Grace," she said. She opened the locket and showed the King's picture to the queen.

Queen Anne turned pale at the sight of it. Then she turned scarlet with anger and humiliation. "How dare you flaunt this in my presence?" she raged. "You are a shameless creature. You will leave the court at once!"

"The King does not wish me to leave, your Grace," she replied. "He says that I bring him comfort."

"So, you admit your guilt, you shameless hussy," she snapped. "How dare you make eyes at his Majesty?"

She yanked the locket so hard that the chain snapped. Jane cried out in pain. The Queen threw the costly jewel upon the floor and stamped on it. "Get out of here, you little slut," she ordered. "I don't want to see your pasty face ever again."

Jane was stricken by the loss of her jewel. She curtsied and withdrew at once. But the Queen's triumph was short-lived. The King commanded her to receive Jane back into her service and treat her with courtesy. The Queen's eyes were red with weeping and she could not bring herself to speak a word to Jane.

Edward was elated by this proof of Jane's standing. "Look at the honours that the King granted Sir Thomas Boleyn," he said. "He made him Viscount Rochford, earl of Wiltshire and Lord Privy Seal for the sake of his daughter. Lady Boleyn became a countess. We shall receive similar honours if we promote Jane in the King's affections."

"But Jane is nothing like Anne Boleyn," I protested. I could not imagine Jane upholding the rank and dignity of the Queen of England.

"The King does not want another wife like Anne," he insisted. "He wants a conventional wife who is virtuous, submissive and obedient. Jane will be perfect for him as long as she does not yield herself to become his mistress. She must maintain her honour as a gentlewoman. Then he will respect her."

"Surely he will look much higher for a bride," I said doubtfully.

"Anne Boleyn was only the daughter of a knight," he said. "Why should he not raise Jane just as high?"

"If she can succeed in maintaining his interest," I said. "But it is a difficult game to play. Bessie Blount and Mary Boleyn were beautiful and charming women but the King cast them both aside after a time."

"That was because they submitted to his desires," he said. "Jane must resist his courtship and show herself as a pure and gentle lady. When he sees that she does not surrender then he will make her an honourable offer of marriage."

"Then you must teach her some pretty speeches that will beguile him," I said. "Jane can hardly put two words together by herself."

"I shall think of something," he said. "We cannot allow such a golden opportunity to slip from our grasp."

The King's favour towards Jane had not gone unnoticed in the court. The following day, Sir Nicholas Carew came to call on us. He was the Master of the Horse and one of the King's favourite gentlemen.

He swept into the chamber with the easy grace of a man born to the tiltyard and the royal privy chamber alike. He was every inch the courtier—tall, broad-shouldered, with a hawkish nose and eyes as sharp and appraising as a falcon. His beard was neatly trimmed in the French fashion and his russet hair curled just beneath a black velvet cap adorned with pearl spangles. He wore a doublet of dark crimson velvet edged with slashes of gold damask that revealed glimpses of cloth-of-silver beneath. A heavy chain of office hung across his chest with a heavy medallion set with a Tudor rose. His hose was made of fine black wool, and his boots were fashioned of the finest Spanish leather. At his side hung a jewelled dagger that had been a present from the King.

He bowed with practiced elegance. "Mistress Seymour," he said with a smile that never quite reached his eyes, "it seems your star is rising faster than Jupiter's. Even the stags in Windsor Forest have heard whispers of your beauty and sweet nature." But there was a cunning in Carew's charm, like a blade hidden in a fan, and I knew well that his visit was not merely one of courtesy.

Jane blushed at his flattery and lowered her head. Her hands twisted nervously in the folds of her gown. "I seek only to serve His Grace with humility," she replied.

Sir Nicholas inclined his head, but there was calculation in his smile. "Then you are wiser than most of those who walk in satin and dream of crowns."

"We are honoured by your visit, Sir Nicholas," said Edward. "Please take a chair and sit with us. May I offer you a cup of wine?"

Sir Nicholas sat upon a high-backed chair and waved aside the offer of wine. He leaned forward, gloved hands clasped on his knee, his gaze sharp and probing. "The court breathes Mistress Seymour's name as though she were an angel of radiant light descended to bless us all."

Edward met his eyes squarely. "It is not her beauty alone that commands attention," he said. "She is modest, virtuous, and—above all—obedient. She offers what the Queen does not—quiet counsel and untroubled grace."

"I would rejoice to see the King set Anne Boleyn aside," he said. "He would be far more contented if he had a gentle and pious lady like Jane as his Queen. But there is an art to persuading him to take this course. Any pretty girl may receive a trinket from the King. But only a clever woman can obtain all the jewels of the Queen of England."

"We would be grateful to receive your counsel, Sir Nicholas," Edward replied. "What do you advise?"

"I have served the King for many years," he boasted. "He is a romantic at heart. He has a fantasy in his mind about meeting a fair lady from the days of chivalry. He wishes to prove his love for her by his courtesy and knightly deeds. He sees himself as being just as honourable as she is virtuous."

"I see you have a great understanding of his mind," he said.

"He is attracted to Jane for her beauty and mildness," he continued. "Now she must demonstrate her unassailable virtue. This will show that she is his ideal lady. An easy conquest would only be a disappointment to him. So, in future, she must decline his gifts and protest her integrity. She will gain his respect and he will desire her all the more."

"So, she must be an unattainable lady," he said.

"She must play her part in the courtly dance," he said. "Anne Boleyn was no great beauty but she knew how to intrigue him. She embodied his fantasy so convincingly that he made her his queen instead of his mistress. And where she succeeded, Jane can follow."

"It is a stroke of genius," Edward said. "How can I ever thank you?"

"I would ask only one thing in return," he said. "Jane must persuade the King to restore Lady Mary to his favour."

"I agree most willingly," he said. "And I shall tell my sister that henceforth she must refuse all the King's gifts."

"By your leave, Sir Edward," he said. "It is not just the words that matter. It is about creating the right image in the King's mind. A delightful picture of a virtuous damsel who kneels and weeps and prays before him. Call your sister here and I will play the part of an ardent suitor. She must practice how to make pretty refusals and reluctant denials that will stir the King's affections. I swear that within three days I will teach her the whole craft of courtly love. He will not be able to resist her charms."

The following week, the King sent a letter and a purse of gold sovereigns to Jane. I knew this was his formal offer asking her to become his *maitresse-en-titre*. I watched intently as she enacted her reply with such solemn grace that even the candles seemed to bow their heads. She received the gift just as she had been instructed with humble gratitude and maidenly tears. She took the letter and kissed it with great reverence. Then she returned it unopened to the messenger and fell upon her knees before him. Her pale gown pooled around her like moonlight, her face was framed by a velvet hood and a single pearl trembled at her throat. This was Jane's moment, and she played it as surely as a lute in the hands of a master.

"Good Sir, I pray you tell his Majesty the King to consider that I am a gentlewoman of good and honourable parents," she said. "I have served at court for many years without any reproach to my name. I have no greater riches in the world than my honour, which I would not injure for a thousand deaths."

"Will you not accept this purse, Mistress Seymour?" he asked in surprise.

If his Grace wishes to make me some present in money, I beg that it might be when God enables me to make an honourable marriage", she replied.

"I will tell his Majesty what you have said," he said.

"I give you my thanks, good Sir," she answered and he took his leave. She remained kneeling, her head bowed as if in prayer. Her modest refusal was like a gauntlet dropped before the throne itself. She was not the King's for purchase. She was more. She was purity incarnate, or so she wished to be seen.

The following day, the King sent for Edward and myself to attend him in his privy chamber. "Let everyone withdraw," he commanded. His attendants departed at once, leaving us alone.

"I wish to speak to you about your sister Jane," he said. "I had thought to exalt her by making her my mistress. But I have come to realise that she is a lady of extraordinary virtue. I would not stain her honour for all the world. So, I am determined to win her love through an honourable courtship."

"I am sure that my sister would be honoured to receive your addresses, your Majesty" he replied.

The King's face brightened. "I am glad to hear you say so," he said. "I have taken thought upon the matter. Master Cromwell has agreed to give up his apartments to you and your wife. They are near to my own and connected by a private gallery. In this manner, I can visit her whenever I wish and persuade her to bestow her affections upon me. I trust that this arrangement would be agreeable to you."

"It would give us the greatest pleasure to oblige your Majesty," he said.

"You are a good servant, Sir Edward," he replied. "As a token of my goodwill I have decided to appoint you as one of my gentlemen of the privy chamber."

Edward made a deep bow. "I shall serve your Majesty most faithfully," he said.

"Pray take this message to your worthy sister," he replied. "Tell her that she has conducted herself most virtuously and henceforth I do not intend to speak with her except in your presence. It is my hope that this will reassure her that my intentions are wholly good and sincere."

"I will urge her to comply with your Majesty's wishes," he said. "If you permit us to take our leave, we will go to her at once."

"Yes, go to her and tell her of my heartfelt regard and affection," he said.

We made our obeisances and departed. Nothing had been said about the Queen. It was as if she did not exist. Edward was too wise to raise the subject. This was a matter that could only be resolved by the King. We stood in the corridor and looked at each other in suppressed excitement. The King had asked for Edward's consent. It was as good as a formal offer of marriage!

"What a wonderful chance for your family, Edward," I said.

"Absolutely", he replied. A faint smile hovered upon his lips. He was already dreaming of the riches and honours that would come his way once he was the brother-in-law of the King.

"You will have to take charge of the situation and make sure that no advantage is taken of Jane," I cautioned. "She must be treated with the respect that is due to a future queen."

"I will accept nothing less," he said, jutting his chin. "Since she has been fortunate enough to attract the attention of his Majesty, I will make sure that she takes her place at his side. No sister of mine shall become the King's mistress. Their courtship will be conducted with the utmost propriety. I shall see to it myself. Jane will say and do exactly what I tell her. I will not allow her to make a fool of herself."

"We will stand beside her and protect her from the hazards of the court," I agreed. "We shall be her closest advisers and friends. She will be grateful and reward us as our loyalty deserves." *From now on we would be part of the royal circle. Nothing and no-one would stand in our way.*

We took possession of our new apartments within a few days. They were splendidly furnished with furnishings brought from the royal stores. The walls were adorned with rich tapestries imported from Flanders, their coloured threads depicting scenes of classical mythology and courtly love—Venus reclining among roses, Perseus rescuing Andromeda and knights seeking their lady's favour. The fabric shimmered in the morning light, lending an almost otherworldly vibrancy to the chambers. Polished oak panels lined the lower walls, carved with Tudor roses and Latin mottoes extolling virtue, honour, and divine right. Above, the heavy-beamed ceiling was painted with the King's arms and *fleur-de-lis*, the paint still fresh enough to give off a faint tang of oil and pigment.

The fireplace was built of pale Caen stone carved with grotesques and acanthus leaves. In the hearth a fire crackled merrily, filling the space with warmth and the spicy scent of burning juniper. Upon the mantelpiece stood an ornate mirror, newly arrived from Venice. A wide velvet-covered settle was set near the hearth, piled with embroidered cushions of crimson satin and cloth-of-gold. Next to it stood a table of inlaid walnut with a crystal vase of fresh gillyflowers—Jane's favourite. The chamber floors were covered with a layer of woven rush mats edged in green silk braid and strewn with costly Turkey rugs. In the window seats long cushions of soft grey and rose damask were set against the glass-panelled shutters. It was a stage set for romance and Jane was its heroine.

Edward walked around the chambers with a calculating look in his eyes. "We must have a new wardrobe of gowns made for Jane," he said. "If she is the King's new favourite, then she must dress the part."

"But have you considered the cost, Edward?" I asked in dismay.

"Hang the cost!" he replied. "I would rather get into debt than lose this chance!"

And so, Jane was the beneficiary of a splendid trousseau. She looked quite passable in her new gowns of pale blue silk, straw-coloured satin and white cloth of silver. I had to admit that Edward was right. It sent a clear message to the world that Jane was now a person of consequence. And when the King visited her apartments, he gazed at her with even greater admiration.

"You look as fair as a blossom on a pear tree, my dear," he sighed.

Jane curtsied low, her silvery skirts spilling like moonlight across the Turkey rugs on the floor. She smiled demurely, but I saw the tremor in her fingers as she gathered them at her waist. She played the innocent well, but I knew her dreams had grown bolder with each new gown and admiring glance.

"I have never seen a woman more fit for court," the King declared, stepping closer. His voice had dropped to a tone meant only for her, but we heard it all the same.

I watched as Jane's lashes fluttered downwards modestly. She was learning fast.

He took her hand, pressing it between his own. "You are a balm to my soul, sweetheart."

At that, Edward's eyes flicked to mine in triumph. The King was thoroughly ensnared! He adored Jane just as much as he had once idolised Anne Boleyn.

Later, after the King had taken his leave and the door had closed behind him, Jane turned to us. Her cheeks were aglow and her eyes were filled with pride.

"He kissed my hand," she whispered, almost reverently.

Edward clapped his hands together as though he had won a great tourney. "You will be Queen yet," he beamed, "if you play the part to perfection."

As soon as it was known that we had moved into apartments near the King, everyone at court wanted to visit us. Overnight we had become a notable family and Jane's name was upon everyone's lips. Edward was determined to make the most of the opportunity. He wanted to redeem his promise to Sir Nicholas Carew and build an alliance with the supporters of the Lady Mary.

"There are many people at court who sympathise with Lady Mary and detest Anne Boleyn," he said. "They would support you to become the next Queen if you interceded with the King to reinstate Lady Mary at court."

"The King does not like anyone to interfere in his family affairs," she replied.

"Master Cromwell would support you too," he said. "He wants an alliance with the emperor of Spain. But Anne Boleyn favours an alliance with France."

"These are political matters," she said stubbornly. "They are not my concern."

"This is your chance to show that you are different from Anne Boleyn," he insisted. "That you would be a good influence upon the King. You would be a peacemaker and heal the divisions at court."

She shook her head. "It will only make him angry," she replied.

"Not if you do it in the right way, Jane," he said. "Wait for the right moment to come. Then use your powers of gentle persuasion. Tell him that nothing would make you happier than to see him reconciled with his daughter."

"You ask too much of me, Edward," she said petulantly.

"You must show that you are worthy to be Queen," he said. "This will be seen as a sign of your goodwill. It will gain you powerful friends in the court including the Spanish ambassador."

Jane turned to me in distress at his demands. "Anne, you can understand why I can't do it," she pleaded.

"What sort of a queen do you want to be?" I asked. "Queen Catherine of Aragon was beloved because she cared for the welfare of others. Whereas Queen Anne is despised because she only considers the interests of herself and her family. Don't you want to be a queen who is popular with the court and the people?"

"I only wish to please his Majesty the King," she protested.

"If you only want to please the King, then you can become his mistress," said Edward brutally. "But if you want to become a queen, then you must influence the King for his own good. I have made promises and given assurances on your behalf. So, you must make good on them and show that you are trustworthy."

"Very well, I will ask him," she agreed. "But not because of politics. Only because it will increase the King's happiness and out of pity for the Lady Mary."

The following day, King Henry paid a visit to Jane's chambers. His expression was a blend of satisfaction and longing as he took his place at the fireside. I stood at her side knowing that this was a moment of great consequence. His gaze bore into hers, and when he spoke, his voice was rich with affection.

"Good morrow, sweetheart," he said. "Last night, I could not sleep for thinking of you. And so, I wrote a verse to express the joy and pain of my great love. Shall I read it to you?"

Jane bowed her head slightly. "If it pleases your Majesty," she murmured.

The King reached into his sleeve, drew out a carefully folded scroll, and unfurled it before us. His eyes gleamed with satisfaction as he read aloud: *"To my fair lady.*

O radiant jewel of purest hue,
Thy beauty shines both bright and true.
The world may turn, the seasons fade,
Yet in thine eyes my heart is laid.

A queen thou art in grace untold,
Thy virtues shine in burnished gold.
Let love endure, unyielding, bright,
For thee, my Jane, my soul takes flight."

As the words fell upon Jane's ears, a single tear traced the curve of her cheek. She gazed at him as if he were the centre of the universe itself.

"It is wonderful, Your Majesty," she breathed. "I am deeply touched by your tender sentiments. No lady was ever courted like this."

"My heart is burning with love for you," he declared, leaning forward ever so slightly. "Do you think that you could ever learn to return my affections?"

"I believe so, Your Grace," Jane replied softly. "I am more inclined towards you every day."

His sigh of satisfaction was audible, a man pleased with his conquest. "Your gracious words are my reward," he said. "I did not spend the long hours of the night labouring in vain."

Jane hesitated, and I could feel the tension in her posture. Then, after a brief pause, she spoke, her voice careful, deliberate.

"Your Grace, I wish to ask a favour of you."

His indulgence was immediate. "You may ask me for anything you like, my dear," he said, his voice warm. "I would willingly give you the golden sun, the silver moon, and the glittering stars of the firmament."

She took a steadying breath. "Then I pray that you would restore the Lady Mary to your good graces again. Let her come back to court and regain her former position of honour."

The transformation in the King was swift and terrifying. The tenderness drained from his expression, his eyes darkening like a storm gathering with sudden force.

"Who has been talking to you?" he demanded, suspicion lacing his words. His gaze locked onto her, searching her face for betrayal.

"No-one, Your Majesty," Jane answered quickly. "It was my own thought entirely."

His expression hardened. "Then you are a fool," he snapped. "You should solicit my favour on behalf of your own children, not those of others."

Jane faltered but did not back down. "I fear that Your Majesty has mistaken my intention," she said, voice trembling. "My only wish is for your future happiness and that of the realm."

"You may leave the affairs of the realm to me," he growled. "I do not wish to think of the past but only of the happy future that is to come. And I have no desire to see the Lady Mary."

A silence settled between them, brittle and dangerous. Jane lowered her eyes. "Of course, Your Majesty," she murmured. "May I offer you some wine?"

His mood had turned sour beyond repair. "It is time that I took my leave," he said coldly. "I have important business to conduct."

With a sharp movement, he rose to his feet, and we hurriedly followed, bending into our curtseys as he departed with heavy, unforgiving steps.

The moment the door shut, Jane turned on me in fury, her cheeks flushed with frustration. "See what you have done?" she hissed. "Now he is offended and it is all because of you and Edward. You are both consumed with ambition. I wish that I had never listened to either of you!"

I caught her hands gently in mine. "He will come back," I reassured her.

"But what if he doesn't?" she whispered, her voice raw with fear. "What if he changes his mind about me?"

I considered her words, then offered a solution. "Then give him some encouragement," I said. "Send him a verse in return."

She hesitated. "But I don't know how to write a love poem."

I smiled. "Leave it to me."

And so, I took up my quill, the weight of courtly intrigue heavy upon me, and penned the words that would soothe a king's wounded pride.

It was a simple matter to pen a verse. Jane was probably the only lady at court who lacked the skill. I had no doubt that Anne Boleyn could have managed it at the age of twelve. I wrote it down and she copied it out in her round childish hand.

"To my true love,

Thy words, like silver, sweetly gleam,
Upon my heart they dance and dream.
Through courtly halls, through days so bright,
Thy love doth set my soul alight.

If fate shall weave our hearts as one,
Through time and tide, through moon and sun,
Then in thy arms, my vow shall stay—
My love, my king, till end of day."

I took it up and scrutinized it carefully. Then I rolled it up. "Give me your ribbon," I said. She unfastened it from her hair and handed it to me. I wrapped it around the parchment and tied it deftly in a lover's knot. Then I summoned the page boy and told him to take it to the King at once. The King replied with an invitation for us to come to supper in his privy chamber. He was quite enraptured by Jane's poem. His tyrannical nature had been placated and now he was ready to play the ardent lover again.

Jane was quite unnerved by the volatility of the King's moods. She clutched at my arm with anxious fingers as we made our way to his privy chamber. The flickering torches along the corridor threw long shadows, dancing like spectres upon the stone walls, mirroring the tumult of emotions within her. The great doors swung open, and there he stood—King Henry, resplendent in deep crimson velvet, a golden chain heavy across his broad chest. His mood had shifted entirely; gone was the sharp-tempered monarch of the morning. His eyes glowed with approval, a man content with his conquest.

"Ah, my fair Jane," he said, his voice rich with satisfaction. "Your words have touched me to the core. I had not thought to find such poetry in your gentle soul." He gestured to the long table, set with goblets of spiced wine and an array of delicacies fit for a king. "Come, sit beside me."

We took our places, Jane at his right hand, myself farther down the table, watchful. A string of musicians struck up a delicate melody, the air filled with the scent of roasted meats and honeyed fruits. The King, leaning toward Jane, traced a finger along the embroidered edge of her sleeve.

"I know the depths of my devotion," he murmured, "but to know that you, too, feel such stirring within your heart touches me deeply." He sighed in contentment, as if transported by the romance of the moment. "It binds us, does it not?"

Jane nodded demurely. "It is my hope that Your Majesty shall always find joy in my words."

He smiled with pleasure. "Joy, indeed! I shall have your poem copied and set within a jewelled book for my keeping." He raised his goblet. "A toast! To my Jane, the light of my heart, the promise of my future!"

We lifted our cups, though the air around us felt heavy with expectation. Jane, despite her graceful exterior, knew that his affection was as fickle as the tide. But for this night, she had secured his favour. And for now, that was enough.

Afterwards Edward congratulated me for my efforts. "I never knew you had such a gift for verse, my dear," he said.

"I can play these courtly games as well as any noble-woman," I replied. But although I had soothed the tempest, I felt uneasy. King Henry's romance with Jane was a great risk for Edward and myself.

"The King is notoriously fickle," I said. "Suppose he gets the Queen with child again? What then? Or suppose he sees another beautiful young lady at court? Jane would end up as one more of his passing fancies." I wondered if we were overreaching ourselves. If something went wrong, then we would lose everything.

"He can't abide the Queen anymore," he said. "He will never share a bed with her again."

"She is clever," I reminded him. "She has beguiled him back before."

"Her attractions are worn out," he said bluntly. "She looks like a tired old woman. He will never return to her again. He wants Jane."

"But how can they get married?" I said. "The King tore the kingdom apart to wed the Queen. He would look foolish if he changed his mind about her."

"The King has told the privy council that he was beguiled into this marriage by sortileges," he said. "He said that it was no true marriage."

"But what grounds does he have to end it?" I asked.

"He has told Cromwell to arrange the matter," he said. "He has never failed the king and he won't disappoint him now."

On the day of the May Day joust, Jane and I took our places in the Queen's pavilion to watch the festivities. We were now the Seymour ladies, her acknowledged enemies, and she treated us with an icy disdain. She had dressed herself with especial care for the occasion in a gown of crimson cloth of gold and sleeves of crimson velvet. A messenger arrived with a letter for the King. He read the missive and then got up and left his pavilion immediately. He did not come and bid farewell to the Queen as courtesy demanded.

"The King must be feeling unwell," said the Queen. She was perturbed by his sudden departure. He had never been known to leave the jousts early before. It was his favourite pastime to watch the knights compete, to congratulate the winners and to bring the competitors back to the palace to drink with him. She continued to preside over the contest alone. But the zest had gone out of the occasion. As the jousts wore on, the atmosphere grew heavier. Without the King's laughter to echo through the grounds, or his booming voice to announce the victor, the contest seemed hollow—a mere pantomime of its former glory. The Queen's efforts to maintain the day's energy faltered, her forced smiles failing to ignite the enthusiasm of the gathered court. When the final challenge took place, it was greeted by a thin scattering of applause.

Queen Anne rose from her seat with practiced poise, her rich crimson gown billowing lightly as she stepped forward to present the prizes to the victorious knights. Her expression was carefully composed—a regal mask of dignity—but the sharp observer would notice the faint tremble in her hands as she clasped the gilded laurel wreath meant for the champion. Each prize was handed over with an air of strained formality, her smile tight and fleeting as she congratulated the winners in clipped tones. "Well done, Sir William," she murmured, her voice carrying just enough to be heard over the din. Yet her gaze darted briefly toward the empty space where the King's pavilion stood, a silent reminder of his departure. She moved on to the next recipient, her pace deliberate but lacking its usual assured grace. The courtiers exchanged glances, sensing the unease that emanated from her. When one of the knights, bold and flushed from victory, offered her a sweeping bow and a jest about her favour, she faltered for the briefest moment, her lips pressing together as though to suppress a retort.

Her eyes flickered towards Jane whose composed elegance had drawn considerable attention. The Queen's grip tightened on the silk sash she held, the tremor in her fingers unmistakable now as she extended it to the next recipient. By the time the last prize was distributed, her face betrayed the faintest sheen of perspiration, her carefully curated confidence beginning to unravel. She returned to her throne with her head held high, yet there was a tension in her posture, a stiffness in her movements that betrayed her struggle to maintain the image of regal authority. The knights cheered, and the spectators applauded politely, but the atmosphere was subdued—laden with whispers and speculations about the King's sudden departure and the Queen's mounting unease. The day, once meant to celebrate triumph and chivalry, had become a stage for her faltering composure, and the court took note.

The festivities of May Day drew to a close and the jousts concluded with none of the revelry that usually accompanied them. The knights withdrew quietly and the crowds dispersed in a subdued manner. As the Queen rose to retire to her chambers, she looked pale and strained. She did not have the heart to make jests in order to arouse a sense of merriment. Her ladies followed her in silence back to the palace. The occasion was a feeble imitation of the joyous celebrations of the past. Everyone was wondering what had happened to the King. Whatever had prompted his sudden departure remained unknown, but it created a sense of foreboding in the court.

I had to give credit to Master Cromwell. His plot was so well-laid that there was no escape. The blow fell with unexpected force and speed. The following day, the Queen was watching a tennis match at Greenwich when she was charged with treason and conveyed to the Tower in the space of a few hours. She had no opportunity to appeal to the king or rally her supporters. Her brother Viscount Rochford and Henry Norris were both arrested on the same day. Two days later there was more shocking news.

"Sir Francis Weston and William Brereton have both been arrested," said Edward. "And the Queen's musician, Mark Smeaton, is also in the Tower."

I gasped. William Brereton was the brother of my former fiancé Urian. "What has Brereton done?" I asked. "He wasn't of the Queen's favourites."

"Nothing that I know of," he replied. "I suspect that Master Cromwell is settling his scores in the privy chamber."

King Henry spared Jane from the unpleasantness of the situation by sending her to lodge at Chelsea. Edward and I kept her company there. The King provided royal cooks for her board and took a barge down the river to dine with her. He wanted to be merry, so he brought a party of musicians and singers to drive away all melancholy from his thoughts. The revelry continued until long past midnight and into the early hours of the morning. The evening was so long and the music was so loud that I ended up with a dreadful headache. But I kept a pleasant smile on my face. I had to share in the happiness of the King and his future bride. There was no mention of the fact that the Queen was a prisoner in the Tower. I had to wait until Edward and I were quite alone in our bedchamber to ask the question that was burning in my mind.

"Has the Queen confessed yet?" I asked.

He shook his head. "No," he replied. "She has sent the King a letter protesting her innocence. But it will do her no good. Master Cromwell has shown him a signed confession from Mark Smeaton admitting their adultery. She is as good as condemned already. Jane has only to hold her nerve for a few weeks and the crown of the queen consort will be hers."

"There is terror in the court over the arrests," I said. "Every member of the Queen's household fears that they will lose their lives or their posts."

"There won't be any more arrests," he said. "The case is now complete. But they are right to fear for their positions. As soon as the Queen is found guilty, the King will dismiss her entire household. He wants no reminders of his life with the former Queen. He will engage a new staff to serve Jane.

It is better that way. They will be loyal only to her and he can enjoy a fresh start with his new wife."

"Of course, that is very wise," I said. "The close servants of the Queen would be bound to resent Jane. But I wonder if an exception could be made for Margery? She is my dearest friend at court and an outstanding needlewoman."

"Jane would not want to be served by any of the former Queen's attendants," he said impatiently.

"Margery would serve her loyally and she is a very useful person," I persisted. "There must be some experienced ladies around the Queen. Otherwise, she will not be well served. Margery is an expert in the making of court dresses. If she was a noblewoman, she would have made an ideal Mistress of the Robes."

"I'll make a bargain with you," he said. "You can keep your Margery if she does something to prove her loyalty. Master Cromwell has persuaded two chamberers to testify about the immoral life of the Queen. The testimony of a maid of honour would be even more convincing. If she is willing to give a deposition, then she may have a place in Jane's household."

"Thank you, Edward," I said. "She will not fail us."

The following day I sent for Margery to come to my apartments. She looked at me with anxious eyes. The balance of power in the court had changed as completely as it had done once before. Now I was on the winning side and she knew it.

"There are rumours that the Queen will never return from the Tower," she said. "What will happen to her ladies if she is condemned to death?"

"They will share in her disgrace," I replied. "The King will not be disposed to be gracious to any of them."

She flinched at the thought of the King's vengeance. "We were always good friends, Anne," she said desperately. "I swear that I would serve Mistress Seymour just as faithful as I served the Queen. Please persuade her to grant me a place in her household."

"The Queen is finished," I said. "And everyone associated with her will be dismissed. But a place could be found for you if you were willing to show your loyalty to Jane."

"What do you want from me?" she asked.

"Master Cromwell wants testimonies from the Queen's ladies," I said. "Statements about her immoral life. If you agree, he will come here tomorrow to take your deposition. It is little enough in order to secure a bright future for yourself."

"Tell me what to say and I'll say it," she agreed.

"The King will be grateful to you," I said. "And Jane will appreciate your efforts. She will need capable ladies like you. There will be many opportunities in the new court."

And so, the bargain was struck between us. Margery was always a woman of good sense. But just when I was congratulating myself on my perspicacity, the hammer-blow fell. Master Cromwell arrested two more courtiers and sent them to join the others in the Tower. One was the poet, Sir Thomas Wyatt. And the other was my stepfather, Sir Richard Page. I was distraught at the terrible news and turned my anger upon Edward.

"You said there wouldn't be any more arrests," I reproached him. "Why didn't you warn me that my stepfather was in danger?"

"I didn't know he would be accused," said Edward. "This is entirely Master Cromwell's affair. The other men must have named him in their confessions."

"But my stepfather is a good man," I protested. "He does not deserve to be caught in this net."

"Stay out of it, Anne," he replied. "There is nothing you can do for him. If he is in the Tower, then it is already too late."

"There must be something we can do," I insisted. "It will kill my mother when she hears the news. She will never be able to hold up her head again."

"I can't afford to get involved," he retorted. "It would tarnish Jane if I did. She must be kept out of the whole sordid affair."

"We can't let Sir Richard perish," I said. "You must go to the King and plead on his behalf."

"The King doesn't want to know anything about it," he said irritably. "Why do you think he tasked Master Cromwell with getting it done? Henry Norris was his closest friend. If he hasn't spared Norris, then he won't spare Page."

"You could speak to Master Cromwell," I urged him. "He is a venal man. You could offer him money, land, favours. Give him whatever he wants to have."

"He is playing for higher stakes than Sir Richard," he retorted. "Don't you understand? These seven men are being sacrificed in order to bring down the Queen. And she has to be brought down. It is necessary in order to advance Jane. It is either Queen Anne or Queen Jane. I'm sorry about your stepfather, but he is a dead man." He walked out of the chamber leaving me to my tears.

Gradually, I became calmer. Time was running out to save my stepfather and I needed to think of a plan. I wondered if I should go to see Master Cromwell and try to bargain with him for Sir Richard's life. But then I realised that I would have to be much bolder. Only the King could save his life. And Jane was the key to the King. He was deeply in love with her. Surely, he would not refuse a request from his beloved lady? I left my tears unchecked and went to speak to Jane. She was astonished to see me in such a distressed state. I was always so calm and composed. I never permitted myself to weep. I considered it a foolish weakness.

"Whatever is the matter, Anne?" she asked. "Has something happened to Edward? Or to your children?"

"Please let me speak to you alone," I said.

"Of course, Anne," she said. "Let us go into my closet."

She sat in a chair and I collapsed to my knees. I took her by the sleeve. "I need a great favour from you, Jane. Please say that you will grant it."

She looked at me in concern. "What is this favour?"

"My stepfather is one of the men arrested with the Queen," I said. "But he is entirely innocent. He is a good and loyal man. Master Cromwell must have some grudge against him. But he does not deserve to die a traitor's death. I need you to intercede with the King. He will not refuse to grant your request."

"But I could not possibly interfere in the matter," she said, turning pale at the very thought. "The King would be greatly distressed. He depends upon me to keep his mind away from this sad business. He made me promise that I would not talk to anyone about it. He does not want me to know what is going on. He only wants me to have pleasant thoughts about our future happiness together. So, you see, it is quite impossible."

"The King will be more distressed if he finds out about this mistake when it is too late," I urged her. "I am your sister-in-law and Sir Richard is my stepfather. So, you are related to him by marriage. Any stain upon my family name is a stain upon yours. My disgrace will be your disgrace."

She shook her head. "It would be most improper of me," she insisted. "It is my place to show complete loyalty to the King. And it is your place too. But for your sake, I shall forget that this conversation ever took place. Now leave me, Anne. I must get ready to meet with his Majesty."

Her eyes were cold and her face was set. The King would not have recognised his sweet lady. I knew that it was no use saying anything more. I took my leave without another word. We were sisters-in-law who were bound together by obligation and mutual self-interest. But I would never forgive Jane for refusing my request.

The following day, I rose before daybreak and took a barge upriver to the north of London. The morning was bitter and damp, the river's chill seeping into my bones as the water churned under the oars. I was dressed in a gown of deep burgundy wool, trimmed with black velvet at the cuffs and neckline. My bodice was tightly laced, the skirt heavy with its lining, and my hood was pulled low over my face to guard against the sharp breeze. The barge pulled up at the shore and I made my way to Master Cromwell's house at Austin Friars. Upon my arrival, I was halted at the entrance by his doorman who regarded me with disdain. My demands to see his master were met with indifference until I handed him a costly jewel. This was no time to stick at trifles.

Master Cromwell's reception chamber was dimly lit, the heavy shutters drawn to block the outside world. The air was thick with the scent of beeswax polish and parchment, mingling with the faint tang of woodsmoke from the fireplace. The chamber was dominated by a long table of dark, carved oak, its surface strewn with papers, seals, and ledgers. Above it, a tapestry depicting a hunting scene hung in muted colours, adding an air of solemnity to the room. Candles flickered in wrought-iron sconces along the walls, casting dancing shadows over the space. The floor was tiled with faded stone, uneven in places, and my shoes clicked faintly as I stepped forward.

Cromwell himself sat at the head of the table, his presence commanding despite his plain attire. He wore a black doublet with silver embroidery at the edges, paired with a robe of sombre grey that pooled around his chair. His white linen shirt was visible at the throat, and a heavy chain of office glinted against his chest. Yet, it was his expression that truly held dominion—sharp-eyed and unreadable, his mouth a firm line that betrayed neither warmth nor weakness. I could tell that he was not pleased to see me. He pursed his lips when I told him the reason for my visit.

"Lady Seymour," he said in a cutting tone, "you should leave this well alone. There is nothing you can do for your stepfather. The matter is grave, and it does not concern you."

I lifted my chin. My pulse quickened, but I refused to let him see my fear. "Sir Richard is loyal to his Majesty," I insisted. "He is an innocent man. He has never cast his eyes upon the Queen."

He sighed with exasperation. "I tell you again, leave this matter to me," he snapped. "You should leave before your presence is remarked."

My heart beat harder against my ribcage. I pressed forward, desperation lending me courage. "Why was Sir Richard arrested? How has he offended you?"

His gaze darkened. "He has been arrested for offences against his Majesty," he said coldly.

"But his guilt has not been proved," I countered, my voice firm despite the tremor threatening to betray me. "He could still be set free."

In an instant, his hand slammed down upon the table, the sound reverberating through the room. "Do you think you are the only one who seeks a pardon?" he said, his voice rising with frustration. "I have listened to pleas from countless families, many of them with powerful allies. Why should I listen to you?"

His words stung, but I would not yield. "Because the new court will be a court of Seymours," I said, my voice steady and deliberate. "Do you truly wish to wound me so gravely? I never forget injuries—and I always remember favours."

He leaned back slightly, studying me with newfound interest. "I had heard that you were a bold lady," he said, his tone softening only enough to betray surprise. "But you seem so demure, that I did not give it credence."

I met his gaze squarely. "I shall stand at the side of Queen Jane," I said firmly. "And she will stand beside his Majesty. So, I think it a small request to ask for the freedom of one man."

For a moment, silence hung between us as he paused to consider my words. "I make no promise, Lady Seymour," he said abruptly. "I will see what can be done."

I dipped my head slightly, masking my triumph beneath a veil of decorum. "Thank you, Master Cromwell," I replied evenly. "You will not regret your consideration. It will serve you well in days to come."

As I turned to take my leave, I felt an overwhelming sense of relief. Few people could boast that they had faced down Master Cromwell in his own lair. If he kept his word, then I would be indebted to a dangerous man. But I counted on Edward and Jane to protect me, no matter what storms might come.

Master Cromwell did not communicate with me by letter or by verbal message. I was left to await the outcome of events. On 12th May 1536, Henry Norris, William Brereton, Sir Francis Weston and Mark Smeaton were tried in Westminster Hall. They were all found guilty and sentenced to be executed. Three days later, Queen Anne Boleyn and her brother George stood trial before their peers. They were both sentenced to death by their own uncle, the duke of Norfolk. Now that the legal proceedings were over, I persuaded myself that my stepfather was out of danger.

Edward thought so too. "You need not have been so concerned about the fate of Sir Richard," he remarked complaisantly. "You see how well everything has turned out."

The following day, the Queen's household was dismissed from court. I sent for Margery to come and join me at Chelsea. I had persuaded Edward that she would be needed to attire Jane in the appropriate regal manner.

"What has been happening at the palace?" I asked.

She shook her head. "It is as lamentable as the fall of Jerusalem," she replied. "I hardly have the heart to recount it."

"Is there any news of the Queen?" I said. "I have not heard anything."

"I saw her in the Tower," she said. "I was sent a message to bring some of her garments. You would not recognise her, Anne. She said that she had hoped to go abroad and enter a convent. But now she looks so forlorn and resigned that I pitied her. She is a ghost of the woman she once was."

"The King would never agree to send her to a convent," I said. "How could he marry again and have a legitimate son? He can only have one lawful wife."

"It is a judgement upon her for what she did to Queen Catherine," she whispered. "Everyone in the palace thinks it is divine retribution for rejoicing at her death."

"You must try to forget it, Margery," I said. "The King is so determined to be merry that he has forgotten her already. Nobody mentions her name anymore. She has passed out of memory."

Lady Carey was the only one who dared to intercede with the King on behalf of the Queen. But he was not moved to mercy by her pleas. Two days later Edward told me that the five accused men had been beheaded in the Tower yard. As the highest in rank, George Boleyn, Viscount Rochford, was the first to be executed.

"What of the Queen?" I asked.

"It will take place tomorrow," Edward said. "Then nothing will stand in the way of Jane's happiness. Or of ours."

We waited all day in a state of increasing tension. But there was no sound from the cannons at the Tower. Word came that the swordsman was delayed on the road and the execution was postponed until the following day. The King was furious at the debacle. He was in no humour for merry-making that night. And Jane was in no mood for polite conversation. She dined with Edward and I in sullen silence and then retired to bed early.

"It is only a temporary delay," said Edward in a nonchalant manner. "Tomorrow will mark the end of the whole affair. Patience is the key to everything."

But I passed an uneasy night. It had been a mistake for the King to make the grandiose gesture of a sword. It would have far been better to have dispatched everyone on the same day. Then we would have been celebrating tonight instead of flinching at shadows. As the dawn broke, I turned to see that Edward was just as wakeful as myself. His face looked strained and his eyes were bloodshot. I wondered how Jane was feeling this morning.

"Do you think Jane really wants to marry him?" I asked.

He gave me an incredulous look. "Why wouldn't she want to marry him?" he said. "He is the best match in England. She will be the Queen. Now she can snap her fingers in the face of William Dormer and his mother - and everyone else who looked down on her!"

"The King is much older than she is," I said. "It might not be easy for her."

"He is a man in his prime," he snapped. "What is the matter with you Anne? This is the best fortune that could befall our family. Don't you realise what this means? We shall have the ear of the King. It means that we shall have positions, titles, lands, houses and riches. Look at what it did for the Boleyn family!"

"What did it do for them?" I asked.

He scowled at my words. "They were too foolish to hold onto their good fortune," he retorted. "We shall not become careless and greedy like they did. Now we must dress and go to join Jane. The King will come here to meet her as soon as he hears the signal. It is the start of a new chapter in all our lives!"

At nine in the morning, it was the Queen's turn to die. The French swordsman had done his work and the King was now a widower.

"Do you think she spoke against us on the scaffold?" I asked. "You know how fearless she was."

"She would not have dared to complain," he replied confidently. "She had her child to consider."

As soon as he heard the booming roar of the cannons, Henry rode out to meet his new love. Edward and I stood beside Jane in the entrance chamber dressed in our best clothes and our best smiles. We heard the pounding of the horses' hooves and the barking of the dogs as he approached the manor with his retinue of favourite courtiers. Then the door was flung open and the King made his entrance. We all made a deep obeisance before him. He stepped forward and raised Jane to her feet. Then he planted a passionate kiss upon her lips.

"My dearest Jane, I could not be happier to see you this day," he said. "Tomorrow we shall be betrothed and you must wear your best dress for the occasion. I shall send the Queen's dressmakers to you to prepare a royal wardrobe for the wedding."

The King was in a hurry to enter wedded bliss with his new lady. And so, the morning after Queen Anne's execution, I pinned Jane into her finest dress of white cloth of silver. We took a barge to Hampton Court Palace and I stood beside her as she plighted herself to the King. Afterwards, he kissed her before the assembled company. The sort of kiss meant to silence gossip and signal triumph. "Mine," it seemed to say. "This one is mine." The courtiers shuffled forward with hasty congratulations. Jane stood like an alabaster statue, dazed by her good fortune. I looked at her sidelong and whispered, "It is done." The palace was filled with the sound of hammering as dozens of workmen laboured to remove the initials of the late Queen and replace them with Jane's instead. At all the royal houses, the falcon badges of Anne Boleyn were superseded by Jane's emblem of a phoenix.

The Queen's dressmakers arrived at the royal apartments that afternoon. They brought numerous bales of coloured silks and satins and displayed them before the queen in waiting. To my exasperation she turned away from the gorgeous purples, crimsons and blues that were the prerogative of royalty. She preferred to dress herself in white and the insipid shades of dove grey, pale pink and butter yellow. She had the tastes of a milkmaid. She would make a fool of herself and I would be blamed for it.

"Those are the colours of a gentlewoman, your Grace," I pointed out. "His Majesty will expect you to dress yourself as a queen. Your wardrobe is your source of power as a consort. You are not noble born, but only the daughter of a knight. You must make the noblewomen of the court respect you and the best way to do it is to assert your royal status through your dress. So, order gowns of cloth of silver trimmed with sables and purple velvet embroidered with gold. It will demonstrate your position in the eyes of the world."

She tossed her head at such a notion. "Henry likes me to dress in a simple manner," she insisted. "He does not care for showy and immodest ladies like the late Queen."

"Queen Catherine of Aragon was most virtuous and modest, your Grace," I hissed at her. "But she always dressed herself in cloth of gold and crimson velvet. She knew what was due to her honour and prestige as the Queen of England."

She pouted stubbornly. "Henry does not admire ladies who dress in Spanish fashions," she insisted. "And he does not care for French styles either. He likes me to wear English gowns. I intend to set a new fashion in the court. It will be pure and virtuous and turn the minds of the courtiers to honest living. I intend to be as famed for my modesty as Queen Anne was notorious for her licentiousness."

"His Majesty chose these fabrics himself, your Grace," I warned her. He will be displeased if you scorn his gifts.

Jane hesitated at the thought of displeasing the king. "Show me those bolts of fabric again," she said. I managed to persuade her to select cloth of gold and cloth of silver, scarlet velvet and violet silk as befitted her royal rank.

"Make sure that they are all embroidered with her royal emblems in gold thread," I ordered the palace seamstresses.

"But Lady Seymour, there is no time to embroider the gowns," they protested. "There is barely enough time to complete them."

"Do you wish to dishonour the King on his wedding day?" I demanded. "They must all be embroidered with gold and trimmed with jewels or else his Majesty will dismiss you like the rest of the late Queen's household."

They scurried away to do my bidding and left me alone with Jane.

"There are other matters to consider, your Grace," I said. "You must have ornamented head-dresses, elegant shoes and stockings and fine perfumes. The King likes his wives to wear scent. And you must have the Queen's jewels to wear. What has happened to them?"

"I do not know," she replied. "Perhaps the King will not want to be reminded."

"What nonsense, your Grace," I said impatiently. "They are the prerogative of the Queen and a sign of the King's favour. The court will expect you to wear them. I shall ask Edward to remind his Majesty."

But the King had not forgotten. He intended to make a grand romantic gesture of presenting them to his wife on their wedding day. He sent Edward with a selection of costly jewels for Jane to wear on her wedding day. He did not consider that she might have preferred to make her own choice. But naturally Jane did not complain. Her marriage would make her the Queen of England. The King honoured Edward by appointing him as a member of his privy council. It was a token of his esteem for the brother of his intended wife.

Their wedding took place in the Queen's Closet at Whitehall on 30th May 1536. King Henry wore a surcoat of white cloth-of-gold, its surface stiff with gold embroidery which gleamed in the candlelight. Beneath it, his doublet was fashioned of crimson satin slashed with silver tinsel, and around his shoulders he wore a gold collar with the insignia of the Order of the Garter. At his waist, a sword of state hung from a belt of red velvet studded with rubies, and his cap was clasped with a brooch bearing the Tudor rose and crown and plumed with a single egret's feather.

Queen Jane was a vision of piety and restraint, dressed in a gown of white damask silk, unembellished save for delicate bands of seed pearls at her cuffs and neckline. Her English hood was edged with round pearls and a fine gauze veil fell softly around her shoulders. Upon her slim waist, a girdle of cloth-of-silver fastened with a jewelled pomander swung gently as she walked, releasing the fragrance of rosewater and cloves. On her left hand she wore a wedding ring engraved with her personal motto: *Bound to obey and serve*. Edward had chosen it for her.

"This will best please his Majesty," he said. "The King wants to have an obedient wife, not a wilful one. His pleasure must be your pleasure."

After the wedding ceremony, Jane presided over the court for the first time seated in the Queen's chair beneath the canopy of royal estate. That afternoon the King sent his new Queen a great casket containing the Queen's jewels and a gold standing cup set with diamonds and pearls engraved with the intertwined initials H and J.

"This is your bride gift, your Grace," I said. "I shall take charge of your jewels and your robes. You know that only a member of your family can be trusted with such great responsibilities. It is the wish of your brother Edward."

"Well, let me see the Queen's jewels," she said eagerly.

"Send all the other ladies away, your Grace," I said. It was better than only the Queen and myself had knowledge of the contents of her jewel box.

She lifted the lid of the great casket of carved ebony, its hinges and lock chased with silver filigree. The sight nearly stole the breath from my chest. Nestled in compartments lined with crimson velvet, the Queen's jewels gleamed like treasures from some ancient fable. A priceless collection of royal ornaments lay before us. No wonder Catherine of Aragon and Anne Boleyn had fought each other bitterly to possess it. "Look how splendid it is!" she exclaimed. There were collars of thick gold links set with table-cut diamonds and rubies, gold necklaces studded with amethysts and pearls and brooches shaped like Tudor roses. Costly rings set with coloured gemstones sparkled like captured fire: sapphires the colour of twilight skies, garnets deep as old wine, pale opals glowing like trapped sunlight. She held up a pendant cross inlaid with emeralds, each stone as large as a fingernail, encircled by tiny seed pearls.

"It is magnificent, your Grace," I said. "I remember when I first saw Queen Catherine wearing it. I had newly come to court." To my surprise, the King had sent her everything. There were many pieces marked with the initials and devices of Queen Catherine and Queen Anne.

"These must be sent to the royal goldsmith to be remade," I remarked. "It will give you the opportunity to have some new pieces made."

"I do not wish to destroy the jewels which belonged to Queen Catherine of Aragon," she replied. "I shall treasure them as a keepsake of her blessed memory."

"Very well," I said testily. "I shall only send the jewels with the insignia of Anne Boleyn. There is plenty of other finery you can wear. Look at these splendid brooches, billaments and spangles set with great jewels!"

"I do not care for such ostentatious pieces," she replied obstinately. "I prefer to wear simpler ornaments. His Majesty once told me that pearls were a sign of purity. They are the stones most becoming to a virtuous maid."

"You are a Queen not a young maiden," I snapped. "Do you want the foreign ambassadors to despise you? These are the jewels of the Queen and his Majesty's marriage gift to you. Do you want to scorn them?"

Her foolish face puckered at my words as if she was going to cry like a child. She needed every ounce of dignity that the Queen's jewels could bestow upon her. Queen Catherine had a royal heritage and Queen Anne had the forceful personality of an empress. All Jane had to commend her was her royal wardrobe. But she still behaved as if she was the least worthy daughter of the Seymour family.

But then she jutted her lip. "I will ask his Majesty to honour me with a gift of pearls," she said. "It will testify to my virtue as his Queen and consort."

Jane triumphed on that occasion because King Henry was only too willing to give his new bride a splendid rope of pearls to wear. She decided to make pearls integral her new fashion.

Every lady at the court was ordered to deck themselves in pearls. Unless they wore at least a hundred, they were forbidden to enter her presence. Overnight the court was transformed into a vision of ladies dressed in English hoods edged with pearls. I wondered what the foreign ambassadors would say in their reports to their royal masters. They could hardly praise the new Queen for her beauty, charm or wit. And now she had shown that could not compete with foreign consorts for her regal taste in dress. Even when seated under a royal canopy she looked like a timid little mouse.

"She is making us look ridiculous," I grumbled to Edward.

"It is not so bad," he prevaricated. "His Majesty does not like to be outshone by anyone. He approves of Jane's modest tastes. And she has set a new fashion among the ladies of the court. It is markedly different from her predecessors. It signifies her piety and her virtue that she shuns ostentation. It is the reason that the King chose her as his wife."

"He will soon tire of her simplicity," I said. "His pride will be piqued that she does not compare with Queen Catherine or Queen Anne in splendour. She is supposed to stand out from the other ladies of the court. How will she manage to hold his attention?"

"She will learn how to conduct herself as a queen consort," he said. "You will teach her to become more majestic. When she has filled his nursery with children he will regard her as his most beloved Queen. If she succeeds as well as you have done in that regard, then he will be well satisfied with her. You know that my mother bore ten children to my father. He hopes that Jane will equally blessed."

It all depended upon that one thing. A son. The King sent his physicians to Jane to doctor her health. He ordered the royal cooks to prepare her foods that were good for breeding women. He gave her a mantle of the finest furs so that she would not take a chill. He was a man who was impatient to receive his reward.

CHAPTER 6

Lady Hertford (1537)

"Wives must be modest, wise, chaste, keepers at home, lovers of their husbands and subject to them"

(Peter de la Primaudaye, 1618, *The French Academie*).

The reign of Queen Jane was a golden time for us. It laid the foundation of our fortunes. On 5th June 1536, Edward was granted a title of nobility. He stood in the Presence Chamber of Hampton Court and I watched proudly as the light poured through the tall oriel windows, catching on the golden threads of his doublet and the newly minted coronet resting on its velvet cushion. The heralds called his new title with such splendour that it sent a thrill down my spine: Edward Seymour, *Viscount Beauchamp of Hache*. The court applauded him loudly and the King acknowledged him with a broad smile. Jane sat beside him, her hands folded with delicate composure and her eyes glowing with satisfaction. In honouring her brother, the King had shown his regard for her.

Now I was Lady Beauchamp and the sister-in-law to the Queen. She appointed me as one of her ladies in waiting. The other ladies of the court watched me with narrowed eyes. Some smiled too broadly; others ceased smiling at all. But I disregarded their flattery just as I did their envy. I had a position of honour and trust that none of them could rival. I was no longer Lady Seymour, the wife of a knight. I was Lady Beauchamp of the Queen's household and the winds of fortune were shifting in our favour. I saw that Margery Hallows was allowed to serve as a maid of honour and praised her exceptional skills as a seamstress. She was deeply grateful to me.

The following day, the Imperial ambassador accompanied the King to the apartments of the new Queen. He wore a gown of deep oxblood velvet which hung in careful folds. His sleeves were slashed to reveal silk the colour of dried rose petals, embroidered with the double-headed eagle of the Empire in gold thread. A stiff white collar framed his long, shrewd face, and a black velvet cap, crested with a single ostrich plume tipped in silver, sat precisely at the angle of quiet authority. He was all smiles and congratulations to Queen Jane. He could not have been happier that his detested enemy, Anne Boleyn, had been shamefully put to death.

"Your Majesty, your predecessor bore the device *"La plus heureuse,"* but it is your Grace that shall bear the reality," he said, his voice smooth as well-aged claret. "I am sure that my master, the emperor of Spain, will be immeasurably pleased that his Majesty the King has found so good and virtuous a wife as your Grace."

Queen Jane blushed to hear his flowery words of praise and looked imploring at the King. I was vexed to see her looking so foolishly tongue-tied at her first public reception.

Her predecessors would have known exactly what to say. I stiffened in my place, willing her to speak. But she stood there in silence like a ninny. Seigneur Chapuys's expression did not flicker, but I knew that he had already made his assessment of her. He was an influential man and his letters would be read at the courts of Spain, Austria and the Netherlands. She had thrown away her chance to make a good impression.

King Henry gallantly intervened on her behalf. "You must excuse her Grace the Queen, Seigneur Chapuys," he said. "You are the first ambassador to whom she has spoken, and she is not accustomed to it. I believe that the distinction that would best suit her is the name of *pacific*, for her nature is gentle and inclined to peace."

"Your Majesty is quite right," he agreed. "I hear that the satisfaction of the people with this marriage is incredible and I believe that she will be a great blessing to this realm and to the whole of Christendom."

After his audience with their Majesties, Seigneur Chapuys made a point of coming over to speak to Edward and myself. "Lord Beauchamp, this is a blessed occasion for all of us," he said. "It would do the greatest good to your sister, the Queen, your family and all the realm if the Princess Mary was now restored to her rights."

"There is nothing that would make us happier than to see the King reconciled with his daughter," he replied.

"I am sure that you will use all your good offices to ensure such a happy outcome," he said.

Edward's voice remained measured. "The Queen has the greatest goodwill and friendship for the Lady Mary," he replied.

Seigneur Chapuys, emboldened, pressed harder. "Then I am certain that it will not be long before she takes her proper place at court again," he said.

"There is only one impediment to this joyful outcome, Seigneur," he said. "She must obey her father's wishes."

The ambassador raised his brows with indignation. "But the obstacle has gone," he said. "The King was only estranged from his daughter because of the evil counsel of Anne Boleyn. Now that she is dead, the princess expects to be invited back to court."

Edward was unflinching. "You must convince her to swear the oath," he said. "Only then will the King relent."

At that, the ambassador's cordial mask slipped for a moment. "But that is impossible, Lord Beauchamp," he snapped. "How can a relative of his most Christian Majesty, the emperor Charles V of Spain, deny the authority of the Pope over the Church? She will never agree to commit such an enormity!"

Edward leaned forward slightly. "Then it will be left to Master Cromwell," he said quietly. "He is clever enough to accomplish anything."

Shortly afterwards, Parliament passed the Act for the suppression of the lesser monasteries. Commissioners were dispatched across the realm, armed with royal authority and a mandate to dismantle centuries of monastic tradition. The closures were swift and often brutal. Monks and nuns were expelled, their vows dissolved, their communities scattered. Sacred relics were seized, altars stripped, and libraries were ransacked. The proceeds from the closure of the houses enriched the royal treasury. None of them were converted into schools or almshouses. Lands were sold off to courtiers and merchants, creating a new class of landowners loyal to the Crown but indifferent to the spiritual and social void left behind. The poor, who had once relied on monastic alms and shelter, found themselves adrift, their needs no longer met by the Church nor the state.

"I believe that Master Cromwell intends to close down all the religious houses in the realm," said Edward. "The great monasteries as well as the small ones."

"Surely the King will never go so far," I said. "There are many honest houses and the rest can be amended."

"Cromwell has promised to make him the richest monarch in Europe," he said. "The sale of their goods and lands will give him a fortune even greater than his father had."

"What can we do?" I asked.

"We can't do anything," he said. "We can only hope that the King will be satisfied and spare the greater houses."

At the end of June 1536, Sir Richard Page was finally released from the Tower. The following week, he came to court to present his congratulations to the King upon his marriage.

King Henry received him very affably. "I will be glad to see you back in your old post, Sir Richard," he said. "You have always been a loyal and faithful gentleman."

But Sir Richard had been crushed by his ordeal. He was a broken man. "Your Majesty is most generous," he replied. "But I regret that my health is too poor to allow me to accept your kind offer. If you would grant your gracious permission, I would prefer to withdraw from court and return home."

"It is granted, Sir Richard," he said indifferently.

"Why are you giving up your post?" I asked him. "All our futures will be safe under Queen Jane. There is no need for you to leave court."

"I have no choice, my dear," he said. "Master Cromwell came to see me in the Tower. He told me that he would spare my life on the condition that I resigned my post. He wants to give it to one of his friends. The downfall of Queen Anne Boleyn gave him the chance to place his own supporters around the King. He tortured Mark Smeaton into giving him the names he wanted. None of the accusations were true. It was just a plot that he devised to rid the King of his wife. But you knew that already, didn't you?"

"You must not speak of it," I said. "The whole matter is over and done with. You can go back home to Beechwood and live there peacefully with my mother."

He took my hand and pressed it gently. "Take care of yourself in this place," he said. "The court has become a nest of vipers."

The following month, the King rewarded Master Cromwell for his faithful service. He granted him the post of Lord Privy Seal and the title of Baron Cromwell of Wimbledon. He also gave him Mortlake Palace and its estates. And he appointed several new gentlemen of the privy chamber. They were all the friends and clients of Lord Cromwell. The new Lord Privy Seal stood high in the King's favour. But not even he could convince the King to receive his daughter, Lady Mary, back at court. King Henry insisted that she must first sign a letter submitting to his demands.

"She must swear the oath of supremacy," he insisted. "Only then will I show her the love of a father to an obedient daughter."

Lord Cromwell persuaded Lady Mary to sign the letter of submission without reading it. She was forced to agree that her parents were never lawfully married and that she was illegitimate. She denied the authority of the Pope and acknowledged that the King was the rightful head of the Church of England. King Henry was satisfied that he had quenched any thought of presumption in her head.

In July 1537 the King and Queen and their retinue went to visit Lady Mary at Hackney as a sign of forgiveness. We travelled in a glittering train of silks and velvets, with gilt trappings on the horses and the King's standard stirring above us. Queen Jane sat serenely on her horse, savouring her victory. She had kept her word to her supporters by fostering this reunion. When we reached Lady Mary's lodgings, she emerged to greet us with such grace that my throat tightened. She was dressed in a gown of black velvet with a Spanish hood, her sleeves slashed with crimson and a gold cross around her neck. She curtsied low before her father, her head bowed not only in reverence, but in wary self-control. And the King who had stormed and thundered at her disobedience now stared at her in silence. Then his hand reached down. He lifted her with a gentleness I had rarely seen in him and kissed her brow.

"Well met, daughter," he said. "We have been too long apart. But now we are together again and you shall find me to be a most loving father."

"I am your Grace's most humble and obedient daughter," she replied. "I shall daily pray to God for your welfare and beseech Him to send you children for the comfort of your whole realm."

"I am pleased to hear such a dutiful answer," he said. "You shall have a present of a thousand crowns to spend upon your pleasures."

"I am most grateful for your kindness, your Majesty," she said.

The King glanced around the chamber at his noblemen. "Some of those here wanted me to put this jewel to death," he said in a reproachful tone. Lady Mary turned pale at his words. She realised that her fears over her father's intentions had not been ill-founded.

Queen Jane smiled encouragingly at her. "It would have been a shame to lose England's chiefest jewel, your Grace," she said. She stepped forward and placed into her hands a diamond ring set in rose gold, a work of exquisite craftsmanship. "This is a small token of our harmony and the joy that it brings to me," she said.

Lady Mary stared at it as though the weight of her father's favour had become suddenly real. I saw how her fingers trembled as she slid it onto her hand. And I, who had witnessed the rise and fall of so many at the Tudor court, thought that at last there might be peace in the royal family. Lord Cromwell was instructed to reassemble her household and Lady Margaret Pole was invited to return to her service. Lady Mary came back to court and was given precedence as the first lady after the Queen. King Henry provided her with her own lodgings at Hampton Court and Greenwich Palace. As a result, Queen Jane gained a great reputation as a peacemaker.

I was among the first to make a visit to Lady Mary's apartments. "I am delighted to see you back here at court, my lady," I said. "The entire Seymour family has petitioned for your reinstatement. We shall do everything we can to support and protect you."

"I will never forget your kindness, Lady Beauchamp," she replied. "I pray that one day I will be able to return your goodness to me."

Now that she had accepted all his demands, the King was prepared to treat her generously. She would be his beloved daughter again and she would have her jewels to wear, a wardrobe of costly gowns and money to spend on her pastimes. She was known as "Lady Mary, the King's Daughter" and she received the honour and respect of the first lady at court after the Queen.

But although one crisis had passed, another arose of much greater peril. This time it threatened the security of the King. The people of Yorkshire and Lincolnshire rose up in protest against the closure of the monasteries and the changes to religion. A lawyer named Robert Aske called upon the common people to join the Pilgrimage of Grace. Soon the northern rebellion numbered thirty thousand men. They blamed Cromwell for leading the King astray and burned the books of his commissioners. On 16th October 1536 they seized control of York. If they marched upon London, nothing could stand in their way. The King had no army that was large enough to oppose them.

"The rebels have taken Pontefract Castle," said Edward. "They have sent the King a list of their demands. They want a reversal of the religious policy, the surrender of the King's evil councillors and a Parliament at York."

"Will he agree?" I asked.

"He has no choice but to treat with them," he said. "He is sending Norfolk to Doncaster to meet the rebel leaders. He will promise to grant them a Parliament and a general pardon if they agree to tell their followers to disperse."

"I pray to God that Norfolk can persuade them," I said. "Otherwise, we are lost."

"Cromwell is very much to blame," said Edward. "He assured the King that all the people were eager for the reform of the Church."

"Can't the other councillors persuade the King to change his mind and put a stop to the dissolution of the monasteries?" I asked.

"Cromwell still has the support of the King," he said. "The rest of the council cannot openly oppose him. And the King does not want to lose face by backing down. But Jane might be able to persuade him. I will tell her that it is her duty as the Queen and a good Catholic."

We went to see the Queen in her apartments. I gazed around the privy chamber with a critical eye. All the furnishings and possessions which Anne Boleyn had acquired over the past ten years were now hers. As she had very little experience of fine things she had not changed a thing. I would have to do it for her. The bold magnificence of Anne Boleyn did not suit her in the least. She needed a milder palate to suit her fair colouring. The crimson and gold should be changed to white and gold. She must have bed-hangings, counterpanes and cushions embroidered with her emblem of the phoenix. It would require a great deal of work by her ladies.

Edward scowled to see the circle of attendants around his sister. "I must have some private speech with your Grace," he said.

"Let everyone withdraw," she ordered. "I will talk to my brother and his wife alone."

"The closure of the monasteries has incited a rebellion in the kingdom," he said. "You must intercede with the King on behalf of the Church. Everyone at court will bless you for your goodness."

She shook her head. "It is too dangerous," she said. "It will provoke his Majesty if I challenge him in this way. Let me ask him in private instead."

"It is better to make a public appeal," he insisted. "He will not like to refuse you before the court."

The following morning the court assembled in the Presence Chamber. Queen Jane rose from her chair of estate like a statue stirring to life. She prepared to play the scene with the same serene confidence she had shown when she protested her honour as a virtuous maiden. She moved to stand before the King, her white damask skirts outlining her slender form. A hush descended over the crowd. Every eye was watching her intently. I felt my heart begin to drum behind my stays.

She knelt down before the King and a gasp swept through the assembly. He gazed at her, his brow furrowed, not yet grasping what she meant to do. Then she lifted her eyes, wide and luminous, and fixed them upon him as she made her plea.

"Sire," she said softly, but the words carried nonetheless, "I beg you to restore some of these monasteries. God may have permitted this rebellion as a punishment for the desecration of so many churches."

It was as if the air had been sucked out of the chamber.

The King stared at her in disbelief. Then the colour rose to his cheeks, not the gentle flush of affection, but the dangerous tide that heralded a storm. His eyes narrowed and his jaw worked. His hand clenched the pommel of his sword. I held my breath.

"Get up, Madam," he growled in a menacing tone. "Do not presume to meddle in my affairs. Remember the fate of your predecessor who meddled too much."

His voice cracked like a whip across the assembly and every courtier recoiled from his anger. Jane's lips parted as if to speak again, but no sound came. She rose, trembling, her knees unsteady, and returned to her chair of estate without another word. Her face had gone paper-white. She had glimpsed the monster that lurked beneath the civilised demeanour of the King.

I had witnessed the fall of two queens in succession. Catherine, noble and unyielding, who was cast aside as if constancy were a fault. And Anne, a force of nature, who rose like a phoenix only to be extinguished before her feathers finished burning. Now Jane recognised the peril in which she stood. She had not yet secured her position by giving the King a son. She was entirely dependent upon his favour and goodwill. Now that their courtship was over, the King was not prepared to indulge her whims. Catherine had never made demands upon him and had always subordinated her interests to his own. His comfort and pleasure had been her foremost concern. But Anne had wearied him by throwing scenes and making herself the centre of attention. He would not tolerate any dramas or demands from Jane. He wanted a conformable wife.

Later, in her privy chamber, she turned on Edward with unexpected venom. "I told you it was dangerous," she said resentfully. "Now he has threatened me. He has never done that before."

"He was in an ill-humour today," he said. "Don't make too much of it. Next time you will succeed in winning him over."

"There isn't going to be a next time," she retorted. "I will not be used by you to put your demands to the King. In future, you can ask him yourself."

"We are your family Jane," he blustered. "If it were not for us then you would never have become the Queen. Remember that you owe us everything!"

In late December 1536 the court moved to Greenwich for the Christmas season. That year it was so cold that the river Thames was frozen solid and so King Henry, Queen Jane and Lady Mary rode across the ice from Westminster to Greenwich. The people turned out in great crowds to see the royal party and their entourage pass by.

"God save the King! God save the Queen! God bless Lady Mary!" they cried.

The Lord Chamberlain and his retainers were waiting to greet their Majesties with roaring fires and mulled wine to drive out the chill. The King came to see Queen Jane in her apartments.

"This will be your first Christmas as Queen," he said. "It shall be an even more blessed season with you presiding over the court festivities."

"The people were pleased to see you reunited with your daughter," she replied. "I shall be a kind stepmother and a true friend to her for your sake. Perhaps you would consider restoring her to her former rank as the Princess of Wales?"

He shook his head. "That title belongs to our own daughter," he said. "Although I would rather welcome a little prince. Is there any sign yet that our marriage is fruitful?"

"No, Sire," she said. "I pray that you would be patient with me."

He sighed. "Well, perhaps it is too soon. But I shall hope that next year the court will rejoice at the birth of a true heir to the throne."

Queen Jane informed the supporters of Lady Mary that she had done all that she could to press her case. Henceforth, they must urge her no more to seek the King's favour on her behalf. She took no interest whatsoever in promoting the welfare of Lady Elizabeth. When King allowed her to visit the court for Christmas, Queen Jane ordered her to be placed at a table well away from the rest of the royal family. She had never forgotten Anne Boleyn's unkindness to her and she was not going to favour her daughter. Master Aske had also been invited to spend Christmas at court. King Henry promised him that he would visit Yorkshire in the summer and hold a parliament to satisfy their demands. He promised there would be a general pardon for the rebels. Master Aske was convinced by his sincerity and persuaded them to disperse.

On New Year's day, King Henry gave Queen Jane a pair of jewelled brooches in the shape of phoenixes. She gave him a nightgown worked with vines and Tudor roses that she had embroidered with her own hands. Edward gave me a girdle of gold with six flowers and I gave him a set of gold buttons to wear on his doublet. On Twelfth Night, the court assembled in the Great Hall and buzzed with anticipation to see the masque. A fanfare of trumpets sounded and at the far end of the hall, the draperies parted to reveal a sight so grand it struck murmurs from every throat. The Château d'Or appeared with gilded turrets and carved lattice, glowing like a dream castle in the candlelight.

On the battlements stood Lady Lyonesse and her maidens, dressed in gowns of blue cloth of silver with long veils fluttering like standards in distress. They raised their arms in entreaty. "Aid us, noble lords! We are besieged!" cried Lady Lyonesse. Before the gate of the castle stood the Red Knight and his company, clad in black and scarlet, their helms horned and their swords drawn.

Gasps rippled through the crowd. The Queen gripped the arm of her chair. I felt the thrill of the moment myself, although I knew it was but play.

Then the doors of the hall opened and King Henry strode into view. He was robed in crimson satin sewn with gold, a lion rampant blazoned on his chest. Behind him followed his knights dressed in shimmering cloth of gold. The hall erupted into cheers.

"Forward!" the King cried, and they charged. The Red Knight and his men advanced against them. Gold battled against red and swords clashed in the melee. The King, radiant and fierce, disarmed the Red Knight with a flourish that drew wild applause. Lady Lyonesse descended from the battlements. She curtsied to her saviour and he kissed her hand.

King Henry stood before the court, still clad in his crimson satin from the masque, the heat of triumph in his cheeks and the sparkle of gold upon him like firelight in motion. He stepped forward, his gaze sweeping the gathered throng. "My lords and ladies, what fortress is more sacred than a virtuous heart? What treasure more enduring than a woman's honour? It is not only kings who wear crowns, but every lady who carries herself with grace, constancy, and piety."

He turned then toward Queen Jane. "I speak not merely of courtesy, but of strength—the quiet power that nurtures kingdoms, that endures the storm and steadies the helm. Such is the virtue I honour in my Queen, and such is the virtue that I call all men to defend and uphold."

A murmur stirred through the crowd, gentle as wind through silk. Queen Jane's eyes lowered modestly, but a bloom of colour touched her cheeks.

King Henry's voice warmed. "Let no man scoff at gentle virtue, for it is the surest foundation of a noble realm. And let all ladies know that in their honour, they hold the hearts of England's sons." He spread his arms. "Now let the dancing begin, and let it be known that at this court, virtue shall ever be crowned."

The music of lutes, viols and sackbuts swelled as the knights partnered the ladies in a graceful pavane. I turned to see Queen Jane smiling faintly, one hand pressed to the phoenix at her breast. And in that moment, I thought: the masque was meant to entertain—but it had done more. It had crowned her. Henry had proclaimed her victory before the court and everyone who watched would remember it.

After the end of the festivities, Margery approached me with a proposition. "There are a great many other members of the late Queen's household who have lost their positions through no fault of their own, Lady Beauchamp," she said. "They have nowhere to turn and they are desperate. You have great influence in the court. Surely you can do something to help them."

"There is no question of them remaining in royal service," I said impatiently. "The King would never allow it."

"But you are a great lady now," she said. "And your husband is a great lord. You could employ them in your own household. You must need more servants. They would be faithful and loyal to you."

"I would have to give it some thought, Margery," I said. "But you may give me a list of their names and their former positions."

"They are all highly qualified and trustworthy, my lady," she replied. "I know that they would serve you most faithfully."

I took the list and considered the matter. At first, I thought that I might employ one or two. But then I heard the news that my father-in-law had died and Edward had inherited Wulf Hall. It occurred to me that this was a golden opportunity to reform the entire household. When Queen Anne was executed, all her household servants had been dismissed from court. In my view, it was a grave error for most of them were men and women of the highest calibre. They had valuable skills and decades of useful service ahead of them. Queen Anne had been a most demanding mistress. Now they faced a bleak future to beg on the highways or starve. No household would dare to employ the servants of the notorious Anne Boleyn. But I was emboldened by my position as the Queen's sister-in-law. I saw a golden opportunity and offered them positions in my household at much reduced salaries. They were only too willing to accept.

"Remember what I have done in giving you honest employment and serve me faithfully," I said.

At last, I could rid the household of the idle old retainers and slackers whom long service had corrupted into inefficiency. I pensioned off the old grumblers and dismissed the idle slackers. I would harbour no idle drones not lazy grumblers who undermined my rightful authority and wasted my husband's substance. I undertook to review the household accounts every week. I noticed the difference immediately. The food was better and the costs were lower. The house was kept clean and orderly. The laundry well-aired and the silver was polished until it shone. The servants were respectful and efficient. The children were well-taught and disciplined instead of being over-indulged. My husband was induced to remonstrate with me over my wholesale domestic reforms, but I made my authority in the matter quite clear.

"Am I not the mistress of this household, Edward?" I demanded.

"Of course, but some of these servants have served me faithfully for many years," he replied.

"They should have been dismissed long ago," I insisted. "These old servants served your faithless first wife, but they turned a blind eye to her infamous conduct. I am determined that our children shall be raised in a virtuous household."

He turned pale when I resurrected that ghost from the past and backed down immediately. "As you say, my dear," he replied. "I am sure that you are right."

In January 1537 another crisis erupted in the realm when Sir Francis Bigod led a new uprising. He urged the men of Yorkshire to take possession of Scarborough and Hull until the promised Parliament was held. In response, the King dispatched Norfolk north with an army to suppress the rebellion. He had bided his time but now he intended to destroy every vestige of the Pilgrimage of Grace.

"Is there any news?" I asked Edward.

"Yes," he replied gravely. "The rebellion has been crushed and the King has ordered bloody reprisals. His orders were to cause dreadful execution to be done in every town, village and hamlet and hang the bodies up in trees as a fearful spectacle."

I shuddered at the thought. "But he promised a general pardon," I said.

"The King is a vengeful man," he reminded me. "Since Bigod broke the peace, the King revoked his pardon. All the leaders of the Pilgrimage of Grace have been arrested and executed as rebels. Robert Aske was hung in chains from the walls of York Castle as an example of the King's vengeance."

I pitied Master Aske who had tried to negotiate an honourable peace on behalf of the rebels. But in the King's eyes there was no scope for divided loyalties. His treatment of the rebels was intended to serve as a dreadful example to the realm.

In February 1537 I gave birth to my second daughter. She was no ordinary girl, but the niece of the Queen. We named her Margaret and held a grand christening in the Chapel Royal. Queen Jane Seymour and Princess Mary acted as her godmothers. Afterwards, I sent her to join her sister at Elvetham.

Three months later Queen Jane informed the King that she was expecting a child. He was elated and sent out a proclamation to the realm: *"Our entirely dear and beloved wife, Queen Jane, hath conceived and is great with child. Upon Trinity Sunday, like one given of God, the child quickened in the mother's womb. Let all our loyal subjects give praise unto Almighty God and pray that the child may be a prince."* The court rejoiced to hear the news. The King cancelled his plans for a summer progress in order to remain close to the Queen. He was determined that nothing would go wrong this time. In September 1537, she retired to Hampton Court Palace to prepare for the birth of her child. Edward exhorted me to keep a close watch over his sister.

"Everything depends upon this child," he said. "If she bears the King a son, then she will become his most beloved wife and Queen. We will become his favourite courtiers and he will shower us with benefits. But only if she succeeds in giving him an heir to the throne!"

"Your sister is a healthy young woman," I said. "There is no reason why she should not succeed."

But I was just as anxious as he was. Our fortunes and those of our children were now tied to Jane's. If she succeeded, we would share in her triumph. But if she failed, we would suffer the King's displeasure. There was no guarantee that she would bear a son. She might give him a third daughter instead.

The Queen's pains began on 9th October 1537 and the midwives were summoned to attend her. Her cries began by mid-afternoon. I stood behind the curtain, my fingers clenched in my skirts, willing her to have strength. Now and then I heard her murmuring the words of the litany, between her gasps and groans: *"Domine, miserere nobis. Christe, miserere nobis."*

I added my prayers to hers. *God grant her a healthy child. And let it be a son!* For two nights her labour continued, unbroken by rest and unrelieved by comfort. The King paced outside the chamber door, demanding news at every hour but never daring to enter. His footsteps rang like a drumbeat along the corridor, his voice rising in bursts of temper whenever an answer was not immediately forthcoming.

On the third day, near dawn, the room grew very quiet. No candle flickered. No one breathed. And then—at last—a high, thin cry cut the air like a blade.

The child was born. And it was a son! The midwives wrapped him in swaddling and placed him in the Queen's arms. Jane, pale as marble, managed the faintest of smiles before her head fell back onto the pillows. Her skin was clammy, her pulse light as a whisper.

"God save the Prince," someone murmured.

"Amen," she replied. "May Almighty God bless my son. Bring me my writing desk. I shall write a letter to tell the privy council of the birth of the long-awaited heir."

"You should rest now, your Grace," I said. "I can summon a clerk to write the letter."

"No," she insisted stubbornly. "It is my right as the Queen of England to inform the council of this blessed outcome."

Laboriously she penned the words. This was her testimony to her achievement. She had fulfilled her duty as the queen and she wanted the whole world to know of her triumph:

"Right trusty and well beloved, we greet you well. By the inestimable goodness and grace of Almighty God, we are delivered and brought in child-bed of a Prince, conceived in lawful matrimony. We doubt not, but that for the love and affection you bear unto us and to the commonwealth of this realm, this knowledge shall be joyous, and glad tidings unto you. We have thought it good to certify you of the same so that you might render unto God thanks and praise for so great a benefit and continually pray for the long continuance and preservation of his life, to the honour of God, the joy and pleasure of the King and the universal tranquillity of the realm. Given under our signet, at my Lord's manor of Hampton Court, the twelfth day of October."

"There," she said, holding it out to me. "Let a messenger take this to them at once!"

"I will have it sent immediately, your Grace," I replied. I took the letter and removed the heavy writing desk from the bed.

She lay back on her pillows in exhaustion. Her eyes were closed and her breath was laboured. The birth of the prince had cost her dearly. Outside the door I could hear the sound of laughter and cheers as the King rejoiced with his friends. Now he had received his heart's desire. I wondered if he knew how much pain and suffering his wife had endured. Before long, the whole of London erupted into celebration at the glad tidings. The church bells were rung, bonfires were lit in the streets and a *Te Deum* was sung at St Paul's cathedral. I felt a pang of envy because I had borne two daughters in a row. It irritated me that Jane should have outshone me. But I did not repine for long for I received the welcome news that the joyful King had granted my husband the earldom of Hertford. I was now Lady Hertford.

Three days later, Prince Edward was christened in the Chapel Royal of Hampton Court. I wore a new gown of cloth of silver in honour of the occasion. He was carried on a cushion held by the Marchioness of Exeter under a canopy of cloth of gold. His long velvet train was borne by the earl of Arundel. Edward was given the honour of taking part in the procession and carrying the four-year-old Lady Elizabeth in his arms. Lady Mary was appointed as his godmother as a sign of the King's favour. Now that he had a lawful son and heir, he was willing to honour his eldest daughter as she deserved. Archbishop Cranmer baptised the prince in a silver-gilt font and a *Te Deum* was sung in thanksgiving. All the courtiers sent splendid presents which were exhibited in a solemn procession and shown to the Queen in her bedchamber. She gave her son her maternal blessing. It was her last act as the Queen. On the same day as the christening, Queen Jane complained of feeling unwell. Within a week she had fallen deathly ill. My husband remained at the King's side night and day.

I brought him the sad tidings of her death. "She's gone," I said numbly. "She died of a childbed fever. We did everything we could to save her life but nothing could quell the burning fire inside her."

"How could she die?" he demanded. "Everything was done for her comfort!"

I crushed the fine velvet of my skirt between my fingers and said nothing. Women died in childbed every day. It made no difference if they were rich or poor. Everyone at court blamed the Queen's ladies for her death. No-one accused the doctors of any carelessness. They were the King's favourite servants and completely above suspicion. Master Cromwell told the other councillors that the Queen had craved sweetmeats and her attendants had foolishly indulged her wishes. As if a woman had ever died from eating marchpane and sugar plate!

The King lamented the death of his beloved wife. "God has seen fit to take her from me, when I would have raised her as high as heaven would allow," he wept. "Leave me! Leave me, all of you!"

He shut himself away in his apartments and refused to see anyone. So, it was the Queen's ladies who performed the proper rites for her. We put on black mourning gowns with white coifs to signify that she had died in childbed and we kept vigil beside her coffin in the Chapel Royal. Her body was wrapped in gold tissue and a crown was placed on her head. Her funeral took place at Windsor and she was buried in his own tomb before the altar in St George's Chapel. A verse was inscribed upon her tombstone:

"Here a phoenix lieth, whose death
To another phoenix gave breath;
It is to be lamented much,
The world at once ne'er knew two such."

In his grief, the King declared that after his own death a splendid memorial would be constructed in their honour. Marble effigies of himself and his beloved Jane would lie together side by side. And statues of children with baskets of red roses would be placed at the four corners of the tomb. The tomb, the steps and the surrounding pavement were to be inlaid with roses of red enamel set with jasper, cornelian and agate. In this way the memory of their love would be preserved into eternity.

Edward took her death almost as hard as the King. "How could she die like that," he complained. "She was a young and healthy woman."

"Some women do not have the strength for child-bearing," I said.

"My mother bore ten children," he grumbled. "And after bearing a son! The King would have certainly granted her a coronation. She would have reigned beside him for the rest of his life. There would have been more honours and rewards in store for me. Now it has all been snatched away!"

"You are still the uncle of the little prince," I reminded him. But he would not be placated.

"But I am not the brother-in-law of the King," he said. "We should have left my sister Elizabeth unmarried. She is wasted on that wastrel son of Cromwell. She might have brought comfort to the King."

I did not think the King would have looked twice at Elizabeth. She was a much more forceful character than Jane. But I said nothing to avoid provoking my husband.

"You will have to do your utmost to ingratiate yourself with the next Queen," he said.

"The King says he will never marry again," I replied.

"He will agree to take another wife in time," he insisted. "And whoever she is, you will have to do your best to please her."

The next few years were a great trial for our family. Since there was no Queen to attend anymore, the ladies returned to their family homes. I thought that I would never serve at court again. In 1538 I bore a son who died in his infancy. Fortunately, the following year another son was born. We named him Edward after my husband. He was pleased to finally have a son who would succeed to his title and estates. I had the reputation of being a stern mistress of my household, but it only took one rotten apple to spoil the barrel. I made sure that the unmarried female servants slept in a separate dormitory from the men. The nurseries were carefully supervised by night and by day. I was determined that there would be no breath of scandal to taint my children. I was a watchful mother and never entrusted my children entirely to the keeping of ignorant servants. I guarded little Edward like a priceless treasure and visited the nursery every morning to ensure that he had clean linen and proper care.

"How is young Lord Beauchamp, Mistress Cobham?" I enquired.

"He is fair and plump, Madam," the nurse replied.

"How is it that he is not yet made ready?" I demanded.

"I have let him sleep this morning, Madam," she said evasively.

"Then unswaddle him and let him be washed in clean water," I said. "I see that his little cheeks are wet. I believe you have left him alone to weep and cry! Did I not give you orders that he was to be watched at all times?"

"Yes, Madam," she said. "I swear to you that I have not left the nursery for a moment. His little lordship is cutting a new tooth, that is all."

"Give him his coral on the small gold chain," I scolded. "Why didn't you think of that yourself? Dress him in his petticoat and cap and give him some suck. Then fetch a clean pillow case and coverlet and make his bed. Put him in his cradle and rock him until he sleeps. I pray you take good care of his lordship!"

"Yes, Madam," she replied. Mistress Cobham was the most foolish creature imaginable. If it were not that my son was thriving upon her milk, I would have sent her away.

After inspecting the nursery, I visited my daughters, Anne and Margaret. I did not hesitate to admonish the governess, Mistress Valdory, if I suspected any failings on her part. On one occasion I found her regaling my eldest daughter with the tale of Patient Griselda. The poor child was round-eyed with horror at the catalogue of misery she had endured at the hands of her monstrous husband.

"Don't tell her such nonsense," I snapped.

"But my lady, it is a most edifying story," she protested. "It teaches young girls the virtues of patience and obedience."

"Are you a fool?" I retorted. "It will make her fearful of marriage. My daughters are to be educated and enlightened, not taught such antiquated myths! I shall write out a list of virtuous women of the Bible and you may tell their stories instead. I am sure that you are familiar with Deborah and Esther who saved the people of Israel. And Tabitha and Phoebe who were praised for their kindness to the poor." I doubted that she was familiar with any of them, but she nodded sagely.

"Yes, my lady," she said. "And there is Hannah, the mother of Samuel, who prayed earnestly to God for a son."

I frowned. "You may omit Hannah," I said. "She had a polygamous marriage with her husband. It is hardly a good Christian example for our times."

"Just as you wish, my lady," she replied.

But it was not so easy to counter the pernicious influence of my mother-in-law when she decided to honour us with a visit. As old Lady Seymour settled into the high-backed chair before the hearth, her fingers delicately traced the worn cover of *The Legend of Good Women*. The girls gathered eagerly at her feet, their wide eyes fixed on her as if she were a prophetess about to reveal some great truth. She related the sorrowful tale of Dido, the Queen of Carthage, with great relish while I stood by the door with my fingers clenched into the silken folds of my skirts. She spared them no detail of her misfortunes as she recounted her love for the hero Aeneas, her tragic abandonment and her death. Her words coiled in the air like venomous snakes, but I forced myself to remain silent. How I longed for her to tell them of Suzannah, who stood firm against wickedness, instead of darkening their innocent minds with such a grim tale. Her storytelling was extremely irritating, but her moralising was even worse.

"Your aunt, Jane Seymour, was also a queen," she sighed. "She was always an obedient daughter to me. And she was a faithful and beloved wife of the King. He loved her the best of all his wives because she gave him a son, Prince Edward. He is my grandson and your cousin. It is thanks to her that you are related to the royal family. You must always do your best to be worthy of that honour. It is a great tragedy that Queen Jane did not live to bear more children to his Majesty. Her death was a loss to the whole realm. You must pray every day for the repose of her soul and ask for the blessing of the same spirit of obedience. If you are as dutiful, faithful and virtuous as Queen Jane, then your father and I will be proud of you." Old Lady Seymour always spoke of her daughter as if she had been a saint rather than the least distinguished maid of honour at the court. But her parting words betrayed how envious she was of me.

"Remember to be worthy of my dear Edward," she said with a faint smile. "His career shines as it does thanks to the sacrifices of his late sister Jane."

I gave a polite nod, though her implication was clear. Her beloved Jane, gone too soon, had set a standard that I could never hope to match. Edward knew as well as I did that it was sheer nonsense, but he did nothing to correct the impression that his sister had been a paragon of virtue.

"Jane was a good woman and a good wife," he said. "If the King found her worthy to be queen, then she was worthy. After all, she was the only wife to bear him a son. So, she deserved her crown. And don't forget that her reputation and standing as the mother of the heir serve to uphold our position at court."

It was pointless to remind him that Jane had never had a coronation. And it was only due to our efforts that she had achieved the rank of a queen. Left to herself she would have been an insignificant mistress like Bessie Blount or Mary Boleyn. And if she had not died when she did, the King would soon have tired of her insipid meekness.

CHAPTER 7

Lady of the Court (1539 – 1547)

"Sends letters from her Ladyship to which he beseeches him to make a speedy answer, for he perceives she will not be merry till she hears from him."

(Sir Thomas Wriothesley to the earl of Hertford, 10th November 1542).

In February 1539 Edward returned to Wulf Hall for a visit. He looked more animated than I had seen him for a long time. "The King is thinking of marrying again," he said. "It is over a year since Jane died. He wants more sons and his children need a mother. There is much discussion among the councillors. If he were to take another wife, then you could return to court."

"What are the councillors saying?" I asked.

"Master Cromwell favours a foreign marriage," he said. "It will have the benefit of bringing a diplomatic alliance. But Archbishop Cranmer does not favour the idea. He thinks it would be better for the King to marry for love rather than for gain."

"He married his first wife for diplomatic reasons," I said. "But he married Anne Boleyn and Jane for the sake of love."

"A foreign match is by far the best option," he said. "It means that no English family will gain favour from the marriage and we will maintain our influence at court."

"Whose names are being put forward?" I asked. "Will it be a French princess?"

"The King considered the idea of a French wife," he said. "He proposed that the most eligible young noblewomen in France should be brought to Calais for his inspection. He wanted to choose a bride for himself in person. But the King of France would not agree to his plan. He thought it would be detrimental to their honour. So, Cromwell is considering ladies from the other royal houses of Europe. You should return to court with me and enter the service of Lady Mary. You do not want to become a forgotten woman."

You should return to court with me and enter the service of Lady Mary. You do not want to become a forgotten woman."

Lady Mary was glad to offer me a place in her household. She was still wearing black mourning clothes in memory of Queen Jane. She was twenty-three years old and her mood was despondent.

"Lady Hertford, it is good to see you again," she said."The court is so lonely without the presence of the ladies.

"I miss life at court, my lady," I said. "Although I have enjoyed spending time at home with my children."

"How many do you have now?" she asked.

"I have a son and two daughters, my lady," I replied proudly.

"Three children," she sighed. "You are most fortunate, Lady Hertford. I would love to marry and have children. But that solace is denied to me. Sometimes I go to visit my sister Elizabeth at Hatfield House and pretend that she is my own little girl. She is a fine child but she is as forsaken as I once was. The King despises her on account of her mother. His only care is for his son Edward."

"How is his Majesty, my lady?" I asked.

"I fear that he is a much changed man since the death of Queen Jane," she replied. "He has no interest in his former sports and pastimes. And he rarely comes to visit me or invites me to dine with him. But there are rumours that he is thinking of marrying again."

"Is there any talk of a marriage for yourself?" I asked cautiously.

She shook her head. "The King will never allow me to marry," she said. "He fears that my husband might seek to claim his throne. As long as my father lives, I shall only be the Lady Mary, the unhappiest lady in Christendom."

In March 1539 Master Holbein was sent to Brussels to paint Christina of Denmark. She was the widow of the duke of Milan and only sixteen years old. He sent her portrait to the King. He became entranced by her portrait immediately. It showed a fair young lady with a mysterious smile upon her lips. She was dressed in black mourning robes faced with dark brown fur. The image appealed to his romantic fantasies. He sent for his musicians and ordered them to play a selection of love ballads. Then he sat in the gallery and gazed at the portrait for hours. The courtiers began to lay bets with each other that the young duchess of Milan would be the next Queen of England. The King sent a proposal of marriage to Princess Christina. But she was a lady with a strong will and a keen sense of humour. She replied that if she had two heads, then one should be at the King's disposal. Thomas Wriothesley, the English diplomat in Brussels, advised that the King should fix his most noble stomach in some other place.

The King was deeply disappointed by the failure of his scheme. He realised that he was no longer the great marriage prize that he had once been. He agreed to send Master Holbein was to the court of Cleves. His orders were to paint the portraits of the two sisters of the duke of Cleves. He sent him two miniatures portraying Lady Anne and Lady Amelia. I accompanied Edward to the King's privy chamber for the viewing. The King was dressed in a doublet of cloth of gold, slashed to reveal a lining of crimson velvet. Around his left arm he wore a thin ribbon of black silk. His black velvet cap was adorned with a spray of egret feathers and a ruby-studded brooch. He was in a good mood and greeted us cheerfully.

"Lord and Lady Hertford," he said. "As you see, I have not forgotten my sorrow for your dear sister. Out of respect for her memory, I would be content to remain a widower for the rest of my days. But my councillors wish me to marry again for the sake of my motherless children."

Lord Cromwell placed the portraits upon two velvet cushions on a table. The King was eager to inspect the likenesses. His eyes were bright with expectation.

"Well then," he boomed, coming to a halt before the table. "Let us see the maidens who may share my crown."

He leaned in, and silence fell. The King's gaze moved over the first miniature—Amalia of Cleves. He nodded, but said nothing.

Then his eyes fell upon the second. Lady Anne. He did not speak at first. He simply stared. Master Holbein had captured her in three-quarter pose, hands folded demurely, her gown a pearl-grey satin edged in dark fur. Her eyes were steady, her mouth poised—not coy, but composed, with a quiet gravity that dared the viewer to dismiss her.

"She is well-favoured," he murmured. "Her countenance is sweet, solemn, and noble. She bears herself with the proper humility – there are no fiery looks nor bold French airs."

He paused and a smile crept over his lips. "She is comely, yes, comely enough for a queen. More than that I can see that Master Holbein has captured her very essence." He tapped the miniature lightly. "There is grace, modesty and obedience in her demeanour. She has every quality that characterises a lady of great virtue. If she is in person as she is in this image, then I may find contentment at last."

"You may rely upon the accuracy of Master Holbein," replied Lord Cromwell. "His talent outshines every other artist in Europe."

The King was so taken by the lovely image of Lady Anne of Cleves that he kept it inside his doublet. He drew it out to gaze upon several times a day. All the gentlemen of his privy chamber agreed that she was as fair as a May morning and fit to be a queen. As a precaution he sent the envoy Christopher Mont to Cleves to write a report on her. He replied that she exceeded her beautiful sister, Sibylle, Duchess of Saxony, as greatly as the golden sun excelled the silver moon. The King was convinced that Lady Anne was a matchless beauty and agreed to negotiate a marriage alliance. The match would create a diplomatic alliance with Cleves and the other Protestant German states. He was so eager to settle the contract that he agreed to forgo the dowry. Now that the agreement was signed, the King was impatient to receive his bride. He ordered Master Holbein to paint a full-sized portrait of the miniature for his privy chamber. He placed it on the mantelpiece and sighed over the merits of his beloved lady.

"I have composed a verse in her praise," he announced. "It is an unworthy tribute, yet it testifies to the deep sincerity of my feelings:

To the Lady Anne of Cleves

As fair as blush upon the pearled dawn sky,
Where noonday sun hath yet to chase the dew,
So shines thy face, serene and soft and high,
That peace and grace in equal measure strew.

The painter's hand no artifice hath made,
He merely caught what Heaven did design—
Those eyes like hush'd cathedral glass array'd,
That modest smile which makes a monarch pine.

My heart, long storm'd, now turns to gentle shore,
Where virtue's form doth beauty's soul embrace.
O Lady Anne, whom realms may yet adore—
England shall bloom beneath thy tempered grace."

"It is a most inspired verse, your Majesty," said Edward. "I found it deeply moving."

King Henry beamed. "I shall read it to her on our wedding night," he said. "I shall tell her that our love began the moment that I first laid eyes upon her lovely face."

"I am sure that you will be extremely happy together, your Majesty," he said.

"The earl of Southampton, the Lord High Admiral of England, is leading the reception at Calais," he said. "You and your good wife shall accompany him. You will greet her in my name and assure her of my most sincere devotion."

"It would be my honour, your Majesty," Edward replied. He was gratified by this proof of the King's trust.

"The wedding will take place at Greenwich," he said. "I shall host a grand reception in her honour. We shall meet for the first time on Blackheath in the presence of the entire court. After the wedding there will be great entertainments for the benefit of the envoys from Cleves. I shall tell the Master of the Revels to prepare a masque and Master of the Horse to organise a tournament. The court will be *en fete* and we shall rejoice as we have not done for many a month!"

"Yes, your Majesty," said Edward. He hurried over to Lady Mary's apartments to tell me the good news.

"You must have a set of new gowns made at once, Anne," he said. "Order a stock of cloth of gold and silk before it sells out. Every noblewoman at court will try look their best at the wedding. But we shall have the opportunity to meet the Lady Anne of Cleves at Calais and so you will have the advantage over them. If you manage to make a good impression on the new Queen, she is certain to appoint you as one of her ladies in waiting."

My heart fluttered with excitement. This was my chance to become a key figure in the Queen's household. I could return to court again and regain my position of a lady of consequence.

King Henry gave orders for ten of his finest ships to sail to Calais and bring the Lady Anne of Cleves to England in all solemnity and triumph. He planned to marry her in mid-December and then celebrate the Christmas season with her at court. She arrived at the city on 11th December 1539. The Lieutenant of Calais, Lord Lisle, and his wife came to meet her. They were accompanied by the earl of Southampton, my husband Edward and myself and thirty other gentlemen of the King's household dressed in blue velvet and crimson satin.

Lady Anne entered the city in her chariot at the Lantern Gate. The English fleet lay in the harbour decked with banners of gold and silk. A peal of cannons was shot in her honour. The main street was lined with five hundred soldiers of the Calais garrison dressed in blue and crimson damask and the merchants of the Staple. She was conveyed to the Exchequer which was the finest building in the city. The mayor and his aldermen presented her with a gift of a hundred gold marks. Lady Anne was escorted by the noblemen and ambassadors of Cleves and accompanied by a great entourage of three hundred and fifty retainers. Her twelve ladies were supervised by the formidable Mother

Lowe. They were dressed in the German fashion which was so heavy and tasteless that it would have made even a beautiful woman appear frightful. For the next two days Lady Anne was entertained with banquets and jousting. But her departure was delayed for two weeks by bad weather.

Lady Anne of Cleves celebrated Christmas at Calais and the wedding was postponed. She sat upright beside the roaring fireplace, her gown a warm crimson trimmed with sable, her hair pinned with pearls that glinted like frost. Outside, the sea wind howled against the shuttered windows, but within, laughter and the clack of wooden dice lent the room a festive pulse. She turned to Lord Southampton, who stood beside her in a doublet of deep green velvet, fingering a deck of richly painted cards.

"What are the King's favourite pastimes with his gentlemen?" she asked, her voice soft but deliberate, the German accent lending a musical lilt to her English.

Lord Southampton gave a courtly bow. "His Majesty likes to play at cards, dice, draughts and chess, your Grace. When his mood is light, cards are his particular pleasure."

"Please teach me how to play one of these card games," she said, leaning forward. "I wish to take part in the King's amusements."

The nobleman smiled, intrigued by her keenness. ""Noddy, Primeroe, Cent and Trump are all popular at the court, your Grace," he mused. "If I recall, his Majesty is particularly fond of playing Cent. It is a game of points and strategy, where the sharp mind is rewarded and a careless hand punished."

He carefully drew out a pack of cards—hand-painted, thick, and edged with gilt—and laid them before her on the polished oak table.

"Here, we begin with suits: clubs, diamonds, hearts and spades. They are like houses of nobility, each with its own symbolism. Hearts for love and loyalty. Spades for battle and toil. Diamonds for wealth. And clubs—well, some say they stand for the common man, but I think they mean mischief."

Lady Anne laughed, a low melodic sound that turned a few heads. "Then let mischief be my suit tonight."

As the lesson unfolded, she proved a quick study, her brow furrowed in concentration, her hands graceful and sure. Each turn she played was with a quiet elegance and wry smile, her countenance composed and attentive. The candles guttered as she laid down a winning hand, the flicker casting shadows across her face. Behind her, a cluster of gentlemen stood watching with folded arms and hushed voices.

"She is a most gracious lady," said Lord Lisle to Edward. "She has already begun to learn English."

"She is an aimable and agreeable lady," he agreed. "She will make him a fine queen."

The gentlemen were well pleased with Lady Anne of Cleves. But the ladies had their doubts about the match.

"She is a typical German noblewoman," remarked Lady Lisle. "But I wonder if the King will like her. She is not like one of the cultured ladies of France or Spain."

"Her dress does not flatter her in the least," I observed. "She ought to change it before she makes the crossing to England."

"Yes, indeed," she said. "An English or a French gown would be far more becoming. She ought to acquire a new wardrobe before she travels to England."

I shared my concerns with Edward. "Lady Anne of Cleves must change her dress before she arrives in England," I said. "Her garments will appear strange to his Majesty's eyes."

"It will give offence to the envoys from Cleves," he retorted. "Once she is married, she can set aside these clothes and wear the proper gowns of a Queen of England."

"Do you think the King will like her?" I asked Edward.

"Why not?" he replied indifferently. "She is young, fair and virtuous. She is of noble birth. Once she gives him a son, he will be well satisfied."

"But her language is unfamiliar to the King," I said. "And she has no courtly accomplishments. How will they converse and keep company together?"

"She will soon learn to speak our tongue," he said impatiently. "And she can easily learn to play a few card games. A few dancing and riding lessons are all that are required. She does not have to sing or play the lute. Besides, royal marriages are not like other marriages. They are matters of state."

"But the King will expect a lady of greater refinement and sophistication," I said. "She has spent her days with her prayer book and her needle. But it is not enough. I fear that the court of Cleves has not prepared her well for her future life."

"She has the look and manner of a princess, does she not?" he said. "She is a noble, gracious and virtuous lady. What more can his Majesty want in a wife?"

"The King is a great lover of pastimes," I reminded him. "But the court of Cleves is too austere for such amusements."

"She will be grateful to his Majesty for taking her out of such a place," he said.

On 27th December 1539, the fleet finally set sail for England. The morning mist clung to the harbour at Calais like a veil, softening the edges of the ships that bobbed in anticipation. Trumpets rang out from the quay, their notes crisp and jubilant, as Lady Anne stepped aboard the flagship *The Great Harry,* resplendent in its fresh gilding and towering masts. The vessel was festooned with pennants and streamers, its hull painted in Tudor colours, and at its stern flew the Royal Standard of England, golden lions rampant beside the red dragon of Wales, fluttering proudly in the wind. Above the mainmast, the flag of St George snapped sharply—its crimson cross on white a bold declaration of sovereignty and unity. The decks were lined with sailors in satin slops of Bruges blue, their coats trimmed with silver braid, while the officers wore velvet doublets and massy gold chains that gleamed like sunlight on water.

Lady Anne stood at the rail, her gown of deep violet velvet trimmed with ermine, her hood set with pearls that caught the morning light. She raised her hand in farewell to the gathered dignitaries—Lord Lisle, the Deputy of Calais, bowed low, his retinue arrayed in splendour. Behind him, the townspeople cheered, their voices rising in a chorus of goodwill and curiosity. As the anchor was lifted and the sails unfurled, a great peal of guns thundered from the harbour walls as a salute to the future Queen of England. The ship glided forward, cutting through the Channel with stately grace, its banners streaming behind like the train of a royal robe. The Channel was restless, its waves flecked with foam, but the fleet held steady. Seagulls wheeled overhead, and the coast of France faded into mist behind them. Lady Anne spent the long sea-crossing practising card games with Sir Francis Bryan. He was an adept card player who often partnered with the King. He diligently taught her how to play Noddy. She quickly mastered the rules of the game and earnestly thanked him.

"You can see how anxious she is to please him, Anne," Edward said. "Above all else, his Majesty wants to have a quiet and conformable wife. I tell you, she will suit him very well!"

As the fleet neared the Kentish coast, the cliffs rose like pale sentinels, and the harbour at Deal came into view. Bonfires crackled on the shore, and English envoys waited in full regalia. The ship slowed, anchors dropped, and the ceremonial landing began. Lady Anne disembarked the ship at five o'clock in the afternoon. On hearing of her arrival, the duke and duchess of Suffolk rode out to meet her and escort her to Deal Castle for the night. After much travelling she arrived at Rochester at the end of December. There she was met by the duke of Norfolk and Lord Mountjoy and taken to the palace to spend New Year's day.

A banquet was held in her honour and then a bear-baiting took place in the courtyard for her entertainment. She had never seen such a novelty before and stood at the window of her chamber watching the festivities below.

"Are the English fond of such amusements?" she asked the duke of Norfolk.

"Yes, your Grace," he replied. "In London there are often bull-baitings, dog fights and cockfights. They are very popular with the people."

"In Cleves we do not have such entertainments," she remarked.

"The King is very fond of pastimes and recreations," he said. "He often likes to go out hunting. When you arrive at Greenwich you will enjoy the pleasures of life at the court."

While they were talking a stranger wearing a hooded cloak approached. He made a courtly bow before her.

"Your Grace, I pray that you will allow me to present you with this ring," he said. "It is a token of the King's regard." He placed it in her hand.

"Thank you, Sir," she replied nonchalantly and continued to watch the spectacle through the window. A great mastiff had been brought out to fight with the bear.

The stranger stood there looking nonplussed at her response. Then he stepped forward and embraced her in his arms. Queen Catherine of Aragon would have recognised her cue immediately. She would have sunk to her knees in astonishment and protested that she was overwhelmed to behold her true love at last. But Lady Anne had never read a chivalric romance in her life and the court of Cleves had no knowledge of masques. She recoiled from the uncouth stranger in disgust. He was crestfallen by her reaction. He left the chamber and returned dressed openly in his doublet and hose of purple velvet embroidered with purls of damask gold and silver thread. The company sank to their knees and hailed him as *Your Majesty*. Lady Anne curtsied low before him and he extended his hand to raised her up. The courtiers applauded their meeting.

"I heard that you had arrived, your Grace," he said. "So, I could not refrain from riding here to greet you."

"Your Majesty is most gracious," replied Lady Anne.

But the occasion had fallen sadly flat and nothing could revive it. The King's bold fantasies about his true love had dissolved into thin air. His intended bride was a young woman dressed in outlandish clothes who talked in broken English. She bore no resemblance to the cherished lady of his dreams. He bowed again and took his leave.

Shortly afterward, Sir Anthony Browne entered holding a bundle of rich sable furs. "His Majesty has sent you this New Year gift as a token of his true affection," he said.

"Please convey my thanks to his Majesty," she replied.

He handed the bundle to the duke of Norfolk and made a deep bow. Then he exited the chamber as fast as courtesy permitted. Edward and I followed him out of the door.

"Why didn't his Majesty present the gift himself?" he asked.

"He didn't want to see her again," he said. "He felt humiliated that she did not recognise him."

"But she was expecting to meet his Majesty at Greenwich," Edward protested. "Why did you allow such a madcap escapade?"

"The King said that he wanted to surprise her and nourish love between them," he replied. "He declared that in 1445 King Henry VI had gone in disguise to visit his new bride, Margaret of Anjou, and he intended to do the same."

"But that was a hundred years ago!" Edward protested. "King do not meet their noble brides in such a manner anymore. They are expected to make a dignified entrance. It is a foolish conceit!"

"He had a romantic notion that she would see through his disguise and recognise him," he said. "He is badly disappointed. He says that she is nothing so fair as she has been reported. He is returning to London at once. I must go to join him."

He hurried off to find his master. Edward and I looked at each other in perplexity and dismay. This was not the gracious and joyful meeting that had been expected. It was a bad sign that the King had left without wanting to see his bride's reception of his splendid gift.

"Lady Anne is as fair a princess as any King might wish to see," he said.

"But she has no understanding of courtly love," I replied. "If only we had been forewarned, then I would have prepared her for the encounter. She would have taken delight in receiving his token. Then the King would have been touched and flattered."

"He wanted it to be a surprise," he said. "He thought that she would recognise him as her true-love. Now what is to be done?"

"It is his own fault for not waiting," I said. "If he had met her at Greenwich, Lady Anne would have appeared to advantage and he would have been entirely satisfied."

Lady Anne of Cleves and her retinue slowly made their way to Blackheath for the official reception. The entire court was assembled there in her honour. She rode down Shooter's Hill to meet the King and his train of noblemen. The nobles were arrayed in their best costumes for the occasion. But the royal couple outshone them in splendour. Lady Anne wore a rich gown of cloth of gold, a round cap set with orient pearls and a necklace of glittering jewels. King Henry was dressed in a resplendent coat of purple velvet embroidered with gold. It was slashed to reveal a lining of cloth of gold beneath and fastened with gold buttons set with diamonds, rubies and pearls. His sleeves of cloth of gold were embroidered with diamonds and pearls. His cap was adorned with fine jewels and he wore a gold collar set with magnificent stones. Together they rose to Greenwich palace followed by their retinues. They dismounted in the courtyard and embraced each other. Then the King escorted her through the hall and to her privy chamber in the Queen's apartments.

The courtiers welcomed her as a gracious lady and a worthy queen. She was wholly anxious to please her husband and learn the ways of the English court. But King Henry was sullen and petulant. "I like her not," he complained. He summoned Lord Cromwell and demanded a remedy. But Lord Cromwell insisted that there was none. He could not withdraw from the marriage agreement without giving grave offence to Duke William of Cleves.

In my opinion, Lady Anne was far more attractive than Jane had ever been. If only the King had waited in London to meet her, then the outcome might have been a far happier one. The splendour of the reception would have created a romantic atmosphere. Lady Anne would have been prepared to greet him in a courteous manner. She might have made a graceful speech to win his heart or else swooned for joy in his arms and declared that he was the noblest prince in Christendom. But now it was too late for her to make a good impression. The sweet melody inside his head had turned to discord. He was certain that their union was a ghastly mistake and nothing would convince him otherwise. Lady Anne did not have a chance to gain his affections. Duke William had spent a fortune equipping his sister to arrive in state as the future Queen of England. But his efforts were utterly in vain. The disastrous first encounter had disillusioned the King and the romance of his marriage had been spoiled for him. He felt the same distaste for his new wife as Sir Gawain did for the Loathly Lady. He did not want her in his bed or at his board.

"I have not been well served," he complained. "If it were not to satisfy the world and my realm, I would not make this marriage for any earthly thing,"

On 6th January 1540, they were married in the Queen's Closet at Greenwich Palace. I watched as her German ladies dressed her in her wedding gown of cloth of gold adorned with a design of flowers made of pearls. Around her neck was a border of fine pearls, gold and diamonds. Her long blonde hair hung loose about her shoulders. On her head she wore a coronet of gold and gems set with sprigs of rosemary. King Henry entered the chamber dressed a gown of cloth of gold embossed with silver flowers and trimmed with black fur. His coat was of crimson satin embroidered with gold and fastened with diamond buttons and he had a richly jewelled collar around his neck. They were married by the archbishop of Canterbury and the King set the wedding ring upon her finger. It was engraved with the motto: *Send me well to keep*. The court applauded. Everyone hoped that now they were married, the King would be reconciled to his new wife. She was a gracious and dignified lady with a queenly manner. Few princes would have complained of such a bride. But the King could hardly bear to look at her. He sat through the wedding banquet looking sullen and ill-used. He took no interest in the extravagant entertainments that enlivened the evening.

The following day, Lord Cromwell approached the King in trepidation. "How does your Majesty like the Queen?" he asked.

"I liked her not well before but now I like her much worse," he snapped. "I have felt her belly and her breasts and I judge that she is no maid!"

"I do not know what is to be done," Edward said. "Cromwell sent for the Queen's chamberlain, the earl of Rutland, and told him that he must counsel his mistress to use all pleasantness towards his Majesty."

"The King has only to be patient," I said. "The Queen's ladies can teach her how to assume the manner of a cultured lady of the court. After all, Jane was practically illiterate and the King never complained."

"Jane understood the ways of the court very well," he snapped. "She succeeded in pleasing the King better than any of his other wives. She was fair, she was dutiful and she was fruitful."

I saw that none of the King's gentlemen understood the situation. I decided to take matters into my own hands. I resolved to speak to the Queen myself and made my way to the privy chamber. I found her seated by the oriel window, wrapped in fur, staring out at the grey drizzle that glazed the river like ash. Her gown was of crimson velvet, stiff and cut in the German fashion, high-necked, square-bodied, adorned with stiff gold stitches that caught the light but not the eye. Her hair was braided and bound beneath a pearl-trimmed coif that looked more ceremonial than flattering.

"Your Grace, may I have a word with you," I murmured.

"You may speak, Lady Hertford," she replied graciously.

"The court is not familiar with your Grace's manner of dress," I said. "If you would please the King then you should dress yourself in the English fashion. Let your hair fall loose beneath an English hood, let your bodice curve and your gown flow with softer lines. Let the court see not a duchess of Cleves but a Queen of England."

"If it will please his Majesty, then let it be done," she said. "Send for the tailor to make me a new gown. It is my desire to respect the King's wishes in every particular."

On 11th January 1540 a solemn tournament was held in honour of the new queen and the envoys from Cleves. The tiltyard of Greenwich was ablaze with colour and sound—trumpets blared, banners snapped in the wind, and the young men of the court assembled to joust wearing doublets and hose of white velvet. The courtiers lined the galleries in their richest finery, their eyes fixed on the royal dais where the King sat, broad-faced and brooding beneath a cap of crimson velvet. The envoys from Cleves stood nearby, stiff with ceremony, their expressions unreadable.

Then she appeared.

Queen Anne stepped into view and a hush rippled through the crowd. Gone was the stiff German bodice and heavy coif. She wore a gown of deep rose damask, cut in the English style to flatter her figure, the sleeves slashed to reveal silver silk beneath. Her French hood framed her face with soft velvet and pearls, her hair smoothed and shining beneath its curve. A girdle of gold filigree clasped at her waist, and her train was borne by two young maids of honour in matching livery.

She walked slowly, deliberately, her chin lifted—not defiant, but regal. Murmurs rose like the wind blowing through the reeds. The transformation was striking. It was so much more becoming to her that I regretted that she had not changed her dress sooner. I hoped that this new vision of the Queen would be enough to arouse the King's interest.

King Henry shifted in his seat as she approached. His eyes narrowed, then widened. The courtiers watched him more than they watched her, gauging every flicker of his mood. He leaned forward, lips parted slightly, as if seeing her for the first time. His gaze lingered appraisingly.

Anne curtsied low before him, her gown pooling like rose petals at her feet. "Your Majesty," she said, her voice clear and steady. "I hope that my attire meets with your approval."

King Henry nodded, slowly. "It suits you well, madam." But then his eyes shifted to look at one of the young maids of honour who carried her train. She was strikingly fair and graceful. She smiled and blushed when she saw that he had caught his eye.

Queen Anne took her place in the Queen's pavilion with her ladies. The jousts began with thunderous hooves and splintering lances, but the Queen's appearance remained the talk of the day. Everyone rejoiced to see her looking so elegant in her English dress and French hood. She had played her part, and played it well. Whether it would soften the King's heart towards her was uncertain—but she had shown England that she could wear its crown with grace.

The joust was followed by a banquet and dancing in the Great Hall of Greenwich. Its walls were adorned with tapestries that shimmered in the candlelight. The hammer-beam ceiling echoed with laughter and the music of lutes and viols. The scent of clove-studded oranges mingled with the warmth of mulled wine. Courtiers spun in elegant reels across the polished floor, their silks and satins catching the light like jewels in motion. The sweet voice of a singer rose above the music:

"It was a lover and his lass,
With a hey, and a ho, and a hey nonny-no,
That o'er the green cornfield did pass
In springtime, the only pretty ring time,
When birds do sing, hey ding a ding, ding;
Sweet lovers love the spring."

King Henry sat beside Queen Anne, his mood unreadable, his goblet untouched. The Queen smiled dutifully, her French hood perfectly aligned, her gown of rose damask silk a triumph of diplomacy. Yet the King's gaze wandered.

Across the hall, a young maid of honour danced with a gentleman of the privy chamber—her steps were light and her laughter unguarded. She was the same girl that he had noticed that morning. She wore a gown of pale green, the colour of spring's first shoots, and her fair hair fell in soft waves beneath a modest hood. Her cheeks were flushed with exertion, her eyes bright with mischief.

Henry leaned forward, his breath catching. "Who is that girl?" he murmured.

The Earl of Southampton, standing nearby, bowed slightly. "Her name is Mistress Catherine Howard, Your Majesty. She serves in the Queen's household."

Henry's eyes did not leave her. "She moves like a flame," he said. "And she smiles as if she has never known sorrow."

Catherine twirled, her hand briefly brushing her partner's sleeve, and Henry's fingers tightened around the arm of his chair. The music swelled, and she laughed—a sound that pierced the clamour like silver. When the dance ended, she turned towards the King and curtsied low. Then she looked up at him and gave a radiant smile.

The King's eyes were fixed upon her. He reached out and grasped the stem of his goblet with his fingers. Then he took a deep draught of wine.

"That new maid of honour is a bold girl," I said to Edward. "She is deliberately courting the King's attention."

"It is Norfolk's doing, I'll be bound," he replied. "She is his niece."

Norfolk was not slow to capitalise upon his niece's success. Before long there were whispers in the court that the King frequently crossed the Thames in his barge in the evenings and dined with her at Winchester palace. It reminded me of how the King had visited Jane at Chelsea while Anne Boleyn was in the Tower. The only thing that could save Queen Anne of Cleves from humiliation was to bear him a child. I decided to find out if there was any prospect of one.

"Is your Grace with child yet?" I asked her.

"I know well that I am not," she replied.

"How can your Grace know that when you lie every night with the King?" I said. "Is it possible that your Grace is still a maid?"

"I am not a maid for I sleep every night with the King," she replied. "When he comes to bed, he kisses me and takes me by the hand and bids me "Good night, sweetheart." Is this not enough?"

"Madam, there must be more than this or else it will be long till we have a little duke of York," I said.

"I am quite content as I am," she insisted.

"Did not your mother speak to your Grace of the marriage bed?" I asked.

"Fie for shame!" she snapped. "God forbid that she should speak of such a thing!"

I shared my concerns with Edward. "I do not believe the King's marriage has been consummated," I said.

"Do not say a word to anyone," he replied. "It would shame the King if it were known."

The King's displeasure in his marriage made Cromwell frantic. He could not find a way to placate the King. He regretted that he had not seen Mistress Howard before contracting a foreign match. He complained that if the Queen had not come so far into his realm and for fear of making a ruffle in the world, he would never have married her.

Cromwell sent for Lord Southampton and berated him. "This situation is all your fault," he said. "You praised the Queen so highly in your letters from Calais that the King expected her to be a great beauty."

"My Lord Cromwell," he replied. "The matter had already gone too far for me to have said anything else!"

"The King wants to repudiate the marriage," Edward confided to me.

"He can't do that!" "I replied. What will he say to the duke of Cleves? That his sister is not fair enough to please him? It is unthinkable!"

"Cromwell is blaming Lord Southampton and myself for not intervening at Calais," he said. "He thinks we should have sent her back to Cleves. He believes we failed in our duty."

"You were asked to welcome the new bride, not make a report on her appearance," I replied. "That was the responsibility of the envoys whom he sent to Cleves."

"Well, he is looking for a scapegoat in this matter," he said. "If it is anyone's fault, it is Cromwell's. He is the one who wanted the alliance with Cleves."

"That is right, my dear," I agreed. "It is Cromwell's fault entirely. He cannot possibly blame you!"

I pitied Queen Anne of Cleves who did not know that she was a failure. She thought that the King was entirely content. She did not know that he built his marriages around romantic illusions. Catherine of Aragon had been the forlorn lady in need of rescue. Anne Boleyn had been his tempestuous mistress. And Jane had been the gentle lady whose virtue could tame unicorns. But he could conjure no romance around Anne of Cleves. And so, she was as repugnant to him as if she was a toad.

The King set his mind to freeing himself from the marriage and taking a wife after his own heart. He told Cromwell to find a pretext for annulling the marriage. But he insisted that there was no remedy. It was a fatal mistake. His enemies whispered in the King's ear that Cromwell was a traitor, a heretic and a false servant. On 10th June 1540, Cromwell was charged with treason and taken to the Tower. Edward was present at the council meeting where he was arrested.

"Norfolk confronted him as soon as he arrived," he said. "He told him not to sit at the head of the table for that was no place for him. Traitors do not sit amongst gentlemen. He tore the chain of office off his neck and told the Yeomen Guards to take him away. The King's archers were sent to his house at Austin Friars to seize his money, plate and goods and take them to the Jewel House. It is the end of Cromwell. This is what it means to lose the favour of the King."

I shuddered to hear of the King's vengeance. "Perhaps my stepfather was right to leave the court," I said. "The King has destroyed Wolsey, More and Cromwell in succession. Who knows who might be next?"

"They had become too arrogant," he said. "The King needs capable servants more than ever."

"The court has become more dangerous than ever," I said. "Cromwell was no traitor. He was devoted to the King's service. He made him the richest monarch in Europe. But when he had served his turn, he was cast aside."

"The court has always been a dangerous place for the unwary," he said. "But I am a cautious man. I study the King and I study the times. Through skill and patience, it is possible to rise in his favour."

"And it is equally possible to fall," I said. "The King's favour is short-lived. It cannot be relied upon to last."

"The King is growing old," he said. "We should look ahead to the reign of his son. When King Edward is on the throne, he will look for faithful councillors. And who will he trust more than his own relatives?"

It was treason to imagine the death of the King. But I knew that Edward was right. We were experienced courtiers and our services were valuable. And as the aunt and uncle of King Edward we could expect to be appointed to important positions.

On 25th June 1540 the King sent the Queen away to Richmond on the pretext that the country air would benefit her health. About two weeks later the King sent some lords to Richmond to present Anne with the news that her marriage to him had been judged unlawful. With that the King was free to marry whomever he would like. This was also the day that they informed her that she was no longer allowed to be called Queen and from that point on she was to be called Lady Anne of Cleves. The Queen was so shocked by the news that she fainted. But she did not attempt to dispute the King's wishes. She sent back her wedding ring to the King and asked him to break it into pieces as a thing of no value.

King Henry was so grateful for her acquiescence that he gave her a generous settlement. She received the title of the King's sister and the three royal houses and parks of Richmond, Blechingley and Hever. She was allowed to keep her jewels and wardrobe of royal gowns. In addition, she was provided with a household staff and a quantity of hangings, plate and furniture and an annual income of eight thousand nobles. It meant that she was one of the wealthiest ladies in the realm. She accepted the terms of the settlement which required her to remain in England for the rest of her life. It was a humiliation and a tragedy for her. She could never marry again for it would have been a slight upon the King's honour. But of course, he could remarry and he did so at once. On 28th July 1540 he married Mistress Catherine Howard at Oatlands palace.

She stood beneath a canopy of estate dressed in a gown of crimson silk with sleeves of cloth of silver. Her bodice, square and tight, was stitched with seed pearls and Howard lions. Her hair was parted cleanly at the centre and fell in soft chestnut coils around her shoulders. A circlet of ruby and enamel rested upon her brow. It was said to have belonged to Anne Boleyn. His Grace the Duke of Norfolk stood at her side, every inch a peacock of state. His cloak, heavy with sable, shimmered with stitched banners and his own rampant lion. He looked as pleased as if it were his own wedding day. He leaned over and kissed her gloved hand, his voice filled with pride: "Today, niece, you raise us all."

A fanfare of trumpets blew and King Henry shuffled in stiffly and slowly. He had aged dreadfully. He wore a robe of cloth-of-gold, so densely woven that it caught the light like hammered brass. It was embroidered with a tapestry of red and white Tudor roses and edged with black satin piping. His doublet of yellow satin was so wide that it could fit three normal men and his hose strained at the buttons. Around his neck he wore the collar of the Order of the Garter, its linked pieces studded with diamonds and rubies. On his head he wore a cap of black velvet with a single white plume and a glittering emerald brooch. He cast a loving glance at his bride and she curtsied low before him. She had adopted the French motto *"Non autre volonté que la sienne,"* meaning "No other will but his."

After the wedding ceremony, he celebrated his joy with the court. Inwardly, I regretted the repudiation of Lady Anne. But as a courtier it was my duty to share in the King's happiness. The Great Hall shimmered with torchlight, casting golden ripples across the tapestries that lined the walls. Queen Catherine sat in a chair of carved walnut, its arms shaped like griffins, their gilded talons clutching spheres. I took my place on the dias behind my new mistress. The King strode towards her, his gait slow but deliberate, his eyes alight with admiration. The hush that fell upon the court was palpable. Even the musicians, sensing the weight of the moment, let their melodies dwindle into silence. In his thick, bejewelled fingers, the King held a small box, its lacquered surface gleaming beneath the candle flames.

Queen Catherine lowered her gaze demurely, yet I could see the excitement in her face—the slight parting of her lips, the flutter of her breath.

"My most beloved wife," Henry intoned, his voice deep and resounding. "Here is a gift, to mark our union."

He opened the box with great ceremony, revealing the jewel nestled within—a pendant of rubies, diamonds and pearls, set in the shape of a Tudor rose. Gasps rippled through the assembled courtiers, and I, too, could not contain my awe. The craftsmanship was exquisite, each stone seeming to hold a fire of its own. He took it out and held it up to the light so that everyone could admire the costly ornament. He fastened the necklace around her throat himself, his fingers lingering upon the delicate skin at her nape. Then he stepped back to gaze at the Tudor rose resting against the pale column of her throat.

"You are as radiant as the dawn," he murmured, and for a moment, he looked at her as though nothing else in the world existed.

The Queen lifted a hand to trace her fingers over the jewel, her touch light as a whisper. Her eyes flickered upward, meeting the King's gaze with something that might have been admiration—or careful calculation. The court, still hushed, waited with bated breath.

"It is the most exquisite gift I have ever received, Your Majesty," she said, her voice delicate yet steady. "I shall cherish it always."

The King's broad face split into a satisfied smile, and a ripple of approving murmurs spread through the gathered courtiers. The musicians, sensing the moment had passed, resumed their melody, filling the hall with warm, lilting notes once more. He extended a hand toward her, his rings gleaming under the candlelight.

"Will my Queen honour me with a dance?" he asked, his voice deep, carrying across the hall with ease.

A delighted smile flickered over her lips. She hesitated just long enough to tease him before rising, curtsying low. "Nothing would please me more, Your Majesty."

The courtiers watched as she placed her delicate hand into his larger grasp, and the King, pleased with the eagerness of her reply, led her onto the floor with the slow, deliberate steps of a man who knew he held the attention of all. The court watched in rapt attention as they moved into a stately pavane. His steps were deliberate, commanding, while she glided beside him, her youth lending her a lightness that seemed effortless. He turned her with great care, his gaze lingering upon her as though she were the most precious thing in the world.

"You dance as though the very air carries you," he murmured in admiration.

She laughed, the sound bright as bells. "And you, my King, lead with such grace that I cannot help but follow."

His chest swelled at her words, and a murmur of approval rippled through the watching courtiers. Catherine followed his lead, her movements supple, her laughter soft as she allowed him to guide her. When they came to a pause, she dipped into a graceful bow before him, her ruby pendant catching the light like a flame against her throat.

The King's broad chest swelled with pride, his lips curving into a triumphant smile. "You wear my gift well, sweet Kate," he said, his voice rich with satisfaction. Tonight, his Queen had captured every eye, every heart and the King, basking in her radiance, could not have been more pleased.

The King's marriage to Catherine Howard took place on the same day that Cromwell was executed on Tower Hill. The duke of Norfolk had a double reason to celebrate. He had raised his niece to the dignity of Queen of England and he had defeated his greatest enemy at court. His triumph was the worst possible news for Edward. His alliance with Cromwell had served him well in the past. But now his sister Elizabeth, Lady Cromwell, was forced to withdraw from court as a result of her father-in-law's disgrace.

"Norfolk is the most arrogant and detestable man in the realm," he complained. "We will never regain our influence while he dominates the court. To think that he has contrived to get two of his nieces into the King's bed! Who is this girl anyway?"

"She is the daughter of his brother Edmund," I replied. "Her mother died when she was young and she was brought up in the household of the dowager duchess of Norfolk. But she is a very unsuitable choice as the Queen. She has hardly any accomplishments besides music and dancing. And she is far too young to be his wife. The King must be in his dotage!"

The duke of Norfolk took charge of the privy council. But he lacked the skills of Cromwell for managing the affairs of state. The King was forced to neglect his new bride in order to deal with important matters himself. He blamed Norfolk for having deprived him of the services of his chief minister.

"Cranmer told me that Cromwell always studied to set forward my will and pleasure," he grumbled. "I should have listened to him. But on the pretext of slight offences and false accusations, I was persuaded to put to death the most faithful servant I ever had. Now I am surrounded by dolts and there is no-one to take his place!"

However, his young wife continued to enchant him. He showered her with gifts of splendid dresses, costly jewels and exotic furs. They were far more magnificent that anything he had ever given to Jane. The Queen delighted in dressing up in her new finery. They were far more luxurious than anything that she had ever owned before. She wore her wedding necklace, a French hood set with diamonds and rubies, a girdle with a gold tablet engraved with her initials and a muffler of black velvet set with thirty pearls. She moved through her privy chamber like a butterfly unfurling its wings, her skirts rustling like whispered secrets, her laughter ringing sharp and bright as cut crystal. Her maids of honour chattered and giggled with admiration as they praised her beauty, her finery and her good fortune.

She stood before the mirror, tilting her head to admire the sparkle of rubies upon her brow. The Tudor rose pendant gleamed at her throat. She stretched out her arm, letting the black velvet muffler, weighted with pearls, slip softly down her wrist.

"His Majesty is besotted with me," she murmured, her voice full of satisfaction. "He calls me his rose without a thorn—his jewel of womanhood."

Lady Herbert, the Keeper of the Queen's Jewels, adjusted the border of gems upon her velvet hood and gave a playful sigh. "Would that every woman could be so adored!"

The Queen turned around, her eyes dancing. "But no woman has ever been so adored," she declared. "No other queen has ever received such finery as this." She twirled, skirts flaring, dazzling in the golden glow of the chamber's candlelight. "This evening, I shall dress myself like an empress! And his Majesty shall see that he has never chosen so wisely before." Her joy was infectious, and her maids of honour clapped their hands, their laughter joining hers, filling the chamber with the sound of pleasure.

I watched her in silence with my hands clasped before me. This was not the way that a Queen should receive the King's favours. She had neither dignity or decorum. She reminded me of a foolish child who had discovered her mother's jewel-box and adorned herself with the entire contents. How did she expect to command the respect of the court? Queen Catherine of Aragon and Queen Anne of Cleves had been the daughters of noble houses. Queen Anne Boleyn had the graces of the French court to distinguish her. And Queen Jane Seymour had been renowned for her virtue and modesty. But what did Queen Catherine Howard have to recommend her?

"The Queen's household is little more than a nursery," I grumbled to Edward. "She has no idea how to order her ladies. She spends her time frolicking with her attendants. She is like a little girl playing with her dolls. The Lady Anne of Cleves was a much better queen!"

"You must ingratiate yourself with her," demanded Edward. "Find a way to make yourself indispensable. I can't get anywhere near the King and he never asks for me anymore. So, it depends on you to establish our influence with his wife."

But the Queen had her own circle of ladies who were connected to the Howards. She was surrounded by her sisters and her companions from her grandmother's household. Her closest attendants were her sister Lady Margaret Arundell, her half-sister Lady Isabel Baynton, her gentlewoman Alice Wilkes and her chamberer Catherine Tylney. They were much younger than I was and more adept at entertaining her. She often withdrew into her privy chamber with her favourites and spent her time in gossiping, dancing and listening to music. I barely had a chance to speak to the Queen. The only one of the older ladies that she favoured was Lady Rochford. She had wormed her way into her good graces by telling her salacious stories about the courtiers. I was left to pass my time in the Presence Chamber with the rabble of the court. Edward was frustrated by our lack of influence in the new regime. He blamed me for failing to please the Queen.

I was not the only one who despised Queen Catherine Howard. Lady Mary had welcomed the arrival of the Lady Anne of Cleves as the daughter of a royal house. But now she was appalled to learn that now she had a stepmother who was younger than herself. She was not impressed by her childish conduct and could barely bring herself to be civil to her. The new Queen complained to the King that his daughter did not show any respect for her. He made his displeasure known by dismissing two of his daughter's favourite ladies. She was deeply grieved to lose her loyal friends. I went to visit her and found her in a dejected mood.

The tension in the air was palpable, thick with the weight of courtly intrigue and simmering resentment. Lady Mary sat in her richly adorned chamber, the flickering candlelight casting deep shadows over her face. Though her gown was of the finest tawny velvet, it did little to conceal her weariness. The burdens she carried were not of fabric or jewels but of sorrow and disappointment. Her hands trembled slightly as she spoke, each word heavy with despair.

"Sometimes I wish that I had died with my mother," she confided, her voice a whisper barely audible above the crackling fire. "I live in the estate of a King's daughter, but my father will not give me the title of a princess nor will he allow me to marry. And now I have to bear the indignity of having a stepmother who is even younger than I am!"

My heart clenched at such a statement, yet I knew well that her suffering was genuine. She was a princess by birth, yet stripped of the title by her own father's cruel decree. It was an injustice that gnawed at her very soul. Of course, she ought to have been married long ago. But the King feared that if Lady Mary took a husband he would reach for the crown. He was determined that only his son Prince Edward should succeed him. I glanced around the chamber. Several attendants and servants were hovering within earshot. Any one of them could be a spy and report our conversation to the King. As I hesitated, one of the servants drew closer. I knew that the slightest mistake could lead to an accusation of treason. I decided to take precautions.

Feigning light-heartedness, I spoke in a voice meant for all to hear. "Perhaps some music would lift your spirits, my lady," I said. "Why don't you send for your musicians?"

It was the safest way to have a private conversation. Lady Mary's brows knitted in brief confusion, but she nodded. Within moments, her players entered, their instruments in hand. As they struck up a lively tune, I leaned in, lowering my voice so only she could hear.

"You must not despair, my lady," I murmured, my words urgent but soft. "You must have faith that your life was spared for a good purpose."

She sighed, her dark eyes haunted by doubt. "That is what my chaplain says. But I fail to see what purpose that could be. Nothing would make me happier than to be a wife and a mother. And yet I am already twenty-six, with no prospect of a husband."

I hesitated, knowing I must tread carefully. "Queen Jane Seymour was your good friend, my lady. When she died, she left behind a motherless son. You can honour her memory by taking care of him."

Her expression softened, yet sorrow remained. "I do what I can for Prince Edward and Lady Elizabeth. But they have servants aplenty; they do not need me."

I would not relent. "But there are many children who do need care. The poor have suffered since the monasteries were dismantled. You could be their patroness, as your dear mother was."

A flicker of resolution appeared in Lady Mary's eyes, the fire of duty rekindling beneath her grief. She nodded slowly. "You are right, Lady Hertford. I was thinking only of my own misery. But there are many who suffer. I will send for my chaplain. He will advise me on how best to help. I do not possess great means, but I will offer food and clothing to the most needy."

Relief washed over me. "May it bring you comfort, my lady."

She reached for my hand, squeezing it gently. "You are a true friend, Lady Hertford. I will not forget your kindness."

I smiled, though my heart remained burdened. The tides of fortune in this court were fickle, and Lady Mary's future was still uncertain. Yet for tonight, at least, I had given her a measure of hope.

The King celebrated the Christmas season with splendid entertainments. He was so content that he invited Lady Anne of Cleves to come to court at New Year. She sent the King a gift of two fine horses trapped in mauve velvet which delighted him. The Great Hall of Hampton Court glittered like the court of paradise that New Year's Eve. Fir boughs swathed the gilded beams, and the scent of frankincense hung heavy in the air, mingling with roasted meats and mulled wine. Flickering candlelight danced across polished floors and brocaded tapestries; everything spoke of triumph—of a King restored to merriment.

I stood behind Queen Catherine's chair of estate as Lady Anne of Cleves entered the Great Hall. Her gown was of deep wine-coloured velvet lined with ermine, and her black velvet hood was elegantly set with garnets. She walked slowly at first, her step dignified, her expression serene. Then, as she reached Queen Catherine, she sank to her knees with grace so profound the air itself seemed to hush.

Her Majesty extended her hand, and Anne took it, pressing it to her lips in homage. I saw a look of surprise flicker across the Queen's face and then she smiled.

When the King arrived, the hall stirred as if lit from within. He wore a surcoat of gold tissue embroidered with crimson thistles, and his boots rang against the stone like a royal drumbeat. All eyes turned as he crossed the floor and embraced Lady Anne. It was exactly a year since their first ill-fated meeting had taken place in Rochester.

They dined together beneath a canopy of estate and conversed as if they were the best of friends. There was no trace of old wounds. Only civility and warmth. At the end of the banquet, the King presented Queen Catherine with a gift—a ring set with diamonds and two white spaniels with matching velvet collars—Her Majesty, with eyes shining, turned and placed the ring in Lady Anne's palm, and handed her the leash of the dogs.

"A token for you, dear sister," she said, with impulsive generosity.

Lady Anne accepted them with gentle courtesy. Her composure was unmatched. I was impressed by her grace and fortitude. She had every excuse for self-pity or bitterness, but she had such nobility of mind that she displayed no sign of unease.

When the King retired to his own apartments, the Queen and Lady Anne remained. The music of viols and sackbuts swelled and the two danced together with their hands clasped. They spent the evening in laughter and making good cheer. I watched Lady Anne closely. She was neither proud nor bashful. She took pleasure in taking part in the festivities of the court. I thought then, that her unfortunate marriage had not left her diminished. No crown rested on her head, yet she bore herself with such dignity that all who watched her saw something finer than royalty. My mother would have said that she was a true example of a noble-woman.

In February 1541 King Henry fell so ill from the ulcer on his leg that his face turned black. His doctors were forced to lance the swelling which caused him great pain. He gradually recovered but became ill-tempered and melancholy. He refused to see anyone, but remained shut away in his apartments. Not even the Queen was allowed to visit him. She feared that the worst might happen and begged to be kept informed of his Majesty's health. The King told one of his gentlemen ushers to report to the Queen every day and compose her mind.

The morning sun spilled across the polished floor like gold dust, and laughter—high, bright, and utterly unchecked—tumbled from the lips of Her Majesty and her ladies-in-waiting. I had never seen Queen Catherine so radiant; her golden hair sparkled with tiny pearls, and her cheeks carried the bloom of a girl who hadn't yet tired of being adored. We were gathered in the privy chamber, the air perfumed with crushed rose petals and the scent of sweet almond oil. The lute player sat cross-legged by the hearth, plucking a tune so merry that even Lady Rochford tapped her foot in time. Queen Catherine leaned back against her cushions, eyes shining, and clapped her hands in delight.

> *"Now is the month of maying,*
> *When merry lads are playing,*
> *Each with his bonny lass*
> *Upon the greeny grass.*
> *The Spring, clad all in gladness*
> *Doth laugh at Winter's sadness.*
> *Fie then! why sit we musing*
> *Youth's sweet delight refusing?*
> *Say, dainty nymphs, and speak*
> *Shall we play barley break?"*

Master Thomas Culpeper entered the Queen's privy chamber with a stride too confident for the shadowed times. His doublet was bottle-green silk, slashed at the sleeves with tawny velvet, a chain of fine gold resting against his chest like a promise. His dark auburn hair was curled and perfumed, and his boots polished to a sheen that caught the sunlight. He bowed low to the Queen—an elegant dip with just a touch of insolence. She watched him closely.

"My lady," he said. "I come bearing news of his Majesty."

Her fingers clenched about the embroidery frame she had not touched in hours. "Speak."

"His fever has broken. The physicians are hopeful. His humour remains a shade sour, but the swelling lessens."

She sighed in relief. "You will come again tomorrow?"

He smiled—a slow, crooked thing that lit his hazel eyes. "If Your Grace desires it."

She nodded. And Culpeper did come, day after day. He lingered after others left. He stood too near her chair of estate. She laughed more easily when he was in the room, a laugh tinged with melancholy, as if he brought both comfort and reminder. One afternoon, I found her in the gallery, Culpeper reclining in the window seat with a lute across his lap. His fingers brushed the strings as he told some tale of the King's youth, his voice low and intimate.

"Did he really ride from Greenwich to Windsor in two hours?" she asked, leaning forward.

"He did," Culpeper replied, "though I'd wager no-one has attempted the feat ever since."

They laughed and his gaze rested on her face a shade too long for decorum.

I stepped forward with a cough. "My lady, the goldsmith awaits your opinion on the new pomander."

She blinked, startled, and Culpeper rose. "Then I shall leave Your Grace to her duties."

He bowed, and as he departed, I saw her eyes follow him with something dangerously close to longing. Queen Catherine ought to have remembered that her cousin, Queen Anne Boleyn, had been denounced for being over familiar with her courtiers.

By the summer of 1541, the King had recovered his health again. He made plans to take the Queen on a great progress to the North. He intended to remind his rebellious subjects of their duty to the Crown. But before he left, he took the precaution of executing the notable prisoners who were kept in the Tower of London. These included the elderly Lady Margaret Pole, Sir John Neville and Lord Dacre. No-one at court dared to show any sign of sadness at their deaths. The King regarded them as traitors.

"Poor lady," the Queen whispered to Lady Rochford. "I asked the King to spare her life but he said that she was the most treacherous woman in the kingdom."

"Once someone has been condemned to the Tower, your Grace, they never get out of it alive," she replied.

I turned away and crossed over to the latticed window. Below in the tiltyard, I saw the King's men saddling horses for the northern progress. Pennants flapped in the breeze—bright, careless things, oblivious to the blood recently spilled.

The royal court set out from Greenwich at the end of June. The entourage comprised one thousand courtiers and a guard of five thousand horsemen and the line of carts stretched along the road for over a mile. Two hundred tents were packed in the baggage together with the royal wardrobes and the richest pieces of tapestry and plate. The weather was cold and rainy and the roads were flooded which made the journey particularly arduous. At the end of July, Queen Catherine caught a chill and the progress had to halt for several days at Grafton Regis until she recovered.

On 9th August the royal party arrived at the city of Lincoln. A pavilion had been erected to receive the King and Queen. There they changed their apparel from green and crimson velvet to cloth of gold and silver. Then they processed into the city where the Mayor and his officers knelt down and cried out, "Jesus save your Grace!" The King pardoned the citizens for their part in the rebellion. Then the King and Queen went to hear mass in the Cathedral. Afterwards, they retired to the Bishop's Palace for the night. Queen Catherine sat before the fire in her privy chamber warming her hands.

"How cold it is here in the north!" she said.

"You must ask his Majesty to take you on a progress in the south next summer, your Grace," said Lady Rochford.

Queen Catherine reached down beside her chair and drew out a parcel wrapped in scarlet silk. Its weight made the fabric sag as she held it out.

"I pray you take this gift to Master Culpeper, Lady Rochford," she said.

Lady Rochford took it in her hands. "What makes it so heavy?" she asked. "Is there a piece of armour inside?"

The Queen smiled, not her courtly smile, but more secretive. "No, it is a gold chain and a black velvet cap set with gold brooches," she said.

"He will feel like a nobleman when he wears such finery," she replied.

"Well, he is a gentleman and has done me good service," she said. "He deserves to have some reward."

I am sure that he will be very grateful to your Grace, she replied with a smirk.

I stepped forward, clearing my throat softly. "Your Grace," I said, "if you are chilled, perhaps I might fetch your fur mantle from the wardrobe."

She turned toward me, the firelight catching her face in gold and shadow. For a moment, her eyes met mine, not with the playful expression she wore in public, but something more guarded.

"Thank you, Lady Hertford," she said. "Bring me the grey sable."

As I left the chamber, I cast one more glance behind me. Lady Rochford still held the parcel, her fingers resting lightly on the silk as though she measured its worth in secrets rather than coin.

At Hatfield in Yorkshire the King went out hunting deer in the park with his nobles and gentlemen. They were accompanied by a great pack of greyhounds and their keepers. Queen Catherine did not join them but remained in her chamber. As the hunting party set out, she stood at her chamber window and watched them depart. She was dressed in a gown of scarlet satin with a border of crimson velvet. Her sleeves of white silk were embroidered with golden hearts. Around her neck she wore a string of crystal beads with spacers of enamelled gold. Her breath clouded faintly on the leaded glass. Below, the King's retinue galloped forward with a swagger that only the hunt affords—plumed caps bouncing, greyhounds straining against their leashes and horns calling out in jubilant fanfare.

Master Culpeper rode past, the gold chain glinting at his neck like the morning sun on a field of buttercups. His velvet cap sat bold and rakish on his head, and he saluted the Queen as he rode by. Catherine's lips parted slightly. She gazed down upon at him with a look of love. "Does he not look fine?" she murmured.

I made no answer. Lady Rochford gave a slight smirk, but did not reply either. We knew the tone in her voice too well.

The King returned that evening in triumph. The hunters had slain two hundred stags and does. That evening there was a banquet in the Great Hall with roast venison and pasties aplenty. I saw the sweat glisten on Henry's brow as he laughed, boisterous and red-faced, beside the Queen. She smiled dutifully, adorned in a gown of crimson cloth of silver stiff with gold thread and pearls. But her smile faded when he produced the jewel. It was a brooch—heavy and grotesque in its splendour. A miniature ark, decked in diamonds and rubies.

"How good you are to me, Sir!" she said, her voice tight with sweetness.

"Do you know what it signifies, sweetheart?" he asked.

"It is the ark of the prophet Noah, Sir," she replied. "A sign of God's salvation and forgiveness."

"Aye," he declared. "You shall be the barque of England and replenish the House of Tudor with your progeny just as Noah replenished the earth after the flood."

I watched as he fastened it to her bodice, pressing a kiss just above it. His mouth curved into a grin. Queen Catherine turned pale and fingered it nervously.

"It is a wonderful ornament," she said with a tentative smile. "It shall have pride of place in my jewel casket." But I saw that her eyes were filled with unease and her mouth struggled to hold its curve. For the rest of the evening the King drank heartily and made jests with his companions while the brooch glittered upon her breast like a beacon.

On 23rd August the royal party arrived at the great fortress of Pontefract Castle. Five years ago, its guardian, Lord Darcy, had surrendered it to the leaders of the Pilgrimage of Grace. He had been executed as a traitor. An oppressive atmosphere of gloom still pervaded the stronghold. The musicians did their best to lighten the mood by performing ballads in the gallery. But King Henry ate his supper in a glowering silence. There was no dancing that evening and the King retired to bed early.

Queen Catherine likewise returned to her privy chamber. She sat in her chair of estate before the hearth, her shoulders drawn close in her ermine-lined mantle. Her gaze was fixed not on the fire, but on a parchment she held in her hands. When I approached her with a steaming cup of mulled wine, she quickly folded it up and tucked it into the sleeve of her bodice with practiced discretion.

"Let everyone withdraw, she said. "I wish to be alone in my chamber to pray this evening."

I hesitated, noting her pallor. "But what about your chamberers, your Grace? They ought to prepare your bedchamber and heat the bed with a warming pan."

"I have no need of them," she insisted, her voice cool with finality.

"Yes, your Grace," I replied.

"Lady Rochford, you may remain," she said.

It seemed that Lady Rochford had become the Queen's favourite confidante. She preferred her company above any of the younger ladies, even those of her own family. Later that evening, I passed by her privy chamber on the way to my own chamber. I paused before the tapestry of St. Margaret beside the entrance. I heard the sound of whispers and suppressed laughter behind the closed door. The sort that belonged more to jesters than to prayers. I wondered if Lady Rochford was entertaining the Queen with more of her scurrilous stories. I moved on before anyone saw me, but I could not shake my sense of unease.

On 16th September 1541 the progress finally arrived at York. A fanfare of trumpets sounded and the royal banners flew overhead in a riot of crimson and gold as we passed beneath the ancient city gate. The crowd surged forward, pressed tight by excitement and fear. The King and Queen rode side by side, shining like icons in a pageant, though Henry's eyes were sharp with judgment. The cavalcade halted and the mayor and his aldermen begged the king's forgiveness upon their knees. Sir Robert Bowes stood before the King and made a speech on their behalf:

"We your humble subjects, the inhabitants of this your Grace's county of York, confess that we have most grievously, heinously and wantonly offended your Majesty in the unnatural, most odious and detestable offences of outrageous disobedience and traitorous rebellion. We thank your Majesty for granting us your gracious pardon for so great an offence and we declare that we will henceforth pray for the preservation of your Majesty, Queen Catharine, and Prince Edward."

The King rose and surveyed the company kneeling abjectly before him. He was gratified to see their humble submission.

"I harbour no indignation in my heart against you," he said. "I freely forgive your offences and assure the citizens of York of my loving affection as their sovereign."

The mayor of York rose to his feet and presented the King and the Queen with gold cups filled to the brim with gold coins. King Henry accepted his cup with a nod, but did not smile. Instead, he turned it slightly in his hand, inspecting the workmanship, the weight of gold against his palm. He raised the cup briefly, like a conqueror acknowledging tribute, and then passed it to a servant with barely a glance. His eyes surveyed the crowd, his face a mask of stern magnanimity. When he finally spoke, his voice rang out like a bell of judgment:

"Your token has pleased me," he declared. "York shall have its peace, and I shall have its loyalty."

A ripple of relief moved through the gathered citizens and they sent up a great cheer: *"God save the King! Long live the King!"*

Suddenly I noticed Master Culpeper standing close to the Queen's party. He had drifted away from the King's circle as quietly as smoke from a candle. He gazed at the Queen with a gleam in his eyes. His cap, ornamented with gold spangles, sat proudly atop his curls. His presence drew disapproving looks from the ladies.

"That young man hovers around the Queen like a bee around honeysuckle," said Lady Margaret Howard indignantly. "Someone should send him about his business!"

He bowed to Queen Catherine, and she acknowledged him with a fleeting look. *Lady Margaret is right*, I thought to myself. *He is much too bold.*

The royal party stayed the night at the King's Manor House. It had once been the abbot's lodgings of St Mary's Abbey. The great reception at York was the climax of the progress. Afterwards, the royal party wound its way southward across a patchwork of meadows and golden stubble. The weather had improved with the onset of autumn and the farmers were bringing the last of the harvest in from the fields. The hedgerows brimmed with late flowering blooms and slow-turning berries, and carts laden with hay trundled along nearby lanes.

The Queen's litter moved at a stately pace and its silk curtains rippled faintly in the breeze. She sat composed in a gown of pale damask embroidered with silver threads, her head tilted slightly and her eyes flitting between the passing countryside and the cluster of mounted courtiers.

Then he appeared.

Master Culpeper broke from the pack of gentlemen with deliberate ease, his horse sleek and restless beneath him. He held a nosegay in his hand—a posy of wildflowers gathered from the roadside. He rode up alongside the Queen's litter, lifting the bundle as if offering a relic.

"Your Grace, I have brought you a nosegay," he said. "It will sweeten the air inside your palanquin."

I saw her eyes brighten and her lips curve into a beaming smile. "How thoughtful of you, Master Culpeper," she replied, her voice lilting like a minstrel's tune. "It is indeed a gallant gesture."

She accepted the posy, her fingers brushing against his as she took it. She turned her face toward the petals, inhaling the scent, while Master Culpeper lingered beside her litter. His face shone with triumph as he softly murmured the words of a song:

"Ah Robin, gentle Robin,
Tell me how thy leman doth,
And thou shalt know of mine.
My lady is most kind, I wis,

With eyes that softly glow;
She loveth none so well as me,
And she will not say no."

At the end of October, the King and Queen returned to Hampton Court Palace. King Henry was so content that he ordered a service of thanksgiving to be celebrated for his happy marriage. I sat behind the Queen's pew during the service, watching the light play over her features—serene, almost regal in their composure. It was the last time I saw her truly calm. The next day, Archbishop Cranmer reported that accusations had been made concerning the chastity of the Queen. The King ordered him to conduct an investigation into the matter. Queen Catherine was confined to her apartments until her reputation was cleared. Guards were placed at the doors. That night, Hampton Court was quiet and the Queen's apartments became a gilded cage. Queen Catherine sat not in her usual chair of estate, but upon the window seat, bundled in her fur-lined cloak. Her face was pale and her hands clutched at her pet spaniel in her lap. Her ladies stood around in fearful silence. There was no more music or dancing.

It turned out that Queen Catherine Howard had grown up in a lax household. Her step-grandmother, the dowager duchess of Norfolk, was too old to supervise her women properly. They had contrived to lay their hands on the key to the maid's dormitory. And they invited their sweethearts to visit them at night and make good cheer. I had chafed under the moral restraint of my pious mother, but there were far worse environments for a girl. Queen Catherine Howard had a damaged reputation and it would undoubtedly cost her both her marriage and the crown. There were no convents any more, but she would end up living out her days in solitude and disgrace in some remote house like Edward's first wife, Catherine Fillol, had done.

I expected that the annulment of their marriage would be announced. But worse was to come. The investigation of the Queen's life discovered not only an immoral youth, but adultery during her marriage to the King. It was decided that all her ladies would be rigorously questioned about what they had seen and heard during the summer progress. Fear washed over me. Things were different from the investigation of Queen Anne Boleyn. I had never been questioned then. I had witnessed signs of partiality between Queen Catherine and Thomas Culpeper, but no actual misconduct. I decided that it was better to remain silent than risk being accused of collusion. If they were looking for accomplices, then I would not take the blame. The Queen was responsible for her own folly!

The King's Secretary, Thomas Wriothesley, conducted the interview with me. His pale blue eyes surveyed me confidently. I had no doubt that he intended to implicate me in the Queen's disgrace. But I kept my head. The years of teaching on modesty, humility and silence that I had imbibed bore fruit. My best defence was to answer in the manner of a lowly woman. One who would not presume to parade her knowledge before men.

"You claim to be a godly woman, Lady Hertford," he said. "Were you a righteous servant to the King and Queen?"

"I am only an ignorant woman, Master Wriothesley," I replied. "But I do my best to keep the oath of loyalty that I swore to their Majesties."

"It is said that you take much pleasure in the reading of books," he said. "Surely you know the words and teachings of the holy scriptures?"

"I was brought up to respect and obey God's Word," I replied. "I always wear my prayer book at my girdle."

"That might be just for show," he sneered. "Tell me what you have learned from your virtuous reading."

"Sarah was obedient to her husband and called him lord," I answered.

He was perplexed for a moment. My words reminded him that I had a powerful husband who was highly regarded by the King.

"Indeed, that is a godly text," he agreed. "Would that Mistress Howard had taken it to heart."

"You mean her Grace the Queen," I corrected him.

"She has forfeited that honourable title," he snapped. "What conversations did you have with the former Queen?"

"I showed her how to embroider linen collars and cuffs in blackwork and she thanked me," I said.

He waved his hand in irritation. "I mean what treasonous conversations did you have?" he said. "Think carefully and give me an honest answer. Your words will be checked against the testimonies of the rest of her household. Now is the time to confess your errors of judgement and seek mercy from the King."

He scrutinised me with his cold eyes and tapped his quill pen insistently on the table. Was I really under suspicion?

It could not be possible! I was the aunt of Prince Edward and part of the royal circle. My loyalty was beyond reproach. Anger surged up within me. I would not be played for a fool.

"I have never participated in any treasonous conversations with the former Queen," I said firmly. "Our interactions were always practical in nature. I carried out the duties of a lady in waiting and assisted her with her dress. I kept her company in her privy chamber and played card games with her whenever she wished."

"Then what treasonous conversations did you overhear," he demanded.

"I never overheard any treasonous words," I replied steadily. "If I had, then I would have reported them at once."

"Reported them to whom?" he asked

"To my husband who is my lawful master and head," I said. "And I would have begged him to lay the matter before the King."

"So, you said and heard no treason," he remarked. "Then what treasonous behaviour did you witness?"

"None, Master Wriothesley," I replied. "Her unlawful conduct took place in great secrecy. I was not privy to any of it."

"So, say all her ladies," he sneered. "And yet she did not act alone. She had accomplices among the members of her household. I want you to name them for me. Then perhaps I will believe in your innocence."

He looked at me with a gleam in his eyes and I knew that death had entered the chamber. I could not afford to falter for an instant.

"I was not admitted to the former Queen's secrets," I insisted. "If I had suspected anyone of leading her astray then I would have reported it immediately."

"To your husband?" he taunted me.

I finally lost patience with his game of cat and mouse. I was no simple maid but Lady Hertford. I would never forgive him for his attempts to implicate me. I vowed that one day I would settle the score between us.

"Who better than Lord Hertford?" I retorted. "He is the King's most trusted and loyal councillor!"

"It is my duty to ask these questions," he replied defensively.

"And I have given you honest answers, Master Wriothesley," I said. "You have sifted me very narrowly and now you should be content. I have served all five of his Majesty's wives with honour."

"Indeed, Lady Hertford, that is known to the whole court," he conceded. "You may go."

I stood up and took my leave without another word. I made my way blindly to my apartments and shut myself in my bedchamber. I did not want anyone to see that I was trembling with fear and revulsion. I thanked my good fortune that I was not one of the young Queen's confidantes. I wondered how many mice Master Wriothesley would succeed in capturing in his toils.

I did not have to wonder for long. I was in the Queen's gallery, tidying a stack of prayer books that no hand would touch again, when Lady Margaret Howard swept in with her mouth tight and her eyes wide.

"Lady Rochford has been arrested," she hissed. "They say she kept watch at night while the Queen met with Culpeper."

I froze with a book in my hands. The gold thread embroidery on its cover shimmered faintly in the firelight. So, she was guilty after all! My thoughts turned to the parcel, the nosegay, the whispered laughter behind the door at Pontefract. The gifts had been an exchange of love-tokens. How careless they had been to flaunt their romance in public. And how foolish of Lady Rochford to abet them!

"She is a widow," I murmured, setting the book down. "Her place at court was all that she had."

Lady Margaret snorted. "She should have prized it more dearly."

I walked from the gallery without another word and made my way toward my chamber. The air was heavy like the hush before a sermon. When I passed the guards outside Lady Rochford's rooms, one turned his head but said nothing. Their silence was enough. She was now a prisoner of the state.

Inside my chamber, I lit a taper and sat by the hearth. The flames threw long shadows against the wall, and I stared into them, remembering her sly smile and knowing eyes. I wondered why she had done it? Was it to safeguard her place in the young Queen's circle? Or had Catherine's youth and beauty intoxicated her into folly? I would never know.

But I did know this: the Queen would not survive Lady Rochford's tongue. The court would feast on the scandal until only the bones remained.

Catherine Howard was disgraced and forfeited her title as Queen of England. Her household was discharged and she was ordered to move to Syon Abbey. Her royal wardrobe and casket of jewels were confiscated. Only a few plain gowns without ornaments remained in her possession. I was one of the ladies chosen to attend her in her banishment. It was a mark of the King's confidence in me. A barge conveyed us up the Thames from Hampton Court to her place of exile. We departed with neither trumpets nor farewells, only the measured strokes of the oarsmen and the creak of timber against water. The grey barge rocked gently upon the river's swell, its canopy threaded with rain-dark silk, as if mourning in quiet ceremony. The Thames glinted dully beneath a sullen sky, and the trees along the bank bowed as though in witness

Lady Catherine sat opposite me, swathed not in velvet or gold-threaded brocade, but in a plain gown of brown wool that ill-suited her youth. Her hair, once braided in brilliance, now hung in loose waves beneath a modest hood. The tears ran down her cheeks in silence, leaving pale tracks upon her face. I pressed a handkerchief into her fingers, and she clutched it with trembling gratitude but made no effort to blot out her sorrow. The barge passed Isleworth, where the reeds leaned low and the wind carried whispers. I felt a chill, not from the air but from the moment—the severing of identity, the ending of illusion. I wondered, did she remember York? The laughter? The posies? Did she regret Culpeper now, or mourn only her lost crown?

As the barge curved around the bend and Syon's turrets came into view, I leaned closer to the window, studying the structure. Strong walls, high gates and a courtyard lined with linden trees. Syon Abbey had once been a famous convent, but now it was a royal house. I found myself examining the grounds with a surveyor's eye. It occurred to me that it would make any nobleman a splendid country residence. There was ample space for gardens and a fine view of the river. I resolved to mention it to Edward. He was just as worthy of it as anyone at court. Lady Catherine shuddered at the sight of her prison. I reached for her hand once more, and though she did not meet my gaze, she did not pull away. We disembarked in near silence. As she stepped onto the worn stones of Syon, I thought how strange it was to see royalty stripped so swiftly of its radiance. Only weeks ago, she had processed through cities in cloth-of-gold, with trumpets announcing her every step. Now, no fanfare greeted us—only the damp breath of autumn and the grim façade of Syon.

The gates creaked open without ceremony. The guards flanked her impassively. I followed behind, my steps measured, my face composed. But inwardly, I felt each stone beneath my feet like a judgment. Lady Catherine paused at the threshold, her eyes flitting over the ivy-clad walls, the high windows dark and silent. She shivered again, though not from cold. Inside, the steward gestured toward her appointed chamber which was plain and sparsely furnished. A bed, a prayer stool, and a chest. No tapestries. No lute. No cupboard of plate. I helped her remove her cloak. It was damp at the hem, and smelled faintly of river mist. She sank into the chair by the hearth, though the fire had not yet been lit. Her hands rested limply in her lap, the fingers that had once been adorned with fine jewelled rings were now bare. She did not speak. I remained silent too. There was nothing left to say. No reassurance that did not ring hollow. *"This is not the Tower,"* I told myself, over and over. *"There is still hope."*

Lady Catherine was a girl of only nineteen and had been greatly beloved of the King. Surely, he would relent from taking vengeance against her. I whispered a prayer for her soul and for whatever came next. I remembered the brooch in the shape of Noah's Ark, the kiss he pressed above it, the bold promise that she would replenish the House of Tudor. How could that love curdle so swiftly? But King Henry's love, I had come to learn, was a fire that did not mourn what it destroyed. The storm of disappointment, once roused, swept away tenderness as surely as the wind stripped autumn's final leaves. Still, I watched Catherine in her exile—grieving, altered, never fully grasping the depth of her peril—and I clung to the hope that the King's heart might soften. Yet the days passed and no pardon came. What struck me most was the transformation of her spirit. She no longer reached for embroidered gloves or perfume vials. She no longer fussed over her coiffure or asked for music. Her hands, once quick with cards and ribbons, now lay idle on her lap. She sat upon the narrow window seat, gazing not outward, but downward, as if the Thames might carry her regrets away in its current. Sometimes she would ask me, "Do you suppose his Majesty still thinks of me?" I never knew how to answer her.

Archbishop Cranmer came to Syon to hear her confession. She was too shaken and distressed to deny the accusations against her. But he looked more sorrowful than satisfied by her admissions.

"Good ladies, see to your mistress," he said. "She makes such lamentation that it would pity any man's heart to look upon her."

"Will his Majesty have pity on her, your Grace?" I asked.

He shook his head. "It is a matter for the council to decide," he said.

Lady Catherine was distraught. "Alas, that I am still alive!" she wept. "The fear of death does not grieve me so much as the remembrance of the King's goodness. I cannot restrain my tears when I recall what a gracious and loving prince I had. I pray that he will have mercy on me and pardon my faults. If only I could see him again, I am sure that he would forgive me!"

But there was no forgiveness for her. She was not brought to trial. It was considered too degrading to the King's honour. Instead, the guilty parties were proceeded against by acts of attainer. They were all sentenced to death for the crimes of adultery and treason. Catherine Howard was condemned for having led an abominable, voluptuous and vicious life. The King did not grant his fifth wife the mercy of the sword, but ordered her to be executed with the axe on Tower Green. She protested on the scaffold, *"I never intended to dishonour the King, and it is now no time to dissemble, because I am to die."* Lady Rochford followed her to the block. It was rumoured that she had lost her reason in prison but the King was so unrelenting towards her that he insisted that she should be put to death all the same.

I considered that the dowager duchess of Norfolk was greatly to blame for the scandal. She had failed to exercise the proper vigilance over her household. Consequently, she had ruined the reputation of her noble house. I vowed that no-one would ever tarnish the virtuous name of my daughters. Their honour was my greatest care. I wrote an urgent letter to the steward of Wulf Hall:

"Sir John Thynne, I greet you well,

It is my instruction that you undertake a serious moral reform of the household. Everyone shall attend prayers in the morning and in the evening. There shall be no lewd talk or swearing under my roof. If any servants behave in a lascivious manner, they must be dismissed at once. Furthermore, if anyone is found loitering near the maiden's chamber, he is to be discharged. My daughters must never be left alone in the company of male servants or tutors. They are to be strictly chaperoned by day and by night. You must change the locks on the door of the maiden's chamber and give the only copy of the key to the lady governess. She is to keep it on her person at all times. Write to tell me when this has been done. I hold you responsible for upholding the good character of the house.

Anne Hertford."

I did not have to explain my reasons. The sad story of the Queen's downfall was known to all the world. Parliament passed a law making it high treason for any unchaste woman to marry the King. Anyone who supressed this information would be considered equally guilty. The leading members of the Howard family were sent to the Tower for concealing the evil demeanour of the Queen. King Francis wrote a letter of condolence to the King reminding him that the lightness of women could not touch the honour of kings. He crumpled it in his fist and threw it on the floor. There was no court mourning after the execution of Catherine Howard any more than there had been for the death of Anne Boleyn. But the atmosphere at court was as dark and painful as it had been all those years before. No-one at court dared to speak unguardedly, recite a verse or make a jest. In the absence of the ladies, the King's household was as quiet as a monastery. This time there was no substitute wife waiting in the wings. The King was so embittered by his misfortunes that everyone doubted that he would take another wife.

However, the King's daughter, Lady Mary, still maintained a houschold of ladies to attend her. She invited me to enter her service and I was very glad of the opportunity for it meant a return to stability, to a household governed by dignity and devotion. Lady Mary, though a figure touched by sorrow and political strife, possessed a formidable grace. Her household was quieter than the Queen's court had been for there were no reckless flirtations nor treacherous intrigues. In Mary's chambers, the talk was of Latin treatises, of religious observance and of cautious hope for the realm's future. She favoured quiet company, and I gave it willingly.

At New Year 1543 Lady Mary presided over the festivities at court. The Great Hall at Greenwich glittered with candlelight and tapestry. She sat upon the dais beside the King, adorned in crimson damask trimmed with gold and a necklace of rubies and diamonds at her throat—a regal figure, her presence commanding without flourish. I stood behind her chair, my hands folded, watching the festivities. The musicians struck up a brisk allemande, and laughter swirled like perfume through the crowd. Nobles danced. Pages scurried. The scent of rosemary and roasted fowl mingled with the waft of beeswax and wine.

That was when Lady Latimer entered. She was an attractive woman with red-gold hair and brown eyes. She moved with gentle composure, her gown a deep violet that suited mourning yet glowed in the candlelight like polished amethysts. There was something fragile in her bearing—the softened grace of a woman long bowed by duty and illness at home. I saw Lady Mary's eyes brighten at her approach, and she rose slightly to greet her with clasped hands and a warm smile.

"Lady Latimer, you are most welcome to court," she said. "I had not expected to see you, given Lord Latimer's condition."

Lady Latimer gave a graceful curtsey. "Your Grace, I could not let the New Year pass without paying my respects. His suffering is grave, but I felt it right to be here, if only briefly."

But before Lady Latimer could retreat into the quiet margins of the crowd, the King turned. He had been deep in conversation with Lord Norfolk when his gaze shifted.

"Lady Latimer?" he boomed, voice cutting through the music like a herald's horn.

She curtsied, startled, murmuring the proper addresses.

"By God's grace, I had not expected to see you at court," he said. "You honour us with your presence."

"My lord husband's health has kept us away," she replied, steady but subdued. "I came to pay my respects to her Grace, the Lady Mary."

Henry's expression softened—an uncommon thing, these days. "He is fortunate to have such dutiful care," he said. "But you belong at court, madam. Not hidden away with sorrow and privation."

Lady Latimer's cheeks flushed faintly. "I am always grateful to serve when I am called."

"Well then, let it be more often," the King declared, casting a glance toward Lady Mary. "Her Grace has need of loyal women. And so do I."

She bowed low, and murmured, "Your Majesty is most gracious."

Rumours at court travelled faster than fire through straw, and when whispers reached me that Lady Latimer had caught the King's attention, I felt a curious mix of relief and guarded wonder. Unlike the reckless charm of Catherine Howard, or the political shadow of Anne Boleyn, Lady Latimer was steady. A woman of quiet dignity and tested patience. And in the wake of so many calamities—broken marriages, beheadings, intrigues that had poisoned every corridor—I saw in her a kind of anchor the court had long lacked. Still, I kept my thoughts close.

Within weeks, invitations followed. Subtle ones at first—banquets, prayers, private viewings of new tapestries. Lady Mary saw to it that Lady Latimer was regularly in attendance. They shared not only proximity, but lineage and faith.

Lady Maud Parr, Lady Latimer's mother, had once served Queen Catherine of Aragon, and Mary had always held that loyalty close. Lady Latimer comported herself with tempered elegance. Her conversation was measured, her attire modest, yet quietly distinguished. And though she spoke little of Lord Latimer's condition, it was understood that his decline was nearing its end and that soon she would be a widow.

The King began to send her presents as tokens of his favour – pleats for skirts, sleeves and fashionable gowns made in the Italian style. She bowed her head and murmured, "His Majesty honours me more than I deserve."

On 2nd March 1543 Lord Latimer died and his funeral was held at St Paul's Cathedral. After his death, Lady Latimer withdrew briefly from court to mourn. She was now a wealthy widow who owned the manors of Nunmonkton and Hamerton. She was young enough to marry again if she chose. Or else she could live an independent life as a woman of substance. One afternoon in Lady Mary's privy chamber, I heard two ladies murmuring together behind a standing screen embroidered with Tudor roses and griffins.

"The King has asked after her again. Three times this fortnight."

"She's still in mourning. Do you think she'll refuse him?"

I pretended not to hear, but my needle stilled in its work. Later that day, I confided the news to Edward. "It is said that the King will take Lady Latimer as his next wife," I said.

"Indeed," he replied. "My brother Thomas will be desolate. He thinks that Latimer's widow is going to marry him and he will become a wealthy man."

"He had better withdraw his suit," I replied. "Or else he will incur the King's displeasure."

But the King removed his rival by appointing him as his ambassador to the Netherlands. Thomas could hardly refuse such an honour. Shortly afterwards, the King summoned a meeting of the privy council. When it concluded, Edward came to find me in a state of suppressed excitement.

"The reports were true," he said. "The King does intend to marry Lady Latimer."

"What did he say?" I asked.

"He told the councillors: "Gentlemen, I desire company, but I have had more than enough of taking young wives and I am now resolved to marry a widow by the name of Lady Latimer." At once, I rose to my feet and said that his Majesty had chosen well and I knew of no more honourable widow in the realm. Then all the other councillors applauded. It was well spoken, was it not?"

"What if she refuses him?" I asked. "He is no great prospect as a husband. After his behaviour to Anne of Cleves, no foreign bride would have him. And after his treatment of Catherine Howard, no honourable virgin in the realm would dare to take the risk."

"He is still the King," he replied. "How can she possibly refuse his wishes?"

Their wedding took place in the Queen's Closet at Hampton Court on 12th July 1543. Bishop Stephen Gardiner, the Bishop of Winchester, presided at the ceremony. The chamber was adorned with tapestries of David and Solomon at the height of their glory. King Henry VIII liked to compare himself with these famous kings of Israel who were renowned for their valour and riches. But he was not a golden prince any more. His virtues had been overtaken by the vices of tyranny, suspicion and lasciviousness. Queen Catherine Parr wore a robe of cloth of gold with a train that was two yards long. The sleeves were lined with crimson satin and trimmed with crimson velvet. She had a jewelled head-dress and wore a gold cross around her neck.

The King was proud of his refined and elegant wife. She inherited the jewels and gowns of her predecessor. But because she had more experience of the world, she cut a more impressive figure as his queen consort. She persuaded the King to allow all three of his children to attend the court so that he could enjoy a family life. She established close relationships with them and selected the best tutors for Prince Edward and Lady Elizabeth. She even persuaded him to reinstate his daughters in the line of succession. Her serene common sense was just what was needed to set the King and the court at ease again. The Queen appointed her sister, Lady Herbert, as her chief lady-in-waiting. She gave her cousin Lady Tyrwhit and her stepdaughter Lady Lane positions in her privy chamber. I was also offered a place as a lady in waiting in her household.

"You will have more in common with this Queen," said Edward. "She is no foolish butterfly, but a mature woman of culture and learning."

"She has surrounded herself with her own friends and relatives," I said. "I am not part of her inner circle."

"Then make yourself part of her circle," he said. "You must do whatever it takes to win her confidence."

I did my best to gratify my husband's wishes. I discovered that Queen Catherine was interested in the new learning and in church reform. Her circle of ladies included many who shared her opinions. She spent her mornings in the reading and study of the Holy Scriptures, and in the afternoons, she invited one of her chaplains to come to her privy chamber to preach a sermon and discuss the abuses in the church. One of her favourite preachers was Hugh Latimer. He was plainly clad for a man of rising influence, yet every word he spoke carried the weight of thunder. The light fell in latticed bars across the floor, catching the edge of the velvet cushions and vellum-bound Bibles. Around him, the Queen's circle gathered, each lady filled with a thirst for reform. I sat at the side of the group with my hands folded neatly over my prayer book.

"Be not deceived," he said, his eyes fixed upon the Queen. "Ceremony without substance is but gilded straw. Christ's church is no market for indulgence nor theatre for superstition—it is the temple of truth."

A murmur of agreement rustled through the chamber. Queen Catherine nodded, her fingers brushing the edge of a Psalter as if in silent benediction.

Master Latimer paced slowly, the sunlight glancing off his brown hair. "The soul," he declared, "must be fed with the Word, not drowned in Latin that no man may comprehend. Let the Scriptures be as bread to every table, not jewels for the rich alone."

My breath caught. It was bold—dangerous even—but we hung on his words. Then came the moment I remember most.

Master Latimer paused. He looked toward the Queen and then, towards us. "Let no woman shrink from wisdom," he said softly. "God has placed His word in hearts, not ranks. The Spirit moves where it will, whether beneath crown, veil, or simple cap. And when truth calls, let no soul—man or woman—stay silent."

"Your words have moved me deeply, Master Latimer," said the Queen. "I shall do my best to promote the true knowledge of the gospels in the realm."

Latimer lowered his voice. "Your Grace, should consider the piety and courage of Queen Esther who became the salvation of her people," he said. "Who knows if you have gained your high dignity for such a time as this?"

"It is my dearest wish to enlighten the people of England," she replied. "I have decided to sponsor an English translation of *The Paraphrases of the Gospel* by Erasmus in the hope that one day there will be a copy of this excellent work in every church in the land."

"That is a most godly undertaking, your Grace," he said.

I found myself confused by these new ideas. I knew that I needed guidance from someone. But it was useless to approach one of the Queen's relatives. They would not welcome the overtures of an outsider. So, I started to visit the apartments of Lady Catherine Brandon, the duchess of Suffolk. She was a fervent evangelical who encouraged her servants to read the Bible in English and a close friend of the Queen. The duchess delighted in spreading the word of God and she listened sympathetically to my questions.

"My dear Lady Hertford, the one thing that is needed is an open mind," she said. "I rejoice to hear of your sincere desire to understand the Christian faith. You will find it a revelation to read the Bible for yourself. You should begin with the gospels which explain how Christ is the path to our salvation. They will illuminate your soul and give you the peace that passes all understanding."

She gave me the gift of an English Bible. I took it home and read it secretly at night. I learned many things that I had never known before and I began to understand the importance of religious reform. Soon I was able to participate in the Queen's afternoon discussions.

"Why does Psalm 119 say that the Word of God is like honey to our lips and a lamp to our feet?" Queen Catherine asked, her eyes shining with enthusiasm.

"Because it feeds us and guides us," replied Lady Suffolk. "There is nothing sweeter than the true knowledge of the gospels."

"Just so," agreed Queen Catherine. "The scriptures are our greatest source of strength and wisdom. How can we share this knowledge with our fellow citizens?"

"We must encourage them to listen to learned preachers and read the Bible for themselves," I said. "Then they will know the truth and this nation will become a godly people."

She rewarded me with a warm smile of approval. "I am so glad to know that you are one of us, Lady Hertford," she said. "We must put an end to the superstitions and idolatry of Rome. But what about your husband? Is he equally in favour of religious reform?"

"Lord Hertford is a cautious man, your Grace," I said. "He believes that whatever the King says is right. But he is also a man of intellect and high principles. I believe that he could be persuaded by the right person."

"I will ask Archbishop Cranmer to invite him to dinner," she said. "He is a persuasive man. He has been doing his best to convince the King that the Church of England should have an English liturgy instead of the Latin mass which no-one can comprehend. If there were more privy councillors who shared his opinions, it would be better for the realm."

It was not long before Hertford became a convinced evangelical. It meant that I could read my English Bible openly in our apartments and share my opinions with him. He became one of the reformers who wore sober colours as a sign of their temperance.

"All the well-educated people at court are reading the gospels," he said. "It is only the members of the old nobility like Norfolk who disapprove. And I don't think he has ever read a book in his life. He thinks that reading and writing is only for lowborn clerks."

"The Catholic faith is riddled with errors," I said. "Why should we worship in Latin which only the priests can understand? The Church is ripe for reform."

"His Majesty was right to dissolve the monasteries," he agreed. "The monks were only loyal to the Bishop of Rome. He is the enemy of our king. And the Church has stolen the wealth of the kingdom for centuries and hoarded it for the benefit of the clergy. The King was quite justified in taking it back. He can make better use of it. And so can his loyal noblemen."

The court became divided between the Catholic faction who were led by Bishop Gardiner and the duke of Norfolk and the reformers who supported Queen Catherine and Archbishop Cranmer. Both sides vied with each other to gain the ear of the King. In May 1543 the conservatives scored a victory when Parliament passed the *Act for the Advancement of True Religion*. It restricted the reading of the English Bible to the ranks of the nobility and the gentry. The Great Bibles were removed from the parish churches to prevent the common people from reading the scriptures and discussing their meaning.

Lady Suffolk had such disdain for Catholics that she named her pet spaniel Gardiner. I marvelled at her temerity. Bishop Gardiner was known to be a ruthless man with no sense of humour. But the young duchess was fearless.

"I do not need to bow down to any of these pompous prelates," she declared. "My husband is the King's favourite courtier. He would never dare to threaten me. You should not fear him either since you are a countess!"

"He is a detestable man," I said boldly. "He is more interested in gaining power and wealth than in spreading the faith."

Lady Suffolk smiled. "Come to Suffolk House tomorrow," she said. "There is someone I would like you to meet."

The following day I felt an unspoken fire kindling in my breast as I arrived at Suffolk House. Lady Suffolk met me in her gallery, flanked by a tapestry of Saint Paul and wearing a gown of pale blue silk with sleeves slashed in white satin. Her spaniel, Gardiner, snored beneath a side table.

"You've come," she said with a warm smile. "Good. She's waiting."

She led me to her privy chamber, where the light bled through diamond-paned windows and danced across a writing desk scattered with pamphlets. A young woman rose as we entered.

"Lady Hertford," Lady Suffolk said, "allow me to present Mistress Anne Askew. She is a most fearless servant of the gospel." She poured wine into silver chalices and handed them to us.

Mistress Askew was younger than I expected—slender, with sharp eyes that seemed carved from steel rather than glass. Her attire was simple: a dark wool gown and a linen coif, yet her bearing was unmistakably noble.

"Your Ladyship," she said, curtsying with quiet grace.

"Pray sit," I replied, returning the gesture. "Lady Suffolk has spoken highly of your fortitude."

Mistress Askew took her seat, folding her hands with studied calm. "I cannot claim to be brave," she said. "I am only resolved to speak the plain truth. The simple message of the Bible is salvation by faith alone. This is the message that I seek to share with the world. I read the scriptures aloud in public and explain their meaning to anyone who cares to listen. The gospels teach us that Christ is the sufficient and only mediator between God and man. So, there is no need for any of the false rituals of confession, penance, pilgrimages or the veneration of relics. Such things have no power to save the soul."

I leaned forward. "But Bishop Gardiner sees such talk as an attack upon the church. He could burn you for heresy."

"He may," she answered. "But I will not offer incense to error in order to placate him. Scripture does not lie. I would rather face fire than deny it."

Lady Suffolk raised her chalice. "May your courage inspire us all."

Mistress Askew did inspire me. I set aside time every day for prayer and reading of the scriptures. I increased my charitable donations to the poor and I appointed a tutor to train my children in good literature and the knowledge of God's holy laws. My Protestant convictions brought me into the inner circle of the Queen. She longed to convince the King to accept an English Bible and an English liturgy. But the King was unwilling to unleash such radical new ideas upon his subjects. The Catholic faith upheld the divine right of kings to rule and he would do nothing to undermine that belief.

In December 1543 the Scottish Parliament rejected King Henry's proposal that Prince Edward should marry the infant Mary Queen of Scots. The King was incensed by their refusal:

"If they decline my gracious proposal to the Queen of Scots, then she shall have a rough wooing instead!" he declared. "I shall send an army to invade Scotland and impose my wishes by force!"

In March 1544 Edward was appointed as Lieutenant General in the north. He commanded a force of twelve thousand men. He destroyed the town of Leith and then devastated Edinburgh. I took pride in his great victory, but at the same time I was concerned for his future. I did not want him to remain in Scotland indefinitely with the garrisons. The soldiers were poorly supplied and provisioned and Edward had been provided with nothing more than a tent. I feared that he would die of sickness and privation and leave me a widow. I went to speak to the Queen.

"Your Grace, my husband has done his Majesty great service in Scotland," I said. "I pray that you would ask the King to recall him and appoint some other man in his place."

"Have no fear, Lady Hertford," she replied. "His Majesty intends to summon him back to court very soon. He has decided that John Dudley, Viscount Lisle will replace him."

In June 1544 King Henry decided to invade France. He sent an even greater army of forty thousand men to Calais. Queen Catherine was appointed to act as Regent in his place. In the King's absence, she made an English translation of Bishop Fisher's *"Psalms and Prayers taken out of Holy Scripture."* Edward served as one of the Queen's councillors. One of his first duties was to establish a new household for Prince Edward. He was seven years old and it was time for him to leave the care of women and begin his education.

Queen Catherine selected Richard Cox and John Cheke as his tutors. The sons of eighteen noblemen were chosen to join his household including my eldest son, Lord Beauchamp. It meant that his future as a courtier was assured.

In September 1544 King Henry captured Boulogne and returned in triumph to England. Queen Catherine celebrated his return as a conquering hero. Edward was sent to Calais to negotiate terms with the French ambassadors. In February 1545 the French army besieged Boulogne and attempted to recapture it, but Edward rallied the English troops and put the French to flight. King Henry had such confidence in his military prowess that he sent him to wage war in Scotland again. In September 1545 he razed the towns of Ketso and Jedburgh to the ground. The King was in such a mellow mood that he gave Queen Catherine permission to publish an English book entitled *"Prayers and Meditations."* In June 1546 Edward returned to Calais and signed the Treaty of Camp. Its terms enabled King Henry to retain possession of Boulogne until 1554. The wars were now over and Edward had gained a great reputation at court for his valour and diplomacy.

That same month Mistress Askew was arrested for heresy and taken to the Tower. Queen Catherine and her ladies were greatly distressed to hear the news. Her arrest struck dangerously close to home. The Queen's enemies at court, ever watchful, might use this moment to question her own religious sympathies.

"What can we do to help her?" said Lady Suffolk. "Perhaps the Queen could intercede with the King on her behalf?"

"That's just what they want," I replied. "It will prove that she is a heretic."

"But we can't do nothing," she insisted. "She is a gentlewoman. She does not belong in the Tower."

"I will send some money to her in secret," I said.

"What if they force her to give them names?" she said. "They may come to arrest us next."

"She will tell them nothing," I replied. "And they would not dare to arrest the wives of the King's chief courtiers."

I sent a manservant to the Tower with ten shillings to help her. "Be discreet and mention no names," I cautioned him. But the fool wore his coat of blue livery and his visit to the Tower was reported. I might have been investigated if I was not the wife of an important man. But Edward made sure that I did not suffer any consequences.

"Must you parade your sympathies in public?" he complained. "Bishop Gardiner's spies saw your servant visiting the Tower. There is nothing that can be done for her now. The woman has condemned herself by her own folly."

"I do not care what Gardiner thinks," I retorted. But inwardly I fumed that my servant did not have the sense to wear a cloak.

"He has the ear of the King," said Edward. "We must tread carefully. His Majesty does not care for heretics."

Mistress Askew was interrogated by Thomas Wriothesley and Richard Rich. She refused to implicate the Queen or anyone else even when she was tortured on the rack. Neither would she recant her beliefs. On 16th July 1546, she was burned at Smithfield as a heretic. She had to be carried on a chair because she was unable to walk. When she was asked to recant her beliefs, she replied: *"I came not hither to deny my master."* I sent my servant with a bribe for the executioner. He hung a bag of gunpowder around her neck so that her sufferings would be cut short. It was all that I was able to do for her.

But Bishop Gardiner was not satisfied with the execution of Mistress Askew. He remained determined to topple the Queen. One day, he saw his opportunity to denounce her. Queen Catherine was visiting the King in his privy chamber. She wore a white satin gown studded with pearls and embroidered with Tudor roses in gold thread. In her enthusiasm to share the knowledge of the scriptures, she set aside her caution and urged him to proceed with the reformation of the Church.

"Your Majesty gave your subjects a great gift in the English Bible," she said. "But why should this blessing be restricted to the nobility? Surely all of your people should have the chance to read and understand the Word of God?"

I shifted uneasily. Bishop Gardiner stood near the fireplace, his eyes colder than the stone lions that guarded it. King Henry, red-faced and swollen with gout and suspicion, squinted at her through bloodshot eyes. The silence was filled with tension.

"You do not understand these matters, Kate," he snapped. "The common people cannot be entrusted with such a precious jewel. Their ignorance of doctrine leads them astray. The bishops tell me that there are more heretics now than there have ever been. It is enough for the people to attend their parish churches and receive instruction from the priests."

Behind him, Gardiner inclined his head. "Your Majesty is quite right," he agreed. "The Word of God is irreverently disputed and jangled in every alehouse and tavern in the realm. London is flooded with pestilential ballads, rhymes and songs which subvert the true meaning of the scriptures."

The Queen ought to have taken heed of the King's mood. But her ardour led her to plunge headlong into danger. "But think how much your subjects could learn from the study of the scriptures, your Majesty," she replied. "I pray that you would reconsider the matter and restore the English Bibles to the parish churches. It would be to the glory of God to complete this good and godly work."

I saw a vein pulse in the King's temple. He stared at his wife, a cold light flickering in his gaze. Gardiner's expression was triumphant. His enemy had taken the bait. Soon afterwards Queen Catherine took her leave, but I lingered by the door of the privy chamber. King Henry was short-sighted now and Gardiner's attention was entirely focussed upon his royal master. The King was slumped in his great carved chair, upholstered in tawny velvet, his limbs swollen and his face soured with distrust. "Things have gone too far when women become such clerks," he muttered, bitterness etched across his features. "It is little comfort to me in my old age to be taught by my wife."

Bishop Gardiner bowed low, his robes billowing like a storm cloud around him. "It grieves me that the Queen should so forget herself as to argue with Your Majesty, he said." His lips thinned and his fingers tightened around his rosary. "It is an unseemly thing for any subject to contradict their sovereign. Your Majesty knows it is dangerous to cherish a serpent within your bosom. I suspect there are treasons concealed within this cloak of heresy. I fear that the matter has already grown too great for your Majesty's safety."

The King shifted, his face mottled with temper. "You shall investigate this matter with the full rigour of the law," he growled, striking the arm of his chair. "Even if it touches the Queen."

Bishop Gardiner lowered his head reverently. "I am Your Majesty's most faithful servant," he said.

I stepped back into the shadows, my heart pounding and my breath shallow. Then I turned and fled down the corridor. I knew that the Queen was in great danger and so were all the ladies of her household.

"Your Grace, I overheard Bishop Gardiner talking to the King," I said. "He intends to investigate the royal household. We should take precautions in case they search our chambers. We should send all our books and pamphlets out of the palace and hide them in our houses."

"I have been expecting this ever since the death of Anne Askew," she replied. "My lord bishop has grown ambitious in his hatred. He has turned his eyes towards the court."

Queen Catherine heeded my warning and purged her library. The heretical books and pamphlets were removed and her precious notebooks were burned in the fireplace. She invited no more evangelicals to come to her apartments to preach. I hoped that it would be enough to keep us safe. But Bishop Gardiner was a resolute enemy. He did not intend to stop until he had accomplished the destruction of the Queen. There were plenty of witnesses to her unauthorised Bible studies. The investigation continued in secret and the trap was laid. However, Queen Catherine was more fortunate than her predecessors had been. The King's physician, Dr Wendy, was a secret reformer. He visited the Queen to bring her a warning.

"Your Grace is in great peril," he said, his voice low, urgent, and trembling. "The King says that he will no longer be troubled by your heretical doctrines. He has signed a warrant for your arrest. I have seen it lying on the desk in his privy chamber. You must act at once or it will be too late to save yourself."

Queen Catherine's face turned pale, the colour draining like wine from an overturned goblet. She clutched the edge of the carved chair beside her, fingers whitening against the walnut. "Lord have mercy upon me," she whispered. "What shall I do?"

"If you will accept my counsel, you will speak to his Majesty as soon as possible, your Grace," he said. "You must frame and conform yourself to the King's mind. If you show your humble submission to him, I have no doubt that he will be gracious and forgiving. It is your only hope!"

"But I cannot go to see the King for no reason," she faltered.

"I will tell his Majesty that you are in great distress of mind and only his presence will comfort you, your Grace," he replied. "God bless your Majesty." He bowed, deeply, with urgency and reverence, before sweeping from the room like a man fleeing a plague house.

"This is the work of that scoundrel Gardiner!" I said. "He has poisoned the King's mind against you!"

"It was foolish of me to speak my mind so openly," she said. "I fear that I have angered him past recall."

"Dr Wendy is right, your Grace," I said. "You should take to your bed. Let his Majesty find you suffering, not defiant. It will persuade him to take pity on you."

"Very well, Lady Hertford," she said. "Bring me my nightgown and cap."

I hurried to the wardrobe press, unlatched the heavy oak doors, and drew out her finest lawn nightgown, embroidered at the hem with lilies of the valley, and her cap of delicate lace.

She changed her clothes and then lay in her bed weeping. "God grant that the King still remembers how to forgive," she murmured.

I had scarcely folded the edge of the bedcover when the cry rang out beyond the chamber doors: *"Make way for his Majesty the King!"* The words echoed like a summons, hollow and terrifying. I saw Queen Catherine flinch beneath the linen sheet. Her face was pale, eyes glassy with dread.

Moments later, the door swung wide, and the King entered. He clutched a gold-topped walking-stick in his hand, the weight of his body shifting heavily to the right. His breathing came laboured, punctuated by wheezes that betrayed his age and ailments. Everyone made their obeisance before him. The King's eye fell upon the empty chair of estate.

"I have come to visit her Grace," he said. "Where is she?"

I stepped forward, my heart hammering. "The Queen is in her bedchamber, Your Majesty," I said. "I fear that she is very unwell."

"Take me to her, Lady Hertford," he commanded. "I shall go and compose the Queen's mind."

Queen Catherine lay upon her pillows, arranged with all the fragility of a saint in wax. "Your Majesty," she gasped. "Forgive me that I cannot rise to receive you."

"It is no matter, Your Grace," he said, moving toward the bed with slow deliberation. "We heard that you were ill. What is it that troubles you?"

"I feared that you were displeased with me and I was utterly forsaken, your Majesty," she replied. The tears streamed down her face as she spoke.

The King took her hand and patted it clumsily. "There is no need to fear, my dear," he said. "I am here now and all will be well. Tell me of the forebodings that so oppress your mind."

"My conscience smote me, Your Majesty," she began, each word measured like an act of penance. "I realised that I had spoken to you most unadvisedly. God has ordained that weak and ignorant women should be governed by men whose wisdom and understanding is far superior to their own."

King Henry stood beside her bed, his lips drawn into a thin line. "Not so, by St Mary," he retorted. "You have become a doctor of theology to instruct us and not to be directed by us."

I held my breath. A single misstep would unmake her.

But the Queen brushed away her tears and leaned into humility like a practiced courtier. "If your Majesty has taken it so," she replied, "then your Majesty has very much mistaken me." Her voice softened, adopting a deferential tone. "I consider it preposterous for a woman to become an instructor to her husband. It is her part to learn of her husband and be taught by him. I regard your Majesty as my supreme head and governor here on earth."

He scowled, unconvinced. "And yet there have been times when you have seen fit to contradict me," he said.

"I may have seemed to have a difference of opinion with your Majesty," she said gently. "But it was merely to distract you from your painful infirmity. I thought that having a discussion would help to ease your sufferings."

"Is that so, Kate?" he replied. "And did you make your argument to no worse end?"

"I hoped that I might profit from hearing Your Majesty's learned discourse."

His face broke into a beaming smile. "Then we are perfect friends again, sweetheart," he declared. "It has given me more pleasure to hear you say these words than the gift of a hundred thousand pounds. Now that I know the truth of the matter, I swear that I shall never mistake you again!"

King Henry kissed her hand and took his leave. I felt an overwhelming sense of relief. The Queen had been in great peril. But she had succeeded in averting the threat.

"You have saved yourself, your Grace," I whispered.

She turned to me, pale but composed. "May God be praised for directing my words," she said. "He had made up his mind to rid himself of me."

"But now he is entirely reconciled with your Grace," I assured her.

The following afternoon, the King sent the Queen a message to join him in the privy garden. He was sure that she would benefit from taking the air. Queen Catherine dressed in a regal gown of crimson cloth of gold with wide sleeves trimmed with sable fur. She wore a necklace of rubies and pearls and a golden girdle with jewelled pendants. The privy garden shimmered beneath the late afternoon sun, the air ripe with honeysuckle and tension. I stood a pace behind the Queen as she sat beside the King beneath the carved stone arbour.

King Henry spoke amiably at first, gesturing to the red and white roses that hung from the trellis. Queen Catherine answered softly, each word an exercise in serenity. I allowed myself to believe the danger had passed. Then the sound of boots shattered the peace.

A detachment of guards stormed into the garden, their armour clanking, forty strong, and at their head strode Chancellor Wriothesley with a face set like stone. He advanced without preamble, without respect.

"Madam," he said, voice hard as flint, "you are charged with heresy and treason. You must accompany me to the Tower."

Queen Catherine sat motionless, her lips parted in astonishment. I saw the colour drain from her face, leaving it pallid beneath the French hood edged with rubies.

The King rose slowly, his face unreadable, and walked away. My heart turned to stone in my chest. So, he had only pretended to reconcile with the Queen. Now he was taking his revenge upon her.

"Lord Chancellor," Henry called suddenly, his voice sharp and brittle.

Wriothesley turned, lips thin with anticipation, and approached with his warrant outstretched. The parchment fluttered slightly in the breeze like a death sentence about to take flight.

But the King snatched it from him, his eyes blazing, and tore it into ragged pieces.

"Knave!" he thundered. "Varlet, beast and fool! How dare you insult Her Majesty? Get out of my presence at once or it will be the worse for you!"

The garden seemed to vibrate with his fury. Birds burst from the hedges, trilling with alarm. The guards faltered, and then turned, ashen-faced, and departed. Wriothesley trailed behind them like a man sent back to purgatory. The Queen had escaped once more, but now the trap had been sprung and the court had witnessed its failure. Queen Catherine realised that she had escaped disaster by a hair's breadth. But she kept her countenance and spoke calmly.

"I hope that Your Majesty is not offended with the Chancellor," she said. "It seems that he made a mistake and displeased you."

Henry's gaze followed the retreating guards like a hawk watching prey. "He is an utter villain, Kate," he declared. "He does not deserve your concern."

That evening, after supper, I attended the Queen in her privy chamber. The golden light of evening filtered through the mullioned windows, painting the walls with halos of warmth, though none of it reached Catherine's eyes. She sat before the hearth, her fingers clasped over her lap, the crimson of her gown spilling around her.

I poured her a draught of hippocras wine, though I knew she would not drink it. She gazed past me, lips parted slightly, as if she still heard the guards' boots grinding the gravel and saw Wriothesley's face twisted with shame beneath the King's rage.

"That man meant to see me disgraced before all England," she said, quiet but resolute. "And yet I still live and rule."

I sat beside her, my own heartbeat not yet calmed. "Your Grace has won a great victory over your enemies," I replied. "You have humiliated him and Gardiner with him."

Queen Catherine's hand trembled slightly as she touched the rubies at her throat. "I ought to feel triumph," she murmured. "But I feel only exhaustion. I fear the King's mercy is limited. And his temper is as changeable as the wind."

I leaned closer. "But Your Grace has shown him submission and his sense of grievance is pacified," I said.

She turned to me then, and for the first time that day, smiled—a faint, mournful smile. "Then let us hope that my humility is enough to keep me safely in his favour," she replied.

King Henry had made his point clear to everyone at court. He would govern as he saw fit and he alone would decide the religious policy of the kingdom. Bishop Gardiner abandoned his heresy hunts. And Queen Catherine avoided any more talk of reform. The court settled into an uneasy state of quiet. But the King's health continued to decline. He could no longer walk and had to be carried around in a chair by his gentlemen. It was treason for anyone to speak of the death of the King. But the thoughts of the councillors turned to the future. Prince Edward was only a child. Everyone wondered who would govern the kingdom after his father's death. The most prominent member of the old nobility was Thomas Howard, duke of Norfolk. But he was a member of the Catholic party. He was not a popular choice as Regent.

His son Henry Howard, earl of Surrey, could not resist boasting that his father was the best person to take charge of Prince Edward and the realm. His foolish ambition was his downfall. Not long afterwards, Sir Richard Southwell accused him of usurping the royal arms. When the rumours reached King Henry's suspicious ears, he ordered the arrest of both the father and the son. The Howards were sent to the Tower on a charge of treason. Surrey insisted that he had a right to display the royal arms, but he was executed for his presumption. The King was not prepared to take any chances with the future of his son.

CHAPTER 8

Duchess of Somerset (1547)

"The Protector had a wife who was prouder than he was, and she ruled the Protector so completely that he did whatever she wished, and she, finding herself in such great state, became more presumptuous than Lucifer. She thought that as her husband ruled the kingdom, she ought to be more considered than the Queen, and claimed to take precedence of her"

(*The Spanish Chronicle*, 1550).

"The duke had taken to wife Anne Stanhope, a woman for many imperfections intolerable, but for pride monstrous. She was exceeding both subtle and violent in accomplishing her ends, for which she spurned over all respects both of conscience and of shame"

(John Hayward, 1530, *The Life and Reign of King Edward VI*).

King Henry became increasingly withdrawn and would see no-one but his gentlemen and his doctors. He did not want his wife and children to see him in his feeble condition. He decided that they would spend Christmas at Greenwich while he remained at Westminster with his gentlemen. Queen Catherine was beside herself with anxiety. "He has been ill like this before and recovered," she said wringing her hands together. "We must not lose hope." She would have been even more anxious if she had known what was happening in her absence. The King's gentlemen were manoeuvring to exclude her from the regency of Prince Edward. The day after Christmas, I heard the details of the plot from my husband.

"The King asked Sir William Paget, the King's Secretary, to bring him his will," he said exultantly. "He has agreed to appoint a Regency Council to govern the realm during the minority of his son."

"What about the Queen?" I asked. "She is quite convinced that she will act as the regent for her stepson."

"It is too late," he said. "She has missed her chance to rule. Sir William persuaded his Majesty that the Queen could not possibly assume such a grave responsibility. Nature has ordained that only men can have the governance of the state."

"She won't like being set aside," I said.

"She will be left very well endowed," he said. "His Majesty has treated her most generously. She will receive a thousand pounds and the royal manors of Hanworth and Chelsea. She will be styled as the dowager queen and ranked as the first lady in the realm. For the rest of her life, she will continue to be honoured in the same way as if his late Majesty was still alive. She can have no complaints."

"So, who will serve on the council?" I sat impatiently.

"Naturally, I will be one of the councillors," he replied. "Archbishop Cranmer will be another. And so will William

Parr, John Dudley, William Herbert, William Paget, Anthony Denny and Anthony Browne."

"So, there will be a majority of reformers on the council?" I observed.

"Precisely, my dear," he replied. "In the next reign the work of reforming the English church will be completed. There will be no more of these halfway measures and there will be an end to the persecution of heretics."

1547 was as eventful a year as 1536 had been. Queen Catherine spent Christmas and New Year quietly at Greenwich with the royal children. She awaited news of the King's recovery, but none came. After New Year, the King's children returned to their own households. King Henry VIII died on 28th January 1547. But the news was suppressed for three days. My husband had to ensure that a peaceful succession took place.

"I am going to Hertford Castle to fetch my nephew," he said. "The realm must be kept quiet until I have brought him to the Tower of London. There he will be proclaimed as the lawful successor."

"What about the Lady Mary?" I asked. "Should you not to go her and persuade her to resign her claim in his favour?"

He shook his head. "There is no need for any persuasion," he said testily. "The true line of succession is set down by an Act of Parliament and the King's last will and testament."

"But she is the firstborn child of the King," I said. "And she is of an age to rule while her brother is only a minor. Suppose she appeals to the emperor of Spain to uphold her right to the crown?"

"She will not do so," he insisted. "She promised her father that she would protect her little brother and be like a mother to him. She is an honourable lady and accepts his superior claim to the throne."

"Then Godspeed, my dear," I said. "I shall pray for you to be blessed with a prosperous journey."

"When I arrive in London, I shall see my nephew proclaimed as King Edward VI," he declared. "And I shall stand at his side as his most loyal and honoured subject."

I watched him ride through the gate and smiled at the thought of our promising future. Our time had come at last. In the reign of the new King, we would become the foremost family in the realm.

On 31st January 1547 King Edward VI was proclaimed to the citizens of London as the rightful King of England, France and Ireland. A general pardon was granted to prisoners. Sir Anthony Denny rode to Greenwich to inform Queen Catherine that she was now a widow. She was forced to concede to the rule of the council. Not even her brother, William Parr, was willing to defend her right to the regency. The fool did not realise that he would have gained even greater rewards and honours by serving as the Queen's right-hand man. But he was a courtier, not a soldier. He had no stomach for a fight.

On the morning of 1st February 1547, the Tower of London stood hushed beneath a leaden sky. Snow clung to the crenelations like ashes from a dying fire and ice glazed the paving stones. I sat near the latticed window of our apartment in the Tower. The light thin and reluctant, filtered through a skein of fog and frost. Beyond the glass, the Thames moved sluggishly, as if mourning the passing of the late sovereign. Yet here, behind closed doors, the future stirred - not with grief, but with purpose. Edward stood before the fireplace, his silhouette sharp against the flames. I watched his jaw tighten—not in hesitation, but in resolve. William Parr had lingered too long in the shallow waters of favour and indecision. My husband was not such a man. He had moved quickly to take control of the regency council.

"Sir William Paget believes that some special man must have the first and chief place on the council to oversee matters of state," he said. "He thinks that I am the natural choice for that position. Not only am I the young King's uncle, but I have the greatest reputation at court for warfare, diplomacy and statesmanship."

"There could be no better choice," I agreed.

"This afternoon he is going to make the recommendation to the council," he said. "He will propose that I should be appointed as the Lord Protector of the Realm and Governor of the King. It is the usual custom when the King is still a minor."

"Are the rest of the councillors willing to agree?" I asked.

"There will be rewards for our supporters," he said. "The most prominent members of the council will receive titles and lands. It will ensure their loyalty to the new regime."

"Will the young King grant these rewards?" I asked.

"No, Sir William will report them as the last wishes of the late King," he said. "No-one is likely to dispute it. And it is very necessary to make some new creations. The ranks of the nobility have become sadly decayed with the downfall of the Howards, the Poles and the Nevilles. It is time for some new families to come to the fore."

"What will you receive?" I asked eagerly.

"I shall be granted the title of duke of Somerset," he said proudly. "In addition, I shall be appointed Earl Marshall and Lord Treasurer."

"That is wonderful, Edward," I exclaimed. "A dukedom! I am so proud of you!"

His eyes glowed and his mouth quirked into a smile. "It is a signal honour," he said. "But don't say a word to anyone until it has been announced."

On the afternoon of that fateful day, the councillors gathered in the council chamber at the Tower. The flickering torchlight gleamed upon the polished oak table and the tiled floor. The air held an expectancy—as if the walls themselves knew the gravity of the moment. I stood at Edward's side, my fingers folded neatly against my skirts, every inch of me arranged with studied grace. I was dressed in a black gown out of respect for the late King. But it was made of the best quality satin trimmed with velvet with an upstanding collar embroidered with blackwork. My slashed sleeves were lined with black silk and embroidered with black gillyflowers. Around my neck I wore a string of jet beads and a gold pomander on a black ribbon hung from my girdle.

The young King sat by the window upon his great chair of estate. He wore a doublet and hose of black velvet which were elaborately embroidered with Venice gold. Around his neck hung a gold chain of office adorned with Tudor roses in red and white enamel His black velvet cap was set with a row of jewelled aglets and had a white feather plume. His eyes, bright and watchful, swept the chamber as the councillors arrived one by one. John Dudley entered first, his face carefully neutral, though a flicker of calculation shadowed his gaze. Then came William Parr, shoulders too stiff, hands trembling just slightly—he would always be gilded but never gold. Thomas Wriothesley followed, lips pursed, brows furrowed like a man already weighing consequence against advantage. Sir William Paget came last, parchment in hand, his countenance worn but resolute. Edward nodded once, and the ceremony began.

King Edward stood up and addressed the councillors. Although he was only nine years of age, his voice did not tremble. "We are called by God and by the will of our father to wear this crown," he announced. "It shall be worn in duty, not in vanity."

Edward led the way in paying homage to the new King. He knelt down and kissed his hand. "God save your Grace," he declared. One by one, the councillors knelt before the boy king and swore their allegiance. The echoes of those words reverberated in the stones, sealing futures as surely as any decree. King Edward VI resumed his seat looking relieved that the ceremony was over. Then Sir William Paget's voice rose above the murmuring of the councillors.

"In this hour of transition, we are not merely executors of a will, but stewards of a kingdom," he said. "And I say that this realm must be overseen not by an assembly of equals, but by a single figure of proven judgement, loyalty, and authority." He paused. He knew his next words would carve the path forward for decades to come. "I propose that Lord Hertford should be appointed Lord Protector of England, to lead this council, to guard the welfare of his Majesty King Edward, and to steer the governance of this realm with firm and faithful hand."

A silence fell. A breathless, crackling silence.

"This is not a matter to be decided now," said Chancellor Wriothesley. "It is a question that merits much greater deliberation by the members of this council."

Edward did not shift. He did not flinch. His gaze swept the room like a sword unsheathed.

"There is no need of any further deliberation," replied Sir William. "There is no-one who is more worthy of this position than the King's own uncle."

Then Edward spoke, calm and precise. "If the council accepts this burden to be mine, I shall wear it not as an ornament, but as armour."

I felt it then—not in words, but in something stronger. A wave of inevitability. Sir William had manoeuvred well. The assents came like falling dominoes, cautious but unstoppable. The Protector's place was undisputed. When the young King turned and glanced up at my husband, something passed between them—an unspoken confirmation. The boy trusted him and needed him. And I, watching from the margins, felt the charge of that power flicker down my spine. My husband would serve as the Lord Protector of the Realm during the King's minority. He would not come of age until he was sixteen. His uncle would decide the affairs of the realm for the next seven years.

Edward and I returned to our apartment in triumph. He turned toward me as the heavy doors closed behind us. The fire hissed against the damp logs, its amber light dancing across Edward's face—stern now, but alight with pleasure.

"I am now the Lord Protector of the Realm," he said, his voice clipped with satisfaction. No louder than a statement, yet no softer than a crown laid upon his own brow.

I stepped forward, the weight of my gown moving like a current around me. "There is no one more fit for the role," I said, watching the fire catch gold along the threads of his doublet. "You are the uncle of the King and you have devoted your whole life to the service of the realm."

He removed his gloves, laying them across the coffered table between us, fingers flexing as though he might still be gripping the neck of power. "Wriothesley tried to object," he said. "He dared to question the vote. The council was unanimous—save for him."

"He is an ambitious man, Edward," I said. "His only loyalty is to himself. You should appoint someone else in his place."

Edward looked at me, his eyes steady and his jaw set. "His days are numbered. Let him cling to relevance while it lasts. I shall not suffer ingratitude." He crossed the room, standing beside the tapestry that bore the rose of England, his shadow fell across it. "But I shall reward my loyal friends and supporters with titles and lands."

Outside, a bell tolled across the courtyard marking the hour for vespers. I turned toward the sound, then back to Edward. "England belongs to a child," I murmured, "but power belongs to you."

He did not refute it. And I knew, as the fire gathered and the flames danced in the hearth, that the Protectorate had truly begun.

Shortly afterwards, Sir William Paget made another speech to the regency council. "His late Majesty wished to bestow certain honours upon his chief councillors in order to increase the ranks of the nobility," he said. "Lord Hertford, the Lord Protector, is to be created duke of Somerset. Lord Essex, brother to the former queen, shall be raised to the dignity of marquess of Northampton. Lord Lisle shall be henceforth known as earl of Warwick. Sir Thomas Seymour, Sir Richard Rich and myself will become barons. Let us honour his final commands and serve young King Edward with loyalty and unity. And let none doubt the gravity of this trust for it was conferred not by whim, but with the weight of a dying king's hand."

Sir William's final words rang through the chamber like the peal of a church bell—resounding, solemn, and unchallenged.

"Hear, hear!" cried the councillors, their voices overlapping, some rising with genuine fervour, others with the practiced tones of duty. But no-one protested. Not even Chancellor Wriothesley who had winced at Edward's rapid ascent. The late King's will, as Sir William had invoked it, had sealed their compliance.

Edward stood tall, his expression resolute. The transformation from earl of Hertford to duke of Somerset was not just a matter of title. It was the culmination of years of diplomacy, warfare, and quietly brokered alliances. And I, who had watched it all from behind velvet curtains and ornamental screens, knew the true weight of the moment. I would not need to linger in the shadows for much longer.

He inclined his head slightly toward the council, not a bow, but a measured acknowledgement of the new order. "I accept these honours not for vainglory," he said, voice steady, "but in devotion to my nephew, the King, and for the peace of the realm."

There was a rustle as the herald stepped forward, unfurling a roll of fresh parchment bearing the King's seal. The names of the newly titled men gleamed with wet ink. Sir William handed the document to the Lord Chancellor to record formally. As the councillors dispersed, murmuring about estates and precedence, Edward turned to me as if no one else existed in the room. There was a kind of solemn triumph in his eyes, not the giddy fire of victory, but the calm steel of arrival. He had scaled the mountain, and now stood on its peak, surveying all beneath.

"They know who holds the reins now," he murmured, his voice pitched low, for me alone.

I stepped closer, letting my fingers graze the edge of his sleeve. "Let them know it," I replied. "Let them feel it every hour in court, in council and in chapel." We departed the chamber arm in arm, not as lord and lady alone, but as the stewards of England's future.

The following day, Edward celebrated his victory at Chester Place. He invited all his friends and supporters to attend and I presented a splendid banquet in his honour. The fires in the Great Hall of burned brightly, scenting the air with spiced pine and orange peel. The musicians played soft music from the minstrel's gallery. The tables were spread with the finest victuals in London. Boars' heads glistened with fruit in their jaws, peacocks were re-plumed and stuffed with herbs and mulled wine flowed freely from great silver ewers into the cups. My lord's rise had drawn a glittering flock—nobles, courtiers, ambassadors—all eager to bask in the triumph of England's new Lord Protector. Edward, seated at the high table beneath our coat of arms, accepted each toast with the quiet command of a man who no longer needed to raise his voice.

But Thomas Seymour sat at the table with his face drawn in petulance. He had dressed well for the occasion, in tawny velvet lined with sable, the medallion of the Garter on a chain around his neck. But nothing could smooth the lines of resentment etched deep into his face. I watched him from my seat beside Edward, the fire casting gold against our goblets and the wine within them glowing like garnets. The hall was crackling with merriment, but Thomas sulked like a schoolboy denied a plum. He poked at his trencher, refusing the venison, the swan pie, even the sweetmeats that he usually devoured without ceremony. With every toast made to his brother, his face grew increasingly sour.

Lord Paget leaned toward him with an indulgent smile. "Do you not wish to toast your brother's success?" he asked. "He has made your family the greatest in the land. Now you will be able to pick and choose a bride from among the noblest houses in the realm!"

Thomas's goblet paused mid-air. "It is always about Edward," he grumbled. "But why should he have everything? What about me?" His fingers curled tighter around the stem of his goblet as if to wring it.

I glanced at Edward. He heard it, of course—every word—but did not stir. His fingers rested on the arms of his chair, his gold rings catching in the candlelight. He remained silent and ignored the ridiculous outburst.

"I am also the King's uncle," Thomas went on, voice rising. "Yet I am not treated with equal honour. Edward has been appointed both Lord Protector and Governor of the King. But when King Henry VI was a minor, his two uncles—Humphrey of Gloucester and John of Bedford—shared the government. I should be appointed as the King's Governor! It is my right!"

It was plain that the aggrieved Thomas thought that he ought to have been appointed a duke like his brother. But it was absurd to think that he ought to have an equal share in the governance of the realm. He had none of the required qualities of experience, prudence and wisdom. King Henry VIII had not even wanted him to be appointed a councillor. I exchanged a glance with Sir Anthony Denny, who set down his cup with a purpose.

"You cannot compare yourself to your brother," he said, his voice firm as iron. "He has waged wars in Scotland and France on behalf of the realm. You should be well satisfied with the honours that you have received. You have been appointed a

Knight of the Garter and granted the title of Baron. John Dudley relinquished the Admiralty for you. Let that be enough."

Thomas's eyes flicked around the hall, searching for sympathy. But none came. Even the laughter at the hearth had grown dim, as if the fire itself disapproved. His shoulders slumped and he stared down into his goblet. The music rose again and the moment slipped past like smoke. The laughter returned, louder this time, soaring toward the carved rafters above. Thomas subsided into a black sulk for the rest of the evening while the future—our future—was toasted in every corner of the hall. I sipped my claret slowly, observing him. He brooded now, but he would act later. He would pick a time to press his claim again. But the realm would not be governed by folly and Edward would not be ruled by a brother who had never learned to govern himself.

I was only mistaken in the speed by which he pursued his grievance. The following day, he went to visit his mother and poured out his woes to her. Old Lady Seymour was foolish enough to take his part. She hurried over to Chester Place at once. The old matriarch entered the privy chamber in a flurry of lace and velvet, her face etched with worry.

"You must be good to Thomas for your father's sake, Edward," she began, plaintively, with the urgency of a mother fearing a quarrel between her sons.

Edward turned from the fireplace, his expression already set in flint. "I have been good to him, Mother," he replied evenly. "I have given him a title of nobility, the residence of Sudeley Castle and its estates, and a position of great responsibility in the realm."

She fluttered a hand as if brushing away dust. "But he says these do not compare with your honours, Edward," she bleated, her eyes growing watery. "You could at least have made him an earl or a marquis. He feels so slighted that he does not know how he will hold his head up among the other councillors."

I stood at the window, unmoving. I watched her words strike Edward like arrows against armour, none penetrating, but each one leaving a mark.

"If it had not been for me," he said coldly, "he would not even have a place on the council. He has no business complaining to you."

The old woman's lips trembled. "He believes he has been deprived of his right, Edward. It would break my heart if there was discord between you. Surely you can agree to share your honours and responsibilities equally with your own brother?"

Edward shook his head. "It reflects very badly upon him to make such unseemly demands. The councillors granted me the supremacy on account of my long years of royal service and my prowess on the battlefield. It was not solely because of my blood ties to the King. They would never consent to appointing Thomas to such high honours. He needs to prove his worth by loyal service before he is given anything more."

She dabbed at her eyes with a handkerchief edged in lace. "I did not think that you would refuse your own mother, Edward," she sighed. "Poor Thomas will be most distressed by your unkindness."

"It is not unkindness, mother, it is justice," he said, with icy restraint. "The realm must be led by those who have earned the right to lead it, not by those who demand it at dinner tables or weep to their mothers."

The old lady, her eyes narrowed by disappointment, said nothing more. She took her leave full of sorrow that she had failed to move her eldest son to show the same indulgence to his brother that she had always done. The silence following her departure lingered like smoke, and Edward now stood brooding before the fireplace, arms folded, his brow furrowed.

"He would split the realm if it suited him," he muttered, half to the flames, half to himself. "Thomas cannot see beyond his own reflection. And now he fills Mother's ears with nonsense."

"He feeds off his sense of injury," I said, crossing the chamber and setting my goblet aside. "And worse, he seeks a way to take control of the young King. That would be dangerous."

He turned toward me abruptly. "We need to appoint someone reliable as Groom of the Privy Stool in the King's household. Someone who will report to us and shield him from unsuitable influences. Whom can we trust with such an important task?"

"I know the ideal candidate," I replied immediately. "My half-brother Sir Michael Stanhope."

Edward's eyes narrowed, not with suspicion, but with measured thought. He considered the suggestion for a moment, a flicker of calculation across his face.

"He is my father's son from his first marriage," I continued. "He would be completely loyal to us. You need not have any

Chapter 8: Duchess of Somerset (1547) | 409

fears that he could be bought or bribed. Moreover, he is discreet, diligent, and obedient. He would understand that the King's household must be guarded like a fortress."

Edward's expression shifted, easing as if the fog in his thoughts had lifted. "As you say, my dear. It is always better to keep such important responsibilities within the family."

I allowed myself a small, satisfied nod. "Then let it be done swiftly. Before Thomas even thinks to make a suggestion."

He crossed to the writing desk and lifted the lid of the inkwell. "I shall write the writ myself. Let the King's household be guarded by strategy and not by sentiment."

As his quill scratched across the parchment, I felt a sense of elation. Thomas thought it would be an easy matter to make himself the power behind the throne. But we would bar the door firmly against him and not allow him anywhere near the young King.

Soon afterwards, Lord Lisle came to see Edward, his cloak still dusted with road grit, his jaw tight beneath the shadow of his hood. The steward had barely announced him before Edward beckoned him in with a wave. I watched from my desk near the window, where I'd been overseeing the writing of household accounts. The ledger lay open but forgotten now.

"Good day, Lord Lisle," he said. "Take a chair and sit down with me. Can I offer you a cup of wine?"

Lord Lisle waved his hospitality aside. He had come on serious business. "You'll want to hear this, my lord," he said, taking off his gloves. "Your brother Thomas asked me—bold as brass—to propose him as *Governor of the King* at the next council meeting."

Edward stood still, his face hardening, but said nothing yet.

Lord Lisle pressed on. "Naturally, I turned him down, my lord. But you should keep a close watch on him. He will always envy your position and seek to overthrow you."

"I am grateful for your loyal service, Lord Lisle," he replied. "I shall not forget your fidelity in this matter."

"I am your true friend, my lord," he replied. "Rest assured that you can always count on me." He bowed and took his leave.

I rose from the desk, my voice clipped and cool. "Your brother is a born troublemaker," I said. "You should send him abroad. Let him serve as ambassador in some distant court. Spain, perhaps. Or Poland."

Edward turned toward the tall window where the sun was just breaking through the clouds over the Thames. "The Seymour family must stick together," he insisted "If I sent him away, it would show my distrust to everyone. He is reckless, but still my blood."

"He may be your blood," I replied, stepping closer. "But he is not your friend."

Edward didn't smile. He stood still for a long moment, his fingers drumming faintly against the window sill. "I am sure Thomas will come round in time," he said, though without conviction. "We must find him a rich bride who will enable him to live as a wealthy nobleman. That will flatter his ego and distract him from his ridiculous obsession."

"A bride," I repeated, considering it aloud. "He'll want nobility. Preferably beauty. And a connection to court."

"You will have to arrange it, my dear," he said. "Find him a bride. Secure the match. But make certain she is wise enough to temper him."

"Don't you want to choose his wife yourself?" I asked.

"I cannot afford to spend any more of my time on Thomas," he said. "There are too many important matters of state demanding my attention. I have to meet with Archbishop Cranmer urgently. We must discuss the arrangements for the late King's funeral and the new King's coronation."

I turned to the steward. "Fetch the book of genealogies," I commanded. "I will begin at once."

He brought it to my desk and I set aside my ledger. This task was far more pressing. I scanned the pages of the volume carefully. There was Lady Catherine Brandon, the dowager duchess of Suffolk. Lady Margaret Clifford, the daughter of the earl of Cumberland. And Lady Mary Howard, the former duchess of Richmond. I wrote down the list of names and sent it to old Lady Seymour for her approval. I hoped that a rich and noble marriage might serve to placate both the mother and the son.

On the morning of 14th February 1547, the funeral cortege of King Henry VIII began its journey from Westminster to Windsor. I followed the procession through the misted dawn, the coffin of our late sovereign veiled in black velvet and cloth of gold that caught the pale light like a dying star. Black-caparisoned horses marched with measured steps, their hooves muffled on the stone causeway, while a thousand horsemen stretched behind us in a silent river of mourning. Each rider sat as still as a statue, their banners lowered, their faces hidden beneath sombre helmets. A hush fell over the citizens of London as the great chariot emerged into view. It was hung with heraldic banners and drawn by eight horses. A collective sob rippled through the crowd as they gazed upon the royal coffin that lay beneath a pall of cloth of gold, its surface embroidered with Tudor roses, the lions of England, and the fleurs-de-lis of France in heavy bullion thread. As the cortege swept onward, they fell back in respectful silence, their heads bared until the last banner had slipped from view. In the atmosphere of awe and lingering sobs, the people joined together in mourning not just a monarch, but the end of an age.

At Syon Abbey we paused for the night, the coffin resting upon trestles in the chapter house. The following day we journeyed onto Windsor. The Yeomen Guards bore the royal coffin into St George's chapel to lie in state overnight. On 16th February 1547 the funeral ceremony took place. I sat beside the dowager queen and watched the proceedings from the Queen's Closet above the choir. The stained-glass windows spilled coloured light across the stone flagged floor and the scent of incense curled around the arches like pale smoke. They lowered him into the vault with care and I watched as the black velvet brushed against the cold stone and he rested at last beside Queen Jane.

Bishop Gardiner recited the words of the Latin requiem mass. I bowed my head, feeling the steady pulse of the chant against my throat, remembering King Henry in his riotous triumphs and terrible rages. The music wove through my memories—his golden crown, his glittering court, the splendour and the terror of his reign. Tears pricked my eyes, and I dared not glance at the dowager queen for fear her tears would find mine. At the close of the service, the chief officers of the household stepped forward with their white staves of office. Each one broke their rods in two and then cast them down to lie upon the lid of the coffin. Silence swallowed the chapel, broken only by the distant tolling of the great bell. When the final Amen echoed and the clergy filed away, I lingered in the doorway of the Queen's Closet staring down at the open vault. King Henry VIII lay before the altar next to his third wife as he had wished. But his project for an extravagant tomb was quietly set aside. The expense of a royal funeral and a coronation was quite enough of a burden upon the treasury.

The following day, the councillors gathered in the council chamber at the Tower of London to receive their honours. Its vaulted ceiling cast shadows across the tapestry-lined walls. Young Edward sat upon his chair of estate of crimson velvet beneath a canopy of crimson cloth of gold. He wore a buttoned jacket of black satin with a high collar and a heavy surcoat of black velvet trimmed and faced with ermine. Around his neck he wore a gold collar of office set with rubies and pearls and at his waist was a ceremonial dagger. His black velvet cap was set with rubies brooches. His expression was grave and remote.

The Garter Knight advanced, his robes sweeping the stone like waves across a shore, clutching the letters patent like sacred scriptures. Edward followed behind with solemn grace escorted by the earls of Dorset and Suffolk. How carefully the courtiers masked their envy. How perfectly he played the part.

When he knelt before the King, the chamber held its breath. Lord Paget unfolded the heavy parchment with deliberate grace. His voice rang out in the words of the proclamation:

"Edward the Sixth, by the Grace of God, King of England, France, and Ireland, Defender of the Faith, and of the Holy Church of England and also of Ireland in earth the Supreme Head, do by these our Letters Patent advance our right trusty and well-beloved uncle, Edward Seymour, to the estate, dignity, and honour of Duke of Somerset."

The King rose and bestowed upon him the cloak, the sword, the golden rod, and at last the cap of estate. Edward rose to his feet clothed in the splendour of his ducal office. He stood beside the King like a black lion at the throne's right hand. Elevated, adorned, transformed. The chamber murmured their approval; some bowed, others nodded with studied neutrality. I clutched the embroidered edge of my sleeve to keep from trembling. He assisted the King with the other creations of noblemen. But I had eyes only for him. The cut of his collar, the quiet authority in the set of his shoulders and the way he did not smile. The younger courtiers looked to him with careful admiration, many already shifting their allegiance not toward the throne but to the man beside it.

The sunlight spilled through the high windows of Somerset Place casting a glow over the tapestries and polished oak that lined our parlour. We had renamed our house in honour of Edward's new title. We intended to extend the building and create a vast Renaissance palace that was worthy of our new rank. I stood by the fireplace, twisting a sprig of dried lavender between my fingers. Edward was seated in the high-backed chair beneath the crest of our house, newly embroidered and flanked by red damask—still a Seymour, but now elevated, gilded, *fortified*.

"You must commission a new coat of arms," I said, folding my hands together with studied ease. "One that expresses the honour of the House of Somerset."

His gaze flicked toward me, thoughtful, brow furrowing beneath the black velvet cap he had come to favour. "Yes, my dear," he murmured, the corner of his mouth curving. "I shall consult with the Master of Arms about selecting a suitable device."

I stepped closer, lifting the edge of my sleeve to reveal the fine stitching of wings—the Seymour emblem, bold and proud. "It is a simple matter," I replied, voice steady. "You need only quarter the Seymour arms with the royal arms of Queen Jane."

He hesitated. I saw it in the stillness of his hands, the way his fingers paused mid-rest against the arm of the chair. "That might be considered presumptuous," he said slowly. "Remember the fate of the earl of Surrey. His pride was his undoing."

I did not flinch. "Queen Jane Seymour was your sister," I reminded him. "And the title Duke of Somerset is *royal*. You are the highest authority in the realm now. No-one would dare to question your rightful honours."

There was silence but for the crackle of the fire. Then, Edward nodded with quiet conviction. "You are quite right.

I shall quarter the Seymour wings with Queen Jane's lions and fleur-de-lis. After all, I am the King's uncle. Our family *is* the highest in the land."

While Edward summoned the painter and gave orders for his new coat of arms, I commissioned a scribe to draw up an illuminated genealogy. "Begin with the noble descent of my children from King Edward the Third," I instructed. His eyes widened, but he obeyed. When he laid down his quill, the parchment shimmered beneath the glow of my lantern. I moved closer, tracing with my fingertip the delicate lineage as it cascaded in gilded scrolls from Edward III to my own children. Each painted lily and lion told a story of claim and kin, of right and remembrance. I lifted the vellum, holding it aloft as though it were a prayer book, and felt the weight of generations settle onto my shoulders. I carried it down the long gallery of Chester Place and placed it beside the newly painted coat of arms that hung opposite the entrance. There, side by side, our symbols would speak as loudly as any herald's trumpet. Everyone who passed through our doors would recognise our noble ancestry and our illustrious status.

Edward turned his attention to the final preparations for the coronation of King Edward VI. He would be on public view as the Lord Protector just as much as the new monarch. On Saturday 19th February the young King made his formal entry into the city of London. He was dressed in a gown of cloth of silver embroidered with gold, a doublet of white velvet embroidered with silver and a cape trimmed with sable. On his head he wore a cap of white velvet garnished with rubies, diamonds and pearls. His horse was trapped in crimson satin embroidered with gold and pearls. My husband, the Lord Protector, rode beside him dressed in the best furs from the wardrobe of the late King Henry VIII. They were followed by the clergy and nobility of the realm in order of precedence. I took my place in the chariot and watched the succession of city pageants to welcome the new King.

The streets of London were spread with gravel in every place and rails were fixed on one side in which the Guildsmen stood in their order. On the other side of the street, priests and clerks were dressed in their finest robes holding crosses and censers to cense the King. All along the route the houses were adorned with tapestries, cloth of gold, and cloth of silver, streamers and banners. Cornhill Street was hung with rich tapestries and coloured banners and the fountain ran with sweet wine for celebration. King Edward was greeted by a choir of children singing a ballad:

> *"King Edward up springeth from puerility,*
> *And toward us bringeth joy and tranquillity;*
> *Our hearts may be light and merry cheer,*
> *He shall be of such might, that all the world may him fear.*
>
> *Sing up, heart; sing up, heart; sing no more down,*
> *But joy in King Edward that weareth the Crown!*
>
> *His father late our sovereign both day and also hour,*
> *That in joy he might reign like a prince of high power,*
> *By sea and land hath provided for him eke,*
> *That never King of England had ever the leke.*
> *Sing up, heart; sing up, heart; sing no more down,*
> *But joy in King Edward that weareth the Crown!*

Ye children of England, for the honour of the same,
Take bow and shaft in hand, learn shootage to frame.
That you another day may so do your parts,
To serve your King as well with hands as with hearts.

Sing up, heart; sing up, heart; sing no more down,
But joy in King Edward that weareth the Crown!

Ye children that be toward, sing up and not down,
And never play the cowards to him that weareth the crown:
But always be your care his pleasure to fulfil,
Then shall you keep right sure the honour of England still.

Sing up, heart; sing up, heart; sing no more down,
But joy in King Edward that weareth the Crown!"

The crowd surged around the Great Conduit, alive with anticipation, their breath misting in the cool morning air. Draped in fresh garlands and festooned with silks, the fountain itself had been transformed into a marvel: atop its central column sat a gilded crown, gleaming as if newly forged, with streams of red wine cascading from lion-shaped spouts into marble basins. The smell of sweet claret mingled with crushed rose petals filling the square with heady excess. Near the fountain stood four children dressed in rich garments: Regality, in a robe of gold tissue; Justice, in stiff crimson satin; Truth, draped in ivory with a silver girdle; and Mercy, wrapped in soft azure lined with ermine. Each wore a circlet fashioned of gilded leaves, and as the King stopped before them, they stepped forward in turn, their voices bright and rehearsed, rising above the murmurs of the crowd.

Regality took the lead: *"Rule and govern prudently,"* she proclaimed.

Justice, grave-eyed followed. *"And do justice condignly,"* he intoned.

Truth took her turn next, her hands clasped together: *"But mix with mercy,"* she said.

Mercy, the smallest and most solemn, stepped forward last: *"That the truth may stand surely, and your throne may endure permanently."*

The children bowed low and a hush fell on the crowd as thick as velvet. The young King smiled and waved his hand in acknowledgment. Around the fountain, cheering erupted and toasts were drunk. The children retired from view and a tableau of the King's ancestry was presented. It showed a golden phoenix descending from the heavens and landing upon a mount decorated by red and white roses and boughs of hawthorn. A crowned lion then approached, followed by a young cub. Two angels brought a crown which they set upon the head of the young lion. Then the old lion and phoenix vanished away, leaving the young lion alone. I smiled to see the honour that was paid to the Seymours. Queen Jane had been dead for nine years, but her memory still lived on.

The procession moved on to the Standard in Cheapside. It was hung with cloth of gold and tapestries and the market cross was newly painted and gilded. The Mayor of London and his aldermen were assembled there to receive King Edward. He presented him with a purse of a thousand gold marks.

"Why do they give me this?" he asked.

"It is the custom of the city," his uncle replied. He handed the purse to the captain of the guard.

Upon a stage an old man sitting in a chair represented King Edward the Confessor. He was dressed in a gown of cloth of gold with a crown on his head. In his left hand he held an orb and in his right hand he grasped a sceptre. Then St George arrived on horseback dressed in full armour. Beside him stood his page holding his spear and shield and a fair maiden holding a lamb. St George greeted the King and made a speech:

"Most noble and gracious Prince Edward, heir to the crown and hope of England's realm. Behold, I, Saint George, patron saint of this fair land, come forth in peace and fealty to greet thee on the threshold of thy reign. In mine armour I stand not to make war, but to guard thy crown with steadfast heart and sacred vow. This fair maiden with the lamb doth bring token of innocence and mercy — virtues which must ever temper thy justice. And here beside me, the page bears shield and spear, symbols of thy royal charge: to protect the weak, defend the realm, and rule with wisdom. Follow the path of thy forebears who sought counsel and kept faith, and let thy sceptre be guided not by pride, but by virtue. In thee rests England's future — may thy reign be long, thy judgments fair, and thy heart ever true. Thus do I salute thee, King Edward, with sword sheathed and loyal spirit."

When the King arrived at St. Paul's Churchyard, he was greeted by a Spanish tightrope walker who slid down a cable from the church steeple to the ground as swiftly as an arrow from a bow. He bowed to the King and kissed his foot, and then he ran up the rope again until he stood over the midst of the churchyard. There he turned somersaults and jumped from one leg to the other. The young King watched the acrobatics with great pleasure. Afterwards he proceeded to the Great Conduit in Fleet Street where he was greeted by four children, very richly dressed, representing Grace, Nature, Fortune, and Charity. They each gave short speeches of benediction to the King. The last show was at Temple Bar where the gate was painted with coloured battlements and adorned with fourteen flags. Eight French trumpeters blew their trumpets after the fashion of their country, and a choir of children sang a verse:

> *"Good Lord in Heaven to Thee we sing,*
> *Grant our noble King to reign and spring,*
> *From age to age*
> *Like Solomon the sage,*
> *Whom God preserve in peace and war,*
> *And safely keep him from all danger."*

The following morning, King Edward travelled by barge from Westminster to Whitehall. There he dressed in a robe of crimson velvet trimmed with ermine in readiness for the coronation service. He walked to Westminster Abbey under a canopy of state carried by the four Lords of the Cinque Ports. The Lord Protector carried the crown, as was his right. Behind him followed a procession of the Gentlemen of the Privy Chamber, the nobility, the guards and the court servants. I was filled with pride to take my place in the procession at the head of the noble ladies of the court. Only the royal woman took presence before me. Now I knew how Queen Anne Boleyn had felt on her day of triumph. But her mistake was to have entrusted herself to a tyrant. I was married to the finest man in the realm. I knew that I would share his good fortunes and he would never play me false.

The coronation ceremony was cut short to meet the limitations of a nine-year-old king. Archbishop Cranmer preached a sermon proclaiming him as a new Josiah. He was anointed with holy oil before the altar and then he was crowned. The choir then sang a *Te Deum* and a gold ring was set upon his finger. He was presented with the orb, sceptre and staff of St Edward. Then he sat upon a throne of damask and gold with two cushions to raise him up to receive the homage of the nobility. I felt a sense of great satisfaction in the occasion. It was not just the celebration of a Tudor monarch. It was the triumph of the Seymour family. After mass was celebrated, the whole assembly walked from the Abbey to Westminster Hall for the coronation banquet. As I entered the hall the greatest lords and ladies of England gave way before me. But my cup of joy overflowed when my mother approached and curtsied low before me. For once she had forgotten her austere composure. Her eyes brimmed with tears.

"Your noble ancestors would be proud to see you on this glorious day!" she said. I treasured her words as the greatest accolade I could receive. At last, I had made my mother proud!

"You will not forget to do something for your stepfather," she asked. "It was not his fault that he lost his place at court."

"Edward shall find him an even better place," I promised. "After all, Sir Richard is his father-in-law."

"Bless you, my child," she said. "This is the happiest day of my life!"

CHAPTER 9

First Lady of the Realm (1547)

"Am not I wife to the Protector, who is King in power, though not in title; a Duke in order and degree; Lord Treasurer, and Earl Marshal, and what else he pleaseth; and one who hath ennobled his highest honours by his late great victory? And did not Henry marry Catharine Parr in his doting days; when he had brought himself to such a condition by his lusts and cruelty that no lady who stood upon her honour would adventure on him? Do not all knees bow before me, and all tongues celebrate my praises, and all hands pay the tribute of obedience to me, and all eyes look upon me as the first in state?

(Peter Heylyn, History of the Reformation of the Church of England, 1661).

After the coronation I was determined to demonstrate our new status to the world. My family was now pre-eminent in the realm and we needed to dress according to our rank. Edward was a careful man who did not waste his substance upon expensive clothes. But now he was a duke and I was a duchess. It was our duty to impress the court with our grandeur. I had learned from my service to six queens. All of them had dressed in regal style with a splendid wardrobe and costly jewels. I thought of a practical solution. I would obtain my rightful due from the royal stores and then it would cost us nothing. I took a large bedsheet from my linen cupboard and waited until midnight so there would be no-one around to interfere with me. Then I made my way to the fabled Silk House of Whitehall Palace accompanied by my chamberlain, Master Whalley. King Henry VIII had maintained a priceless store of rich and rare fabrics for the royal wardrobe. I did not intend to allow these priceless goods to fall into anyone's hands but my own.

The clerk of the stores did his best to object to my visit. "My lady, I regret to inform you that nothing can be discharged from these stores without a warrant signed by the King," he protested.

I drew myself up to my full height and stared at him. "The old King is dead now," I said coldly. "All his property belongs to his son, King Edward. And my husband is the Lord Protector and governs in his name. So, I will take whatever I please from these stores and be damned to your warrants."

"My lady, this book has been honestly kept", he said.

"There will be no need to make any more entries," I replied. "From this day on, you may set the book aside."

"As your ladyship commands," he conceded.

"Fetch your keys and open all these chests," I ordered. "I want to see everything in this storehouse."

He brought the keys and reluctantly unlocked the row of great chests. I saw the gleam of precious metals as he lifted the lids. They contained bolts of cloth of gold and cloth of silver worth a King's ransom.

"You may leave us," I said. I was eager to explore the riches of the Silk House for myself.

Master Whalley held up his lamp as I examined the priceless textiles. No two bolts were the same for the late King had prided himself upon the striking originality of his wardrobe. The rich fabrics were woven with coloured backgrounds to create a more striking effect. I gasped with wonder as I held up a length of violet cloth of silver. I imagined myself wearing a fabulously rich dress to rival any gown that Queen Catherine Parr had worn. The next time I attended court I was determined that I would outshine every other lady in the land.

Master Whalley coughed. "My lady, the hour is late," he whispered.

I collected myself and placed the splendid cloth upon the great bedsheet. Then I added half a dozen equally splendid rolls. I regretted that I could not take more, but they were too heavy to carry away.

Then I perused the vast array of silks, satins and velvets lying upon the shelves. They were the very best quality that could be obtained from Italy and Flanders. There was every shade imaginable including the royal colours of purple and crimson. I took bolt after bolt from the shelves and laid it upon the great bedsheet. Soon a great heap arose of rose-pink, sea-water, pansy, straw and whey. I could not wait to show them to my seamstress and give my orders. Tomorrow morning, I would give orders to have two dozen new gowns made for my wardrobe. It would be a collection that was worthy of a queen.

I gestured towards the bedsheet. "Tie it up," I ordered. The bundle was so enormous that Master Whalley could barely manage it. I should have brought a couple of other men on the expedition. We made our way to the side entrance where a great wagon stood waiting for me. The Yeomen of the Guard at the door gave me questioning looks when they saw the great bundle, but none of them dared to challenge me. I made my way back to Chester Place on the Strand in triumph. Now I had the pick of the finest imported textiles in the realm at my disposal.

I had the bedsheet taken upstairs to my linen room. Now I would have my own silk store. I had the maids roused from their beds and set them to clearing out the linen and replacing it with the costly rolls of fabric. It was sunrise by the time the task was completed to my satisfaction. In the morning light I could see my treasure in its full glory. The violet cloth of silver shimmered in the light. I knew that it would set off my looks to perfection. I ordered Master Whalley to make a full inventory. The value of the goods was so great I decided to keep my own book. Any of my servants could have made their fortune by stealing one of the bolts.

"None of these items are to leave this room without my express orders," I said. "You shall send for the locksmith and have the strongest possible lock fitted to the door. Only you and I shall have a key. Bring the list to me as soon as it is ready."

"Yes, my lady," he replied. He brought the inventory to me in the late afternoon. I was displeased by the delay.

"What took you so long?" I demanded.

"My lady, there were one hundred and twenty bolts and each one had to be precisely measured," he explained.

"Very well, you may go," I said.

I perused the list carefully. I intended to make a careful selection of the fabric for my two dozen gowns. I remembered the care with which Anne Boleyn had prepared her splendid wardrobe for her visit to France. I intended to create an even greater sensation. No-one would doubt my position in the realm as the Lord Protector's wife. We would be King and Queen in all but name.

The following morning, I sent for my head seamstress and gave my orders. Her first commission was the gown of violet cloth of silver. I decided that it would have sleeves of white silk richly embroidered with silver thread.

"It must be completed by the end of the week," I informed her. "You must cut out the sleeves today and set two women to embroidering them. I will accept no excuses if they are not ready."

"I will not fail you, my lady," she promised.

The following week I attended court dressed in my magnificent violet gown with a necklace of fine amethysts around my neck. I was every inch the duchess of Somerset and the wife of the Lord Protector of the Realm. I prided myself that I was the most splendidly dressed lady in the room. I far outshone the dowager queen. Everyone hastened to pay their court to me and beg me for favours. The highest lords and ladies in the land showed me the greatest respect.

Thomas Seymour entered the Presence Chamber with the swagger of a man far too accustomed to his own charm. His doublet was slashed in the latest fashion, and a jewel sparkled from his cap—a mark of his new elevation to the rank of Baron Seymour of Sudeley. Edward had granted him honours that were far beyond his merits. But they were not enough to satisfy him. He still looked for more.

He bowed to me with mockery flickering in his eyes. "My dear Lady Somerset," he said. "How are the affairs of the realm?"

I answered as coolly as the winter winds that once swept through Syon. "You must enquire of your brother, Lord Sudeley."

He chuckled, low and deliberate, as if my coldness amused him. "Yes, indeed, I will. Edward will be glad of my support at this difficult time."

I gazed at him in chilly disdain. He spoke as if he were the pillar upon which kingdoms might rest. As if his brother did not already bear the full weight of England's fate on his shoulders while he played the courtier.

"Now that you have a title, a position and an estate you ought to find yourself a wife," I reminded him. I was irked that he had made no response to my list of worthy candidates.

"There is no hurry, my lady," he murmured. "You have done your duty by my brother so well that there is no lack of inheritors to the Seymour name. Four is it not?"

"Five," I snapped back. "Two boys and three girls."

His smirk faltered for a heartbeat, but he recovered quickly. "Ah, forgive me. It is difficult to keep count when there are so many blessings."

He gave a charming smile and sauntered off to pay his respects to the dowager queen. I should have remembered that Thomas was a born liar. His words were always lacquered with charm, but beneath the polish lay ambition, coiled and venomous. He had already married her in secret—Catherine Parr, widow of the late King, and a woman of considerable influence and wealth. The match was not merely romantic; it was strategic. With one calculated act, he had bound himself to the legacy of Henry VIII and placed himself within striking distance of young King Edward.

When I learned of his deception, fury surged through me—not the hot, reckless kind, but the cold, deliberate rage of a woman who had been played for a fool. I had offered him counsel, connections, even candidates for marriage, believing—perhaps naively—that he might be steered toward stability. Instead, he had outmanoeuvred us all, slipping past the watchful eyes of council and court to claim a prize that would elevate him far beyond his station.

It was not merely the secrecy that stung, but the insult. He had flaunted his charm in my presence, mocked my loyalty to his brother, and then walked away with a queen on his arm and a smirk on his lips. I saw now that Thomas Seymour did not seek approval—he sought power, and he would wear any mask, speak any lie, and break any bond to grasp it.

The court would soon feel the tremors of his ambition. But I, Anne Somerset, would not forget. And I would not forgive. I made my way to Edward's privy chamber where maps of Scotland lay strewn across the table.

"You must put an end to it at once," I stormed. "It is unfitting for the King's widow to marry anyone, let alone your knave of a brother. He has done this to spite us!"

Edward rose slowly, the crease between his brows deepening. He looked weary, as if the realm's burdens had settled in his bones. Yet he tried to calm me with his usual soft diplomacy. "I am just as angry as you are, but what can I do, my dear? They are lawfully married."

I took a step closer. "She did not have permission to marry," I snapped. "So, it is not lawful!"

Edward sighed, exasperated and resigned. "He claims that he had the permission of the King," he said. "And it does seem to be the case. His Grace said that he thought it would be a good idea for his stepmother to marry his Uncle Thomas."

I gave an incredulous laugh. "He imposed upon the poor boy," I said. "He tricked him and he misled us. The King's daughters will both be shocked when they hear the news. And so will the whole court!"

Edward turned away and rubbed his temples, but I refused to relent. The betrayal was galling and I would not let it pass. I cursed myself for my folly in not keeping a closer watch on the dowager queen's affairs. I ought to have placed a spy in her household. But I had supposed that she was sunk in grief and intended to devote herself entirely to the care and education of her stepdaughter, Lady Elizabeth. So, it had never occurred to me that she would want to remarry. After all, Lady Anne of Cleves had never done so. In my opinion, the dowager queen had shown herself in her true colours. She had married the late King in his doting days when he had brought himself to such a condition by his lusts and cruelty that no decent woman would go near him. And after his death she had failed to honour him by observing two years of mourning. However, every cloud has a silver lining. Since she had chosen not to remain as the King's widow, it meant that she was not the foremost lady in the realm any more. As the wife of the Lord Protector, that position was rightfully mine. She was merely the wife of my husband's younger brother.

"She has shamefully dishonoured the memory of the late King," I said. "She does not deserve to be honoured as the dowager queen. Since she has married your brother, she is only Lady Sudeley. She should no longer have precedence at court. That privilege belongs to me as the wife of the Lord Protector."

"You are quite right, my dear," he agreed. "The former queen has degraded herself to a mere baron's lady. You are the duchess of Somerset. There is no lady of higher rank in the realm."

"Since she is no longer the dowager queen, she cannot expect to wear the royal jewels," I said. "If anyone has the right to wear them, I do."

"She has forfeited her royal privileges," he said. "I will send for the Queen's casket from the Jewel House and you shall wear them at court. There is no-one who may gainsay us and it will remind everyone that my brother and his wife are of no importance whatsoever."

It was a great pleasure for me to receive the royal jewel casket. I had seen it presented to five of the wives of the late King Henry. Now it was my turn to wear them. They adorned my fine new wardrobe admirably and established beyond any doubt that it was the duke and duchess of Somerset who governed this realm. I decided to make my position clear. I returned to court wearing a gown of crimson velvet stitched with silver thread in the shape of Tudor roses and phoenixes rising. My sleeves were made of cloth of gold adorned with gold spangles set with pearls. Every inch of fabric had been chosen with calculation. My regal costume proclaimed my new status as I entered the Presence Chamber at Whitehall. I wore my jewels with dignity—rubies at my throat, diamonds along my sleeves, pearls swinging from my ears. They were not merely ornaments. They were declarations of power.

I felt the eyes of the whole court upon me as I walked through the chamber. My jewels had once adorned queens. I wore them as a symbol of my prestige. At the far end of the chamber, I saw my husband Edward, the Lord Protector. His expression shifted as he caught sight of me. His eyes glowed with pride and he nodded his approval. My grandeur upheld his standing as the *de facto* King of England. Around him, men paused mid-sentence, their discourse halted by my astonishing appearance.

I curtsied slowly, deliberately, allowing the jewels to catch the sunlight. The weight of memories clung to them—Anne

Boleyn's ambition, Jane Seymour's gentleness, Catherine Howard's laughter and Catherine Parr's grace. I rose, meeting the gaze of those gathered around me, my back straight and my head held high. There was silence at first and then the quiet hum of approval, of strategies realigning. In that moment, I was more than a lady. I was a statement. A testimony. A reminder that power did not always wear a crown or wield a sword—it could walk in silk, speak in measured tones, and command with nothing more than a glance. Little Edward Tudor was still a boy learning his lessons in the schoolroom. It would be at least another nine years until he came of age and married. Until that time, the Lord Protector and his wife would preside over the court. The courtiers hurried over to bow and pay their respects to me. At eleven o'clock a fanfare of trumpets blew to signal that it was time to attend morning prayer in the Chapel Royal. I deliberately took my place at the front of the procession.

The dowager queen moved to confront me, her face flushed red with anger. "Lady Somerset, you have mistaken your place", she declared. "As the widow of his late majesty, I have the right of precedence at court. If you ever do that again, I shall drag you back by your skirts!"

"It is you that are mistaken, Lady Sudeley," I replied coldly. "You are no longer the widow of the late King. You are now the wife of Baron Sudeley. He is my husband's younger brother and a person of little rank or consequence at court."

Behind us Lady Mary and Lady Margaret Lennox looked dismayed. Their hands faltered on their prayer books, eyes darting between us like courtiers caught in a storm. Mary's brow furrowed with quiet alarm—she, who knew better than most the cost of public defiance. Margaret, ever calculating, pressed her lips into a thin line, as if weighing the consequences of siding with either woman. But they made no attempt to intervene in our quarrel. One wrong word might shatter the fragile decorum that held the court together.

The other ladies of the procession shifted uneasily, their silks rustling like dry leaves. Some lowered their gazes, pretending not to hear. Others watched with thinly veiled fascination, sensing that this was no mere quarrel over precedence—it was a struggle for power. The dowager queen, once consort to a monarch, now tethered to a man of lesser station. And I, Duchess of Somerset, wife to the Lord Protector, standing at the apex of power in a realm ruled by a boy.

"You have grown proud, Lady Somerset," she said. "You wear the Queen's jewels and you take the Queen's place. But you are a duchess and not the Queen. The will of the late King gave me precedence at court for the rest of my life. You may have the right to walk behind me and carry my train."

"Indeed, I will not, Lady Sudeley," I retorted. "I shall take my place at the head of the procession and Lady Mary shall carry my train. You gave up your rank of your own free will. You should go and take your place with the other baron's wives."

Catherine Parr looked around the court for support. But no-one would meet her eye. They did not wish to offend the Lord Protector by taking her side.

"If this is how I am to be treated, then I shall withdraw from the court," she replied. "I will go to stay at my manor at Chelsea.

And Lady Elizabeth will come and live there with me. The Privy Council has agreed that I should oversee her education."

"As you wish, Lady Sudeley," I said triumphantly.

The trumpets had long since faded, but the echo of our confrontation lingered in the chamber. I felt it in the silence that followed, in the way the company held its breath. I had not merely defended my place—I had claimed it. And though the dowager queen turned away with a stiff back and burning cheeks, I knew the court had seen. They had witnessed the shift. The old order was fading, and I would not yield to its ghosts. The dowager queen turned around and left the court for the last time. She was a defeated woman, and she knew it. I walked at the head of the procession to the Chapel Royal and took my place upon the Queen's chair of estate. Lady Mary carried my train and sat next to me. The whole court recognised my new position and status. I was undoubtedly the first lady of the realm.

The following day, Baron Thomas Seymour of Sudeley came to see us in a rage. "Your insolent wife has insulted my wife before the whole court," he said. "She is the dowager queen and I insist that she is treated with the honour that is her due."

"She *was* the dowager queen," Edward replied. "Now she is only a baroness. Perhaps she should have considered the consequences before making a marriage so far beneath her rank."

"You have taken the Queen's jewels and bestowed them upon your wife," he said. "She has no right to wear them. They are the property of the dowager queen and must be returned to her at once."

"They are state property and Lady Sudeley has no claim upon them," Edward countered. "It is my wife who has the best right to wear these jewels."

"The late King gave her those jewels," he retorted. "So, they belong to her and must be given back."

"They were lent to her during the lifetime of the late King," he said. "But now that he is dead, she is no longer entitled to wear them."

"They were a gift, I tell you," he said. "By God, you shall not cheat her out of her due. I will not stand by and see her humiliated in the eyes of the world."

"She has humiliated herself," he replied coldly. "She forfeited her royal standing and privileges by making a foolish marriage. If she had remained as the King's widow then everyone would have treated her with the honour that she deserved. She has only herself to blame."

"You will regret doing this, Edward", he blustered. "You will rue the day that you demeaned my wife. I shall take my complaint to the Privy Council. The King will hear of this slight to his stepmother!" He gave me a venomous look and stamped out of the door.

"Your brother is a disorderly fool," I said. "He has no respect for either of us. You should send him to the Tower to learn better manners."

"I can hardly disgrace a member of my own family," he replied. "Let him go and stew at Chelsea with his wife. They will not trouble us there."

"But what about the threats that he made?" I asked.

"The councillors will not heed him," he replied. "They all disapprove of his presumptuous marriage. And he will not get anywhere near the King to voice his complaints. I have given strict orders to Sir Michael Stanhope and Sir Richard Page not to admit him to the royal apartments."

I was satisfied that my tiresome brother-in-law was merely an empty reed. His marriage may have brought him wealth, but it had not brought him power. There was no-one who could oppose us. While Edward was occupied with affairs of state, I was equally busy. Every day I rose early and dressed in a costly gown. Then I visited the lady governess to supervise her activities. Anne and Margaret were now eleven and ten years old and I had high hopes for them. I was resolved that my daughters should have a suitable regime of lessons and training. I had seen the efforts that Catherine of Aragon had made to educate Lady Mary. I intended that my daughters should become gracious and accomplished ladies with a reputation for piety and learning. They would become the chief ornaments of the court and marry the best young noblemen in the realm. My daughters rose to greet me as I entered the schoolroom.

"I beseech you, Madam, give me your blessing if it please you," they said courteously. Their good manners pleased me. A courtier needed to master perfect etiquette.

"I pray God to heap His blessings on you and increase His graces in you," I replied. "I see you are holding your books, it is well done."

"God give you good morrow, Madam," said Mistress Champorte. She was a devout and dignified woman who always wore a silver cross around her neck.

"Good morrow, Mistress", I replied. "I am glad to find your scholars so well employed with their books. There is nothing more harmful to youth than idleness. It is the mother of all evils. What have you taught them today?"

"As soon as they had risen, they said the Lord's Prayer and the Creed, Madam," she replied. "Then they read a chapter from the Gospel of St Luke in English and construed some sentences out of Cicero in Latin."

"That is well, Mistress," I replied. "Let them not make haste when they read. The wise scholar reads for their instruction and does not repeat the words senselessly like a parrot."

"Yes, Madam," she replied. "I take for my guiding principle the maxim: *Legere et non intelligere negligere est*. Which is to say, to read and not understand is an unprofitable thing."

"A most excellent maxim," I agreed. "Let it be written out and fixed upon the wall as a daily reminder." I had never been instructed in Latin, so I could not offer a better suggestion. But my daughters would receive all the benefits of a classical education.

I turned my attention back to my daughters. "Anne and Margaret, which one of you writes the best?" I asked.

They exchanged glances with each other. "It is my sister Anne, lady mother," said Margaret.

I reached into my sleeve. "Here is a gilded ink-horn for

you, Anne," I said. "This is given to encourage you to learn all the better."

"I most humbly thank you, lady mother," said Anne.

"Margaret, what say you of your sister's gift," I demanded. "Are you sorry for it?"

She shook her head. "Truly, lady mother, I am not sorry that she has it," she replied. "But if I had the same, I would be gladder."

"Well, I shall see how you profit from your lessons," I said. "However, you should be as glad of your sister's good as your own. If I thought that you envied her good fortune, I would cause you to be soundly whipped for there is nothing more foolish nor reprehensible than envy."

"Yes, lady mother," she agreed.

"I would have you know your duty so that you may do good service to your King, your country and your commonwealth," I admonished them. "Do not think that the nobility of your ancestors frees you to do whatever you please. On the contrary, it requires you to live up to their good example and follow the path of virtue."

"Yes, lady mother," they replied obediently.

"Mistress Champorte, I charge you to look well to my daughters", I ordered. "Let them practice their French conversation for an hour and then embroider their tapestry cushions. This afternoon they may have their singing lesson and play upon the virginals and the lute. And then they may have their dancing lesson. Tomorrow I shall visit in the afternoon to see how well they have progressed."

"Yes, Madam," she replied. "I shall instruct them to become virtuous and accomplished ladies who are worthy of their honourable parents."

Afterwards I retired to my study and dealt with my correspondence. The gate of our house was besieged by crowds of petitioners seeking favours of one kind of another. Naturally, I could not use my influence on behalf of everyone who approached me. I dismissed those who only offered me flattering words. My time was too valuable to spend upon petty matters. The wiser petitioners offered me rich rewards and presents in return for my intervention. My secretaries dealt with the legalities of those requests that I considered to be worthy of my attention.

Edward and I soon became the objects of envy. "My dear, that the lords of the council are displeased that we are offering patronage to clients," he said. "They have accused me of holding an unofficial Court of Requests at Somerset Place."

"Are you not the Lord Protector of England?" I retorted. "The councillors are jealous of your prerogatives. But if they were in your shoes, they would do the very same thing. This is how Wolsey and Cromwell built up their wealth and power and became great men."

Edward had become the wealthiest and most powerful man in the court. He received an annuity of eight thousand marks a year as the Lord Protector. He took the first place on every occasion and two gilt maces were always borne before him in procession. He kept over a hundred servants and two hundred gentlemen retainers who wore his blue livery. I took pleasure in furnishing Somerset House as splendidly as a palace. Edward spent thousand pounds upon a set of silver-gilt bowls and decorated cups so that we could dine in a suitable manner with our noble friends. My privy chamber was adorned with tapestries depicting valiant David clutching his sling and heroic Judith lifting her blade. I bought a pair of playing tables and a set of ivory chessmen. I purchased a pair of virginals and an ivory lute. I even had my own library of books. Our enemies took their revenge by composing a ballad of great derision against us. The common men and women sang it in the streets of London to mock our pretension and greed:

"In Somerset House where gold doth gleam,
With velvet halls and silver seam,
Lord Greed holds court both night and noon,
And Lady Pretence hums a wealthy tune.

Come one, come all, bring coin and plea,
A silken bribe, a princely fee!
They'll smile and nod, they'll sign and bless—
So long as trinkets buy success.

They turned away the poor man's cry,
And bid the flatterers pass them by.
But he who brought a ruby ring,
Was granted audience with the King.

They say he guards the realm's affairs,
Yet stocks his vaults with golden wares.
And she who walks with jewelled grace,
Bestows sweet smiles to save her face.

So let the lords grumble and scowl,
The Lady laughs, the hawks do prowl.
For none may rise in courtly strife,
Without a purse or princely wife.

Sing hey! For Greed, who holds the pen,
To write the fate of poorer men.
And hail to she who charts the course—
With satin cuffs and gilded horse."

Edward was more vexed for my sake than for his own. "I pray you to pay no manner of regard to it, my dear," he said. "I am not at present informed who is the setter forth of this malignant writing, but when he is found out he shall be straitly punished for it."

I had my suspicions that Thomas Seymour was the author of it, for he envied us more than anyone else. But nothing could be proved against him.

Archbishop Cranmer came to visit Edward at Somerset House. "It is time for us to make a general reform of religion, my lord," he urged him. "We should begin by repealing the Act of Six Articles which upholds the tenets of the Catholic faith."

"There is no difficulty about that, your Grace," Edward said. "The majority of the councillors are in favour of reform."

"And we should revoke the prohibition against reading the Bible in English," he insisted. "All of his Majesty's subjects should have the opportunity to read and understand God's Word."

"I intend to abolish the restrictions imposed by the late King," Edward agreed. "The common people have as much right to read the Bible as the nobility."

"We must purify the English Church of its idolatry," he said ardently. "It is time to abolish the Latin mass and replace it with a Book of Common Prayer that can be comprehended by the people."

"Indeed, it is nonsense for the people to worship in an unknown language," Edward said. "They must learn to say the Lord's Prayer, the Creed and the Commandments in English."

"We should remove the superstitions of Catholic worship," he said. "England should be a holy nation without images, crucifixes or shrines of the saints in its churches."

"The young King is in favour of reform," Edward said. "He is certain to agree to the proposals."

"They shall be the crowning glory of his reign," he replied. "He will rule England like a new Josiah and purify the realm of its corruption."

I was just as enthusiastic as Edward to promote the reform of the English church. But Lord Paget was more cautious in his response.

"You are eager to make reforms, my lord," he said. "But it is unwise to make too many changes during the minority of the young King. It will cause too much unrest among the people. It is the first priority of the government to maintain the stability of the realm. We should consider the conservatism of the people and the hostility of the Catholic states that surround us. It would be better to proceed in this matter slowly and by degrees."

"Not so, my lord, Edward retorted. "Our first priority must be the destruction of idolatry and the proclamation of the gospel. We have waited long enough to introduce our reforms."

"I know that His Grace, Archbishop Cranmer is eager to introduce his English liturgy," he sighed.

"So is his Majesty the King," Edward replied.

"Very well, my lord," he conceded. "Let us lay the matter before the next council meeting. But you must be prepared to meet strong resistance from the Catholic bishops."

On 31st July 1547 the dearest wish of the reformers was fulfilled. Every church in the land was ordered to obtain a large Bible in English, a Book of Homilies and a copy of *Paraphrases upon the Gospels* by Erasmus. In the months that followed, the council banned candles, crucifixes and rosaries. Chantry chapels, shrines and relics were abolished. Finally, images in stained-glass, wood, and stone were removed from all the churches across the realm. However, not everyone was pleased by the new reforms. As Lord Paget had foretold, Bishop Gardiner and Bishop Bonner opposed the religious changes. They were both sent to the Tower for preaching against them.

Edward was not satisfied simply to change the religion of the kingdom. He was determined to conduct the foreign affairs of the realm. He was faithful to the late King's wish to marry his son to Mary, Queen of Scots. Since the Scots would not abide by their treaty, he resolved to impose it by force.

Lord Paget tried to counsel restraint. "It is a dangerous policy to wage war, my lord," he said. "Our enemies are strong and the treasury is empty. It would be better to keep the peace at home and abroad until the King comes of age."

"I do not agree, my lord," he replied. "It was the wish of the late King to see his son wed to Mary Stuart and the two realms joined as one. This war will strengthen the kingdom and bring about a lasting peace."

On 11th August 1547 Edward was appointed Lieutenant and Captain General for War. He assembled an army of six thousand and took it north to Scotland with a fleet of ships. In his absence he appointed his Sir Richard Page as the Governor of the King. His brother Thomas was furious about being overlooked. I knew that Edward was a fine soldier but I waited anxiously until I received a letter from him:

"My dear Anne, I have won a great victory at the battle of Pinkie Cleugh. I have no doubt that the Scottish Regent will sue for peace and give Mary Stuart into our keeping. You shall oversee her education and ensure that she is a fit bride for King Edward. The two realms of England and Scotland will be united by their marriage and enjoy lasting peace and prosperity. Your loving husband, Somerset."

It was a worthy ambition and it was not Edward's fault that it did not succeed. He fought most bravely at the head of his troops. But he was cheated of his due. The following year, France joined the war on the side of Scotland. On 16th June 1548 several thousand Frenchmen landed at Leith. By 2nd July the garrison of Haddington was besieged. The treacherous Scots reneged on their promise to send Mary Stuart to England. They smuggled her over to France and she was betrothed to the dauphin. Edward was bitterly disappointed, for despite his success he had nothing to show for his efforts. King Edward was furious to be disappointed of his promised bride. He was so spoiled and wilful a child that nothing had ever been denied him. The privy councillors blamed Edward for the ruinous cost of the war and the failure of his foreign policy. He had been cunningly out-manoeuvred and now Scotland had made an alliance with France instead of England. They began to mutter that the Lord Protector was not as capable as he thought he was.

It was a year filled with misfortunes for us. I lost my dear stepfather Sir Richard Page. My poor mother was widowed yet again. I wept to hear the news. It was forbidden to say prayers for the dead or to light candles in their memory. Such things were now regarded as superstitious nonsense. My mother came to stay at Somerset House and took comfort in sitting in our rose garden. I found her there one afternoon when the roses had begun to fade. Her hands trembled over her prayer book, but her gaze was steady when she looked up.

"He was a good husband," she said, her gaze never leaving the wilting roses. "But after his ordeal in the Tower, he was never the same again. It wounded something in him that never healed."

I knelt beside her. The ground was cold, but I did not care. "His sufferings changed him," I said softly. "But his honour was restored, Mother. Edward saw to that."

She reached out and touched my cheek—something she had not done since I was a child. "I am grateful to you for that," she said. "He needed to die as a gentleman, not as a victim of politics. I am proud that he died in the service of the King."

I saw the flicker in her eyes—a mixture of pride and heartbreak. Behind the dignity lay the truth: she had buried too many husbands, endured too much scandal. Yet still, my mother held her head high. She straightened her shoulders, though weariness clung to them.

"There are no requiem masses for the dead now," she said. "No chantry chapels are left. But I shall still remember him in my heart. I will take the memory of our love to the grave with me."

I placed my hand over hers and we sat there as the afternoon dimmed into twilight. The rose petals fell one by one behind her, soft as snow. I watched them scatter across the path—fragments of summer returning to the soil. I found myself thinking of Sir Richard as he had been in the days of my youth. I owed my stepfather a great deal. If it had not been for his efforts then I would never have come to court, nor made such an advantageous marriage nor reached such heights of prosperity and success. As the dusk deepened around us, I let my eyes close for a moment and whispered his name into the darkness.

In September 1548 Edward and I received the tragic news of the death of Catherine Parr. She had given birth to a daughter named Mary and died six days later. She was buried in St Mary's Chapel at Sudeley Castle. I sat by the latticed window, my hand clutching the parchment that bore the seal of Sudeley. The autumn breeze stirred the tapestries upon the wall as if they too mourned her passing.

Edward stood beside me, his boots scuffing the rushes. "Poor lady," he murmured. "What a terrible misfortune for her. It is just what happened to my sister Jane!"

"She ought to have remained a royal widow," I replied. "She was too old to bear her first child."

He looked up at me, his pale brow furrowed. "What will become of the infant?" he said softly. "Perhaps we should send for her?"

"She is your brother's responsibility," I snapped. "He must do his duty as a father."

Edward looked away, shifting uncomfortably. "He will lose his wife's income now," he said at last. "His marriage did not bring him the advantages he had expected."

"Yes," I agreed. "Thomas has lost everything. Now he is poor and inconsequential again." I crushed the letter in my fist.

I thought that my brother-in-law's misfortunes would humble him. But his sense of pride and envy still gnawed away at him. He devised another clever scheme to revive his fortunes. Lord Russell warned Edward that his brother intended to marry Lady Elizabeth. Edward was determined not to let Thomas get away with another presumptuous royal marriage. He summoned him to Somerset House at once.

I watched from the window as his figure emerged beneath the archway, the shoulders braced as if marching into battle rather than a brother's rebuke. His hat sported a jaunty feather, his opulent velvet cloak proclaimed his vanity. He knew what awaited him, but pride burned undimmed in his eyes.

Edward stood beside me, his hands clasped behind his back, his jaw set firm. "He'll bluster," he murmured. "He always does."

The doors opened. Thomas entered without bowing, his gaze sweeping the chamber like a man appraising his inheritance. I saw no humility in his countenance, only the smirk of a man who believed fortune would bend to him if he willed it hard enough.

"Brother," Edward said, voice clipped, "we must speak plainly."

Thomas tilted his head. "Must we? I was told you summoned me for a family matter, not a sermon."

"You know very well why you're here," Edward said coldly. "I hear that you have designs on Lady Elizabeth."

Thomas snorted. "Designs? I visited her once or twice, as is courteous."

"You are courting her!" Edward snapped. "Do you think that because you married the King's widow that you can wed his daughter too?"

"Why should I not?" Thomas flared. "I am the best match in the kingdom. Should I not aim higher for myself than other men?"

I could feel Edward stiffen, and I stepped forward. "Higher?" I said quietly. "Is that how you speak of your late wife? As a rung to be climbed and discarded?"

Thomas's eyes flicked to me, and for a moment his bravado faltered.

Edward's voice rang out then, sharp and final. "Listen to me, Thomas. Neither of us was born to be King nor to marry Kings' daughters. So put the idea out of your head."

"And yet you live like a King while I live like a pauper," he replied sulkily. "Why shouldn't I marry a rich wife if I choose?"

I saw Edward's temper flash, the vein in his temple pulsing. "Let me make things quite clear to you," he said. "If you visit Lady Elizabeth again, I shall clap you in the Tower."

The silence was immense. Even the guards seemed to hold their breath.

Thomas laughed once, a bitter, hollow laugh, and turned on his heel. But when he reached the threshold, he looked back over his shoulder, eyes glittering with resentment. "You'll regret this day, Edward," he said. "You'll be sorry that you stood in my way."

Then he was gone, and the storm he carried with him lingered in the air like smoke. Edward looked at me, and I saw not triumph in his expression, but dread. For ambition thwarted leaves resentment in its wake. I knew that Thomas, humbled or not, would not go quietly. He was forced to give up his plans for Elizabeth, but he did not renounce his aspirations. He merely bided his time like a wolf watching for the moment the shepherd turns his back.

When Edward departed for the northern campaign in Scotland, Thomas saw his chance—not to serve the realm, but to seize it. He convinced himself that he was owed more than scraps from his brother's table. That he, not Edward Seymour, should hold the reins of power. That the boy King, so young and impressionable, might be moulded in his image if only he could be spirited away from the Protector's grasp. And so, on the bitter night of 16th January 1549, cloaked in arrogance and desperation, he tried to break into the royal apartments at Hampton Court. Naturally the plot went awry. King Edward's pet spaniel alerted the guards by barking at the intruder. Thomas shot the dog and fled into the darkness. He was arrested the next day for treason and taken to the Tower, where the cold stone walls offered no comfort and no escape.

His treachery was apparent to everyone in the kingdom except for his mother. She pleaded with Edward not to stain his hands with his brother's blood. Edward found it very difficult to take the necessary action against Thomas. But I stood firm on the matter: "My lord, I tell you that if your brother does not die, he will be your death."

He reluctantly agreed to sign the warrant. On 20th March 1549, Thomas Seymour was executed on Tower Green, beneath a sky as grey and unyielding as the stone walls that had confined him. The scaffold was draped in black, but no mourning bells rang. His death was not a tragedy—it was a reckoning. I received the news with grim satisfaction, not because I rejoiced in bloodshed, but because justice, at last, had found its mark. He had played too many games, gambled with too many lives, and fancied himself untouchable. The realm could no longer afford his ambition.

The Lieutenant of the Tower reported that he was unrepentant to the very last. No confession, no plea for mercy. He met the axe with the same arrogance that had led him there, his chin lifted, his gaze defiant. But even in death, Thomas could not resist one final act of treachery. Concealed within the soles of his velvet shoes—stitched with care, hidden from the guards—were letters addressed to Lady Mary and Lady Elizabeth. He urged them to rise against the Lord Protector, to claim their birthright, to cast down the man who had denied him his due. It was a gesture both desperate and calculated. He sought to sow discord even as the executioner sharpened his blade. Thomas was a man undone by his own vanity, and his final act only confirmed what I had always known: he would rather burn the house down than be denied a seat at the table.

I thought that we would be safe after getting rid of Thomas. That his execution would cauterize the wound he had inflicted on the realm, and restore a sense of order. But I was wrong. In truth, it made matters far worse. The privy councillors, once wary allies, now regarded Edward with suspicion. They questioned his fitness to have charge of the young King. Behind closed doors, they whispered that he had become a bloodthirsty tyrant, a man who would sacrifice even his own brother to preserve his grip on power. If he could sign his brother's death warrant with such cold resolve then what loyalty or mercy could they expect to receive from him? The ink on Thomas's warrant had barely dried before the murmurs began—low at first, then louder, like a tide rising beneath the polished floors of council chambers. Some said Edward had lost the moral compass that once guided him. Others feared he had never possessed one at all. Even the way they bowed to him changed—less reverent, more cautious, as if unsure whether they were greeting a statesman or a despot.

That same month Parliament passed the Act for the Uniformity of Religion. The Book of Common Prayer in English replaced the Latin mass throughout the realm. The only exception was the household of Lady Mary. She declared that she would not change her religion until King Edward came of age. The Spanish ambassador Francois van der Delft appeared at Somerset House seething with indignation.

"Lady Mary must be given a written exemption from this law, my lord," he demanded. "She is a member of the Spanish royal family. It is impossible that she should become a heretic. It would be scandalous!"

Edward gazed back with a steely look in his eyes. "None of the King's subjects are exempt from his laws, your Excellency," he replied. "I will put nothing in writing. However, I shall undertake not to enquire how Lady Mary chooses to worship within the privacy of her own chambers."

"Very well, my lord," he replied. "I shall inform his Majesty, the Emperor, that Lady Mary will not be troubled." He bowed and departed with a flourish of his velvet cloak.

"Lady Mary is flagrantly flouting the laws, my lord," reported Lord Paget. "She used to attend mass twice a day in her house. But ever since the prohibition she has celebrated mass three times a day and with greater ostentation."

"Naturally, everyone must conform to the religious reforms," Edward replied testily. "But we are talking about Lady Mary. She is the only person who ever defied King Henry VIII and lived to tell the tale!"

"We can hardly make an exception for her," said Lord Paget.

"And yet we cannot do otherwise," he insisted. "There are special circumstances to consider. She is the King's sister, the heir to the throne and the cousin of the emperor Charles V. If she is persecuted it will inflame public opinion and increase dissent. Moreover, it will create a serious diplomatic issue with Spain."

"This is what encourages her to disobey the law," he grumbled.

"She says that no changes should have been made to the church during her brother's minority," he said.

"Perhaps he could write her a letter enjoining her obedience," suggested Lord Paget.

"I will suggest it to his Majesty," he said. "In the meantime, I am prepared to allow her to celebrate Mass privately within her own chamber."

"The best solution would be to marry her abroad to a Catholic prince," he said.

"I am looking into the matter," he said. "The late King did her a grave injustice by not allowing her to marry. I would like to make amends by finding her a suitable match. Her cousin, Dom Luis of Portugal, is a likely candidate. He is the second son of King Manuel and is said to be an educated and cultured man. He lives in the palace of Salvaterra de Magos and enjoys considerable wealth."

"He sounds extremely suitable," said Lord Paget. "I am sure that Lady Mary would be grateful to you. In Portugal she would be free to practice her Catholic faith. Such a match would spare her brother from any further embarrassment."

The spring of 1549 brought many troubles upon the realm. In June, the simmering tensions in the kingdom burst into open flame. The people of Devon and Cornwall rose in rebellion against the Crown. The new Prayer Book, imposed with haste, was met not with reverence but with fury. The folk of the West declared that they would not have their prayers in English, nor their altars stripped bare. They insisted, with voices sharpened by grief and defiance, that they would have the mass in Latin and the images set up again in the churches. It was not merely a protest—it was a lamentation. The old rites had been woven into their lives like thread into cloth: the incense, the Latin chants, the painted saints gazing down from niches worn smooth by generations of devotion. To take these away was to unmake their world. The new liturgy, cold and unfamiliar, felt like an exile from grace.

And so, they marched—not as traitors, but as mourners. The rebellion spread like wildfire through the parishes and villages, carried by priests who refused to abandon the old ways and by farmers who saw in the new religion not salvation, but sacrilege. Church doors were barricaded. Altars were rebuilt. Processions wound through the lanes with crucifixes held high, as if to summon back the sacred from the shadows. I could not help but wonder: had we pushed too far, too fast? Had the zeal for change blinded us to the cost? The people of the West were not rebels in the usual sense. They were defenders of a vanished world, and their rebellion was a requiem.

At court, the news was met with alarm. "The Cornish rebels have objections to the reforms, my lord," said Lord Paget. "They complain that they do not speak English and so they cannot understand the new prayer book."

"They do not speak Latin either," Edward replied. "So how could they understand the words of the mass? The prayer book is new at present but they will soon become accustomed to it."

But the rebels refused to listen to reason. Edward was forced to suppressed the revolt ruthlessly with the loss of five thousand lives. The following month there was another rebellion in East Anglia against the enclosure of common land. Fences were pulled down and hedges were torn up. A yeoman farmer named Robert Kett led the rebels to a camp near Norwich. The situation was becoming dangerous.

"You must put down this uprising at once, my lord," urged Lord Paget. "It is intolerable for the King's subjects to fall away from their rightful obedience. Rebellion cannot be tolerated. It is treason against the King."

"The poor have genuine grievances," Edward said. "Many local landowners have stolen common land for their own profit. They are only taking back what is their own. I wish to show justice in this matter."

"The situation has gone too far," insisted Lord Paget. "Your leniency is only making things worse. You must use force to suppress the rebels or the violence will spread further."

The rebels succeeded in taking the city of Norwich. Edward sent the Marquis of Northampton to confront them, but he was defeated. The Scottish garrison at Haddington had to be abandoned in order to raise troops. The French took advantage of the opportunity to besiege Boulogne. Edward was forced to send the earl of Warwick to take command of the army. He was a much more effective commander. He crushed the rebels and defeated the rebellion. Robert Kett was hung from the walls of Norwich Castle. But the councillors were dissatisfied that there had been two rebellions in succession. They blamed the Lord Protector for his weak governance. Lord Paget was alarmed and came to Somerset Place to see Edward.

"I would speak with you alone, my lord," he said, his eyes shifting to mine.

"You may speak freely before the duchess," Edward replied. "She has my complete confidence."

"Very well, my lord," he said. "I shall be plain with you. You will recall that you gave me your solemn promise as we stood together in the gallery at Westminster when the old King lay dying. I would persuade the other councillors to appoint you as Lord Protector. And in return you would heed my advice before anyone else's."

"I remember it well, my lord," he replied. "What is your complaint?"

"My complaint is this," he snapped. "Your fellow councillors appointed you to be the first among them but not to rule alone without any consultation."

"They should be well contented," he said. "I have rewarded them well. They never received such titles and lands from the late King for their service. They received these honours from me. And I expect to receive their loyalty in return."

"And you have rewarded yourself most handsomely," he said. "A dukedom, lands worth three thousand pounds a year and this splendid palace of Somerset Place."

"Why should I not be compensated for my labours?" Edward replied. "I work night and day on behalf of the King and the commonwealth."

"No-one objects to your standing," he said. "But your fellow councillors are growing discontented. They have grievances against you. You need to treat them with more courtesy."

"What are these grievances, my lord?" he asked.

"You cannot be unaware," he said. "You are far too ambitious in your plans. In one stroke you seek to reform religion, wage war with Scotland and improve the lot of the poor. Did I not warn you against stretching your grasp too wide?"

"It would have been wrong to have neglected these matters," Edward insisted.

"My lord, you seem to disregard the counsel and concerns of your fellow councillors," he said. "Lord Wriothesley has never forgiven you for depriving him of the office of Lord Chancellor. Lord Parr is aggrieved because you would not consent to let him divorce his wife and marry again. Lord Warwick is offended that you have refused to grant any patronage to his family and friends. As for the others they complain that you have grown arrogant. You do not brook any contradiction and you become angered if you are gainsaid. Take my advice and listen to the opinions of your fellow councillors. Cultivate their friendship and build a bulwark of support for yourself. Then the realm will be well governed and your position will be unassailable."

Edward hesitated and bit his lip. I could see that he was affected by the appeal of his old friend. I stepped into the breach before he wavered and offered concessions.

"The Lord Protector does not need to court anyone's favour," I retorted. "He is the uncle of the king and he has his complete confidence. It seems to me that these councillors have grown too greedy and demanding. They should remember the fate of Thomas Seymour who over-reached himself!"

"It is only too clear where the Lord Protector receives his counsel," he snapped. "I see that it is quite useless to advise you for your good. You should reflect upon the fate of Thomas Cromwell who despised his fellow councillors and lorded it over them. But when he lost the favour of the King, they all turned upon him."

"Those were different times, my lord," he replied. "The old King became tyrannical in his latter years. No-one in the court was safe from his suspicions. But King Edward is wise and just despite his youth. He would never consent to cast aside his chief minister for trifling causes."

"I bid you good day, my lord," he said. He bowed and took his leave.

"The presumption of the man!" I exclaimed. "How dare he come here and make such absurd demands."

"And yet Lord Paget has been my good friend," he said, frowning. "It is true that I promised to heed his advice. Perhaps I should send a messenger after him and call him back."

"Would you appear weak in the eyes of the world?" I said. "Lord Paget has served his purpose and has been well rewarded in return. You have no more need of him. You are quite capable of governing the realm by yourself."

"You are right, my dear," he said. "I have treated the councillors most generously. They have no right to expect any more."

The rebellion had been suppressed, but the danger was not over. When Lord Warwick returned to London, he did not disband his forces. His victory over the rebels had given him a great conceit of himself. He started plotting with the other councillors to depose Edward from his position as the Lord Protector. Edward suspected that a conspiracy was brewing against him. On 5th October 1549 he issued a proclamation ordering all the King's loyal subjects to hasten to Hampton Court to defend him against a conspiracy. The following day four thousand people had arrived there. Edward made a speech telling them that Lord Warwick intended to depose him and make Lady Mary the regent. He sent Edward Wolf to secure the Tower of London. But St John had already reached the Tower before him and placed it under the control of the council.

"It is not safe here, my dear," Edward said, his brow furrowed. "I shall have to take the King to Windsor where he can be better defended. It is better for you leave here and go to stay in the country. Make your way to Beddington Manor in Surrey and place yourself under the protection of your brother, Sir Michael Stanhope."

"My place is at your side, Edward," I protested. "If any of these fine lords dare to come here, I shall remind them of your good service to them and to the realm."

"You must think of our children, my dear," he said. "If they arrest me there will be no-one to protect them except for you."

"How bad do you think it will be?" I asked.

"You should prepare yourself for the worst," he warned me. "These men are out for my blood. And if I am executed, they will seize all my property and goods."

"What should I do?" I exclaimed.

"You must try to save some of our valuables so that you are not left destitute," he replied. "Go secretly to Somerset Place and pack up some chests of goods. Then take them by barge down the Thames to the house of our chamberlain. He will conceal them from our enemies."

I wept as I left the palace leaving Edward behind. I feared that I might never see him again. As I took my barge from Hampton Court to Somerset Place the crowds jeered at me. *Jezebel! She-wolf! Vixen!* I was enraged by their insolence, but I had no choice than to disregard their taunts and depart as quickly as possible. As soon as I arrived at Somerset Place, I packed four great chests full of our finest possessions. I put the silver plate and jewels in the bottom of the chests and placed my wardrobe of gowns on top. At least our enemies should not seize my best gowns, jewels or silverware from me. My servants loaded them onto the barge and we travelled downriver to the house of Richard Whalley at Wimbledon. I ordered his servants to take the chests up to the attic and store them there.

"Please take a cup of wine with me, my lady," he said.

I sat before the fireplace in his privy chamber and sipped the wine appreciatively. "Send the servants away, Master Whalley," I said.

"Yes, my lady," he replied. He shut the door and took his place beside the fireplace.

"Is there any news from Windsor?" I asked.

"His lordship has dispersed his forces and surrendered to the council, my lady," he replied. "He had no choice in the matter. He only had the support of Archbishop Cranmer, Paget and Smith. The rest of the council have gone over to the side of Lord Warwick. He has taken the title of Lord President of the Council."

"He has always envied my husband for his greatness," I said bitterly. "What has he done with him?"

"They have taken him to the Tower, my lady," he said. "He has been deposed from his position as Lord Protector and Governor of the King."

My heart pounded at the mention of the Tower. "He does not deserve such treatment," I said, "He is a faithful servant of the realm and no traitor. I must write to Lord Paget at once and ask him to intercede with the councillors."

I hurriedly composed my letter: *"Lord Paget, What hath my lord done to any of these noble men that they should thus rage and seek the extremity against him? All this trouble has been caused by wicked men, but I am sure that God will defend my lord from his enemies as He hath always done. Anne Somerset."*

I anxiously awaited his reply. My greatest fear was that my poor Edward would be murdered by those rogues upon the council. They had long envied his rank and privileges. Now was their opportunity to take revenge. But there was little that Lord Paget could do for him. Sir Michael Stanhope was also arrested and taken to the Tower. I feared that I would lose both my husband and my brother. I decided to make a direct appeal to Lord Warwick and his wife. I dressed myself in a plain black gown. Then I opened my jewel chest and selected the finest diamond brooch in my collection. It had been a gift from King Henry VIII to Queen Catherine Howard. Master Whalley escorted me to Ely Place in Holborn. A crowd of petitioners were waiting outside to see Lord Warwick. I could not afford to wait. I forced my way to the front and spoke to the steward.

"I am the duchess of Somerset," I declared. "I am here to see Lord Warwick."

"His lordship is occupied, my lady," he replied. "I will inform him that you are here."

"Conduct me to him at once," I demanded. "You know who I am."

"Yes, my lady," he said. "Please come this way."

He brought me to his private study. As soon as he opened the door, I saw the look of surprise on Lord Warwick's face. He had not expected that I would be so bold as to seek him out in his own house. I fell upon my knees before him.

"Have pity upon me, Lord Warwick," I said. "Do not make me a widow. My husband is a good man. He has done nothing that deserves death!"

"Rise, my lady," he said. "Take a chair and then we can talk."

I got up and took my place in a chair. "I beg you to spare my husband, my lord," I said. "He was always a good friend to you."

He pursed his lips. "I can make you no promises, my lady," he replied. "There are serious charges against him. He has ruined the kingdom by his mismanagement of affairs. He has plundered the King's treasury to build houses for himself. And for lack of money we have lost the forts at Boulogne and the garrisons in Scotland. For the least of these things, he deserves death!"

"My lord, I pray you consider that he is the King's uncle," I said. "If you execute him then there will be an accounting for his blood one day."

"My lady, you should go to your house," he said. "You must leave the matter in my hands. I will speak to the council and do my best for him."

"Please give me leave to pay my regards to the countess," I said.

"As you wish, my lady," he replied.

I made my way through the narrow gallery, my shoes striking the polished tiles with quiet determination. The scent of lavender hung in the air from the rush matting, mingling with the distant waft of roasted quince from the kitchens below. Outside, the autumn sky was low and pewter-grey, casting a chill into the stone corridors.

Lady Warwick's apartments were warm and immaculately ordered, panelled in oak and adorned with Flanders tapestries depicting pastoral tableaux. My eyes fell upon the scene of a huntsman spearing a stag beneath twisted oaks, with falconers at the margin and hounds in mid-leap. In the corners were emblems of strength and vigilance: lions, eagles, and chained griffins. She rose from her cushioned chair, a small embroidery hoop slipping from her lap. Her gown was of dark russet satin trimmed in mink, her sleeves stiff with goldwork and lined in poppy-red damask silk. The string of pearls around her neck was of the finest quality.

"My dear Anne," she exclaimed, startled but composed. "What brings you here?"

I removed my gloves slowly, feeling the tremor in my fingers. "It is a matter of the utmost importance, Jane," I said, willing my voice steady. "Please allow me to speak to you in private."

She frowned—not unkindly—but nodded. "Let everyone withdraw."

The chamberlain bowed and swept the door closed behind him. Her maids cast curious glances as they departed, silk whispering against stone, the faint sound of their laughter fading down the hall.

At last, we were alone.

I stepped forward and curtsied low, the silk hem of my gown brushing the edge of her Turkey carpet. "I beg you to speak to Lord Warwick on behalf of my husband," I said, voice breaking as I reached for her hand. "He is no traitor, but an innocent man."

Jane's mouth tightened. She turned slightly away, her eyes settling on the fire where the embers glowed like watchful eyes.

She shook her head. "His lordship will not listen to me," she said, each word dropping like stone into a well. "This is a matter of state."

Her reply cut sharper than I expected. I felt the warmth drain from my face. The fire crackled behind us as if in warning, and outside the casement, a raven croaked in the dying light.

But I had not come this far to leave unheard.

"He does not deserve to die a shameful death," I said. "We have always been good friends, have we not? You would not want to see me left a poor widow, my children orphaned, my goods and properties confiscated?"

"What do you want me to do?" she asked.

"Ask Lord Warwick to spare his life," I said. "He has already deprived him of the Protectorate. Isn't that enough? My husband and I will withdraw from public affairs. We will retire to live at our country house at Syon."

She hesitated and I pressed my advantage. I drew the diamond brooch out of my sleeve and placed it in her hands. It was shaped like a Tudor rose and the gold framework was finely chased with scrolling acanthus leaves. At its centre blazed a flawless table-cut diamond set in a sunken gold bezel. It was surrounded by a circle of smaller stones which encircled it like a halo. Nestled between the petals, were four tiny rubies, so deep and bloodred they caught the firelight with an almost ominous flicker. They looked like drops of spilled wine against the snow. I saw her eyes widen at the sight of the opulent jewel.

"Take this as a token of my gratitude," I said. "I will be forever in your debt if you intercede with Lord Warwick. But you must speak to him tonight or it will be too late."

"I promise to speak to his lordship," she said. "But I can't accept such a costly present. It is much too valuable."

I rose to my feet. "Keep it to remind you of your promise," I said. I knew the power of gifts and I was confident that I had accomplished the purpose of my visit.

Jane did not fail me. She spoke to Lord Warwick that very night and persuaded him to show favour my husband. He granted me permission to visit my husband in the Tower. On Christmas Day 1549 I went to see Edward in his apartments.

"My dear Edward, how long it has been!" I said. "I feared that I would never see your face again!"

"I rejoice to see you, my dear Anne," he replied. "How are the children?"

"They are all well, but they miss you," I said. "There is no good cheer at home without you."

"I have signed a document admitting to the charges against me," he said. "I have submitted myself to the mercy of the King and the council. I am sure that the King will never consent to my death."

"No, he will not," I insisted. "I swear that I will get you out of this place. I have been to see Warwick. He is in charge of the council now and he has promised to speak on your behalf."

"You are the bravest lady in the kingdom," he said. "I still have good friends on the council. So, we must hope for the best."

"You are kept in better state than I had expected," I said. "But I have brought you some good victuals from home. You must celebrate Christmas even if we are apart from each other."

"The wardens of the Tower have done their best to make me comfortable," he said. "I shall see that they are well rewarded for their kindness if I ever get out of this place."

On 6th February 1550 Edward was released from the Tower. He was brought before the council to receive the King's pardon. Afterwards, we retired to live at our country house at Syon. In spite of all our setbacks I continued to educate my children to the highest standards. I engaged a French scholar named Nicholas Denisot to give a classical education to my daughters Anne, Margaret and Jane. They became so proficient in their studies that they composed a set of Latin verses to commemorate the death of Queen Marguerite of Navarre. The renown of their scholarship circulated around Europe. I was satisfied that they would have splendid futures. But Edward felt discouraged and restless in his exile. He longed to return to the centre of affairs.

"Lord Warwick is the absolute master of everything," he said. "He has made himself head of the council and Lord Great Chamberlain. The councillors go every day to attend him at Ely Place."

"He has usurped your rightful place," I said. "You are the King's uncle and you ought to be the one in charge of affairs."

"I still have friends and supporters," he said. "I intend to regain my position in the government one day."

At the end of March 1550, we were allowed to return to court. Warwick signed a peace treaty with France which returned Boulogne in return for four hundred thousand French crowns. It was far less than the cost of the wars which had been waged to win it. The following month, Edward was reinstated as a member of the privy council and a gentleman of the privy chamber. His restoration did more than turn heads, it opened doors. The seal was fresh on his letter of appointment when I set out for Ely Place with carefully chosen words and the faint scent of triumph stitched into every hem of my gown. Lady Warwick received me in a chamber adorned with tapestries depicting ancestral battles won—perhaps a silent reminder that political alliances were forged not by sentiment, but by necessity. Yet she smiled graciously and took my hands warmly.

"My dear Jane," I said, heart pounding with intent, "I have never forgotten your kindness to me."

She nodded, her expression soft. "I was glad to assist you and your husband in your time of need."

And so, I pressed forward. "Our families are the greatest in the realm," I said with quiet conviction. "We have both been blessed with many children. We should unite ourselves in a lasting bond of friendship. A marriage would ensure peace and amity between our husbands."

She looked at me not just as a peer, but as a mother. "It is a wonderful idea," she said. "Our oldest children are both of an age to wed."

"That was exactly what I thought," I replied, and could not suppress a smile. "Your son John can marry my daughter Anne. Their wedding shall be the greatest celebration in the kingdom."

I returned home with elation dancing through my limbs. At last, a worthy alliance, a sign to the court that the Seymours were not only restored, but ascendant. I summoned my daughter Anne at once.

She stepped into the room, still flushed from riding, her cheeks bright with health and youth. I held out my hands.

"I have good news, my dear," I said. "You are to be married to John Dudley, Viscount Lisle. It is an excellent match!"

Her brow furrowed. "But Mother, how could I possibly marry him?" she exclaimed. Her voice wavered with disbelief. "Lord Warwick is our father's worst enemy. It is because of him that he lost his position as Lord Protector and was sent to the Tower."

I steadied myself. "Lady Warwick and I intend to make a reconciliation," I said firmly. "This marriage will make them the best of friends again. Don't you want to help your dear father?"

She looked down, her jaw clenched. "I would rather marry anyone than a son of Lord Warwick."

I crossed the room and placed a hand on her shoulder. "You are the daughter of a duke," I said, measured and resolute. "Viscount Lisle is a very suitable husband. One day he will be the Earl of Warwick and you will be the Countess. He is young, noble, and well educated. And his mother has promised that she will treat you as if you were her own daughter. There is nothing for you to fear."

Still, she said nothing, only stared out the window as if hoping her future might flee with the wind.

"Your father will give you a worthy dowry," I continued. "And you shall have the most splendid wedding in living memory. It will remind everyone at court that the Seymours are the greatest family in the realm."

The silence lingered. I saw the protest still flickering in her eyes, but beneath it, the weight of duty had begun to settle.

In truth, I was relieved to make such a good match for my daughter. It would heal old wounds and elevate our name once more. I had high hopes that it would enable me to negotiate more prestigious alliances for my children. If Anne bore it with grace, as I knew she must, then her sacrifice would be our triumph. It would restore our standing in the sight of the world and enable me to build the future that I had long envisioned for our family.

The wedding took place at Sheen on 3rd June 1551. The day dawned bright and mercifully fair, as if the heavens themselves approved the union. Sheen Palace, garlanded with silks and fresh summer blooms, had been transformed into a theatre of triumph. Every shrub seemed sculpted, every herald polished. The Seymours and Dudleys—once bitter rivals—now stood side by side in costly velvet and embroidered emblems. I felt the weight of every glance, every whisper. Let them watch. Let them see what reconciliation looked like, crowned in splendour.

Anne looked radiant, her gown of silver tissue catching light with every step. She carried herself with more composure than I had dared hope, her chin lifted, her smile poised—a true daughter of ambition and grace. The celebrations were magnificent and the whole court was present for the occasion. I had insisted that everyone should attend, and so they came: lords, ladies, even bishops, each one compelled to acknowledge our family's restored grandeur. King Edward himself graced us with his presence, youthful yet regal, his smile warm as he pressed a sapphire ring worth forty pounds into my hand as a sign of his favour.

The banquet gleamed like a tapestry come to life. Platters of spiced meats and sugar sculptures towered across the tables. Goblets clinked beneath tapestries that whispered of power regained. Behind every toast, every polished phrase, I could feel the old resentments softening. Lady Warwick and I exchanged courtesies that tasted faintly of victory. After dinner, the court spilled onto the lawns where the summer air shimmered with energy. Two arbours had been built of tree boughs—woven thick with roses and sweet herb to shade the noble spectators. From there we watched the joust, the clatter of hooves and gleam of armour setting hearts racing. Young courtiers took their lances with pride; every shattered lance another cheer for peace, for prestige, for our alliance. And as the trumpets rang and banners waved, I knew: this wedding would be spoken of for years. Not merely as a union of youth, but as a masterstroke—

crafted in strategy, draped in silk, sealed with joy. There was only one fly in the ointment. Lord Warwick did not attend the celebrations. His absence made me uneasy. Perhaps he did not want to give his approval for the match.

"Why didn't Lord Warwick come to see his son's wedding?" I asked Edward. "It was a great honour for his family."

"His wife said that he was feeling unwell," he replied.

I wondered if that was really the case. Jane and I had done our best to stage a public reconciliation between our families. But it seemed that he did not want to participate. It did not bode well for the future. However, Edward was encouraged by the success of the marriage.

"We must forge other suitable alliances for our children," he said. "I would like to match Jane with King Edward. They are of age and they are cousins."

"That would be my dearest wish," I replied. "Do you really think that you can arrange it?"

"I will ask his companions and gentlemen to persuade him," he said. "I think the wedding made a great impression upon him. It is high time that he was married."

"How marvellous if there could be another Queen Jane Seymour on the throne," I said.

"Nothing would be more appropriate," he said. "There has been talk on the council of matching him with Princess Elizabeth, the eldest daughter of King Henri II of France. But to my mind, an English match would be far better than a foreign marriage."

"Certainly, it would," I said. "King Henry VIII was never fortunate in his foreign marriages."

"I intend to marry our eldest son Edward to Lady Jane Grey," he said. "She is the best catch in the kingdom. She is a Tudor lady and has a great reputation for piety and learning."

"Yes, she would make him an ideal bride," I agreed.

"Our daughter Margaret can marry Lord Strange, the son of the earl of Derby," he said. "And our son Henry can marry Lady Catherine de Vere, the daughter of the earl of Oxford. I intend to speak with Lord Oxford on the matter and agree the dowry."

"These marriages will assure our children's futures," I said. "They will make us the greatest family in the land!"

"It will cost me a pretty penny," he replied. "But I do not begrudge the cost of making noble marriages. Our grandchildren will be the highest lords and ladies in the kingdom. They will become the next generation of courtiers and participate in the affairs of the realm."

However, in August 1550 a rumour began to circulate that my husband had declared himself King. I knew the source of the rumour. Warwick was determined not to allow his rival to regain his power.

"It is outrageous," I fumed. "Warwick thinks that he can rule us all. He will find that he is badly mistaken!"

Edward sighed. "I must bow my head and endure until a better time, my dear Anne," he said.

"But what about our plans?" I said. "Nothing must prevent us from making these marriages."

"I will do what I can," he said. "But Warwick is equally ambitious for his children."

In October 1550, old Lady Seymour died. Edward was deeply grieved to lose his mother. He requested a state funeral to honour her as the grandmother of the King. But the council refused his petition.

"It is an insult," he stormed. "If I was still the Lord Protector they would not have dared to refuse me!"

In May 1551 the council deprived him of his separate table at mealtimes. They claimed that it was necessary to reduce the King's expenses.

"You may be sure that Warwick is behind it," I said. "He cannot bear to see you being honoured as you deserve."

"His behaviour is intolerable," he said. "But he will not succeed in humiliating me. I will regain my honours in spite of his opposition."

"Master Whalley is a member of the House of Commons," I said. "You were always popular with the people. He can persuade Parliament to support you. It will demand that you are restored to your rightful position as the Lord Protector."

But Master Whalley's efforts were frustrated. The earl of Rutland reported him to the council and he was sent to the Fleet prison.

"Something must be done before we are entirely ruined," said Edward. "I will speak to my friends on the council and win them back to my side."

"Start with your strongest friend," I said. "Someone who can be replied upon to support you."

"I will send for the earl of Arundel," he said. "He was always my staunchest ally. We will devise a plan to overthrow Lord Warwick and his friends Northampton and Herbert."

"Yes, you must trample on that snake or else he will trample you," I said.

But Edward failed to act quickly enough to defeat his enemy. In the meantime, Lord Warwick took steps to secure his position and reward his friends. On 11th October 1550 he was created duke of Northumberland at a grand ceremony at Hampton Court palace. Dorset became duke of Suffolk, Wiltshire became Marquis of Winchester and Herbert became earl of Pembroke.

Five days later, Edward came to court to attend a council meeting. He was arrested and taken to the Tower. I knew that this time it would be useless to approach the duke of Northumberland and plead for mercy. I decided that I would appeal to the King to save his uncle. But the wily duke forestalled my intentions. This time he was taking no chances. He was not prepared to let me seek justice from the King.

CHAPTER 10

The Tower of London (1551-1553)

"Some have fallen from being princes to being prisoners in this place"

(Queen Elizabeth I, 1558).

I was sitting in my privy chamber when they came to Somerset Place to arrest me. I was working intently at my writing desk which was covered in green velvet and embroidered with Venice gold. The parchment before me bore my petition to the King on behalf of his uncle. It was an earnest appeal for justice, carefully framed and worded. Sunlight slanted across the chamber, catching the gold filigree of my seal and the gilded frame of my husband's miniature which lay beside the inkwell. The door opened not with ceremony, but with purpose, and the lords of Suffolk, Winchester, and Pembroke entered with slow, deliberate steps. They did not bow. Suffolk gazed at me with a look of pity in his eyes. He wore black damask embroidered with gold thread, his heavy chain of office gleaming around his shoulders. Pembroke's face was carved from granite, and Winchester did not look at me at all.

"My lady, we have our orders," Suffolk said quietly. "I regret to inform you that you must accompany us to the Tower. A barge is waiting to conduct you there."

The words struck me with the force of a cannon volley. I rose from my carved oaken chair and confronted them. "Why have I been arrested?" I demanded. My voice was clear, but beneath it ran ice.

"You are charged with conspiring with your husband against the King's counsellors," he replied, placing his hand upon the pommel of his sword.

I held my head up high and stood my ground. "I know nothing of any conspiracy," I insisted. "I am innocent and so is my husband." Winchester flinched and Pembroke's eyes flickered toward the door where the guards were waiting.

"You are to be detained until the investigation has been concluded," Suffolk said. He bowed, but it was hollow. I knew what lay behind my arrest. That snake Northumberland was afraid that I would make an appeal to the King. He did not want anything to interfere with his plot. I glanced down at my unfinished petition with regret. I could only pray that Edward's friends and supporters would come to his assistance. I picked up the miniature of my husband and my prayer book from the desk. They would accompany me into my captivity.

The sky was a pale pewter when they led me to the waiting barge. Already the light was fading. The lords of the council did not want to parade me before the eyes of the curious in broad daylight. I stepped on board and my captors followed me. A guard stationed himself at either side, their cloaks sodden at the hem. Not a word passed between us. The Thames was swollen, its surface bruised by the wind. Barges moved sluggishly alongside us—merchants and messengers, oblivious to the silent prisoner being ferried downriver. I gazed at the grey ribbon of water and thought of how often it had borne queens and traitors alike. Once, I had travelled these waters to attend the coronation feast. Now, I was journeying into shadow.

A strong wind blew across the water making me shiver. I wished that I had had the foresight to bring a heavy woollen mantle with me. My gown of claret damask was unsuited to the chill and I clutched my prayer book tightly to my chest. I refused a blanket when it was offered. I was the duchess of Somerset and I would not be swaddled like a beggar woman. We passed beneath London Bridge, its arches narrow and snarling, the houses jutting out like crooked teeth overhead. I could hear fishwives calling out their wares beyond the stone embankment, their cries shrill in the rising mist. Somewhere a bell tolled, sonorous and slow. The Tower appeared gradually, vast and solemn as a tomb. Its walls reared up from the water, pale and forbidding. Grey clouds hung low over its ramparts, and the air smelt of river silt and apprehension. The barge drew up to the landing place and there was a sharp slap of water against the stone steps.

Sir Arthur Darcy, the Lieutenant of the Tower was waiting to receive me at the Water Gate. He stood with his cloak pressed close against the wind, a trim figure in dark wool lined with fox fur. The livery of the Tower gleamed upon his breast—a golden key on a field of black—but his expression was impassive. He bowed, stiffly. "My Lady Somerset," he said. "You must accompany me."

I stepped onto the wet stone, lifting my skirts to keep the embroidered hem from the water. The dress that I wore was much too fine for a prison but I did not regret it. Let them see I was no traitor's wife—I was the duchess of Somerset, the King's aunt and the first lady of the realm.

"Why have I been brought here?" I asked. "I have done nothing that deserves imprisonment. And neither has my husband."

"You have both been accused of conspiring against Lord Warwick, my lady," he replied. "The charge against you is treason."

His words struck colder than the wind. The charge was absurd. Whatever Edward had done, it could never be called treason. I looked ahead to the gatehouse which was defended by an iron portcullis. The Tower Guards flanked the archway, their hands tight on their halberds, their faces impassive. I drew my shoulders back, refusing to let them see me look cowed.

"It is a nonsensical tale," I insisted. "There has been no conspiracy. There is no truth in this charge."

He sighed. "I have received an order from the council to detain you, my lady," he said. "But do not fear. You shall not suffer any ill treatment. You shall be provided for in accordance with a lady of your rank. You will be permitted to have your own cook to prepare your meals and two gentlewomen to attend you."

He escorted me through the gatehouse and along a passageway to my lodgings. The chambers were modest, but not harsh. The stone walls were hung with faded tapestries. A high bed stood draped in blue velvet, its posts carved with Tudor roses and aged finials. A chair had been placed by the window which allowed me to look out over the Thames to the streets and houses of the city of the London which lay beyond it. I touched the linen that lay at the foot of the bed and found that it was clean.

"I was brought here without any of my belongings, Sir Arthur," I said. "Pray allow me to send for some of my goods and clothes."

"You may have whatever you require, my lady," he replied.

I sent for those things that would be practical for my life in the Tower: A thick woollen mantle, a black gown faced with lynx fur, a plain black velvet kirtle, three pairs of knitted hose and sleeves and some newly-made smocks. I also requested a set of plate, my embroidery box and some books to read in my confinement. The following week my mother came to join me in the Tower. It was a noble gesture for such an elderly woman.

"I came as soon as I heard the news," she said. "My poor child, you have suffered such sad trials. There is little that I can do for you, but at least you shall not lack for company."

"I am so glad to see you mother," I said. I am as lonely as a pelican in the desert."

"I have never forgotten your goodness in saving my dear husband from the Tower," she said. "And Edward promoted his career by appointing him to King Edward's household. I am deeply in your debt, my child."

"It was the least that I could do for Sir Richard," I said. "He was a good and worthy man."

"It is outrageous that an innocent lady should be imprisoned in the Tower," she said indignantly. "Northumberland's quarrel was with your husband. It is ignoble of him to revenge himself on you. If the King were of age, he would not permit such villainy. The day will come when Northumberland will be held to account for his crimes."

"There is no-one who has the power to hold him to account," I said. "Now that Edward is in the Tower, the rest of the lords are too fearful to cross Northumberland."

"When the young King gains his majority there will be an accounting," she said. "He will take his revenge upon him for the downfall of his uncle."

"I do not think so," I said. "He is now fourteen years old, but he did not say a word on his behalf."

"Northumberland gained his position by treachery," she insisted. "He does not have the love of the people like your husband did. He will reap what he has sown."

"I fear that he has already destroyed everyone who might have stood in his way," I said. "He has gained complete control of the Council and the young King. His power is absolute."

"He has usurped the rightful place of your husband," she said. "But you must not lose hope. Remember that you are still the duchess of Somerset."

"I shall be his next victim, mother," I said. "You must take care of my children when I am gone."

"He would not dare to execute a lady," she protested.

"He regards me as just as great an enemy as my husband," I said. "He will not be satisfied until he has destroyed our whole house."

"But you are innocent," she said. "There has been no trial. He has no case against you."

"When has that ever mattered?" I asked. "Queen Anne Boleyn and Queen Catherine Howard were both executed. And so was Lady Margaret Pole."

"That was in the reign of the old King," she said. "Such things cannot happen now. Beside you are King Edward's aunt. Northumberland would not dare to touch so high a lady as yourself."

"Perhaps I should not have encouraged Edward to pursue such a dangerous path," I said. "He was not ruthless enough to prevail against the wolves of the court. I fear that my ambition has cost me what I hold most dear - my husband and my children."

"You only did what was right, my dear," she said. "It was your duty to stand at his side like a loyal wife and promote the interests of your family."

My mother's words comforted me. I held onto the hope that the King would send a pardon to save his uncle. But the only mercy he received was death by the axe instead of by hanging. On 22nd January 1552 Sir Arthur Darcy, the Lieutenant of the Tower, brought me the news of his execution.

"Your husband died boldly, my lady," he said. "He was taken by the first stroke of the axe."

"What were his last words, Sir Arthur?" I asked.

"He avowed that he had never offended against the King by word or deed and he had always been faithful and true to the realm."

"He was a loyal servant of the King," I said. "He did not deserve to die such a shameful death! I used to fear that he would perish on the battlefields of Scotland or France. But I had a thousand times rather that he had died in battle than suffer execution on Tower Hill."

Sir Arthur sighed and looked down at the ground. He did not dare to affirm that Edward had died unjustly.

"And shall I follow my husband to the scaffold, Sir Arthur?" I asked.

"I have received no such orders, my lady," he replied.

"Then am I free to leave the Tower and return home?" I said.

"I regret to say that you must remain here, my lady," he said. "But I promise that you shall have an honourable captivity."

"What will happen to my children?" I asked. "They are still young and they need a mother's care."

"You need not fear for them, my lady," he said. "They have become the wards of the King. Lord Paulet has been appointed to take charge of the boys and your sister-in-law, Lady Cromwell, will care for the girls."

The news came as a double blow. I put on black mourning clothes as a tribute to my husband. I did not even have the solace of holding a splendid funeral for him. He was buried without ceremony in the chapel of St Peter ad Vincula. My sole consolation was that my husband had not been condemned as a traitor. Consequently, his titles and properties were not forfeit to the crown. But Northumberland was determined to ruin us entirely. He passed a bill through Parliament confiscating his honours and his goods. His entire life's work of advancement was lost and we were left destitute. I had dreamed of a future in which my children were married into the noblest families of the realm. But calamity followed calamity. The earl of Oxford repudiated the marriage agreement between his daughter and my son Henry. Since we were poor and disgraced, I had no hope of making good marriages for my children. My mother did her best to console me in my misery.

"Edward was a good man," she said. "He did nothing that deserved death. He was a true servant of the state and you can take pride in his memory."

"Yes, mother," I said. "But it is a cold consolation to me. My husband is dead and his property has been taken. Now I am only a poor widow with nothing to give to my children."

"You must not give in to despair," my dear daughter, she said. "Remember that you have children who still need you."

"I am heartbroken by the downfall of our house," I said. "Edward wanted to leave our children an honourable heritage. But now everything that he worked for has been lost. I have failed to uphold my family. I feel that I have betrayed my noble ancestors, mother."

"The great houses of the realm are like mighty oaks," she said. "They weather the storms and they survive to flourish again."

"Edward and I had planned to marry our children to the noblest families in the realm," I said. "But now the Seymour family has been disgraced. I fear that my sons will marry unworthy women and my daughters will never marry at all."

"It is no fault of yours, my dear," she said. "I was proud to see you wearing the coronet of a duchess on the day of King Edward's coronation. But hardly any great family has managed to maintain its fortunes under the Tudors. The noble houses of Stafford, Howard, Pole, Courtenay and Neville have all fallen under royal displeasure and been humbled into the dust."

The following month four of Edward's associates were executed. Among them was my dear half-brother Sir Michael Stanhope. He was an innocent man, but he still fell victim to Northumberland's vengeance. However, Northumberland did not proceed any further against me. He was content to leave me in the Tower. The winter of 1552 was particularly cold. I tried to maintain my spirits, but the fire smoked and the damp chill of the stones bit into my bones. I threw my book on the floor in a temper. My mother regarded me disapprovingly. This was not how she had raised me to conduct myself. She remained undaunted by the hardships of the Tower.

"Whatever is the matter, Anne?" she asked.

"This place is intolerable," I grumbled. "The light is too poor to allow me to read or sew in comfort and we are kept so confined that we never hear any news. I have no idea what is happening in the realm."

"As an oak tree remains unshaken by storms so a noble woman rises above the adversities of life," she reminded me. "If you cannot read or sew, then you may say your prayers."

"For the soul of my husband?" I replied.

"And for justice," she said. "You are an innocent lady and the whole world knows it. One day, King Edward will learn of your plight and have you set free."

But in the end, it was not King Edward who liberated me from my captivity. In the spring of 1553, his health began to decline. At the end of May, Sir Arthur Darcy invited my mother and I to dine at his table. I suspected that he had something of great import to tell me.

"The duke of Northumberland has married his son Lord Guildford Dudley to Lady Jane Grey, my lady," he said. "And his daughter, Lady Catherine Dudley, has married Lord Henry Hastings."

I was filled with anger and bitterness. It should have been my own dear children who made these splendid matches. I had raised them with the greatest care and attention for their education. But now they were poor wards living upon charity. Lord Northumberland had stolen their futures from them. It was deeply unfair. Events followed on quickly from this point. On the afternoon of 10th July 1553, I heard a fanfare of trumpets and I wondered what it portended. But I could not find out for several days. Sir Arthur Darcy, the Lieutenant of the Tower, made a brief visit to my chamber.

"My lady, I regret to inform you that his Majesty King Edward has died," he said.

"May God have mercy upon his soul," I exclaimed. "How did he die? He was only fifteen years old!"

"His Majesty suffered from a most painful malady," he said. "He had the care of the best doctors in the kingdom, but nothing could be done to save him."

"I am most grieved to hear it," I said. "That is the worst news I have heard since the death of my poor husband."

"The council have proclaimed Lady Jane Grey as the rightful Queen, my lady," he said. "She is here in the Tower awaiting her coronation."

I was shocked into silence at his words. Lady Mary was the lawful successor. I wondered what had happened to her. But I hesitated to say anything which might be regarded as treason. Sir Arthur understood my dilemma and forestalled my questions.

"Lady Mary has raised an army in Norfolk to support her claim to the throne," he said. "The duke of Northumberland has set out with an army from London to capture her. Everyone fears there will be civil war in the realm. You are safer in here, my lady."

"God save us all!" I quavered. Despite his comforting words, I knew that I was in great danger. If the crown was in peril, then it was common practice to execute all the notables that were held in the Tower.

"Amen to that, my lady," he replied and took his leave.

I stumbled over to a chair and sat down in it. My head was reeling in terror and confusion. But gradually I became calmer and was able to think. I perceived that with King Edward's decline, the duke of Northumberland had foreseen that he would lose his grip on power. The accession of Queen Mary would certainly have resulted in his downfall. So, he had plotted a means by which he would gain control of the crown for his own house and posterity. He had persuaded the council to proclaim his daughter-in-law as the Queen of England.

My mother was most indignant. "Lady Jane Grey is only the niece of King Henry VIII," she declared in ringing tones. "She has no right to the throne. It is the Lady Mary who is the true and lawful successor!"

"That villain Northumberland has practiced upon her," I said. "He has forced her into it. He thinks that he can get his son Guildford crowned as the next king."

"What are the nobility doing?" she asked. "Will they stand by and see the Lady Mary deprived of her right?"

"They are all afraid of Northumberland," I said. "They saw what he did to my husband. And he was a duke and the uncle of the King."

"They are dastards and cowards if they do not honour their allegiance to the true sovereign," she said. "Will they see a puppet queen set up over them?"

"There is no knowing what may happen, mother," I said. "I fear that Northumberland not only intends to usurp the crown but to put his rivals out of the way." I wondered if he would send King Henry's two daughters to the Tower or have them executed.

On 19th July 1553, I heard the sound of trumpets blowing and a great burst of cannon fire that made my windows tremble in their casements. The air itself seemed to shudder, as if the realm were exhaling after nine days of breathless uncertainty. I rose from my chair, heart quickening, unsure whether the noise heralded triumph or disaster. Shortly afterwards, Sir Arthur Darcy, the Lieutenant of the Tower, burst into my chambers without so much as a knock—his face flushed, his breath short, his eyes alight with urgency.

"There is great news, my lady!" he cried, barely able to contain himself. "The council has proclaimed Lady Mary as the rightful Queen of England. The Duke of Suffolk, Henry Grey, took down his daughter's canopy of state with his own hands. She was queen for only nine days—and those have been most turbulent ones!"

I stood in silence, absorbing the weight of his words. The coup had collapsed. Lady Jane Grey had been cast aside like a pawn sacrificed in a losing game. Her father's ambition had crumbled into shame, and the council, sensing the wind's turn, had scrambled to align themselves with the true heir. Lady Mary Tudor had prevailed against the usurpers of the crown.

"God be praised!" I said. "But what has happened to the duke of Northumberland? Is there still any danger of war?"

"I cannot say, my lady," he replied. "But the citizens of London are rejoicing at the news. All the church bells are ringing and bonfires have been lit in every street. The people have set up tables to drink wine and feast with their neighbours. You may see the glow of the fires from the window of your chamber!"

The celebrations lasted all night long. My mother was greatly heartened by the demonstration. "The citizens of London are good and loyal subjects," she declared. "Would that the lords of the council had shown the same devotion to the true Queen! They must stand in fear of being condemned as traitors to the crown!"

"They richly deserve it," I said. "But I would be well satisfied if only that vile dog Northumberland is executed!"

On 25th July 1553 I heard the noise of a hostile crowd shouting the words *"Traitor and heretic."* I waited impatiently to hear the explanation. But it was not until the following day that Sir Arthur found the time to visit me.

"Pardon me, my lady," he said. "I have had much ado to find lodgings for so many noble prisoners."

"Has Northumberland been arrested?" I asked eagerly.

"Yes, my lady," he replied. "He surrendered five days ago in Cambridge. Thankfully, there was no bloodshed and the armies have now dispersed to their homes. He is imprisoned here with his five sons, his brother Sir Andrew Dudley and the Marquis of Northampton. They will all be put on trial for attempting to usurp the crown. It is the end of the Dudley regime."

"May God be praised," I exclaimed. "He has delivered the realm from the power of a scoundrel. I only wish that I had been a witness to his shame and dishonour yesterday."

"The crowd were most enraged with him," he said. "They hooted at him and threw stones. I believe that they would have torn him in pieces if they had been given the chance."

"I would have liked to spit in his eye!" I said. "What has happened to Lady Jane Grey?"

"Naturally she has renounced all her honours," he said. "She said that she was glad to resign her royal dignity for she knew that the right belonged to Queen Mary, and the part she had played had been prepared for her without her knowledge. She has been moved from the Queen's apartments and is lodged in the house of a warder on Tower Green with her husband Guildford and the wife of the duke of Northumberland."

So, my former friend Jane Dudley, the duchess of Northumberland was here too. I prayed that she would suffer the same misery and humiliation that I had endured at the hands of her wicked husband.

"Shall I be released now, Sir Arthur?" I asked.

"I pray that you will be patient, my lady," he replied. "Queen Mary is on her way to London and she will come straight to the Tower. She is the one who has the rightful authority to liberate all the political prisoners who have been kept here. When she arrives, you can greet her at the gate and request justice from her. I am sure that she will consent to grant you a royal pardon."

"Who are the other prisoners?" I asked.

"There is the old duke of Norfolk who was imprisoned for treason," he said. "There is Bishop Gardiner who was imprisoned for his Catholic faith. And there is Edward Courtenay who was imprisoned for his Plantagenet blood. The poor young man has been kept here since his childhood. But the Queen is a merciful lady and I have no doubt that she will requite you all."

CHAPTER 11

Restoration (1553)

"It is credibly reported that the duke of Norfolke, Courteney, the bushope of Winchester, and my lady Somerset, mette the queenes grace at the Towere gate, and theare they kneelinge downe saluted her grace, and she came unto them and kissed them and sayd, 'Theis are my prisoners.'"

(The anonymous "resident in the Tower of London", *The chronicle of Queen Jane, and of two years of Queen Mary, and especially of the rebellion of Sir Thomas Wyatt,* recorded on 3 August 1553).

The morning of 10th August 1553 was filled with expectancy as I stood at the gate of the fortress. A great crowd of onlookers had gathered there, craning for a glimpse of the anticipated spectacle. The other prisoners were gathered at my side, their faces drawn, their garments worn but hastily mended for this day. I was dressed in my best gown of sapphire velvet embroidered in silver thread, the bodice square-cut to display the fine Flemish lace at my throat. On my head I wore a French hood, adorned with pearls that had once belonged to my mother.

The sun broke through the clouds as the cry rang out: *"God save the Queen! Long live the Queen!"*

A white mare appeared at the head of the procession, its hooves precise, its mane flowing like silk against the royal standard behind. Queen Mary rode as confidently as if she had been born to the saddle. Her gown of purple velvet shimmered, each embroidered gold thread catching the sunlight like fire. Her face was stern, serene and sovereign. All the prisoners fell to their knees as one and raised up their hands to plead for mercy.

"These are my prisoners!" Queen Mary proclaimed, her voice clear as a church bell. "And I decree that you are prisoners no more. You shall attend my court with honour!"

"God save the Queen!" we cried.

She dismounted, the mare snorting softly as a groom came forward to hold its reins. Her steps were measured but quick, her skirts swept with purpose. And then—she stood before me.

She took my hand, warm and firm, and raised me gently. "My dear Anne," she said, brushing my cheek with her lips. "How much you have suffered at the hands of that varlet! But now all your sufferings are over."

"God bless Your Grace!" I said, voice thick with emotion.

I bowed my head in gratitude. At last, my long ordeal was over. Now I could return to court and take my rightful place as the duchess of Somerset. I was certain that Queen Mary would grant me justice and restore the goods and properties that had been stolen from me.

On 22nd August 1553 my hateful enemy, the duke of Northumberland, was executed as a traitor to the realm.

He had converted to Catholicism in an attempt to save his life, but to no avail. He was too dangerous a man to be allowed to live. I rejoiced to hear of the downfall of my enemy. Northumberland was responsible for the deaths of my husband and my brother. He had imprisoned me and stolen my property and goods. He had ruined the fortunes of my entire family. Now the tables were turned on him. All his estates, properties and money were forfeit to the state. Consequently, Somerset House was given to Lady Elizabeth instead of being returned to me.

But Queen Mary granted me an annuity of seven hundred pounds a year and the use of the royal manor of Hanworth during my lifetime so that I could live in comfort for the rest of my days. After Northumberland's execution, I was offered the pick of his household goods. This was my compensation for the seizure of my property. I managed to reclaim my valuable plate, tapestries and linen from the household of his widow Jane. But many of my best things had gone missing. They had probably been stolen by the servants after Northumberland's arrest.

Queen Mary graciously restored my standing as the duchess of Somerset. I became the highest-ranking lady after the royal Tudor ladies Lady Elizabeth Tudor, Lady Anne of Cleves, Lady Lennox and Lady Suffolk. I had once been the first lady of the realm. Now I was only the sixth highest lady in the land. I returned to court, but it was not the same as before. I was still the duchess of Somerset but now I was a widow who had lost her power and influence. Nobody clamoured to attend me or request favours from me.

Worse still, no noble families were eager to marry my sons and daughters. I had no place in the royal circle and my lands and properties had been scattered to the winds. My three eldest daughter attended court with me, but I could not afford to provide them with rich dowries. I felt that I had let them down. I pinned all my hopes on my eldest son Ned Seymour. Queen Mary had agreed to restore him in blood since my poor husband was clearly no traitor. But she did not allow him to inherit his father's titles as I had hoped. She had saved me from penury but I was not one of her favourite courtiers. Edward and I had been ardent reformers and the Queen blamed us for having led her brother and the nation astray. She preferred to promote faithful Catholic houses rather than a prominent Protestant family like the Seymours. Nonetheless I hoped that my son would make a worthy alliance and retrieve the family fortunes one day.

On 1st October 1553, I was invited to attend the coronation of Queen Mary at Westminster Abbey. I had a fine new gown of crimson silk bordered with crimson velvet made for the occasion. The last time I had attended a coronation it had been in the company of my dear husband. This time I was accompanied by my son Ned. Many fortunes were changed after the accession of Queen Mary. The Dudley family and their adherents were cast down in disgrace. I would not have cared a jot were it not for my poor daughter Jane. Her husband John Dudley was imprisoned with the rest of his brothers in the Tower. She expected that soon he would be executed and she would be left a poor widow.

It would have been justice if all the rogues and scoundrels on the privy council had been imprisoned alongside

Northumberland. They had conspired against my husband and against Lady Mary. But the Queen was persuaded to be merciful to them. If all the experienced ministers in the realm were removed, then there would be no-one left to govern the Commonwealth. So, they were pardoned for their treason.

Queen Mary was committed to restoring the Catholic faith to the realm. She triumphantly celebrated mass in the Chapel Royal and all the courtiers were expected to attend. They councillors hastened to demonstrate their loyalty to the new regime by forsaking their Protestant convictions and joining the Queen every day at mass in the Chapel Royal. Everyone else in the court did the same. I regretted having to forsake the principles of my faith, but I was not prepared to take the extreme step of seeking exile abroad in Geneva. I needed to remain at court and rebuild the fortunes of my family. But in return I would have to conform to her wishes as the Queen and accept the restoration of the Catholic church.

However, there was one person who tried to defy the Queen. Her sister Elizabeth thought that her royal status gave her the freedom to worship according to her conscience. She was unwilling to change her faith merely to please her sister. She protested that she had been brought up as a Protestant. But the Queen would not allow any exceptions to be made. The foolish girl tried to insist upon her right to worship as she pleased. The issue became a contest of wills between them.

The Presence Chamber of Greenwich Palace was already crowded with courtiers when I entered. The sunlight gleamed upon the gold and silver threads in the tapestries that celebrated King Henry's victories and Queen Mary's lineage. A fanfare of trumpets pierced the morning quiet, reverberating through the stone corridors of the palace like a summons to judgment. Velvet-clad courtiers emerged from antechambers like chess pieces stirred to life and assembled into the line of procession to attend mass in the royal chapel.

Queen Mary took her place at the head of the procession. She was resplendent in a gown of crimson velvet, her mantle edged with ermine. Behind her, as protocol demanded, walked her sister, Lady Elizabeth, carrying the royal train with measured grace. I had seen her perform the role before, but never with this tightness to her jaw, this fire behind her lashes. I stood in line behind Lady Frances Grey, the widow of Lord Suffolk. Her nod to me was clipped, her eyes already fixed upon Elizabeth. Even she could feel it—the air bristled with something unsaid, as if mass today would be no ordinary ritual. The great procession was complete with bishops in embroidered copes, the lords of the council and the rest of the court in their proper order.

The procession moved, a slow river of devotion and decorum winding through the palace toward the Chapel Royal. Sunlight streamed through high mullioned windows, gilding the Queen's profile as she ascended the dais. She settled into her chair of estate under the royal canopy and banners stitched with the symbols of the crown and Tudor rose. Lady Elizabeth followed, and took her seat beside her sister. I sat behind them with the other ladies, watching every flicker of expression.

The Chapel Royal had been transformed into Queen Mary's vision of restored Catholic majesty. What had once been stripped bare under her brother's reformist reign now gleamed with ceremonial splendour. The High Altar, once vacant save for a Bible and two modest candlesticks, now stood dressed in sumptuous cloth of gold, shimmering with threads worked in pomegranates and vines. Six tall wax candles on tall gold candlesticks flanked its sides, their flames dancing with each whispered prayer. A newly installed crucifix of carved ivory and ebony stood proudly at the centre. The figure of Christ was rendered with exquisite pathos the limbs curved delicately and the face tilted in sorrow. Behind the altar, embroidered reredos panels depicted Saint George with his dragon and Saint Catherine with her wheel in vibrant colours. Silver censers swung gently from their chains, trailing smoke like sacred ribbons through the nave. The Queen's reform was no subtle gesture—it was a declaration. Every ornament reclaimed and restored stood as a rejection of Edward's austere doctrine, a return to ceremony, symbolism, and awe.

Bishop Gardiner began the prayers. The Latin words draped themselves over us like shrouds. The courtiers lowered their heads. I bowed mine. But Lady Elizabeth remained sitting upright. Then, as the Kyrie echoed from the choir loft, she stirred. "I am unwell," she said, her voice threading through the liturgy. "I must leave."

Heads turned, sharp as drawn blades. Her declaration had rung louder than a confession. Queen Mary did not move, but I saw the way her eyes locked onto her sister with thunderous ire. No words passed her lips, but the weight of her gaze was crushing.

Lady Elizabeth stood up. Her shoulders were squared and her stride was too slow and deliberate for one claiming to be faint from illness. As she turned to leave, her eyes met mine briefly in a flash of defiance. I saw then that it was not sickness, but strategy.

"She defies her," whispered Lady Frances beside me, her face pinched with outrage.

The Queen remained seated, her fury contained beneath a mask of royal stillness. But her silence burned. This was no mere breach of etiquette, it was rebellion staged before the altar. As Elizabeth's figure disappeared behind the chapel doors, I felt the hush descend, not reverent but ripe with tension. The mass continued, hollow now, each holy word an echo beneath the shadow of what had transpired.

Afterwards, Queen retired to her privy chamber accompanied by her ladies. As I entered, the scent of incense struck me first, rich with myrrh and frankincense, clinging to the crimson velvet drapes that cloaked the walls like robes of a cardinal. Every corner whispered of Rome, every ornament nodded toward Spain. The Marian emblems embroidered in gold—the crowned M, the Immaculate Heart—shimmered in candlelight, lending the room a devotional hush. Beside the fireplace stood the prayer niche, its sculpted Madonna and Child almost alive in the flicker of taper flames. Upon the mantlepiece gleamed large silver candelabra gleamed nearby, their twisted vines and cherubic details unmistakably Spanish – undoubtedly gifts from the Emperor Charles V of Spain. Even the Virgin of Guadalupe stared down from the tapestry behind the

Queen's chair, her radiant presence proclaiming allegiance not only to Heaven, but to Castile.

Queen Mary took her place on her chair of estate and stared into the flames. Her face was set and her eyes were filled with fury. Her ladies stood around her, their eyes downcast and unwilling to speak. Even Lady Frances Grey, usually as unyielding as stone, shifted uncomfortably beneath the weight of the Queen's silence.

"She shamed me," Mary said at last, her voice not raised—but razor-edged. "Before God, and before my court."

No one dared respond. To contradict her now would be perilous. But I felt the need to speak on her behalf. "Your Majesty," I said quietly, "she may be ill-prepared for such public devotion."

Queen Mary turned her gaze to me, and I felt the full force of her anger. "Ill-prepared is not illness," she replied, voice laden with ice. "She has been raised a princess. She knows precisely what she does."

She rose then, slow and deliberate, as though her own fury needed formal procession. Her hand brushed the back of her chair, but it was her eyes—dark, glinting with storm—that held the court captive.

"She will not disgrace me again." Those words sealed the mood like wax pressed with a signet. Lady Elizabeth's protest in the chapel had wounded not just protocol, but sovereignty.

The chamber door opened, not hurriedly but with intent. Don Simón Renard, the Spanish ambassador, entered with the grace of one who carried more than mere diplomacy. His rich attire rustled softly as he approached the Queen, bowing low before bending toward her ear. His whisper was inaudible to most, but in the hush of that chamber, certain phrases slithered through like smoke.

"Your sister is a heretic at heart," he murmured in Spanish-accented English, his tone smooth and unwavering. "She defies Your Majesty with her rejection of the mass. She seeks to become the Protestant figurehead of the realm, your rival in faith, in loyalty, and in throne."

Queen Mary did not respond at once, but I watched her jaw tighten, her hand clenching the quill so fiercely the feather trembled. Her eyes remained fixed forward, yet the lines at her brow deepened with every word.

Simon Renard's gaze drifted briefly toward me and the others, then back to the Queen. "You must not permit her pretence of illness to mask sedition. England watches. So does Spain."

At last, Queen Mary rose, slowly, but with terrible finality. "She shall attend mass tomorrow," she said, her voice low, almost a growl. "And she shall kneel."

Lady Frances drew a quiet breath, clearly unsettled. I could feel the atmosphere shift—where Elizabeth's protest had provoked tension, Renard's words had ignited resolve.

Queen Mary's eyes swept the chamber. "If she refuses again," she said, "she shall answer not only to her Queen, but to Rome."

Then she swept from the privy chamber, her words still burning in our ears. Lady France stiffened beside me, her eyes flicking to mine. We both knew the words were not mere outrage—they were a declaration of intent. In that chamber of relics and alliances, Elizabeth had ceased to be just a sister. She had become a threat.

The moment she departed, I gathered my skirts and made for Lady Elizabeth's apartments with a speed bordering on impropriety. Lady Frances called after me, but I did not stop. This was no time for courtly restraint. Lady Elizabeth's lodgings lay in the western wing, swathed in shadow and silence. Her ladies stood like sentinels outside the door, but they did not bar my entrance. They knew from the expression on my face that I had come to bring a warning. I found her seated in a carved armchair beside the fireplace, one hand resting against her cheek, the other curled around a closed book. She looked up as I entered, brows lifted—not in surprise, but in readiness.

"So, Lady Somerset," she said. "Has Her Majesty decided to send me to the Tower?"

"Not yet, your Grace," I replied. "But you must conform. You must attend mass tomorrow and you must kneel."

She let out a slow breath and leaned back, her gaze drifting to the fire. "Has the Queen said so?"

"Yes, your Grace," I said, stepping forward. "Simon Renard was in the Queen's chamber. He called you a heretic. He claims you mean to lead the Protestant faction at court and conspire against her."

The revelation struck her to the core. I saw it by the tightening at the corner of her mouth and the flicker in her eyes. She set the book aside deliberately.

"And what does my sister believe?" she asked.

"She believes him, your Grace," I said. "She thinks your illness was a performance. That you slighted her before the court and before God."

Lady Elizabeth stood, brushing her gown smooth. Her expression shifted into a calculating look. She walked to the window and stared out into the dim courtyard.

"I will attend mass tomorrow," she said quietly. "I will kneel and conform."

The words did not come easily to her. But they were spoken. I knew that her obedience would be no true submission. It would be survival, dressed in reverence.

I nodded. "You know that I am as ardent a Protestant as yourself, your Grace," I said. "But the Queen must be obeyed. Let them see you pious. Let them believe you obedient. Then you will live long enough to write your own prayer."

She turned then, met my gaze full on. "I will let them see what they want," she said. "But in my heart, I will always remain true to my own beliefs."

"Remember what I have done for you, your Grace," I said.

"I will not forget, Lady Somerset," she promised.

The following morning, Queen Mary summoned Lady Elizabeth to her presence. The Queen's fury had stewed overnight, ripening into something cold and ceremonial. Lady Elizabeth entered the privy chamber looking poised but pale. The room was redolent with Spanish ceremony and piety. Crimson velvet cloaked the walls, embroidered with pomegranates and crowned Marian emblems, while the Virgin of Guadalupe gazed from her tapestry with eternal gravity. The Spanish ambassador, Simón Renard, stood to one side, his hawkish eyes gleaming beneath his brows, already calculating the Queen's victory. Mary sat tall in her chair of estate, her rosary coiled like a serpent in her fingers. Her lips were pressed into a line that had not softened since Elizabeth's protest in the chapel.

Lady Elizabeth hesitated, but only briefly. Then she knelt down before her.

"Your Majesty," she said, voice level. "I beg your pardon. I regret my conduct and ask your forgiveness for any shame I brought upon you and the crown." The silence that followed was carved from ice. I could feel Renard watching her and assessing whether her penitent pose was the truth or only a mask.

Queen Mary studied her sister thoughtfully. Then, after a long moment, she opened the small wooden casket by her side and withdrew a ring of gold. The bezel was engraved with a tiny pomegranate, the symbol of her mother and the old faith.

"You have defied me in public," she said, her voice low and resonant. "But you are my sister. And I will forgive."

She placed the ring in Elizabeth's hand. Her fingers lingered—brief, firm. A gesture not of affection, but sealing.

"Wear it," she said. "As a token of peace. And a proof of loyalty. You are my sister, Elizabeth. But you must be my subject, too."

Lady Elizabeth rose, curtsied with elegance, and murmured, "I shall wear it with honour, your Majesty."

Yet from my place in the shadows, I saw her eyes. They did not shine with relief nor contrition. They burned quietly with calculation. And I knew that peace, in this court, was always written in sand. Lady Elizabeth had been obliged to conform, but her obvious reluctance to embrace the Catholic faith caused her to lose the Queen's favour.

Soon the two sisters had become completely estranged from each other. Queen Mary openly expressed her doubts about Elizabeth's parentage. She began to refer to her as the daughter of Mark Smeaton and not her royal father. She granted the right of precedence to her cousins Lady Margaret Lennox and Lady Frances Grey instead. They were given the privilege of walking behind her in procession and sitting next to her at banquets. Lady Elizabeth was humiliated and requested permission to retire from court and live at her country residence at Hatfield House.

But Hatfield proved to be no sanctuary for her. The following year, Elizabeth was caught up in the toils of the Wyatt conspiracy. Queen Mary's intention to wed Prince Philip of Spain caused consternation in the court. Bishop Gardiner fell to his knees, his voice shaking as he begged her to reconsider.

"I urge your Majesty to take Edward Courtenay as a husband or make some other match for the sake of the tranquillity of the realm," he pleaded.

Queen Mary's knuckles turned white as she gripped the carved oak armrest of her chair. She looked around the chamber. The other councillors nodded in fervent agreement, their faces taut with anxiety.

She rose from her chair, silencing the room with a single, unwavering glance. "I am your Queen," she said in a voice as hard as iron. "I will marry my cousin Philip. We will rule together as Christian monarchs and return the realm to Papal authority. We shall restore the realm to the true faith and secure the Tudor dynasty by our child."

Her resolve shone as brightly as her ruby necklace. The Spanish ambassador standing beside her inclined his head. The courtiers exchanged glances of dread and awe. Even the tapestry of Saint George upon the wall seemed to tremble in its threads. She swept out of the chamber, her crimson velvet gown trailing across the marble floor like a tide of blood.

At the end of October 1553, she announced her betrothal to Prince Philip. But her decision to marry a Spaniard was widely unpopular in the realm. The people muttered that England would fall under the rule of a foreign Catholic. A conspiracy arose to depose the Queen and put Lady Elizabeth and Edward Courtenay on the throne. It was led by Thomas Wyatt, the son of the famous poet Thomas Wyatt. In January 1554 he raised his standard at Maidstone and declared that Queen Mary's marriage to Prince Philip would bring miserable servitude upon the realm and establish popish religion. He urged the townsfolk to march on London and preserve their liberty against the Spaniards.

A force of six hundred men was sent out from London under the command of Norfolk. But when they met the rebels, they heard the cry, *"We are all Englishmen!"* The royal army promptly deserted to join the other side. Norfolk was forced to retreat back to London and report the bad news. He burst into the Queen's privy chamber without ceremony, his doublet torn, his eyes wild with urgency.

"Wyatt is on his way here to London," he gasped. "I could not stop him. Those lily-livered dogs of mine—they've turned!"

The rebels advanced further taking the towns of Rochester and Dartford. A royal herald was dispatched to offer a pardon if the rebels dispersed. Wyatt dismissed the proposal and demanded the custody of the Tower of London with the Queen in it. The court was shaken to hear his reply. But Queen Mary refused to leave the capital. She issued a proclamation naming Wyatt a traitor and offering a reward of a hundred pounds for his capture. Then she mounted her horse, her face pale but resolute, and her crimson mantle billowing like a banner of defiance. She showed the same fearless dignity that I had seen in her mother, Queen Catherine, when she stood firm against Henry's divorce. Whatever my doubts about Spain, I could not deny the courage that burned in her. She was the Queen. And she would fight for her crown. She rode to the Guildhall to address the people of London:

"I am your Queen, to whom at my coronation, when I was wedded to the realm and laws of the same you promised your allegiance and obedience to me. My father, as you all know, possessed the same regal state, which now rightly is descended unto me; and to him always you showed yourselves most faithful

and loving subjects, and therefore I doubt not, but you will show yourselves likewise to me, and that you will not suffer a vile traitor to have the order and governance of our person and to occupy our estate. And I say to you, on the word of a Prince, that certainly, if a Prince and Governor may as naturally and earnestly love her subjects as the mother doth love the child, then assure yourselves that I, being your lady and mistress, do as earnestly and tenderly love and favour you. And I, thus loving you, cannot but think that ye as heartily and faithfully love me; and then I doubt not but we shall give these rebels a short and speedy overthrow."

The Queen's speech inspired the citizens of London to resist the rebels. When Wyatt and his forces arrived at London, he found the city guarded and barricaded against him. He was forced to surrender and was taken to the Tower. Henry Grey, the duke of Suffolk, was also arrested and executed for taking part in the rebellion. His downfall was not sudden—it was the inevitable consequence of ambition untethered from wisdom. He had courted power recklessly and he had lost.

But the true cost of his treachery was written in the blood of his daughter Lady Jane, and her young husband, Guildford Dudley. Queen Mary was forced to accept that they posed too great a liability to remain alive. On 12th February 1554, the nine day's queen and her husband died upon the scaffold. In the game of crowns, it was not only the guilty who paid the price. Sometimes, it was the innocent who suffered for their actions. That night, I lit a candle in the chapel and prayed for their souls.

The Spanish ambassador, Simon Renard, urged Queen Mary to send Elizabeth to the block and rid herself of all her enemies. Elizabeth was a rallying point for Protestant dissent, a Tudor by blood but a heretic by inclination. The crown could not rest easy while a rival claimant lived. The Queen ordered her sister to be arrested and taken to the Tower. But she hesitated to shed her blood. She had no clear proof of her guilt

Bishop Gardiner exhorted her not to waver in her duty. "Lady Elizabeth is a danger to the realm," he stated. "The rebellion rose in her name."

Lord Paget opposed him resolutely. "Lady Elizabeth is no traitor," he insisted. "She has neither plotted nor conspired. She suffers for the ambitions of others."

Queen Mary's face was drawn and her eyes were shadowed. She had endured betrayal, unrest and the burden of restoring the old faith. And now, she stood at a crossroads between justice or vengeance, mercy or fear. She rose slowly, the room holding its breath.

"I will not shed innocent blood," she said. "But I will not be blind to danger. Elizabeth shall remain in the Tower until I am satisfied of her loyalty."

In March 1554 Wyatt was tried for treason at Westminster Hall and sentenced to death. The following month he was executed at Tower Hill. On the scaffold he proclaimed the innocence of Lady Elizabeth and Edward Courtenay to the crowds:

"Whereas it is said and whistled abroad that I should accuse my lady Elizabeth's grace and my lord Courtenay; it is not so,

good people. For I assure you neither they nor any other now in yonder hold or durance was privy of my rising or commotion before I began. As I have declared no less to the Queen's council. And this is most true."

Elizabeth's loyal servant, Sir William St Loe, requested the honour of an audience with the Queen. She granted his petition. The privy chamber was hushed, heavy with the scent of beeswax and rose oil. The Queen sat beneath the canopy of estate, her crimson gown pooling around her like the petals of a crushed rose, her face indecipherable in the candlelight. Courtiers lined the walls, silent as statues, their eyes flicking between the Queen and the man who stood before her.

Sir William St Loe stepped forward, his boots echoing against the polished floor. He bowed low, then straightened with quiet resolve. In his gloved hand, he held a small velvet pouch.

"Your Majesty," he said, his voice firm but respectful, "my mistress requested that I present you with this ring that you once gave her as a sign of your favour."

He drew the ring from the pouch—a delicate band of gold, its bezel engraved with the device of a pomegranate, the symbol of Queen Catherine of Aragon. The light caught its surface, and for a moment, it seemed to glow.

"She said that you would recognise it."

He bowed again and extended the ring. Queen Mary did not move at first. Then, slowly, she reached out and closed her fingers around it. Her hand trembled ever so slightly. The chamber held its breath.

"Is that the whole of her message, Sir William?" she asked, her voice low, almost too calm.

"Yes, your Grace," he replied, meeting her gaze.

Queen Mary's eyes narrowed. "Did she say that you would receive a reward in return for your services?"

"No, Your Majesty," he said, his voice steady. "I was only too glad to do what I could on her behalf."

A long silence followed. The Queen's fingers closed around the ring. Her gaze drifted to the fire, where the flames danced like restless spirits.

"Very well, Sir William," she said at last. "You may withdraw."

He bowed deeply. "I thank Your Grace for receiving me."

As he turned and walked from the chamber, the Queen opened her hand and stared down at the ring. The device of the pomegranate glinted faintly in the torchlight. She remembered how she had once given the token to her sister. The death of her cousin Jane still troubled her greatly. "I will not have her blood on my conscience too," she murmured.

She summoned a meeting of the privy council and spoke with clarity and resolve. Elizabeth would be removed from the Tower and placed under house arrest. There was no dissent. It was agreed that Sir Henry Bedingfield would serve as Elizabeth's keeper at the palace of Woodstock. Edward Courtenay would be sent abroad—exiled, but spared.

Queen Mary nodded, her eyes glancing at the pomegranate ring upon her finger. "Let it be done, my lords," she commanded. "Thus, we will show firmness without cruelty and vigilance without tyranny."

On 25th July 1554 Queen Mary married Prince Philip of Spain at Winchester Cathedral. By all accounts, it was a grand and costly celebration. But neither Lady Anne of Cleves nor I were invited to attend the wedding. We were suspected of harbouring sympathies for Lady Elizabeth. We took the hint that the Queen regarded us with displeasure. We retired from the court and lived quietly in our own residences. My eldest son Ned kept me informed of the events at court. He was now a handsome young man of fifteen. I focussed my attention upon caring for my younger children.

In April 1555 Lady Elizabeth was released from detention at Woodstock and allowed to reside at Hatfield House again. The doors of her childhood home stood open once more, but not to embrace her freedom. Queen Mary sent Sir Thomas Pope to reside with her to prevent any more conspiracies or plots. No-one dared to visit her or send any messages for fear of arousing suspicion. She received no New Year gifts or greetings. Her amusements were very few. She was limited to the simple pleasures of reading her books, riding her horse and sitting in her garden. She walked through its halls like a prisoner instead of a great lady. It was a sad life for the sister of the Queen.

After her marriage to the Spanish prince, Queen Mary had become even more ardent in her Catholic faith. The altars were restored, Latin chanted once more through vaulted chapels, and the shadow of the Inquisition crept across the realm. Many devout Protestants were executed for their beliefs and others left the realm and fled into exile. In October 1555 Bishop Hugh Latimer and Bishop Nicholas Ridley were burned at the stake for heresy. The following year, Thomas Cranmer, once Primate of All England and architect of reform, followed them into martyrdom. My dear husband Edward would have been grieved to the heart. He had believed in the necessity for reform and enlightenment. To see the realm unravel into smoke and blood would have cut him deeper than any blade.

In July 1557 Lady Anne of Cleves died and was buried at Westminster Abbey. Queen Mary had ordered the rites herself, and spared no dignity. The bells tolled low and solemn as last of King Henry VIII's wives was carried beneath the vaulted arches. She had not lived the life of a queen consort, but she was now honoured in death with regal splendour. Draped in cloth-of-gold and surrounded by wax torches and tapers, her bier was borne through the nave to the echo of Latin chant and placed before the High Altar. The heralds marched in precise step, their tabards flashing with the royal arms, while black banners fluttered above the mourners like reminders of ambition undone and civility preserved.

I stood among them, robed in black in her memory for I had been one of her ladies in waiting. She had survived the difficulties of Henry's reign with quiet wisdom, living with grace and without scandal. I blessed her as a good and worthy lady. That same month Prince Philip departed from the realm to attend to the affairs of Spain and its territories. Queen Mary was left heartbroken. She failed to bear a child and her health steadily declined. The courtiers began to resort in ever greater numbers to Hatfield in order to secure their futures with Lady Elizabeth, the queen in waiting. I sent her a message of goodwill by a trusted courier.

"Your Grace, I look forward to the time when the rising sun shall replace the setting sun and the radiant light of the gospel shall once more shed its bright beams across this forsaken realm of England. Your assured and true friend, Anne Somerset."

CHAPTER 12

The Secret Marriage (1560)

"The Queen claims that the marriage is not to be considered valid as there was no witness, although both Catherine and the earl (Hertford) declare they are married"

(Letter of Bishop Quadra to the Duchess of Parma, 27 Sept 1561, Calendar of State Papers Spain).

In November 1558, Queen Elizabeth succeeded her sister Mary on the throne. With the accession of a Protestant Queen, Cranmer's English rites once again replaced the Latin mass across the realm. The religious exiles returned to England from their sanctuaries abroad. I was now free to practice my faith as I chose. I drew the coral rosary from my girdle and set it aside. Then I opened a silk-lined chest in my bedchamber and took out my English prayer book. I turned the pages and saw with pleasure how its gilded edges caught the morning light. I felt as if I had reclaimed a piece of my soul. I made my way to the chapel and waited for the chaplain to arrive to conduct the first office of Prime. The chapel door creaked open and Master Becon entered holding a candle in his hand. I handed him the book and saw the look of amazement on his face. But he knew better than to make any protest. It was the third time in succession that the realm had altered its faith.

"From now on you shall read the service of morning prayer at this hour," I ordered. "You shall speak the words of good King Edward's order instead of the papist Latin liturgy. And you shall put aside these gaudy vestments and wear a plain black cassock and a white surplice as befits a man of God."

He nodded reverently before turning to face the small congregation of our household. As he began the opening responses in English, the very syllables felt like liberation, echoing against the frescoed walls of the chapel. Afterwards, I returned to my chamber and reclaimed my precious English New Testament and Book of Psalms from the chest. I seated myself before the high window, where the pale winter light slanted onto the pages. My fingertips brushed against the text and I marvelled at how strange it was to read God's Word in my own tongue again. The familiar phrases of the gospels sank into me like a soothing balm, and I murmured the words of the psalms aloud, revelling in the clarity of meaning that once had been veiled. I blessed good Queen Elizabeth for restoring the true faith back to the kingdom and prayed that she might long reign over us. I soon had another reason to be grateful to her. The Queen had not forgotten my loyalty to her. She gave my eldest son Ned the title of earl of Hertford and restored his father's lands to him. I was delighted that the Seymour line was made noble once again. I trusted that Ned would prosper and thrive with the goodwill of the new Queen.

"Do not make my mistakes, my dear," I urged him. "Your father was once King in all but name, but he made the error of parading his wealth before the court and the people. His fine palace at Somerset House aroused envy. He did not listen to the advice of his friends nor reward his colleagues as they felt they deserved. That snake in the grass, Northumberland, usurped his position. It is a comfort to me that I lived to see his downfall. His pride has been humbled just as he had humbled mine."

"Northumberland was a traitor to the realm," he said. "But my father is remembered as the Good Duke. The people still honour us for his sake."

"Our family is no longer in disgrace, but it is still ruined," I said. "We have lost our titles, our properties and our fortune. We are no longer a great name in the land. I counsel you to live quietly and avoid provoking the displeasure of the Queen."

"Father was cheated of his rightful place as the Lord Protector," he said. "But I will regain our family's rightful place in the realm."

I should have paid more attention to him. How could I guess that he would embroil us in another disaster? And this time it would have terrible consequences for the next generation of our family. My daughter Jane served as a maid of honour to Queen Elizabeth. She became a close friend of Lady Catherine Grey. She introduced her to her brother Ned. The two of them soon fell in love with each other. Ned came to visit me at Hanworth.

"I have come to ask your approval to get married, mother," he said. "I wish to marry Lady Catherine Grey."

"It is a worthy match," I replied. "Your father would have approved of your choice. But this matter must be carefully handled. We must take care not to provoke the Queen. I have no great standing at court, but Lady Frances Grey is the Queen's cousin. You must go to see her and ask her consent. If she agrees, then you must leave it to her to persuade the Queen."

"Naturally, I will request the permission of her mother," he agreed. "Yet I fear that Queen Elizabeth will never agree to the match. She does not like any of her ladies to marry and Lady Catherine Grey is the next in line to the throne."

"The alliance of our two families is a very great matter," I warned him. "Your marriage must be made in the eyes of the whole world if it is to stand. You must promise me that you will not think of making a secret marriage. It is far too dangerous to attempt such a thing. It is treason to marry a member of the royal family without the sovereign's permission. Moreover, it would look dishonourable. Great families do not get married in secret."

"But what if the Queen refuses to give permission for our marriage?" he asked. "It would mean that we had lost our chance for happiness."

"If she denies her permission, then you must accept it with good grace," I said. "In such a case she will very likely make amends by finding you another good match. But on no account should you risk the enmity of the Queen. I forbid you to even think of a secret marriage. It would mean the ruin of us all."

I doubted that the Queen would ever permit either of the Grey sisters to marry. Catherine and Mary Grey stood too close to the throne. The fatal marriage of Lady Jane Grey to Guildford Dudley had cast a dark shadow over the entire Grey family. I had high hopes for my son. I intended him to marry a rich noblewoman whose wealth and connections would enable him to pursue a career at court. He would rebuild the fortunes of the family and uphold the name and honour of the House of Seymour. But my foolish son did not listen to me. He thought that he could find a way to get his heart's desire and raise the fortunes of the family again. Ned rode to Bradgate House to ask the permission of Lady Frances Grey. He returned beaming with joy.

"Lady Frances has given her consent to the match," he said. "She told me that she was glad to receive such an eligible suitor for her daughter."

"But what about the Queen?" I said.

"Lady Frances has promised to write a letter to the Queen on our behalf," he said. "She said that it was her last wish on earth to see her daughter honourable married. She is certain that the Queen will not refuse her."

But Lady Frances Grey was a sick woman. The executions of her daughter and her husband had taken their toll upon her. She died with the letter left unfinished. However, my daughter Jane was determined to secure the happiness of her beloved brother. She pleaded with the Queen to allow him to marry Lady Catherine Grey.

"She is his true love, your Majesty," she said.

Queen Elizabeth pursed her lips. "I shall consider the matter," she replied. Jane reported that she remained immoveable on the subject despite her earnest entreaties.

"You must give it up, my son," I said. "You have done all you can in this matter."

"We can get married in secret and seek permission later," he declared. "Once it is done then the Queen will have to accept it with good grace."

"On no account must you consider a secret marriage," I replied. "If you flout the Queen we will be sent to the Tower. I would not survive such an ordeal for a second time."

"I will leave you out of it, mother," he replied. "If the Queen is offended, then her anger will fall on me alone."

"You would be a fool to risk it, Ned," I said. "Remember that Lord Thomas Howard died in the Tower because of his secret betrothal to Lady Margaret Douglas."

In March 1561, my beloved daughter Jane died of an illness. She was only nineteen years old. It was a great grief to me to lose my beloved child in the flower of her youth. To lose her so young, so full of promise and grace, was a sorrow beyond words. I had hoped she would make a good match at court and know the happiness of having a family of her own. I mourned not only the daughter I had loved, but the future that would never come to pass—the grandchildren I would never hold, the joy she might have known and the legacy she might have left.

The following month, Queen Elizabeth decided to send my son Ned on a tour of the continent to finish his education.

So, I knew nothing of the disaster until it burst upon me. On 5th September 1561 Ned was arrested for treason and taken to the Tower for seducing a virgin of the blood royal. It was the very fate from which I had wanted to protect him. I requested permission to visit him in the Tower.

"What have you done, Ned?" I demanded.

"Lady Catherine and I secretly married each other at Hertford House last November," he admitted. "Afterwards I was sent to France for my education. While I was away, she discovered that she was pregnant. So, she had to confess the truth to the Queen. But she had lost the written jointure that I had given her. And we could not remember the name of the priest who performed the ceremony. We have no proof that we were lawfully married."

"But there must be some proof," I said. "What about the witnesses?"

"My sister Jane was the only witness", he replied.

A dart of pain shot through me at his words. She was dead and now there was no living witness. "How could you have been so careless? I demanded.

"We had to keep our marriage a secret from the world," he said.

I feared that the Queen would take revenge on my whole family. I saw myself condemned to the Tower for the rest of my life and all my goods and property confiscated. My only recourse was to plead ignorance of Ned's folly and throw myself upon the mercy of the Queen. I wrote a heartfelt letter to Sir William Cecil:

> *"Good Master Secretary,*
>
> *I write to you in great distress, having heard the troubling news that my son has married Lady Catherine Grey. This report has grieved me so deeply that I could not remain silent. I must appeal to you, and through you, to Her Majesty. I make my first and most heartfelt request: that the Queen may judge me in this matter according to my true intentions and loyalty. If my son has indeed forgotten the honour Her Majesty once showed him, and has acted so far beyond his duty as a subject—abusing her grace—I beg you to understand that I was never privy to, nor consenting of, such actions.*
>
> *I will not burden this letter with the many ways I have rebuked and tried to persuade him otherwise. Nor do I ask that his youth or fear be used to excuse or lessen his fault. I ask only that Her Majesty may continue to think of me as one who, for neither child nor friend, would ever willingly neglect the duty owed by a faithful subject. Please, good Master Secretary, stand by me now. Let not the wilfulness of my unruly son diminish Her Majesty's favour toward me. I am overwhelmed by this disheartening rumour, unsure how to proceed or what steps to take. I therefore ask you to let me hear some comfort from Her Majesty, and some counsel from yourself. I commend you to God, and remain,*
>
> *Your assured friend to the best of my power, Anne Somerset."*

Fortunately, the Queen believed my fervent protestations and she spared me from her wrath. But she had no mercy upon poor foolish Ned or Lady Catherine. On 24th September 1561 Catherine gave birth to a son in the

Tower. She named him Edward. It enraged the Queen that her cousin should presume to bear a child when she had none. She saw it as an attack upon the throne. I bitterly regretted having encouraged their match. The Grey's were an ill-starred family. They had destroyed two great houses – the Dudleys and now the Seymours.

The disaster of my son's disgrace broke my spirit. I could no longer bear the burden of my family affairs alone. So, I married a second husband. He was Francis Newdigate, the former steward of my late husband. He would take care of all my lands and properties on my behalf. It was whispered at court that it was shameful for such a great lady as myself to demean myself by marrying a common man. But I no longer cared for the opinions of others. I had always vowed that one day I would be free to do and say as I pleased. After all, Lady Frances Grey had been better born than I, and she had married her horse master after the death of her husband. My marriage sent a signal to Queen Elizabeth that she need not regard the Seymour family as a threat to the succession. We were no longer a powerful family at the court with dangerous ambitions.

In June 1562 the marriage of Ned and Catherine was declared unlawful and their offspring illegitimate. They were condemned to perpetual imprisonment in the Tower. It was a great grief to me. I had spent my lifetime working for the honour of the family name and the prosperity of my descendants. Now Ned had thrown it all away. However, the gaoler had pity on the unfortunate young couple and allowed them to visit each other. In February 1563 Catherine bore a second child named Thomas. When the secret came to light, the Queen's anger was terrible. She ordered that Ned and Catherine should be kept apart and never allowed to see each other again. I feared that the unfortunate couple would grow old and die in their prison. My anxiety prompted me to write another letter to Sir William Cecil:

> *"Good Master Secretary,*
>
> *After a long silence, I presume to take up my pen to renew my suit to the Queen's Majesty on behalf of my son Ned. I pray as his mother that you would grant me your assistance in resolving his plight. How long will Her Highness continue to bear her displeasure against him? Shall he live out his days in the misery of the Tower? Would it not be better for him to gain his liberty and serve Her Majesty? I know that there is no cause that by your earnest counsel has not failed to reach a good outcome. So, I pray that you may urge Her Highness to show her plentiful mercy to him. The more sincere you show yourself in this matter, the more you shall set forth Her Majesty's honour and the better you shall discharge your office. And so, I end with a prayer that God will bless your endeavours to a gracious end.*
>
> *Your assured loving friend, Anne Somerset."*

However, the Queen would not relent. Ned and Catherine remained in prison with their children. But that summer there was a deadly outbreak of plague in London. The Queen sent Catherine and her youngest son Thomas to live under house arrest at the house of her uncle Lord John Grey at Pirgo in Essex. I was terrified that my son Ned would perish if he remained in the Tower and I asked Sir William Cecil to arrange an audience for me with the Queen. I curtsied low before her chair of estate. Her face was inscrutable beneath its mask of paint and her dark eyes surveyed me dispassionately.

"My Lady of Somerset," she said. "It is not often that I see you at my court."

"I am an old woman, your Majesty," I said. "During my life I have served under eight queens and my husband died as a loyal servant of the state. All that I have left to me are my children. I pray that you will show mercy to my son Hertford and my unfortunate grandson and release them into my care. I fear that if they remain in the Tower they will perish miserably of the plague."

"Your son Hertford is a traitor," she replied. "He seduced a lady of the blood royal. He is fortunate only to suffer imprisonment and not execution for his crimes. If he must languish in the Tower, it is no concern of mine. He brought this on himself."

"My concern is not only for my son," I said. "I have an even greater care for your Majesty's reputation. You are renowned for your goodness and clemency. I am sure that you would not want it to be blamed for the deaths of a foolish young boy and an innocent child. They are the descendants of the noble house of Somerset. My husband treated you well when he was the Lord Protector. I humbly ask you in his name to be good to his son."

"Your son is unworthy to bear his father's name," she snapped. "It is better that such a knave should perish. You have other children who are more deserving of your care. It would be more fitting for you to seek my favour on their behalf instead."

"This is the only favour that I will ever ask of your Majesty," I said. "Is it so much to ask for my son and my grandson to be given into my care? I swear that they will live quietly at my house at Hanworth and will never leave its precincts. They will never trouble your Majesty for as long as they live."

"Very well, Lady Somerset," she said. "I will grant your suit. But I do it for your sake and not for theirs. You shall be entirely responsible for their future conduct. And if Hertford should dare to set one foot outside your door, he will return to the Tower for the rest of his life."

"I shall be eternally grateful to your Majesty," I said. "I thank you for sparing them to me. They shall be my comfort in my old age."

"I pity you for your troubles, Lady Somerset," she said. "If Hertford had been a worthy son he could have made an honourable marriage and brought honour to your house and your name instead of so much sorrow and disgrace. But I shall say no more on the matter lest I repent of my leniency. I shall send a warrant to the Lieutenant of the Tower and he will see that they are conducted to Hanworth. It is not safe to linger here in London. You should return home and wait for them there."

"I shall never forget your Majesty's goodness to me," I said.

"Farewell, Lady Somerset," she replied. "You are a lady of great qualities. I regret that fate has not treated you more kindly."

I curtsied to her and took my leave. I left the palace and returned to Hanworth. The Queen kept her word and released Ned and his son Edward into my custody. It was a joyful day when I received them into my home.

"Forgive me for the anguish I have caused you, mother," said Ned.

The years in the Tower had aged him and he was no longer the light-hearted and merry boy that he had once been. He was only twenty-four but he stood before me as solemn as a winter morning—his youth dimmed and his spirit tempered by years of shadow. His face was lined with disappointment and grief. My heart went out to him. He was so young and had suffered so much! I reached for his hand and clasped it with the urgency of everything left unsaid. His fingers were cold, his skin pale from years without sunlight. I wanted to gather him into my arms, to shield him from the world's judgment, but I knew that some wounds could not be mended by a mother's embrace. Still, I held his hand, and in that moment, I hoped he felt something of the love that had never left him, not even in his darkest hour.

"I do forgive you, my son," I replied.

"This place is like a paradise," he said, gazing around at the magnificent gardens.

"You must forget your troubles and think of your future," I said. "You are still a young man and you still have time to amend your life."

He shook his head. "I can never be happy while I am kept apart from my beloved wife," he said.

"Perhaps one day the Queen will forgive her and set her free," I said. "It is a blessing that you are both clear of the Tower."

But the Queen would not consent to show any more clemency towards Lady Catherine. She pined away from sorrow in her detention. On 27th January 1568 she died at the age of only twenty-eight. The Queen ordered a suitably grand funeral for her cousin befitting her royal status. But she was buried in the parish church of Yoxford, rather than in Westminster Abbey with her mother. Ned was not permitted to attend the funeral nor allowed to pay a visit to her grave. But the Queen allowed his younger son Thomas to come and reside with him at Hanworth. Little Edward and Thomas wandered around the lawn chasing pall-mall balls with their nurse. The poor boys were strangers to each other.

Ned drew a round miniature out of his sleeve and sighed deeply. It was a portrait of Lady Catherine holding her infant son Edward in her arms. She wore a black velvet gown with an ermine collar. Her red-gold Tudor hair was covered by a cap of white lace. She gazed ahead with a sweet expression upon her delicate pink and white face.

"I was sorry to hear of the death of your wife," I said.

"She was the finest lady in the kingdom," he said. Tears glistened in his eyes. "She wrote a letter to me before she died saying that she was my most loving and faithful wife and it was a hard fate to be deprived of so good a man as I. She said she longed to be merry with me as when our little sweet boy in the Tower was begotten and declared that she would willingly bear the pain of further childbirth because of her boundless love for me. But alas, it was not to be! She was too frail to survive the rigours of her long confinement.

Her loving heart was crushed by the pain of our separation and the unrelenting anger of the Queen against her."

"You must forget your sorrow and think of your children," I said. "You must love them and care for them for her sake."

"They are all that I have left of my beloved Catherine," he said. "I shall never love any other woman but her."

Little Edward picked up a ball and threw it to his nurse. His brother Thomas rolled upon the grass laughing with pleasure. They were both fine boys who were worthy of their royal heritage. They ought to have been honoured as princes of the realm. It cut me to the heart to think that they had been named illegitimate. They were not only disbarred from the succession, but from inheriting the title of earl of Hertford. Now the noble house of Seymour would perish with the death of my son. Queen Elizabeth was every bit as vengeful as her tyrannical father had been.

Now that I am advanced in years, I do not care to attend the glittering court of the last Tudor monarch. I have turned aside from that nest of intrigue and betrayal. I prefer to live quietly at my beautiful manor of Hanworth. Here I spend my days in the company of my husband, my son and my dear grandson. And I regret that my ambitious folly has repeated itself in the next generation of my family. All that I now desire for myself and my children are good marriages and peaceful prosperity. I have learned from my own bitter experience that grasping at power is a fatal endeavour. The sword of state will pierce the hand that over-reaches itself to seize it.

I rose from obscurity to become the first lady of the realm. For four years I stood at the pinnacle of power beside my husband, the Lord Protector of England and the uncle of the King. But he was struck down by envy and violence. Northumberland conspired to take our place and plotted to seize the crown, before being overthrown in his turn. Since that hazardous time, the realm has been peaceful. It has been ruled by two Tudor Queen, the daughters of the old tyrant Henry. For a brief moment, I dreamed that we would lead our family to greatness. I urged my husband to seize the opportunity to marry our daughter to King Edward VI and our son to Lady Jane Grey. Just think of it! We had a chance to place our children on the throne! But our ambitious plans did not come to fruition. The envy of our rivals put a stop to our designs. If we had succeeded, then the realm would now be ruled by a line of Seymours.

I did not realise how greatly our downfall must have burdened my son. It was a desperate folly to marry a daughter of the House of Grey in secret. Lady Catherine lacked the guile to succeed in changing her fortunes. I blame her for the carelessness which left my grandson without a name and my son without an heir. At a single stroke, the lifetime efforts of my husband and myself to found a noble line of descendants was ruined.

The candles burn low as I sit alone in my privy chamber at Hanworth. I stare into the flames of the fireplace and reflect upon the events of my life. Once, ambition gowned me in ermine and raised me up to sit beside the Lord Protector, Edward Seymour. But ambition is a fickle sovereign. It flatters, then forsakes. It has lifted me on high only to dash me down low. It has cost me a husband executed, a son broken by scandal and grandsons who are left nameless in history's ledger. Now our house has no honour and no future. I will never be able to raise up our family again. My sons will be poor and my daughters will die unmarried. I have learned that greatness sought too fiercely becomes a trap, and glory chased without mercy leaves only grief in its wake. The pageant has passed me by and I do not grieve its lost glitter. Let others strive for power and glory. I seek no crown but that of peace. And so, I end my days in quiet, among roses and regrets, no longer the First Lady of the Realm, but only mother, grandmother and guardian of what remains.

THE END

EPILOGUE

Anne Stanhope, Duchess of Somerset died on 16th April 1587 at Hanworth Place, Middlesex, at the age of seventy-seven. In accordance with her wishes, her eldest son Edward executed her will, and she was buried with great ceremony in a funeral at Westminster Abbey. In 1588 Edward commissioned an elaborate alabaster monument with a tomb effigy and inscription which stands in St Nicholas' Chapel.

Her son Edward Seymour, first earl of Hertford, married twice more to Frances Howard and Frances Pranell, but had no more children. He died in 1621.

Her grandson Edward Seymour was given the courtesy title of Lord Beauchamp. In 1608 he was finally acknowledged as legitimate, but by then it was too late for him to assert his claim to the throne.

Her great-grandson William Seymour secretly married Lady Arbella Stuart in 1610. They were sent to the Tower but managed to escape. He succeeded in reaching safety on the continent. But she was intercepted on her way to France. She died in the Tower in 1615 at the age of forty.

APPENDIX 1:

The funeral of Anne Stanhope, duchess of Somerset, at Westminster Abbey in 1587:

At the sompteous and stately funeralls of the last Anne duchesse of Somerset, which were performed by the right honorable Edward earle of Hertford hir executor, anno 1587, there was a portraieture of the same duchesse made in robes of her estate, with a coronicall to a duchesse, and the same representation bore under a canopie; and all the other ceremonyes accomplished; and bycause there was no duchesse to assist thereat, the queen's majesty gave her royal consent that the countesse of Hartford his wife should have all honour done to her after that estate during the funeral. As by warrant directed to me under her majesty's hand appears.

(William Dethick, Garter Principal King of Arms, 1600).

APPENDIX 2:

The epitaph on the tomb of Anne Stanhope, duchess of Somerset, in Westminster Abbey:

Heare lieth entombed the noble duchesse of Somerset, Anne, deere spouse unto the renowned prince Edward Duke of Somerset, Earle of Hertford, Viscount Beauchampe and Baron Seymour, Compaignon [Companion] of the most famous knightly Order of the Garter: uncle to King Edward the Sixt, Gouvernor of His Roial Person and most worthie Protector of all his realmes, dominions, and subiectes: Leiutenant Generall of all his armies: threasoror and Erle Marschall of England, Gouvernor and capitayne of the Isles of Guernsey and Jersey: under whose prosperous conduct, glorious victory hath ben so often and so fortunatly obteyned over the Scottes, vanquished at Edinburgh, Leth [Leith], and Musselborough Field.

A princesse discended of noble lignage, beinge daughter of the worthie knight Sr Edward Stanhope, by Elizabeth his wyfe that was daughter of Sr Foulke Bourghchier Lord Fitzwarin, from whome our moderne earles of Bathe ar spronge, sonne was he unto Willm. Lord Fitzwarin, that was brother to Henry, Earle of Essex and Ihon [John] Lord Berners: whome Willm. their sire sometyme Earle of Ev in Normandy, begat Anne the sole heire of Thomas of Woodstock, Duke of Gloucester, yonger sonne to the mighty Prince, Kinge Edward the Third, and of his wyfe Aleanore, coheire unto the tenth Humphrey De Bohun that was Erle of Hereford, Essex and Northampton, High Constable of England.

Many children bare this lady unto her Lord, of either sort: to witte Edward, Erle of Hertford, Henry, and a younger Edward: Anne, Countesse of Warwike, Margaret, Jane, Mary, Katherine, and Elizabeth. And with firme faith in Christ in most mylde maner renred she this life at XC yeres of age on Easter day, the sixtenth of Aprill Anno.M.CCCCC.LXXXVII.

The Erle of Hertford, Edward her eldest sonne, in this dolefull dutie carefull and diligent, doth consecrate this monument to his deere parent: not for her honor wherewith lyvinge she did abounde and nowe departed flourisheth: but for the dutifull love he beareth her, and for his laste testification therof.

APPENDIX 3:

Accounts of King Henry VIII's courtship of Jane Seymour:

(1) The Worthies of England by Thomas Fuller 1661 pub 1662:

JANE SEYMOUR, daughter to Sir John Seymour, knight, (honourably descended from the lords Beauchamps), was born at Wulf-hall in this county, and after was married to king Henry the Eighth. It is currently traditioned, that at her first coming to court, queen Anne Boleyn, espying a jewel pendant about her neck, snatched thereat (desirous to see, the other unwilling to show it,) and casually hurt her hand with her own violence; but it grieved her heart more, when she perceived it the king's picture by himself bestowed upon her, who from this day forward dated her own *declining*, and the other's *ascending*, in her husband's affection.

(2) The Life of Jane Dormer, duchess of Feria by Henry Clifford 1610:

The king seeming to affect Jane Seymour, and having her on his knee, as Queen Anne espied, who then was thought to be with child, she for anger and distain miscarried, as she said, betwitting the king with it, who willed her to pardon him.

(3) The Letters of the Imperial Ambassador Eustace Chapuys to the emperor Charles V:

10th February 1536:

> *On the day of the interment [of Queen Catherine of Aragon on 29th January 1536] the Concubine had an abortion which seemed to be a male child which she had not borne 3½ months, at which the King has shown great distress. The said concubine wished to lay the blame on the duke of Norfolk, whom she hates, saying he frightened her by bringing the news of the fall the King had six days before. But it is well known that is not the cause, for it was told her in a way that she should not be alarmed or attach much importance to it. Some think it was owing to her own incapacity to bear children, others to a fear that the King would treat her like the late Queen, especially considering the treatment shown to a lady of the Court, named Mistress Semel, to whom, as many say, he has lately made great presents.*

25th February 1536:

> *I learn from several persons of this Court that for more than three months this King has not spoken ten times to the Concubine, and that when she miscarried, he scarcely said anything to her, except that he saw clearly that God did not wish to give him male children; and in leaving her he told her, as if for spite, that he would speak to her after she was "releuize." The said Concubine attributed the misfortune to two causes: first, the King's fall; and, secondly, that the love she bore him was far greater than that of the late Queen, so that her heart broke when she saw that he loved others.*

18th March 1536: Chapuys to Cardinal Granvelle:

> *The new amours of this King with the young lady of whom I have before written still go on, to the intense*

rage of the concubine; and the King 15 days ago put into his chamber the young lady's brother.

1st April 1536:

At this instant the Marchioness has sent to me to say what Mr. Gelyot (qu. Elyot?) had already told me, viz., that the King being lately in this town, and the young lady, Mrs. Semel, whom he serves, at Greenwich, he sent her a purse full of sovereigns, and with it a letter, and that the young lady, after kissing the letter, returned it unopened to the messenger, and throwing herself on her knees before him, begged the said messenger that he would pray the King on her part to consider that she was a gentlewoman of good and honourable parents, without reproach, and that she had no greater riches in the world than her honour, which she would not injure for a thousand deaths, and that if he wished to make her some present in money she begged it might be when God enabled her to make some honourable match.

The said Marchioness has sent to me to say that by this the King's love and desire towards the said lady was wonderfully increased, and that he had said she had behaved most virtuously, and to show her that he only loved her honourably, he did not intend henceforth to speak with her except in presence of some of her kin; for which reason the King has caused Cromwell to remove from a chamber to which the King can go by certain galleries without being perceived, and has lodged there the eldest brother of the said lady with his wife, in order to bring thither the same young lady, who has been well taught for the most part by those intimate with the King, who hate the concubine, that she must by no means comply with the

King's wishes except by way of marriage; in which she is quite firm. She is also advised to tell the King boldly how his marriage is detested by the people, and none consider it lawful; and on the occasion when she shall bring forward the subject, there ought to be present none but titled persons, who will say the same if the King put them upon their oath of fealty.

And the said Marchioness would like that I or someone else, on the part of your Majesty, should assist in the matter; and certainly it appears to me that if it succeed, it will be a great thing both for the security of the Princess and to remedy the heresies here, of which the Concubine is the cause and principal nurse, and also to pluck the King from such an abominable and more than incestuous marriage. The Princess would be very happy, even if she were excluded from her inheritance by male issue.

29th April 1536:

The Grand Ecuyer, Mr. Carew, had on St. George's day the Order of the Garter in the place of the deceased M. de Burgain (lord Abergavenny), to the great disappointment of Rochford, who was seeking for it, and all the more because the Concubine has not had sufficient influence to get it for her brother; and it will not be the fault of the said Ecuyer if the Concubine, although his cousin (quelque, qu. quoique? cousine) be not dismounted. He continually counsels Mrs. Semel and other conspirators "pour luy faire une venue," and only four days ago he and some persons of the chamber sent to tell the Princess to be of good cheer, for shortly the opposite party would put water in their wine, for the King was already as sick and tired of the concubine as could be; and the brother of lord Montague told me yesterday at dinner that the day before the bishop of London had been asked if the King could abandon the said concubine, and he would not give any opinion to anyone but the King himself, and before doing so he would like to know the King's own inclination, meaning to intimate that the King might leave the said concubine, but that, knowing his fickleness, he would not put himself in danger. The said Bishop was the principal cause and instrument of the first divorce, of which he heartily repents, and would still more gladly promote this, the said concubine and all her race are such abominable Lutherans.

18th May 1536: Chapuys to Antoine Perrenot:

I have no news to add to what I write to his Majesty, except to tell you something of the quality of the King's new lady, which the Emperor and Granvelle would perhaps like to hear. She is sister of one Edward Semel, "qua este a sa mate," of middle stature and no great beauty, so fair that one would call her rather pale than otherwise. She is over 25 years old. I leave you to judge whether, being English and having long frequented the Court, "si elle ne tiendroit pas a conscience de navoir pourveu et prevenu de savoir que cest de faire nopces." Perhaps this King will only be too glad to be so far relieved from trouble. Also, according to the account given of him by the Concubine, he has neither vigour nor virtue; and besides he may make a condition in the marriage that she be a virgin, and when he has a mind to divorce her he will find enough of witnesses. The said Semel is not a woman of great wit, but she may have good understanding (un bel enigm, qu. engin?). It is said

> she inclines to be proud and haughty. She bears great love and reverence to the Princess. I know not if honours will make her change hereafter.

19th May 1536:

> The joy shown by this people every day not only at the ruin of the Concubine but at the hope of the Princess' restoration, is inconceivable, but as yet the King shows no great disposition towards the latter; indeed, he has twice shown himself obstinate when spoken to on the subject by his Council.

> I hear that, even before the arrest of the Concubine, the King, speaking with Mistress Jane Semel of their future marriage, the latter suggested that the Princess should be replaced in her former position; and the King told her she was a fool, and ought to solicit the advancement of the children they would have between them, and not any others. She replied that in asking for the restoration of the Princess she conceived she was seeking the rest and tranquillity of the King, herself, her future children, and the whole realm; for, without that, neither your Majesty nor this people would ever be content.

> Although everybody rejoices at the execution of the putain, there are some who murmur at the mode of procedure against her and the others, and people speak variously of the King; and it will not pacify the world when it is known what has passed and is passing between him and Mrs. Jane Semel.

> Already it sounds ill in the ears of the people, that the King, having received such ignominy, has shown himself more glad than ever since the arrest of the putain; for he has been going about banqueting with ladies, sometimes remaining

after midnight, and returning by the river. Most part of the time he was accompanied by various musical instruments, and, on the other hand, by the singers of his chamber, which many interpret as showing his delight at getting rid of a "maigre vieille et mechante bague," with hope of change, which is a thing specially agreeable to this King.

He supped lately with several ladies in the house of the bishop of Carlisle, and showed an extravagant joy, as the said Bishop came to tell me next morning, who reported, moreover, that the King had said to him, among other things, that he had long expected the issue of these affairs, and that thereupon he had before composed a tragedy, which he carried with him; and, so saying, the King drew from his bosom a little book written in his own hand, but the Bishop did not read the contents. It may have been certain ballads that the King has composed, at which the putain and her brother laughed as foolish things, which was objected to them as a great crime.

The day before the putain's condemnation he sent for Mrs. Semel by the Grand Esquire and some others, and made her come within a mile of his lodging, where she is splendidly served by the King's cook and other officers. She is most richly dressed. One of her relations, who dined with her on the day of the said condemnation, told me that the King sent that morning to tell her that he would send her news at 3 o'clock of the condemnation of the putain, which he did by Mr. Briant, whom he sent in all haste. To judge by appearances, there is no doubt that he will take the said Semel to wife; and some think the agreements and promises are already made.

20th May 1536: Chapuys to Cardinal Granvelle

Wrote yesterday very fully to the Emperor and Granvelle. Has just been informed, the bearer of this having already mounted, that Mrs. Semel came secretly by river this morning to the King's lodging, and that the promise and betrothal (desponsacion) was made at 9 o'clock. The King means it to be kept secret till Whitsuntide; but everybody begins already to murmur by suspicion, and several affirm that long before the death of the other there was some arrangement which sounds ill in the ears of the people; who will certainly be displeased at what has been told me, if it be true, viz., that yesterday the King, immediately on receiving news of the decapitation of the putain entered his barge and went to the said Semel, whom he has lodged a mile from him, in a house by the river.

6 June 1536:

On his return from mass I accompanied the King to the chamber of the Queen, whom, for the King's satisfaction, I kissed, and congratulated her on her marriage, and said that her predecessor had borne the device La plus heureuse, but that she would bear the reality, and that I was sure your Majesty would be immeasurably pleased that the King had found so good and virtuous a wife, especially as her brother had been in your Majesty's service, and the satisfaction of this people with the marriage was incredible, especially at the restoration of the Princess to the King's favour and to her former condition; and, among other congratulations, I told the Queen that it was not her least happiness that, without having had the labour of giving birth to her, she had such a daughter as the Princess, of whom she would receive more joy and consolation than of all those she could have herself; and I begged her to favour her interests; which she said she would do, and especially that she would labour to obtain that honourable name I wished for her of "pacific," i.e., of author and conservatrix of the peace. After speaking to the Queen, the King, who had been talking to the other ladies, approached, and wished to excuse her, saying I was the first ambassador to whom she had spoken, and she was not accustomed to it, that he quite believed she desired to obtain the name of "pacific," for, besides that her nature was gentle and inclined to peace, she would not for the world that he were engaged in war, that she might not be separated from him…I went to talk with this Queen's brother, whom I left very well informed of the great good it would be, not only to the Queen his sister and all their kin, but also to the realm and all Christendom likewise, if the Princess were restored to her rights; and I am sure he will use his good offices therein.

(4) Letter of Sir John Russell to Lord Lisle on 3rd June 1536:

I assure you she is as gentle a lady as ever I knew, and as fair a Queen as any in Christendom. The King has come out of hell into heaven for the gentleness of this and the cursedness and unhappiness of the other.

Book Group Discussion Guide for "First Lady of the Realm"

(1) Was Anne Stanhope Seymour a heroine or a villain?

(2) What were her greatest strengths and weaknesses?

(3) How did she succeed in rising at the Tudor court?

(4) What did she learn from her service to the six wives of King Henry VIII?

(5) How did Edward Seymour become Lord Protector of England?

(6) Was Thomas Seymour a genuine threat to the Somersets?

(7) Why did Edward Seymour fail to retain power?

(8) What caused the downfall of John Dudley?

(9) Why did Queen Mary and Queen Elizabeth both show favour to Anne?

(10) Was Anne complicit in the dangerous liaison of her son with Lady Catherine Grey?

(11) Who is your favourite Tudor character, and why?

(12) What other books by this author have you read? How did they compare to this book?

BIBLIOGRAPHY

Primary Sources

John Foxe, *Acts and Monuments*, 1563.

Antonio de Guaras, *The Accession of Queen Mary*, 1554, trans. R. Garmett 1844.

John Hayward, *The Life and Reigne of King Edward the Sixth*, 1630.

Peter Heylyn, *History of the Reformation of the Church of England*, 1661.

Claudius Hollyband and Peter Erondell, *The Elizabethan Home*, 1573 (Methuen Books, 1949).

Martin Andrew Sharp Hume ed, *Chronicle of King Henry VIII of England* (George Bell and Sons, 1889).

J.B. Nichols ed, *The Diary of Henry Machyn, Citizen and Merchant-Taylor of London, from A.D. 1550 to A.D. 1563* (Camden Society, 1848).

John Gough Nichols ed, *The Chronicle of Queen Jane by a resident of the Tower of London, July 1553 to October 1554* (Camden Society, 1850).

John Gough Nichols ed, *London pageants. Accounts of fifty-five royal processions and entertainments in the city of London; chiefly extracted from contemporary writers* (J. B.

Nichols and Son, 1831).

David Starkey ed, *The Inventory of King Henry VIII, Volume I, The Transcript* (Harvey Miller Publishers, 1998).

Robert Wingfield, *The Life of Queen Mary of England, 1533-1561.*

Mary Anne Everett Wood, *Letters of Royal and Illustrious Ladies of Great Britain, Vols 1 and 2* (Forgotten books, 1846).

Secondary Sources

Conor Byrne, Lady Katherine Grey: *A Dynastic Tragedy* (The History Press, 2023).

Nicola Clark, The Waiting Game: *The Untold Story of the Women Who Served the Tudor Queens,* 2024, Weidenfeld & Nicolson.

Janette Dillon, *Performance and Spectacle in Hall's Chronicle* (The Society for Theatre Research, 2002).

John Edwards, *Mary I: England's Catholic Queen* (Yale University Press, 2011).

Antonia Fraser, *The Six Wives of Henry VIII* (Arrow Books, 1998).

Maria Hayward, *"Gift giving at the court of Henry VIII: the 1539 New Year's gift roll in context,"* The Antiquaries Journal, 85, 125-175, (2005).

Suzannah Lipscomb, *The King is Dead: The Last Will and*

Testament of Henry VIII (Head of Zeus, 2015).

Jennifer Loach, *Edward VI* (Yale University Press, 2002).

David Loades, *The Seymours of Wolf Hall: A Tudor Family Story* (Amberley Publishing, 2025).

David Loades, *Mary Tudor* (Amberley, 2012).

David Loades, *Intrigue and Treason: The Tudor Court, 1547–1558* (London: Pearson Longman, 2004).

David Loades, *John Dudley Duke of Northumberland, 1504–155* (Oxford: Clarendon Press, 1996).

Christine Hartweg, *John Dudley* (Create Space Independent Publishing Platform, 2016).

Suzanne W. Hull, *Chaste, Silent and Obedient: English Books for Women 1475-1640* (The Huntingdon Library, 1982).

Elizabeth Norton, *The Anne Boleyn Papers* (Amberley Publishing, 2013).

Elizabeth Norton, *Anne of Cleves: Henry VIII's Discarded Bride* (Amberley Publishing, 2010).

Joanne Paul, *The House of Dudley: A New History of Tudor England* (Penguin Random House UK, 2022).

Alison Plowden, *Lady Jane Grey* (Sutton Publishing, 2004).

Linda Porter, *Mary Tudor: The First Queen* (Piatkus, 2009).

H.M.F. Prescott, *Mary Tudor: The Spanish Tudor* (Phoenix, 2003).

A.L. Rowse, *The Tower of London in the History of the Nation* (Weidenfeld & Nicholson, 1972).

Margaret Scard, *Edward Seymour, Lord Protector: Tudor King in All But Name* (The History Press, 2016).

Chris Skidmore, *Edward VI: The Lost King of England* (Weidenfeld & Nicholson, 2008).

Sylvia Barbara Soberton, *The Forgotten Tudor Women: Anne Seymour, Jane Dudley and Elisabeth Parr* (Independently published, 2018).

Valerie Schutte, *Princesses Mary and Elizabeth Tudor and the Gift Book Exchange* (Arc Humanities Press, 2021).

Retha M. Warnicke, *Wicked Women of Tudor England: Queens, Aristocrats, Commoners* (Palgrave Macmillan 2012).

Alison Weir, *The Six Wives of Henry VIII* (Vintage, 1991).

Anna Whitelock, *Mary Tudor: England's First Queen* (Bloomsbury, 2010).

Derek Wilson, *The Queen and the Heretic: How two women changed the religion of England* (Lion Hudson Limited, 2018).

Derek Wilson, *The Uncrowned Kings of England: The Black Legend of the Dudleys* (Constable and Robertson, 2005).

Printed in Dunstable, United Kingdom